PARTICIPATION AND TRANSPARENCY IN INTERGOVERNMENTAL SECURITY ORGANIZATIONS

Resource and Norm Driven Opening in the IAEA and OPCW

Tobias Weise

Universität Bremen, Fachbereich Sozialwissenschaften

Dissertation zur Erlangung der Doktorwürde durch den Promotionsausschuss Dr. rer. pol. der Universität Bremen

Vorgelegt von Tobias Weise

Datum der Abgabe: 29. September 2015

Erstgutachter: *Prof. Dr. Klaus Dingwerth*
Zweitgutachterin: *Prof. Dr. Andrea Liese*

Datum des Promotionskolloquiums: 20. Juni 2016

https://book.tobiasweise.de

Contents

List of Tables

List of Figures

Acknowledgements

This book has been written in the context of the very inspiring and encouraging *Changing Norms of Global Governance* research project, funded by the German Research Foundation (DFG). I express my deepest gratitude to all persons that have contributed some of their precious time to help me improve and develop my ideas on transparency and non-state participation in intergovernmental security organizations. First of all, I would like to express my great appreciation to Klaus Dingwerth for his skilled and enthusiastic guidance and encouragement during my work on this book. The same applies to Andrea Liese, who has continuously contributed helpful critique of my thought. Further, I thank my colleagues Ellen Reichel, Ina Lehmann, and Antonia Witt who also contributed tremendously by commenting and discussing my research and giving sound advice. Next, I thank the many people who have read and commented on my work as it matured over the years. In addition, I am grateful to the staff of the IAEA Archives and Library and the OPCW's media and document section for helping me finding sources and providing insights into the inner workings of those two organizations. Further, I am happy to call a number of people my friends. They have helped me keep an open eye to other, non-academic issues. Finally, most thanks goes to my family who have always supported me. Anne, Ella, this book would not have been possible without you. Thank you.

1   *Introduction*

Since the end of the Second World War, there is an expansion of globalized political rule-making. In the expansion of global governance, intergovernmental organizations (IGOs) have played an important role. IGOs were one of the first institutionalized arrangements between states to battle complex political problems. Further, since their creation, they have become important actors of global governance themselves (cf. e.g. Rosenau and Czempiel 1992; Martin and Simmons 1998; Barnett and Finnemore 2004; Hawkins et al. 2006; Hurd 2011). While IGOs produce a growing output of formal and informal regulation for a variety of actors and policy fields, one can also witness changes in their internal processes of policy-making. Starting in the 1970s, but especially since the 1990s, IGOs are no longer exclusive places of state diplomacy (Charnovitz 1997; Willetts 2011). Instead, non-state actors like NGOs, scientists and lobbyists are participating at formal and informal IGO meetings in all policy fields (cf. e.g. Steffek and Nanz 2008; Tallberg et al. 2013). Furthermore, there is a trend of increasing IGO transparency towards states, stakeholders and the general public (cf. e.g. Grigorescu 2003). I will refer to these developments towards more non-state participation and transparency in IGO governance as *organizational opening* in this study. Some welcome opening as a moment of emerging global democracy. Others are more skeptical, criticizing the growth of opaque and unaccountable governance arrangements. Whatever the normative evaluation, organizational opening is a large scale trend, changing the workings of global rule-making and creating important implications for the legitimacy of global governance.

Why and when does organizational opening occur? Why do state representatives and IGO administrations, the main gatekeepers of change in IGOs, increase transparency and allow more non-state participation? In this study, I try to answer these questions. I develop an analytical framework that combines two basic explanations of why IGOs open up: *resource based* explanations and *norm based* explanations. The former logic sees resource gains of increasing openness as a driving factor. The latter argues that open governance has become an indispensable element of *good* and thus legitimate rule-making beyond the state. To assess the explanatory power of both logics, I conceptualize organizational opening as a multi-dimensional phenomenon. I do so by focusing on opening of an IGO's *talk, decisions* and *actions*, allowing for a fine-grained analysis of processes of opening up. I apply the framework to explain the opening of the *International Atomic Energy Agency* (IAEA) and the *Organization for the Prohibition of Chemical Weapons* (OPCW). Both organizations are active in the security field that, so far, has received little attention in the study of organizational opening. Further, both cases are particularly interesting because on the one hand, their activities in technical issue areas require lots of external expertise. On the other hand, both IGOs need to assure high levels of confidentiality of information to their member states as they deal with sensible industry and national security information. Organizational openness is thus less likely in these organizations.

My main findings are the following: *First*, I show that organizational opening does happen in both organizations and that the phenomenon thus has relevance for the study of IGOs active in the policy field of security. *Second*, when looking at possible explanations for the openness of the IAEA and OPCW, the study shows that both the norm and resource based logics are powerful in explaining organizational opening. Yet, norm based mechanisms are particularly strong in explaining changes in the transparency of the OPCW and IAEA, while the resource based mechanisms are more powerful in explaining patterns of non-state participation in security IGOs.

ORGANIZATIONAL OPENNESS AS A MULTI-DIMENSIONAL CONCEPT

Recent studies have shown that the two aspects of organizational opening, i.e. transparency and participation, have become more common features of the design of international institutions. Looking at *transparency* first, early research illustrates that transparency has become a common norm for the conduct of governance beyond the state, where IGOs take a special position because they are "demanding greater transparency from others but [are, TW] often resisting the application of transparency's principles to themselves" (Florini 2002, 23). Building on the spread of the transparency norm, studies have shown that IGOs began to resolve the contradiction noted by Ann Florini and started to not only demand transparency from others, but also to become more transparent themselves. For example, Alex Grigorescu (2007) shows that in a growing share of IGOs, procedures have become more transparent in the 2000s. Also, more recent rankings of IGO transparency, like the *Aid Transparency Index* for organizations active in development aid or the *Global Accountability Reports*[1] both underline the same finding. However, the studies show that there is considerable variation among IGOs' commitments to transparency.

---

[1] See `http://ati.publishwhatyoufund.org/index-2014/results/` for the most recent version of the Aid Transparency Index and `http://www.oneworldtrust.org/globalaccountability/gar/2008gar-mock` for the 2008 Global Accountability Report.

Looking at *participation*, research has focused both on the effects of non-state participation in IGOs and on the rules that govern it. For example, the recent and comprehensive study by Tallberg et al. (2013) shows that there has been a large scale increase in the access rights that non-state actors are granted in international organizations. Especially since the 1990s, providing at least minimal participation opportunities for NGOs, experts and business groups is common for most international organizations. Again, there is some variance between organizations and between issue areas. Participation appears to be more common in the field of human rights, and development than in finance and security.

There is thus an empirical trend towards increasing organizational opening. Why should we study this phenomenon in more detail? *First*, organizational opening has important normative implications. Transparency is often understood as a crucial mechanism to increase IGO accountability and thus general democratic oversight. This is especially important for those processes of global rule-making in organizations that are difficult to control by citizens (see for an overview Hale 2008). Knowledge about the rules and practices of transparency in IGOs thus is essential in assessing implications of transparency for the (democratic) legitimacy of global governance and its institutions. Further, participation is often applauded as leading to more democratic governance (see e.g. Scholte 2002) because it has the potential to let groups take part in global rule making that are not adequately represented by member states. Again, a better understanding of the empirical phenomenon of non-state participation will help evaluating the democratic quality of intergovernmental organizations.

Second, analyzing the processes of opening up helps us to understand mechanisms of decision-making and politics in intergovernmental organizations. IGOs have gained power as independent actors in global politics (see e.g. Barnett and Finnemore 1999), shaping politics and policies that guide national policy making and thus have direct implications for people. Insights into organizational opening thus highlight processes of policy-making and the influence of non-state actors on global politics. Also, focusing on IGOs as bureaucracies (see e.g. Barnett and Finnemore 2004), organizational opening is an important power channel for IGO administrations. Selecting experts and allowing specific voices to be heard can shape the outcome of policy-making processes in IGOs to the bureaucracies' favor. Also, selective uses of information provision may shape perceptions of member-states and the public on topics that the IGO has a special interest in. In summary, organizational opening *matters* in many ways. Increased transparency and participation help us to evaluate the normative quality of global rule making and to better understand political processes in IGOs, the forums with growing authority and power in global politics (see e.g. Zürn, Binder and Ecker-Ehrhardt 2012).

In this study, I focus on empirical questions related to organizational opening. *I ask which mechanisms explain growing participation and increasing transparency in IGOs.* For analytical reasons, I divide the literature on opening up into two strands: *norm based* and *resource based* explanations. To answer my research question, I build on the work of two major studies. In the *first*, Tallberg, Sommerer, Squatrito and Jönsson (2013) study non-state participation in 50 IGOs over time. They show that non-state participation has strongly grown over time. Over the past 60 years, more actors get access. Further, their participation rights increased both in quantity and quality across different policy fields, world regions and policy functions. Tallberg et al. (2013) explain this pattern by a number of mechanisms. First, they turn to resource based explanations. Here, opening-up increases the resources of an IGO at comparatively low costs (also see Raustiala 1997). The expected resource benefits of non-state participation are thus a powerful explanation. As IGOs implement more policies, they rely on non-state actors for implementation and monitoring assistance. However, participation is constrained by states' concerns for national sovereignty. Their study highlights that decision-making bodies of IGOs and organizations active in the field of security are less open because of high implied sovereignty effects.

The study also assesses norm based explanations. This approach argues that shifts in changing normative reference frames explain the behavior and rules of IGOs. Those frames prescribe forms of good and appropriate governance (also see Reimann 2006; Böhmelt 2013). However, Tallberg et al. (2013) show that the emergence of a global norm of participatory governance only has a limited influence on participation rules. A growing public discourse on participation only explains increasing participation after 1990. Another explanation is thus needed to account for variation across IGOs. Yet, they find strong effects of domestic democracy. Here, one can argue that democratic member states upload their democratic values to IGOs and thus influence IGO design. Therefore, growing participation is also connected to the growth of democratic values across member states. Overall, Tallberg et al. (2013) thus illustrate that both resource and norm based logics are important for understanding organizational opening.

Second, my study builds on Alex Grigorescu's work (2015). Exploring norm based explanations, he analyses IGO reactions to normative democratic pressure. He argues that the growth of democracy on the national level has caused normative pressures on IGOs to adopt democratic procedures and principles in their decision-making rules. However, responses to normative pressure vary. Demands to become more democratic, e.g. more transparent or participative, are not simply translated into new rules. Instead, there is considerable normative contestation among member states and IGO bureaucracies on how such norms should apply to the organization. For example, the study illustrates that protest about nontransparent development projects at the World Bank translate into normative pressure for more transparency and publicity at its top decision-making level (Grigorescu 2015, ch. 5). This pressure leads to the creation of formal information policies at the World Bank and other international development banks that had no such policies before. Similar normative pressure was build by both state and non-state actors at other IGOs like the International Monetary Fund, the Food and Agricultural Organization or the Organization of American States. The pressure resulted in change in the formal transparency rules despite resistance from bureaucracies and member states (also see Grigorescu 2007). Regarding non-state participation, Grigorescu (2015, ch. 6) shows that the democratic linkage between democracy and participation is less strong than in the case of transparency. Consequently, many IGOs rather allowed participation on the basis of the functional benefits of non-state actors' expertise and organizational capacities. The case of non-state participation thus shows how some IGOs and their member states narrowed normative pressures for more participation by removing participation from the nexus of democracy norms. In consequence, they did not allow non-state access in decision-making but in the functional areas of policy implementation and monitoring.

With my study, I contribute to the understanding of organizational opening by combining both resource and norm based approaches. In addition, I examine the explanatory power of the main findings of the studies by Tallberg et al. (2013) and Grigorescu (2015) and add additional theoretical approaches for understanding organizational openness. Further, I develop a novel multidimensional conceptualization of organizational opening. First, I understand organizational opening as comprising *both* transparency and participation. Transparency and participation are closely related, because transparency is often a pre-condition for participation. Further, allowing participation often increases an organization's transparency when it provides information to a wider range of actors. Looking at both aspects fills a gap in the research of organizational opening that has so far focused on individual aspects of opening up. Integrating participation and transparency provides new insights into the processes of opening up that otherwise remain hidden.

Second, I understand organizational opening as a process of institutional change. This process is visible on the *talk, decision* and *action* dimensions of an IGO. This conceptualization also allows to paint a more detailed picture of organizational opening. Organizations have multiple ways to commit to participation and transparency. Referring to transparency or participation in its talk, an organization promises to adhere to these norms and is held accountable for their commitments by their audiences (Risse 2000; Risse-Kappen 1995). Increasing openness on the decision dimension, i.e. creating formal rules, is the strongest indicator of opening up. Yet in many IGOs, high-level rules only change through consensus or a majority vote which is hard to achieve in organizations with a large membership. However, change in rules of IGO administrations are more likely because they have more independence in setting low-level rules. Looking at decisions only would thus hide a large share of opening up. Finally, analyzing the actions of IGOs highlights how transparency and participation are enacted in day-to-day activities. Have IGO activities indeed become more open, or are rules not enforced? In summary, my multi-dimensional understanding of organizational opening expands current conceptualizations of organizational opening. IGOs can strategically use opening on either of their output channels in response to demands from their environments. Disentangling opening talk, decision and action thus also allows an analysis of possible *organizational hyprocrisy* (Brunsson 2002), highlighting internal processes of opening up.

This study analyzes the opening up of two organizations active in the security field. Both the IAEA and OPCW are verifying non-proliferation regimes through inspections. The IAEA assures that nuclear technologies are used for peaceful purposes in its member states. The OPCW inspects national chemical industries to prevent the proliferation of chemical weapons. It also verifies the destruction of chemical weapons. Both IGOs thus have a relatively high level of political authority. Their activities thus come with high sovereignty costs for member states as inspections have a strong effect on national sovereignty (see e.g. Abbott and Snidal 2000; Bradley and Kelley 2008). During inspections, states give up parts of their sovereignty and submit their nuclear or chemical industries to oversight by a supranational body. Due to the high sovereignty implications, both organizations have strong standards for the confidentiality of information. Those relate to sensitive information which states and industries provide. Opening up of these two IGOs in the security field is thus not as likely as in other policy areas with comparatively lower authority and sovereignty implications (for studies in other policy fields, see e.g. Bäckstrand 2003; Steffek, Kissling and Nanz 2008; Jönsson and Tallberg 2010; Vabulas 2011; Böhmelt 2013; Nasiritousi and Linnér 2014). My study, however, shows that organizational opening also matters in security politics. This finding illustrates that the change in global governance relating to opening up is indeed a wide-spread phenomenon.

THE OPENING UP OF THE IAEA AND OCPW AND ITS IMPLICATIONS

The empirical findings of this study make two contributions to international relations research. First, the study provides an in-depth analysis of transparency and participation of the OPCW and IAEA. Both organizations are active in the security sector and have received little attention outside security studies. Second, I assess and test hypotheses and mechanisms of the resource and norm based explanations of organizational opening. My study shows that mechanisms from both strands of the literature are necessary for understanding organizational opening. In addition, I point to some gaps in the proposed mechanisms and highlight avenues of future research.

This study shows that the IAEA and OPCW have opened up since their creation. The general trend of organizational opening thus is also visible in the security sector. For the IAEA, I find increased rhetorical commitments to participation and transparency since the 1990s. The same is true for the OPCW. On the decision dimension there is little change in formal access rules for non-state actors. This was expected for these high-level rules. Both IGOs provide active and indirect access to NGOs and have only weak selection criteria for admitted NGOs. Compared to other IGOs, they thus are not completely closed, but they also do not provide the highest possible levels of participation rules for non-state participation (see Tallberg et al. 2013). However, transparency rules expand at the IAEA since the 1980s and since the 2000s at the OPCW. Also, the day-to-day activities of the IAEA and OPCW have become more participative at the same periods. Transparency on the action dimension is particularly strong since 2000 in both organizations. Overall, the development over time thus shows a growth in organizational openness since 1990. This illustrates that the main empirical findings of the two studies discussed above also hold for the IAEA and OPCW. On the interactions of opening up on the talk, decision and action dimensions, I find that there is no sign of large scale decoupling or hypocrisy. Opening on the talk and action dimensions largely overlap. Also, talk about transparency and transparency decisions are closely coupled. This illustrates that opening up has deep impacts on all levels of the two IGOs and is more than cheap talk.

Turning to the explanation of the observed processes of opening, I argue that while norm based mechanisms are particularly strong for explaining changes in transparency, resource based mechanisms fit the patterns of participation. This is the main finding of this study. In more detail, I find that the presence of the norm of open governance, prescribing participation and transparency as important principles for appropriate governance, is a necessary condition for the occurrence of opening talk, opening decisions and transparency action. The existence of a strong norm in the environment of IGOs thus appears to be a strong driver for IGOs to open up. Further, I identify three particularly strong causal mechanisms that explain organizational opening. First, there is a *norm based mechanism* that is strong in the IAEA. When the Agency gained more authority, it became more visible in the wider public and became politicized. As a result, the legitimacy of the Agency is contested in the public and among its member states. Both member states and actors in the environment voiced a growing number of demands that the Agency had to respond to. It did so by increasing its transparency to present itself as an open and accountable organization, thus trying to defuse internal and external normative pressures. Second, there is a *resource based mechanism* that explains opening of the OPCW particularly well. Here, opening up occurs although the organization is hardly visible to the general public and hardly ever is confronted with strong demands for change from the public. Under these conditions, opening is caused by high inequality between the members of the chemical weapons regime. Inequality creates high transparency demands that members direct towards the OPCW Secretariat. This gives the bureaucracy the chance to increase transparency to a much larger extent than the members demanded. Third, a *second resource based mechanism* explains participation at both OPCW and IAEA. Especially in the IAEA case, a resource based logic dominates the Agency's discourse about participation and defines the patterns of non-state participation in day-to-day activities and at the Agency's highest policy-making organ, the General Conference. For example, in times of budgetary constraints, the IAEA invites more non-state advice to gather information and evaluations on its activities.

What are the larger implications of these findings? In particular, they speak to two debates in international relations research. *First,* this study illustrates the relevance of processes of opening up. As Tallberg et al. (2013) have shown, rules of participation are changing. I also show that for the IAEA and OPCW, these rule changes have an effect on the organizations' work. Both IGOs become more open in their day-to-day activities. In addition, rhetorical commitments to the norms of open governance are more than cheap talk. At both IGOs, talk about opening up is accompanied by the opening in decisions and actions. Further, this study shows that opening up is also relevant in the security field, although it may be weaker than in other policy fields like human rights or environmental governance. However, the findings underline that ideas and practices of transparent and participative governance matter there, too. Further, the findings illustrate that the processes of normative pressure and IGO responses to it presented by Grigorescu (2015) matter in security IGOs, too.

Second, these findings speaks to the power of norms in IGOs and international relations (Finnemore and Sikkink 1998). The results are a strong example for the influential spread of norms. As I show, especially transparency is acknowledged in the rhetoric of the two IGOs as an important reference point for appropriate rule-making. The spread of the idea of transparency here thus illustrates a global norm spread. In both organizations, the norm competes with strong norms of confidentiality and high sovereignty costs. Nevertheless, transparency is acknowledged and enacted in both IGOs. However, when looking at participation, the limits of norm driven opening up also become visible. In the OPCW and IAEA, participation is rarely seen as a principle to increase the inclusion of marginalized interests. Rather, functional demands for expertise are used to justify participation. Thus, for opening up as a phenomenon, at best some parts can be ascribed to changing norms of good and appropriate global governance.

THE THREE-STEP RESEARCH DESIGN

This study first describes processes of opening up in the IAEA and OPCW since the creation of the organization. Second, it tests the explanatory power of hypotheses derived from the norm and resource based literatures of organizational opening. The focus is more on describing and explaining organizational opening than on an extensive study of the influence of single explanatory factor. The study thus follows a *y-centered research design* (Gerring 2007, 71). Further, the study is split into three steps. In the first step, I describe changes in the openness of the IAEA and OPCW since their creation until 2011. In the second step, I systematically compare the opening up of the IAEA and OPCW and test explanatory hypotheses, using *crisp-set qualitative comparative analysis* (QCA) (Ragin 1987). The third step checks the explanations that the QCA identified for plausibility in qualitative case studies.

For the first step, I create a data-set for each organization year. It contains values for the dependent and independent variables. Data for the variables is taken from both existing data-sets and created through qualitative methods. Especially for the dependent variables on the talk, decision and action dimensions, I rely on *qualitative content analysis* as a method (see e.g. Krippendorf 1980). In the printed and electronic appendix (http://dx.doi. org/10.5281/zenodo.31245), I provide material for the replication of the data-set, with full reproducibility as a goal (for an overview of the current debate, see e.g. Lupia and Elman 2014; Moravcsik 2014; Elman and Kapiszewski 2014). For the analysis of the data in the second step, I use QCA as a methodology. QCA helps with identifying necessary and sufficient conditions of organizational opening. The method fits my research question well. It focuses on the causal power of *combinations* of explanatory factors of organizational opening, allowing multiple causalities. However, like in regression analysis, the mechanisms identified by the QCA method need to be carefully tested for their actual causal explanatory power. Therefore, I use short qualitative case studies of the main combinations that the QCA identified to test their plausibility and explanatory power in the third step.

OUTLINE

This study proceeds as follows. In Chapter 2, I discuss the literature on organizational opening in more detail. In addition, I elaborate my multi-dimensional approach to organizational opening. Further, I re-construct testable hypotheses of the norm and resource based literatures. Chapter 2 builds a model of organizational opening. It thus prepares the theoretical ground for Chapter 3, where I discuss my methodological approach in more detail. Further, the chapter discusses the case selection of the IAEA and

OPCW and its implications. The chapter closes with an operationalization of the dependent and independent variables.

Chapter 4 is a *descriptive*, empirical chapter. It first discusses patterns of organizational opening for both organizations. In addition, it illustrates changes in the environments of both IGOs that could potentially have caused organizational opening. Chapter 5 is the first *analytical* chapter. It discusses QCA methodology in more detail. Further, it shows how I translate the data-set into crisp-sets for the QCA. Next, it presents the results of the QCA. There, I identify and discuss the norm and resource based configurations leading to more organizational openness.

Chapter 6 is the second analytical chapter. There, I have a closer look at the causal combinations that the QCA identified. My goal is to establish the causality of the combinations and to test possible alternative explanations. In a first case study, I examine the power of the norm based mechanism which explains transparency talk and decisions in the IAEA. In the second case study, I scrutinize a resource based mechanism built on state inequaltiy to explain transparency and participation in the OPCW. In the third study, I show that participation at the IAEA is resulting from resource concerns and that it is used as a functional tool to counter legitimacy challenges, raised after the IAEA's politicization. I conclude this study in Chapter 7. There, I summarize the main findings and discuss the effects and influence of the norms and practices of participation and transparency on the democratic legitimacy of the OPCW and IAEA.

2 Conceptualizing Organizational Opennness

In the following chapter, I will discuss the basic concepts of this study and develop a framework to explain organizational opening. I understand organizational opening as a process of institutional change on three dimensions of an organization's output: talk, decision and action. Further, I conceptualize openness as a quality of an international organization with transparency and participation as its major elements. My analytical framework concentrates on two kinds of explanations for organizational opening, which I label resource and norm based explanations of organizational opening. These will be used to derive the central categories of the comparative analysis of the opening of the IAEA and OPCW (ch. 4). Figure 2.1 summarizes the main hypotheses.

To summarize, according to the *resource based explanations,* openness is likely in organizations that work in issue areas where there is high demand for expertise and operational resources. Openness then reduces information asymmetries, implementation gaps and improves the monitoring of compliance with rules. These explanations rest on the assumption that main actors in IGOs follow a functional logic of consequence: states, their diplomats and NGO administrations want to assure that the organization survives and continues to solve the problems it was set up to solve.

On the other hand, *norm based explanations* start with the assumption that there is a norm of open governance and that this norm has some relevance in the environment of IGOs. If this is the case, actors open the organization because they are following a logic of appropriateness and are convinced that participation and transparency are important principles of global rule-making. As a second possibility, when there are demands for participation and transparency formulated in an organization's environment, it will increase its transparency and participation to manage its legitimacy. This response to demands for openness may either follow a logic of consequence or appropriateness. In both cases, one would expect to see open organizations when their rules strongly effect individuals and when their members are democratic states.

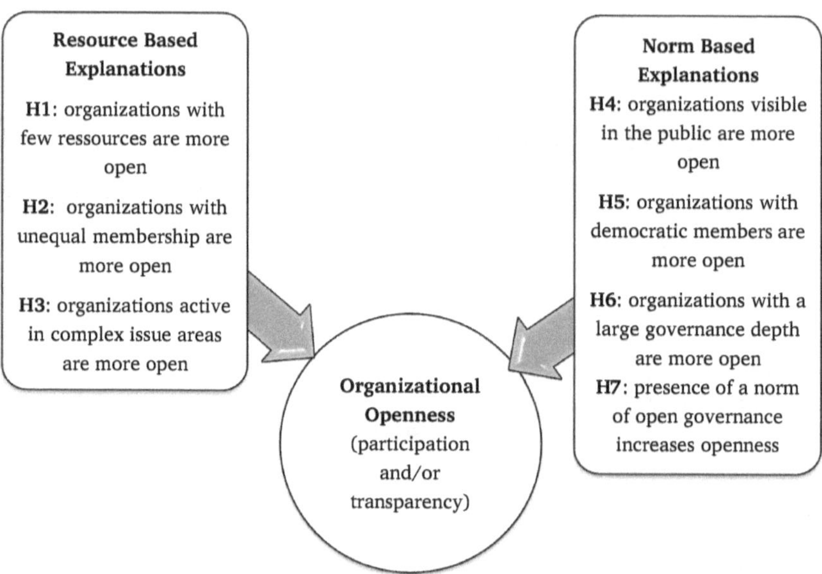

Figure 2.1: Hypothesis for Explaining Organizational Opening

In the following sections, I will discuss and explain my analytical framework in more detail. *First*, I discuss and embed the concept of organizational openness in organization theory. Basically, changes in organizational openness, i.e. organizational opening will be regarded as a process of institutional change in talk, decisions and actions of organizations. *Second*, I will present resource and norm based explanations of organizational openness. Both explanations provide sets of explanatory factors on the level of IGO openness and on reasons actors may have to open up an organization or to keep it closed.

2.1   WHAT IS ORGANIZATIONAL OPENNESS?

2.1.1   TALK, DECISION, AND ACTION AS DIMENSIONS OF ORGANIZATIONAL OUTPUT

My understanding of organizations follows the tradition of sociological institutionalism. Here, organizations are considered as social facts that are not only created to overcome cooperation problems or information gaps. Rather, "organizations may be created and supported for reasons of legitimacy and normative fit rather than efficient output; they may be created not for what they do but for what they are – for what they represent symbolically and the values they embody" (Barnett and Finnemore 1999, 703). I develop an output- and organization-centered concept of organizational openness that reflects the various effects that IGOs have on global politics. Not only do they provide structures for state cooperation, they also structure knowledge by ordering actors and action in the social world, by continuously ascribing meaning to social objects and by articulating and promoting norms, rules and principles (*ibid.*, 710). These material and ideational effects of IGOs become visible by focusing on how organizations influence their environment with their output and *vice versa*. This focus is especially sensitive to the political impact of international organizations, but also to the politics that happen inside an IGO.

Organizational openness is a quality of IGOs. Open IGOs are cooperating with non-state actors, are transparent and underline the importance of participation and transparency in their public discourse. When IGOs increasingly cooperate with non-state actors or become more transparent or when they begin to acknowledge the values of participation and transparency in their public communication, *organizational opening* has occurred. I understand organizational opening as a special type of institutional change. An organization has opened when its institutional output has changed, so that the organization is more transparent and/or more inclusive than before. Also, it has opened if in its discourse, the organization addresses issues of transparency and participation. Opening up thus captures change in the quality of openness. Openness is visible on the following three dimensions of IGO output:

- *talk*, which is what IGOs publicly say to their environments,
- *decisions*, which is written rules that the IGO has decided to follow, and
- *action*, which is what the IGO does in its daily operations.

Talk is what IGOs say about the world and about themselves. Through talk, organizations frame their own output and self-image as well as the output and self-image of others. Therefore, talk of IGOs can be expected to constitute and reflect normative values and meanings that are relevant in global governance. For example, speeches of Secretary Generals, public relations brochures and annual reports are outputs on the talk dimension. Talk is transparent by definition and cannot be opened for participation as only the IGO can speak for itself. Nevertheless, organizations can refer to openness in their talk. Their talk about participation and transparency can have effects on their decisions or actions and on the IGO's perception in its environment. Further, in its talk, IGOs can directly justify their other output dimensions to their environments, thus reflecting the norms and values they and their audiences believe in. Organizational talk therefore deserves analysis.

Decisions of IGOs are conserved as rules. A decision, needs to be perceived as binding by the organization and not as a merely symbolic statements. Decisions can be used as an instrument to interact with the organization's environment. For example, they create opportunities of participation for non-state actors. Examples for decisions are General Conference Resolutions that pass rules for NGO consultative status or media policies that regulate the quality of information provided to the public.

Finally, an IGO's *actions* are those activities that create its products. The variety of IGO products comprises international law, regulations and standards, but also fact-finding, humanitarian and military missions. Actions are thus activities that an organization performs to reach material goals. For example, in order to create new regulation, an organization needs to host consultations, fund expert commissions and negotiate with different representatives. Like decisions, actions are reflecting and constituting power structures in world politics and have direct effects on individuals. Consequently, IGOs are often criticized or praised for their actions, e.g. for un-scientific deliberations or effective inspections.

The *talk, decision, action* distinction is helpful for the analysis of organizational openness and opening as a heuristic device for two reasons. *First*, it highlights complexity in organizations and thus highlights multiple paths of organizational change. The distinction has prominently been discussed by Nils Brunsson (2002) and other students of organization theory (cf. for an overview e.g. Scott 2003). For Brunsson, there are a number of processes, structures and normative frameworks in an organization and in its environment. To better understand organizations, these need to be analyzed separately to see how they work together and influence the organization's production. When organizations produce their output, e.g. political rules or inspections, they struggle with various demands from their environment about what output should be produced and how the processes of generating output should be organized. Yet, these ideal images of how organizations should handle aspects of their production may be in conflict with the organization's perception of their own output. Furthermore, they are confronted with a given set of changing environmental structures that they can only partially influence directly, yet need to cope with to uphold their production. For example, an IGO like the IAEA may have a self-image as a technical organization, providing scientific information and expert inspection assessments. This self-image may conflict with demands for more political assessments of inspection results, e.g. put forward in the global news media.

How can organizations survive under these conditions? For Brunsson, organizations need to creatively respond to the conflicts caused by the competing demands and structures they receive from their environment and their self-image. On the level of organizational output, they can do so by engaging in *organized hypocrisy*, i.e. "talk in one way, decide in another and act in a third" (Brunsson 2002, xiii). The advantages of hypocrisy are that on each of these dimensions, organizations can react to demands from their environment, gaining legitimacy and support, while only minimally altering their self-images. Similarly, organizations can organize hypocrisy for their internal aspects that must not necessarily become visible in the organizational output. The IAEA could thus e.g. respond to the clashing demand for political analysis by providing more focused information on political conflicts to the press while continuing to refrain from political analysis itself. This response is hypocritical in Brunsson's sense because the response on the decision dimension, i.e. changes in the public information policy, does not fundamentally change the IGO's mode of production but responds and possibly defuses demands from its environment.

Scholars like Meyer and Rowan (1977, 356-357) have discussed such processes of *decoupling*, i.e. the deliberate surrender of unitary talk, decision, and action, as strategic tools of organizations to minimize conflicts: by setting up their formal structures in accordance with demands of their environment, they may shield their actions from critique, especially when actions are harder to assess than formal structures. Again, an IGO's reaction to modify information formats is easier to understand for the audience than tracing changes in the daily activities of the IGO. However, Brunsson also shows that two of the three dimensions of organizational output are closely coupled. Often, one can find that one kind of talk and decision leads to less actions of the same kind and vice versa. Accordingly, one would not be surprised to see organizations e.g. talk and make decisions about opening, but not seeing this reflected in their actions; or witnessing characteristics of organization's actions that are not reflected in their talk and decisions. In fact, as Michael Lipson (2007) illustrates, these dimensions are often *counter-coupled*: talking and deciding in one way can be a means to be able to act in another. This is what the IAEA could do. It decides to change its information policies and probably will communicate this step to its environments in terms that the audience understands in order to not change its modus operandi of a-political work. Therefore, there is a qualitative shift from decoupling to counter-coupling. While the former is primarily a defensive strategy to shield action from environmental demands, the latter is a creative strategy to engage in certain kinds of action that are only possible because special kinds of talk and decisions are used.

Second, the talk, decision, action distinction also helps the analyst in showing how different actors inside the IGO influence processes of opening up. Who is responsible for changes in an organization's talk, decision and actions? In IGOs, there are two groups of actors that can bring about institutional opening: state representatives and IGO administrations (cf. for an early analysis e.g. Cox and Jacobson 1973). Both of these groups have a different set of incentives, goals and constraints when they act in IGOs.

Each of these groups also has different chances to influence talk, decisions and actions.

State representatives, i.e. diplomats or national officials delegated to the organization, are central actors in IGOs. IGOs are created by states and states contribute resources to an organization's budget. Consequently – at least Principal-Agent literature tells us – state representatives are important members in the top-level decision-making bodies of IGOs. In IGOs, governments of states primarily want to develop government tools like international regulations and standards. Secondly, governments may also have the goal to solve global problems, like climate change or nuclear proliferation. Third, because IGOs can be understood as institutions of a globalized community of states, representing shared values and behavioral expectations about state governments, governments do not only use IGOs as functional tools. They also build their own reputation as valuable members of the international system by contributing resources to the maintenance of IGOs (cf. e.g. Abbott and Snidal 1998). Because of these various motivation for states to participate in IGOs, decisions to open an IGO are carefully weighted. Because the benefits of opened organizations vary from government to government, and because of the set of strict rules on how to make binding decisions in IGOs, decision-making by state representatives is often slow. Finding a consensus is difficult, implementing this consensus into formal rules is demanding. Especially when opening requires changes in the constitutional documents of IGOs, decisions for opening are less likely because of the high costs involved. The influence of state representatives on the other two dimensions of organizational opening is weaker. IGO talk can only indirectly be influenced because talk is basically produced by officials of the IGO. IGO actions are subject of mixed state influence. IGO production strongly depends on the operational support of governments. Most IGOs cannot act independently of state resources, so states can try to shape large portions of IGO action by threatening to stop material support. Consequently, when looking at how and why IGOs open, explanations of organizational opening need to acknowledge the direct influences of state representatives on decisions, the indirect influences on talk and mixed influence on actions.

Organizations' administrations are the second central group that can decide about institutional opening. As professional administrators, they usually have an interest in maintaining and enlarging their organization's resources and functions (cf. e.g. Bauer et al. 2009). Second, administrations may, like state representatives, also have an interest in contributing to global problem solving. Third, IGO administrations may also want to develop a certain reputation as respected members of an imagined community of IGOs. In questions of openness, some organizations may have a reputation of being more open than others, creating some form of pressure for other IGOs to also become more open. Consequently, also from the administrations' perspectives, increasing IGO openness is a complex decision. Administrations are the main producers of talk. On the level of decisions, administrations are usually involved in top-level decision-making, but their main impact is on the creation of low-level rules. Administrations often have the discretion to translate general, constitutional rules of IGOs into operational rules. Questions of opening are often subject of such low level decision making. Concerning the action dimension, administrations of operational organizations develop guidelines for their field personnel, thus directly shaping the action dimensions. Yet, their freedom of behavior is limited by state-made constitutional rules and by the material support of state governments. Therefore, IGO administrations have a direct influence on low-level decisions and IGO talk, but a mixed influence on action.

2.1.2 Transparency and Participation as Dimensions of Organizational Openness

Next to the talk, decision, action differentiation, I introduce two properties of organizational openness that can operate on all three dimensions. Compared to other IGOs, by more *open* organizations I mean IGOs with

- more participation of non-state actors (i.e. inclusive organizations),
- and more transparently organized processes of governance (i.e. transparent organizations).

Participation is a concept often discussed in debates of global democracy. While the general debate on whether democracy should be a principle of global rule making and how democratic rule making in international institutions should be designed is strongly contested, participation remains a central category of discussion. Students of global governance consider participation to be a central principle of democratic rule-making (cf. e.g. Zürn 2000). Here, the central idea is that people that are affected by political decisions should have the possibility to participate in the decision making process (cf. e.g. Held 1995, 103). As we witness a growth in the power and influence of IGOs, there is also a growing expectation that IGOs should be democratic. For IGOs, calls for more participation can be found on two levels. First, IGOs may be criticized because they lack appropriate state representation, a critique e.g. often voiced with regard to the UN Security Council. Second, concerns of participation may also be voiced with regard to the inclusion of non-state actors in the decision making process. While the first issue was particularly an issue in times of de-colonialization, non-state actors' participation receives growing attention since the 1990s.

However, it is debated whether participation really qualifies as a "good", democratic principle. To some observers, participation rather represents a new form of "tyranny" (Cooke and Kothari 2001). In their critique, practices of participation "can both conceal and reinforce oppressions and injustices

[. . .]" (*ibid.*, p.13) that are present in global rule making. This critique is also reflected in analyses that highlight how Northern individuals and NGOs dominate as actors when participation is practiced (cf. e.g. Collingwood and Logister 2005; Bluemel 2005; Bexell, Tallberg and Uhlin 2010). Thus, participation as a principle needs to be analyzed with care. Especially in political discourses, it may be couched in a language of democracy, thus hiding e.g. the exclusion of non-mainstream actors or unfair opportunities of participation that some groups face. Thus, a thorough analysis of participation not only requires asking *how much* participation, but also *who* participates.

Empirical definitions of participation are also largely discussed. Generally, questions of participation demand answers on how to balance needs for effective government and democratic participation (cf. e.g. Dahl 1994). This also applies to IGOs because a maximum of participation could render decision-making processes highly ineffective, especially when voting rules, organizational processes or resources are not adapted to the risen number of actors participating in decision-making processes. Further, there are whole set of different qualities of activities that IGOs or other actors label as participation. Consequently, an analytic scale is needed to order different forms of participation.

For example, Tallberg et al. (2013, 28,64) have proposed a five-step scale to measure the participation of non-state actors. It primarily answers the *how much* participation and *who* participates questions (see Table 2.1). The lowest point on the scale is *no access*, where IGOs and non-state actors do not interact. Second are information-sharing arrangements where IGOs unidirectionally provide information to the public but do not interact with specific organizations to reflect and discuss the information they provide. This is done on the third level, where consultation on specific issues between various actors are common. Here, NGOs and similar actors may be granted access to events hosted by IGOs. On the next level, NGOs may also directly get involved with the IO. There may e.g. be consultative bodies manned with non-state experts or formal complaints mechanisms where the non-state public can directly address the IGO. Finally, representing the highest level of their scale, there is the possibility of formal collaboration between IGOs and non-state actors. This full and autonomous form of access can e.g. be witnessed when NGOs and others are granted private access to judicial bodies where they can launch appeals that have the same weight that state appeals have (cf. also Kissling 2008; Tallberg and Jönsson 2010). The scale for the *range of access* describes who is provided with participation opportunities. On its highest level, there is no selection by the IGO and all NGOs may participate. The range decreases with the amount of selection criteria that the IGO applies, e.g. limiting NGO access by membership, size or the issue area it is active in, or only allowing selected experts or professionals express their views.

Table 2.1: Levels of Non-State Participation. Source: Tallberg et al. (2013, 64)

Depth of Access	Range of Access
full and autonomous involvement	no selection
active and direct involvement	formal selection criteria
active and indirect involvement	comprehensive selection criteria
passive involvement	demanding selection criteria
no access	no access

Leaving aside democracy theory considerations for now, the minimum level of participation that an organization needs to provide in order to qualify under my concept of organizational openness is *active and indirect involvement*. Providing information sharing capabilities (passive involvement) does increase transparency – discussed in more detail in the following paragraphs – but it is not a form of direct interaction where non-state actors have a possibility to voice their own concerns. Therefore, participation could alternatively be understood as the bi-directional flow of information between IGOs and non-state actors, coupled with formal rules that assure that information reaching IGOs are either at least heard or even acted upon. Further, taking into consideration the "tyranny" critique and answering the *who* participates question, I will consider all IOs that at least adhere to demanding selection criteria to be open. Yet, I will critically discuss the range of access for each case.

Transparency is another important principle of open organizations. Transparency often is a precondition for the participation of non-state actors. Yet, I consider transparency and participation as different categories because there may be arrangements where NGOs have access to high levels of decision-making but are not granted the right to discuss their activities publicly. Transparency has become an important issue for the evaluation of systems of political decision making since the beginning of the 20th century, when it was usually applied to national bureaucracies. Later, with the extension of governance activities to the global realm, transparency was also expected from processes in IGOs like the IMF and the World Bank System (cf. Hale 2008, 73f). However, despite the common referral to transparency, the definition of appropriate levels and forms of transparency is debated.

Alex Grigorescu conceptualizes transparency as possibilities for successful exchanges of information between two separate actors (see Table 2.2).

The focus is on a successful exchange of information, and not just the provision of information, that may not be comprehensible for other actors. Therefore, transparency is understood as "the ability of B to access information rather than of A [only, TW] offering it" (Grigorescu 2007, 626). This requires IGOs to provide information so that it is accessible to audiences in their organizational environment. Grigorescu further makes a distinction between different information channels that IGOs supply. Each of these channels can be used to achieve transparency. First, IGOs may be transparent towards member states, e.g. by issuing classified reports or answering to questions of state representatives in a closed environment. Second, IGOs can be transparent towards groups of non-state actors. For example, an IGO may provide information to private accounting firms for review, but not allowing the public dissemination of the same information. Of course, there may also be arrangements of IGOs providing detailed information to NGOs for review where the results, but not all material, may be shared with the public. Finally, IGOs can be transparent toward the general public, i.e. providing information directly to the public without state or non-state intermediaries.

Table 2.2: Levels of Transparency. Source: Grigorescu (2007, 627)

Level of Transparency
IGO transparency towards the general public
IGO transparency towards international non-governmental organizations
IGO transparency towards a government
NGO transparency towards the public (acting as IGO information broker)
Government transparency towards the public (acting as IGO information broker)

When talking about organizational openness, it is especially the information channel to the public that will need to be strong. I will classify organizations as open if they provide information for the general public and not only to selected groups of states or non-state actors. Relevant pieces of information that should be made available concern the decision-making processes, especially of decisions that have a direct influence on the lives of people. This understanding of transparency acknowledges that some information need to remain classified, for example when the rights of individuals or business secrets may be endangered, or when legitimate security concerns are present. As discussed above, the information that is provided needs to be provided in an accessible form. Information should e.g. be formulated in a language that the main targeted audiences can be expected to understand. This refers both to the complexity (e.g. technical vs. common language) and the kind of natural language (e.g. Global English vs. the language of the concerned). Further, information should be easily accessible, for example in electronic form rather than as paper in archives. Thus, like participation, transparency consists of two dimensions. One is describing *what* information is disclosed. The other assesses *to whom* information is provided.

When comparing the three discussed dimensions, opening on the talk dimensions takes another form than opening on the action and decision dimensions. On the talk dimensions, one can witness talk *about* transparency and talk *about* participation. Talk as such is transparent – because it is directed towards the public and wants to be understood by the public – and not participative – because only the organization itself can produce talk. Yet, an organization is opening on its discursive, i.e. on its talk dimension when it has started to or increasingly talks about participation and/or transparency (*how much*), or has talked about new aspects of these principles (*how detailed*).

Table 2.3: Conceptualization of Organizational Opening

Opening occurs when...	Participation	Transparency
Talk	*how much:* participation is discussed more often *how detailed:* participation is discussed in more detail	*how much:* transparency is discussed more often *how detailed:* transparency is discussed in more detail
Decision	*how much:* more opportunities for participation are formally created *who:* opportunities for participation for more non-state actors are formally created	*what:* rules are created that require the disclosure of more information *to whom:* rules are created that require the disclosure of information to more audiences
Action	*how much:* non-state actors are increasingly participating in the organization's production process *who:* a wider range of non-state actors is participating in the organization's production process	*what:* during its production, the organization discloses more information *to whom:* during its production, the organization discloses information to more audiences

Table 2.3 summarizes my conceptualization of organizational opening. To illustrate, a fictional organization would be said to have undergone organizational opening if:

- in its talk, it talks more or in more detail about participation and/or transparency. For example, participation or transparency are first acknowledged as important principles for the organization in an Annual Report.
- its decisions, in the form of rules have changed so that rules now grant more access or access to more actors; or if it has decided to disclose either more information or provide information to a larger group of people. For example, the organization has amended its rules for the general conference so that working groups are now also opened for non-state actors; or so that now, human rights organizations are allowed to participate, where only experts were before. Further, the organization may have decided to now disclose transcripts of the governing body's meetings or to provide meeting protocols to the public and not only to its member states.
- its actions have changed so that it now more often allows direct participation or is more transparent. For example, a body of the organization has begun to host meetings with non-state actors and has provided transcripts of these meetings to a mailing list. Alternatively, the actions may now allow participation of a wider range of actors or provide information to a wider public. In the same example, the organization's body now also allows the participation of business networks and puts the transcripts of these meetings on their website, thus making them available to the general public.

To summarize, what are the main strengths of the multi-dimensional concept of organizational openness that I propose? First, with participation and transparency, I limit my analysis to two fundamental principles of good democratic governance (cf. e.g. Scholte 2002, 285). At least from a normative point of view, they should be respected when global rules are made. Further, they are important pre-requisites of other democratic principles like accountability or the reversibility of decisions. Also, when rule making follows democratic principles, chances for the rules being regarded as legitimate rules are higher, thus lowering the need for coercion or other less democratic ways of authoritative rule-making (cf. e.g. Hurd 1999, 379). Whether rules made following these principles are indeed regarded as more legitimate by the people that are affected remains an open, and primarily empirical question.

Second, participation and transparency are principles that can be observed directly in the empirical world. They are thus directly accessible for analysis over time. Further, looking at both principles together may answer some interesting questions on the legitimacy management of IGOs, as discussed below in more detail. For example, it may be interesting to analyze why and when organizational opening actually means more transparency, more participation or both and which dimensions (talk, decision, action) are referred to in which situations. Third, my multidimensional concept allows for a very fine-grained analysis of organizational openness. Table 2.3 presents 12 kinds of organizational opening, thus disentangling the complex phenomenon of organizational openness. Zooming in on those micro-instances of opening allows to select individual causal stories for explaining them and to provide a thick description, looking e.g. at the interplay of various actors inside an organization that leads to more openness. At the same time, aggregation and thus zooming out of the micro-findings is also possible, revealing larger empirical trends and explanations of organizational opening as a phenomenon of global governance.

2.2 WHY DO IGOS OPEN UP?

How and why do organizations change? Why would state governments or IGO administrations, the main actors in IGOs, want to make their organizations more transparent and inclusive? The first question requires a look into insights of theories of institutional change (2.2.1), the second one into explanations of organizational opening (2.2.2, 2.2.3). Further, the first question embeds this study in the broader theoretical context of institutional change theory. The second one focuses on the more detailed questions I want to ask to explain the variation in the opening of intergovernmental security organizations. In addition, both questions help to contextualize my findings and enrich the analysis of processes of IGO opening. In section 2.2.4, I will discuss alternative explanations for IGO openness. Finally, I will put together and discuss the analytical framework for this study.

2.2.1 INSTITUTIONAL CHANGE THEORY

The following discussion of institutionalisms provides two secondary, explanatory factors that an explanation of organizational opening needs to consider: the impulses for change (endogenous vs. exogenous) and the scope of change (incremental vs. radical). Furthermore, the three theories of institutional change I discuss below propose to look at the equilibria of state interests, the contestation of normative bases of institutions and the history of previous decisions when assessing explanations for the opening of IGOs. These issues will be taken up when discussing the two kinds of explanations in the following sections and when compiling the explanatory framework of this study.

In general, theories of institutional change differentiate between *endogenous and exogenous impulses for institutional change* (cf. e.g. Rixen and Viola 2009, 20). Endogenous impulses for change emanate from processes within an organization. Exogenous impulses for change are caused by shocks – understood here as sudden, unforeseeable changes in an organization's environment. The concepts of endogenously and exogenously caused institutional change do not only classify different classes of causes for institutional change but also highlight different mechanisms inside institutions that lead to change. For example, when trying to explain opening up, it may be important to notice if a need for openness was primarily formulated as a demand in an organization's environment or if first came up in internal deliberations. Both impulses may then lead to different processes inside the organization. When opening is an environmental demand, one can expect to witness other processes and discussions leading to changes in talk, decisions and actions.

Furthermore, institutional change theory makes a distinction between two forms of change: *incremental* and *radical change*. Incremental change can be understood as the standard mode of change: talk, decision and action change gradually. For example, if an organization already has created participative mechanisms for non-state actors and extends those, one would speak of incremental change. In contrast, radical change is also possible. In these cases, organizations show very strong changes in their output. Those could be, for example, talking about transparency, opening deliberations for non-state actors or cooperating with local groups for the first time. The distinction between incremental and radical change helps with classifying the overall scope of organizational opening and also with asking for explanations why change in one instance is radical, but incremental in another. Institutional change as such can be explained by three kinds of *institutionalisms* (Fioretos 2011, 374) (cf. Table 2.4).

Table 2.4: Institutionalisms

institutionalism	impulses for endogenous change	impulses for exogenous change
rational choice	changes in organization's balance of power	changes in state preferences and power structures
sociological	learning, socialization	new norms
historical	layering and accumulation of rules	changes in structures of environment

Rational choice institutionalism assumes that organizations are based on formally organized equilibria of state preferences. These equilibria were negotiated when IGOs were first created or when major reforms were passed. Once equilibria are reached, they are formulated in the organization's founding documents and are only rarely changed. Therefore, institutional change is expected to be caused by shifts in state preferences and state power relations in an organization's environment. As state preferences change, the once established equilibria start to deteriorate and need to be re-negotiated. The same is true when there are shifts in power. Strengthened states may then try to establish a new equilibrium that more closely fits their own agenda. Because IGOs are mainly organized by states, these exogenous changes will also have an impact on IGO structures. Changes could be radical in nature, e.g. when the IGO's statute is changed, but they also could be caused by changing distributions of resources that states provide.

Sociological institutionalism assumes that IGOs are based on a normative consensus on how to govern a distinct issue area. For example, secret negotiations between powerful states may once have been the consensus form of governing international security. Yet, with the experience of the Cold War and the emergence of a multipolar international system, some may think that transparent negotiations with broad state and non-state participation may be more appropriate to achieve world peace. Change in the normative consensus can thus be caused by learning from experiences. Further, it can also change due to learning from more successful models, e.g. institutional arrangements that have lead to results perceived as more appropriate or legitimate with different institutional tools. In addition, change in the normative consensus may also be caused by socialization with new ideas, when local ownership as an idea heavily influenced the way how development aid should be handled (cf. e.g. Saxby 2003). Radical changes in the normative consensus can be caused by a wide-spread emergence of new norms that challenge the consensus an organization is based on. Yet, such ground braking shifts in the normative environment can be expected to be rather rare. Thus, the opening of an IGO on the talk, decision and action dimension – so sociological institutionalism tells us – may be caused by shifts in normative frameworks.

Finally, *historical institutionalism* understands IGOs as sets of achieved agreements. These agreements represent investments states and administrations have made in an organization. Making agreements in multilateral settings, as when establishing IGOs, is costly. Finding a consensus, or at least a necessary majority for the creation of a new institution requires material and human resources. Further, negotiations come with political costs, for example when political agreements for one project need to be bought with political support for other projects – a practice of package deals known to be at work in international negotiations (cf. e.g. Sebenius 1983). As agreements are costly, there need to be good reasons – and resources – to change them. Consequently, decisions once taken structure possible paths of future development (path dependency). As a result, change in an organization can be understood as consequences of the persistence of agreements and the high costs for new ones. Because new arrangements are often hard to design, there is a tendency to add new layers of rules to existing ones, instead of radically changing them from scratch. This layering e.g. adds new bodies to organizations that are to deal with new problems. Once a number of these new layers have accumulated, organizations may need more substantial reforms because the layered arrangements have become ineffective or cause conflicts. Under these circumstances, radical change is only likely when it inflicts less costs than the multi-layered institutional structures that are available.

2.2.2 RESOURCE BASED EXPLANATIONS

Why do state-representatives and administrations open up organizations? This question has been partially answered by previous research on how the growing participation of non-state actors in IGOs can be explained. For example, Kal Raustiala (1997) shows how states can benefit from NGO participation because they provide valuable resources during important phases of IGO policy making. By opening, states gain political resources and become more active global regulators. From a top-down perspective, Kim Reimann (2006) sees structural and normative changes in the global governance system that explain rising NGO participation. On the one hand, it is growing opportunities for funding and special programs that have created incentives for the creation and participation of NGOs. On the other hand, Reimann describes the emergence of a new norm prescribing NGO participation because they are crucial partners in the field and function as enforcers of good, democratic governance. In a rich way, the edited volume by Jönsson and Tallberg (2010) presents a selection of empirical analyses on how NGOs and other actors participate in different IGOs. For example, Andrea Liese (2010) shows that next to improved access to resources, IGO opening also needs to be compatible with an IGO's culture, i.e. with norms that prescribe appropriate behavior within the organization. Building on this work, the study by Tallberg et al. (2013) test a number of explanations on a sample of 50 IGOs. Finally, concerning transparency, Grigorescu (2007) shows how states, IGO administrations and NGOs influence IGOs to commit to more transparent processes. He also suggests that there is a causal relation between shared democratic norms of IGO member states and the likelihood of the IGO to adopt more transparent processes.

These approaches can be subsumed under two basic explanations of why IGOs are opened: *resource based* explanations and *norm based* explanations. Both provide different causal stories why states and administrations decide to open IGOs. In their explanations, they make different claims about the causal power of norms. For resource based explanations, they are rather epiphenomenal. For norm based explanations, they have explanatory power in processes of institutional change. I will discuss resource based explanations first.

A basic assumption of resource based explanations is that actors in international politics follow a logic of consequence (March and Olsen 2004).

They have a more or less fixed list of preferences that assists them in deciding which of the options available to them they want to realize. Therefore, opening an organization needs to be understood as a deliberate choice of actors. Opening is not something that just happens automatically over time, it requires purposeful choices and decisions. As discussed above, both state representatives and IGO administrations have incentives to organize IGOs in an effective way. This puts resources at the center of analysis of resource based explanations. The general aim of the two actor groups is to secure resources and use them effectively to achieve their goals. Different state governments and actors in an IGO administration have different resources at their disposal. This represents different levels of power that actors have to achieve their goals. In this case, control of resources equals power (cf. e.g. Keohane and Nye 1977).

I formulate three hypotheses that explain IGO openness from the perspective of resource based explanations:

H1 Organizations with few resources allow more participation and/or transparency

H2 Organizations with unequal membership allow more participation and/or transparency

H3 Organizations that deal in complex issues areas allow more participation and/or transparency

Further, the resource based literature provides the following set of mechanisms that explain why choices for opening organizations are made (cf. Tallberg 2010, 47ff). Each of those mechanism is related to one or more of the hypotheses, listed above.

Information Gathering and Provision

IGOs act in complex policy areas. To effectively develop tools of governance, IGOs need to gather information. The more complex situations become, the more costly it will be to gather information. Including non-state actors that either already posses required information, or are capable of generating information at low costs thus saves IGO resources (H1, H3). This gathering of information is especially important for IGO administrations that would otherwise have to use their own resources for this task. Furthermore, as gathering information is delegated to non-state actors, all member states and all subunits of the IGO receive the same information. For example, in arms control IGOs, administrations and member states need to be kept up-to-date in developments in technology and sciences to respond to possible new ways of proliferation. By e.g. setting up a scientific advisory board, the organizations get this information at lower cost compared to employing their own scientists. Further, reports of the board are available to all member states which is especially important for small states that do not have strong analytical capacities in their national administrations. The provision of information thus is an important incentive for state representatives to open IGOs, especially for weaker states (H2). Furthermore, an equal distribution of information reduces information asymmetries between both states and states, and states and IGO administrations. Minimal information asymmetries render joint decision making more effective (cf. Raustiala 1997). The study by Tallberg et al. (2013, 214f.) shows that effects of information asymmetries are especially important for organizations that require high quality scientific information to fulfill their tasks.

Increasing the transparency of IGOs can only partially be explained by resource based explanations and especially by the information mechanism (cf. Grigorescu 2007, 629). Both IGO administrations and state representatives understand information as a valuable resource. As such, disclosing it to a wider public is not necessary, especially if one is certain that pieces of IGO information have a good quality. On the other hand, especially weak states may profit from transparency because open processes provide information on other states and on IGO-state interactions thus lowering information asymmetries (H2). For example, a weak state in a weapons control IGO profits from transparent accounting of weapons material – in contrast to a system were such information is treated confidentially – of all member states because it does not need to gather the information on its own. Consequently, the information gathering and information provision mechanism of resource based explanations posits that organizational opening occurs when participation increases organizational access to information and/or when the transparent disclosure of information decreases information asymmetries in the organization.

IMPROVING IMPLEMENTATION

Both states and IGO administrations have an interest in seeing their policies implemented in the field. For governments, this fulfills the main goal of developing effective tools for governance. For administrations, effective operations additionally lead to a better reputation. If IGOs do a good job on their action dimension, they will secure resources for future operations. Because IGOs and states often lack funds and know-how on how to best achieve an effective operation (cf. e.g. Barnett and Finnemore 1999, 706), increasing participation may be an option. It allows the inclusion of external actors that may have the capabilities required in the field (H1, H3). For example, in arms control IGOs, implementation of regulations covers diverse areas like industry inspections, weapons destruction verification or introducing international regulations. For those implementation activities which are usually supervised by the IGO, non-state actors may provide advise, evaluations or technical support, like scientific analyses and the development of technologies. This saves states and IGO administrations resources while assuring effective implementation of their policies. Tallberg et al. (2013) show a strong effect of implementation needs of IGO policies on participation decisions at IGOs.

Transparency also is an important mechanism to improve implementation. This is especially true for states, because transparent IGO processes make controlling IGO agents much easier. Again, states would rather push for IGO-state transparency, not for transparency towards the general public. From this perspective, including the general public only means increasing costs for information provision but no gains in principal-agent control. For IGO administrations, raising the transparency for both the public and states would only be beneficial if they were convinced that their actions create the right products in an effective way. If this is the case, transparency will raise an IGOs reputation as an efficient partner of states, providing an advantage for further allocations on the global governance market. Consequently, the improving implementation mechanisms predicts that organizational opening on the transparency dimension is likely to occurs when actors try to influence the organizations' reputation as an implementation agent.

MONITORING COMMITMENTS

Finally, another reason why states organize IGOs is to effectively bind themselves and other states to agreed commitments (cf. Tallberg 2002). In complex issue areas, it is not always easy to assess if everyone fulfills its commitments (H3). If it is not clear if a large number of states indeed cooperate, no state would have an incentive to fulfill its commitments and cooperation would cease. Here, including actors that engage in monitoring state commitments can be a solution. Some non-state actors have special know-how on how to assess state commitments via their local or global networks. Consequently, especially weak states may push for the inclusion for monitoring purposes because they do not possess sufficient resources for monitoring (H2). The same is true for administrations. Opening the IGO for monitoring by third actors saves resources that the administration would have to spend for their own monitoring system (H1). Again, this also improves the reputation of IGOs because cooperation works well, thus securing the future support of the IGO by states. For example, an arms control IGO's administration will have a strong interest in using information from non-state sources on undeclared weapons material that does not fall under its own verification and implementation system. This becomes even more important when the IGO does not have the authority or resources to run its own independent investigations in the country. Again, Tallberg et al. (2013) find that IGO rules indeed allow more participation when the policies of IGOs have high incentives for non-compliance and thus external actors are needed to monitor commitments.

Transparency is also functional for monitoring state commitments because the results of monitoring, be they executed by non-state actors or IGO administrations, need to be available to states (H2). Again, like under the improving implementation mechanism, transparency needs not necessarily be directed towards the general public. For states, this would mean having to contribute more resources to the IGO. For administrations, public transparency will only be beneficial if the results build a reputation of the IGO as a good coordination facility where states fulfill their commitments.

CONDITIONING FACTORS

To both norm and resource based explanations, one can ascribe conditioning factors, i.e. conditions of the social reality that enhance or hinder the causal mechanisms that lead to opening. Thus, the discussed conditioning factors help in explaining why certain organizations are generally less open than others. Under a resource logic, there are two scope conditions that raise the chances for organizational opening.

First, decisions for or against opening depend on the *demand for expertise* that is necessary to govern an issue area (H3). Here, it is especially organizations that need to govern highly technical issues and want to set appropriate rules for highly technical processes that will have a high demand for external expertise. Other organizations that are e.g. rather trying to harmonize political decision-making processes on a more abstract level may be less dependent on information and resources provided by non-state actors. Thus, a high demand for expertise may lead to more participation of experts or non-state organizations that possess the required expertise. A higher demand for expertise may also be important for the level of an organization's transparency. To profit from external expertise, the organization will have to disclose some information to those that are supposed to provide the expertise. Of course, this does not necessarily imply improving transparency towards the public but rather towards groups of non-state actors or states.

Second, organizations with a high *demand for operational resources* will more likely open their organization (H1). It is especially organizations with larger operations in the field that require resources for monitoring and implementing their rules and decisions. For example, an IGO that only consists of a decision-making body for the harmonization of state policies but does not implement these decisions on its own will have a relatively low demand for the expertise and operational support that non-state actors may provide. Thus, one would expect to see more participation in organizations if they rely heavily on expertise and external resources for governance or if their activities become more dependent on expertise and resources over time. Additionally, transparency may raise in organizations with a higher demand for operational resources to signal this demand effectively to its environment.

2.2.3 Norm based Explanations

While resource based explanations are build on a logic of consequence, norm based explanations assume that actors follow a logic of appropriateness (March and Olsen 2004). Actors do not only rationally calculate the gains and losses of their actions, they also decide which option would be appropriate to choose. The standards for measuring appropriateness of options are norms, understood here as "shared expectations about appropriate behavior held by a community of actors" (Finnemore 1996, 22). Norms can be understood to be generated in processes of argumentation. During such argumentations and as results of consensual argumentations, norms can be conceptualized as social artifacts, structuring behavior and opinions of individuals (cf. Wiener 2007, 48).

Norm based explanations build on two mechanisms. The *first* one is that there is a norm of open governance. This norm prescribes transparency and participation as important features of global governance institutions and has an impact on the behavior of state representatives and IGO bureaucracies. Organizational opening may then occur whenever the norm of open governance is influential according to the logic of appropriateness and when normative pressure is put on the IGO to adhere to the norm. *Second*, norm based explanations may also work on the level of organizations. As organizations constantly struggle for legitimacy, they need to respond to normative expectations about appropriate global governance of their environment. Consequently, when claims for more transparency and participation are voiced in the environment of IGOs, the organizations need to respond to these claims to maintain, repair or build their organizational legitimacy. Both mechanisms and their conditioning factors are described in the following subsections.

On the basis of the norm based mechanisms, I formulate the following hypotheses for my analysis:

H4 Organizations that have high media attention allow more participation and/or transparency

H5 Organizations with a high share of democratic members allow more participation and/or transparency

H6 Organizations with large governance depth, i.e. high authority, allow more participation and/or transparency

H7 The general presence of a norm of open governance increases participation and/or transparency

The Norm of Open Governance and Openness

A basic assumption of norm based explanations is that there are norms prescribing only those government arrangements as appropriate that are open, i.e. transparent and participative (H7). Such a norm would prescribe *who* can legitimately set rules and *how* the rule-setting process should be constructed (cf. Clark 2005). A norm of open governance would therefore prescribe an IGO to allow participation of a wide range of concerned actors (*who*) and to establish transparent processes to be considered as a legitimate rule making institution (*how*). Kim Reimann (2006) describes how such a new norm has evolved and has been expanded to global governance institutions as a result of debates in the field of development aid. There, ideas like local ownership, transparency and participation became strong and got institutionalized in the organizations of the UN system. From there, they spread to a wider range of IGOs, rendering participative and transparent modes of governance the appropriate models for IGOs (cf. also Stiles 1998; Dingwerth et al. 2015; Dingwerth and Weise 2012). Alex Grigorescu's recent study (2015) discusses how norm changes can cause normative pressures from an IGO's environment and thus may lead to democratic change in IGOs. First, he shows that change in IGOs like opening up is most likely when the challenging norm is strong in the environment and when there is a large mismatch between that norm and its actual application at the IGO. Thus, we can expect to see opening up when the norm of open governance is strong (H7). Further, opening is most likely to occur the lower the current level of organizational openness: organizations that already were transparent when transparency became an important governance norm are under less pressure to react by opening up further.

While the described mechanisms potentially work for many kinds of normative demands, I limit my analysis to the effects of the norm of open governance. It consist of a number of elements, each making assumptions about the appropriateness of different dimensions of political rule. Such elements are observable in political discourses. In questions of IGO opening, I posit that there are at least three important norm elements. First, political discourses should make assumptions about and qualify possible sources of *authority* beyond the nation state. Under a traditional understanding of governance, authority rests in states only. There, states are perceived as the only actors that may legitimately set binding rules for a larger group of individuals. Under a norm of open governance, however, new modes of authority arise. For example, private authority as witnessed in transnational private regulatory institutions may be accepted as a legitimate form of authority (cf. e.g. Hall and Biersteker 2002). Further, authority may legitimately be shared between states and non-state actors in joint authoritative activities, as e.g. witnessed in public-private partnerships.

As a second element, one would expect to find statements about the appropriate *role of non-state actors* in IGOs. Traditionally, there would be statements positioning NGOs and others as functional tools for improved governance. There, a functional logic concludes that non-state actors provide information and resources to IGOs whenever states and IGOs request them to do so. Yet, under a norm of open governance, non-state actors are perceived as partners of IGOs, not as their instruments. Here, NGOs are valuable actors in global rule making. This rather reflects the need of meaningful representation than the traditional functional understanding of non-state participation.

Finally, a third element of the norm of open governance can be analyzed by looking at statements about the appropriate *mode of cooperation* between states, IGO administrations and non-state actors in IGO contexts. Here, a traditional understanding would – in accordance with the other norm elements described above – see NGOs as having very limited chances to participate in IGO governance processes: non-state actors may participate on an ad-hoc basis if states or IGO administrations demand their services. Under a norm of open governance however, non-state actors are granted institutionalized and guaranteed possibilities for cooperation. These may e.g. be specialized, participative bodies in IGOs, but may also include the right to make statements and vote in decision-making processes.

ORGANIZATIONAL OPENNESS AND THE STRUGGLE FOR ORGANIZATIONAL LEGITIMACY

Norm based explanations can focus their explanatory power either on the level of individuals or on the level of organizations as a whole. On the individual level, one would try to explain why a single state representative or IGO administrator decides to push for organizational opening. Of course, this raises the broader question of why individuals follow norms. There are generally two reasons for this. First, individuals may follow norms because they are convinced of their appropriateness. State representatives and IGO administrators may personally think – due to socialization or personal convictions – that transparency and participation are important values for governing globally. This mechanism lies behind the impact of a norm of open governance, as described above. Second, both kinds of actors may also react strategically to normative demands. IGO administrators and state representatives may then push for more transparency and participation because they know that these values are demanded by the organization's environment. In this understanding, norms are used instrumentally to assure the effective functioning of the organizations.

While these individual level explanations are convincing and offer interesting research questions, assessing them would require a methodology that is primarily based on the analysis of individual decision-making processes and convictions of individuals at the time of these decisions. Yet, I will look at explanations of opening on the level of organizations, putting a focus on organizational logics and structural factors influencing decisions for organizational opening.

IGOs are organizations that struggle with issues comparable to organizations known from the national and transnational realm. Under a norm based logic, a central goal of organizations is to be considered as legitimate. I follow Mark Suchman (1995) in making a distinction between three kinds of legitimacy that are relevant for IGOs. First, *pragmatic legitimacy* is a kind of legitimacy attributed to an IGO when it fulfills certain valued functions for its environment. For example, the WTO may be considered to be pragmatically legitimate by a liberal business audience because it provides mechanisms for free trade. Yet, it may be considered pragmatically illegitimate by protectionist business audiences because it does not ensure strong protection of national economies.

Second, IGOs may have *moral legitimacy*. This form of legitimacy is a central category of norm based explanations of organizational opening. Audiences will attribute moral legitimacy to an IGO if its output does not conflict with the audiences' expectations about appropriate IGO behavior. For example, the UN Security Council may be regarded as morally illegitimate by an audience holding that equal representation of member states is the most important principle of international decision-making. Still, it may be considered as morally legitimate by another audience that is convinced of the idea of strong leadership and powerful state representation to solve global problems. Thus, moral legitimacy strongly depends on norms that structure how the output and production of IGOs is evaluated. Transparency and participation are values that are basically subject to evaluations of moral legitimacy because they describe the processes of rule making and not primarily the effects of authoritative action.

Finally, *cognitive legitimacy* is a third form of legitimacy that audiences can attribute to IGOs. It is ascribed to IGOs when they are taken for granted as valuable institutions of global governance. For example, the United Nations may be considered as cognitively legitimate when an audience is taking its contribution to international peace for granted and where ideas to shut down the UN would be hardly thinkable. Provided that there is a norm of open governance, audiences may attribute cognitive legitimacy to organizations that fulfill these demands more easily because they perceive the organization as a whole to be appropriate to regulate global problems. If an organization is rather closed, its existence may be much eagerly contested by an audience that adheres to a norm of open governance, thus questioning the legitimacy of the organization on a more fundamental level.

My discussion of these three kinds of legitimacy proposes a view of legitimacy as an empirical concept. Legitimacy is attributed by audiences for pragmatic, moral or cognitive reasons. Fur the purpose of this study, I will not primarily look at legitimacy from a moral point of view. I am more concerned with looking empirically at evaluations and standards for evaluations that organizations' audiences formulate. This approach does not conclude that moral standards of legitimacy are irrelevant, but they are problems of another kind, requiring different methodological approaches to the opening of IGOs.

Suchman also describes a number of different strategies for organizations to manage their legitimacy. Legitimacy management is an important task of all organizations because it guarantees their survival. This is especially true for IGOs that are competing with other organizations – i.e. other IGOs, non-state organizations, or public-private partnerships – for resources in the global governance market (cf. e.g. Barnett and Finnemore 1999, 704). Basically, there are three types of legitimacy management. First, *gaining legitimacy* becomes important when new IGOs are founded or whenever an existing IGO either starts acting in new areas – e.g. engages with regulating new issue areas – or when it tries to reach out to new audiences and to build new constituencies. In these situations, organizations become active in new environments where they often do not yet have pragmatic, moral or cognitive legitimacy. Consequently, organizations need to become active themselves to either comply with existing expectations of the environment or of selected audiences about legitimate governance, or actively shape these expectations themselves.

Concerning opening, organizations may be confronted with the norm of open governance in two ways. First, when organizations try to gain legitimacy in environments where the norm of open governance is present, they could try to present themselves as very open organizations to signal their environment that they are playing by the rules that their audience holds as appropriate (*emulation*). For example, an IGO that would start acting in the field of development aid where it has not been active before, would be well advised to emulate practices and standards of transparency and participation that other organizations already practice in the field. Second, when IGOs expand their activities into new environments where a norm of open governance is not present, they can nevertheless create open organizations and introduce the norm to the new environment (*innovation*). As innovators, both state representatives and IGO administrations increase the IGO's reputation as an appropriate governance arrangement. This is especially successful when the norm of open governance is known to and appreciated by audiences from other policy fields, e.g. climate governance, but then transported to new issue areas, as for example security politics.

In situations of crises (cf. Reus-Smit 2007), when the legitimacy of IGOs is challenged by larger audiences, they need to use the management strategy of *repairing legitimacy*. In such situations, organizations have a number of options to react to these challenges. A first one could be to convince the audience that the organization is performing better than the audience perceives it. For example, an IGO that is challenged because it has not provided adequate quality of expertise, may try to communicate that it has, contrary to public beliefs, provided the best expertise possible given the limited mandate it has. Another possibility for repairing legitimacy can be to restructure the organization to re-render it compatible with the audiences' expectations. For example, an organization built on moral legitimacy may be challenged because it does not allow participation of certain marginalized groups. To repair, opening the organization to increase participation can be an option. Finally, not acting, or acting very carefully only, can also be a successful strategy to repair legitimacy. As legitimacy crises are also volatile, doing little more than business as usual can also be successful. An IGO that is e.g. publicly challenged by the press may also wait until media attention has shifted toward other topics and trust in its previously built legitimacy. The mechanisms that may lead to the opening of IGOs under the repairing strategy resemble those under the gaining strategy. The only difference is that a repairing legitimacy strategy is followed in an environment that actively challenges the organization and therefore puts state representatives and IGO administration under pressure. Thus, emulation and innovation are also plausible reasons for opening up while repairing legitimacy.

As a third strategy, IGOs constantly need to *maintain legitimacy*. Because IGOs operate in complex environments with a multitude of audiences and deal with complex political issues, the legitimacy of IGOs is very likely constantly challenged by some audiences. Therefore, IGOs need to pay attention to changes in their environments. Only organizations that are sensible to how their output is perceived by broad audiences can react to new challenges of their legitimacy. Further, IGOs can try to maintain their legitimacy by actively strengthening whatever their legitimacy is currently built upon. For example, for IGOs that are known for their high expertise and consequently are considered as pragmatically legitimate, a maintaining strategy could be to constantly improve its internal processes to maintain or improve their expertise. The same applies to organizations with high levels of moral legitimacy: they should maintain highest moral standards in their output.

Concerning organizational opening, maintaining legitimacy strategies will only rarely lead to large scale changes in the openness of organizations. Large scale changes as e.g. the creation of new participatory bodies or the invention of transparency guidelines are rather expected in situations where legitimacy needs to be build or repaired. While maintaining legitimacy, state representatives and administrations may only push for smaller improvements on the organization's participation and transparency record (*continued improvements*). For example, one may expect to see smaller increases in transparency like more kinds of documents that are made available, or participation of a larger number of actors at organization venues. Continued improvements can be understood as the continuation of previous practices and decisions.

CONDITIONING FACTORS

Following a norm based logic, there are also two important conditioning factors to consider. First, the *depth of governance activities* is important (H6). Here, the argument is that the more rules an organization passes and the stronger these rules effect the lives of individuals, the more they require a good legitimacy record. Also, legitimacy challenges are more likely to occur for organizations with a larger impact. For example, an organization that harmonizes standards of industrial products may be less evaluated on the basis of its legitimacy by a broader audience than an organization where working standards of industrial workers are negotiated. Therefore, organizational opening is likely when the organization's governing activities are deep, i.e. when it has high authority.

Second, one can expect more opening the more *democratic member states* an organization has (H5). Here, the idea is that when IGOs act in democratic societies and are controlled by democratic principles, the IGO's environment will more likely raise demands of open governance. This assumption can be plausible when one assumes that democratically governed audiences have more chances to raise these concerns and address them directly to their governments. To contrast, in an IGO composed of mainly autocratic national systems, the audiences in the immediate environment would not have the opportunity to voice their concerns, because their opinions are most likely oppressed. Consequently, organizational opening is likely when the member states of the organization are democratic. Tallberg et al.'s study (2013) shows some support for this factor. They show that e.g. the normative upload of democratic values to IGOs can explain why parliamentary assemblies and organizations in the human rights field – both are places of global governance where the presence of democratic values is very likely – in general are more open on their participation dimension than other IOs. The factor also relates to Alex Grigorescu's study (2015) on normative pressures for change in international organizations. There, he argues that pressure for democratic change in IGOs often relies on the application of domestic analogies. Thus, in IGOs with many democratic members in the decision making organs, members are likely to use their knowledge and convictions of good governance from home when reforming IGO rule-making.

Third, the *visibility in global discourses* of an IGO is important (H4). The mechanisms described in the legitimacy management section are most likely to be influential when IGOs are visible to a large audience. Only for visible IOs it is likely to assume that there is large-scale public contestation of the quality of an organizations openness. Without public contestation, strong needs to repair or build legitimacy on the basis of open governance are less likely. Of course, expert discourses may be influential, yet, they are more likely to be based on pragmatic conceptions of the IGOs legitimacy. For this factor, Tallberg et al. (2013) only provide limited evidence. For most IGOs in their sample, opening up started without protest. Only for the 2000s and for the field of economic governance, they show that high public contestation of IGOs like the World Bank, the IMF or the WTO causes an increase in participation rights for non-state actors.

2.2.4 ALTERNATIVE EXPLANATIONS

There are also a number of alternatives explanations for organizational openness. Here, I will discuss state power relations, bureaucratic politics, political culture, and world culture approaches as alternative explanations. These explanations will help to keep the analytical framework open for other explanatory factors, especially in the third, case-study based part of this study.

First, *state power* is a central category of all political activities. Therefore, its working should also be analyzed as an alternative explanation when looking at decisions in organizations. Power can have various effects on both state representatives and IGO administrations and thus on opening up. For state representatives, power differentials between states may be a very strong and very present fact of policy making. Weaker states may be pressured by stronger states to support strong state political agendas. Strong states have various sources to exert power over weaker ones. Those could be military threats – although this is a less likely category in questions of opening IGOs –, and questions of political and economic support. Especially in the IGO realm where successful political decision-making often needs to rely on the organization of majorities, linkages between different multilateral decisions and side payments to buy support are likely to be at work. Thus, from a power perspective, organizational opening occurs more likely when powerful states push for it. When weaker states want to open organizations, they will rather have to organize broad coalitions with other states, the public or IGO administrations to be successful (cf. e.g. Tallberg 2010, 61).

A second alternative explanation focuses on *bureaucratic politics* and thus on power struggles inside the organization. A basic assumption of the bureaucratic politics approach, as e.g. formulated by Allison and Zelikow (1999, 255), is that decisions inside organizations are to be understood as political struggles, as "bargaining along regular circuits among players positioned hierarchically within" an organization. As typical for political bargaining, different players inside organizations, for example different bodies, committees or individuals, have different interests and goals that they try to get through by playing along the rules of organizations. Yet, each actor or group of actors has mixed resources that they can invest in influencing decision making. Accordingly, when analyzing organizational opening, one should put a focus on who actually decides, e.g. which bodies try to open organizations, how these actors can influence decision making, which rules shape the decision making process and on how external factors like time constraints may have an impact on the decision-making process. One would thus expect organizational opening to occur when powerful actors in the administration, e.g. the Director-General push for more transparency and participation.

A third alternative explanation puts *organizational culture* center stage. Authors like Edgar Schein (1996, 236) understand organizational culture as a "set of shared, taken-for-granted implicit assumptions that a group holds and that determines how it perceives, thinks about, and reacts to its various environments". For the analysis of organizational opening, such a perspective encourages an analysis of how different actors inside the organization or the organization as a whole perceives participation and transparency. For example, actors inside IGO administrations may share the assumption that participation is an important value and may therefore push for opening up. Yet, it may also be possible that different organs of an IGO have different assumptions about openness, causing internal discussions and conflicts. Further, a view at an organization's culture may indicate how an IGO generally reacts to demands from its environment. Organizations may have a culture that rather isolates them from their environment, e.g. because actors do not perceive the environment as very important partners for discussions as opposed to states. Compared to the bureaucratic politics view that looks at power balances inside the organization, organizational culture explanations tend to first look at the general ideas that give meaning to an administration as a whole and second at possible clashes of these meanings between subunits of the organization. Consequently, according to organizational culture explanations, one will expect to see opening in organizations with a culture that values openness and is less isolated from its environment.

Next, *world culture approaches*, as e.g. discussed by Meyer, Drori and Hwang (2006), offer another perspective on the explanatory power of a norm of open governance and its genesis. Here, one of the main arguments is that we witness a growth of a world culture. World culture as a global reference frame includes at least three distinct sets of values: "the role of the empowered individual human person, the notion of scientized universality, and the sense of the social authority of rational models" (*ibid.* 37). In this context of globally shared understandings of the world, there is a general trend to accept formal organizations as a universal model for good authoritative coordination of human life. The organization as a global template is bound to a set of values prescribing what a good organization is, i.e. how good organizational behavior and good organizational processes should look like. These organizational values are closely linked to the values of a world society, comprising ideas of interdependence and mutual responsibility. Theories of world culture therefore conclude that organizations need to take individuals inside and outside the organization serious, that they need to formulate and legitimize their goals, need to follow a scientific-managerial approach in accounting for their resources and that they also need to address the limits of their range of activities (*ibid.* 44-45).

These demands closely correspond with the values of transparency and participation. Transparency is required to successfully legitimize an organization's goals and its use of resources. For example, legitimate organizations need to provide a public account of their budget and a report of their activities. Further, they should be able to describe transparently how they make decisions and justify their activities. Participation fulfills claims to take concerns for individuals and their rights serious. For example, organizations should be able to show that their activities and rules have been discussed with the people that are effected by those very rules. Therefore, both values of organizational opening can be expected to be part of IGO cultures and a broader set of public expectations about IGOs. Opposed to the norm based mechanisms discussed in Section 2.2.3, the world culture approach relies less on the existence of environmental pressures or legitimation challenges. Here, opening up occurs gradually over time through the socialization of actors in IGOs with scripts of rationality. Given this trend towards global culture, corresponding imaginations of global organizations and institutionalized experiences of development aid, one would expect to see a general trend towards more opening in all IGOs over time. Further, justifications of opening up from the organization and its members should be based on ideas of organizational rationality. Yet, as an empirical observation of opening shows (cf. e.g. Tallberg et al. 2013), this is not exactly the case. Variation in opening can be observed. For this reason, the more detailed explanations that I discussed above are required to account for these variations.

Finally, *historical institutionalism*, as discussed above, invites the analyst to have a close look at the historical development of openness in the organizations. Talk, decision and action are confined by historically contingent processes. Changes in talk are thus more likely to occur gradually. The same is true for participation and transparency on the action dimensions. Similarly, changes in the rules governing openness are more likely when they build on existing participation and transparency arrangements. For the case studies, this approach invites an analysis that explains the level of openness at an organization's creation and a reconstruction of the processes that lead to changes in existing rules, talk and activities.

Conclusions

In this chapter, I discussed the theoretical framework for my study. I understand organizational opening as a process of institutional change. I will look for change, i.e. increased openness, on three dimensions of IGO output: talk, decision and action. Further, I discussed resource and norm based explanations of organizational opening. I also showed theoretically how these explanations lead to IGO opening. Overall, the proposed framework will help me to understand IGO opening as a complex and multidimensional process. Through the use of the talk, decision, action differentiation, I am able to see micro-processes of opening, e.g. when a formerly decoupled transparency talk and decisions will in fact lead to more transparent actions after a few years. Also, I focus on dynamics inside the organizations to identify how state representatives and administrations struggle to make their voices heard and if they position themselves as gatekeepers or door-openers for non-state actors and the general public. The following chapter (3) translates the hypotheses to empirical research questions and explains the general 3-step set-up of this study.

3 Designing the Study and Operationalizing Organizational Openness

This chapter first discusses the general design of the study. It follows a three-step research design (see Figure 3.1). In the first step, I gather data on the openness of the IAEA and OPCW and *describe* changes in the explanatory conditions over time. In the second step, I will look at the IGOs from a comparative perspective to *explain* the observed opening up . I will apply *crisp set qualitative comparative analysis (QCA)* (Ragin 2000) as a heuristic tool to better understand similarities and differences between the processes of opening. In this comparative step, I will test the hypotheses that I developed in the previous chapter. The comparative study will reveal interesting combinations of the independent variables, called conditions in QCA parlance. These configurations of conditions will show when organizational opening (the dependent variable, or outcome in QCA language) occurs on the talk, decision and action dimensions. These combinations then guide the third step, the in-depth case studies. They *check the plausibility* of the explanations developed in the second step. Here, I will look at explanatory mechanisms of opening that the QCA identified. In the comparative case studies, I will also check for the explanatory power of the alternative explanations discussed in the previous chapter. This research design thus follows the principle of *triangulation* (cf. e.g. Flick 2007). Further, it connects insights of *small* and *medium-n* research designs (cf. e.g. Gerring 2007, Ch. 3). In the next sections, I will discuss the three-step approach in more detail (3.1). Next, I will justify my case selection (3.2). Finally, I will operationalize the outcomes and conditions developed in Chapter 2 for the comparative analysis (3.3). This operationalization will focus on developing measurements of *openness*. I will discuss how I operationalize the qualitative changes in the openness, i.e. *opening* in Chapter 5 while describing my translation of the data into crisp sets, required for the QCA.

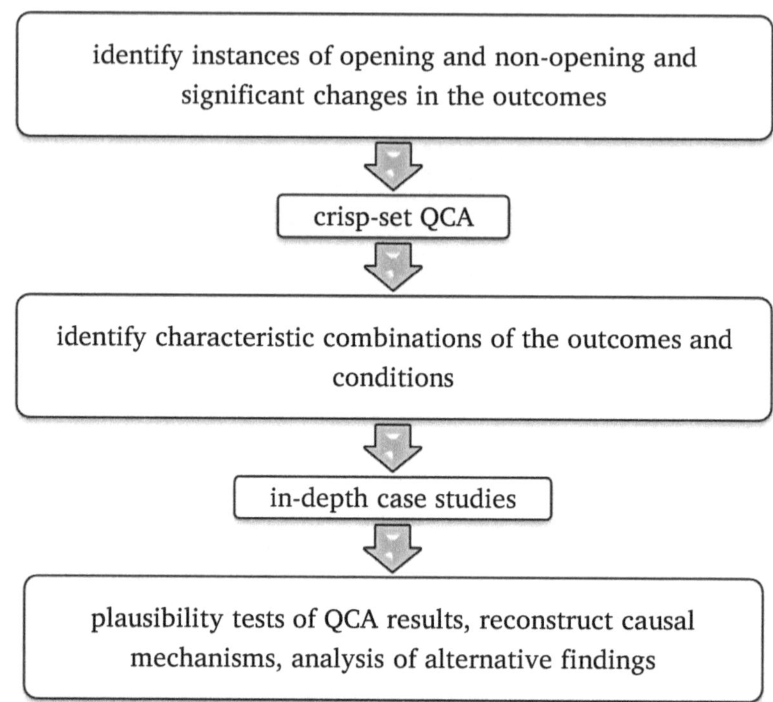

Figure 3.1: Three-Step Study Design

3.1   THE THREE-STEP APPROACH

The fist step asks if – and if yes on which dimensions of organizational output – the quality of IGO openness has changed since the IGOs' creation. I treat each organization year as an individual case and gather variables on an annual basis. This analysis helps me to identify organizational change and variation in the conditions. All cases are added to a dataset (see Appendix A). This method prevents case selection on the dependent variable (King, Keohane and Verba 1994, 129f), also because there is additional variation on the three dimensions of the dependent variable (talk, decision and action).

For the second step, the comparative study, QCA is a helpful heuristic tool. QCA follows a specific logic of causality. It assumes *multiple conjunctural causation*. For example, an explanatory system with one dependent variable under analysis (the outcome) and two independent variables (conditions A, B), the multiple conjectural causation approach states that multiple combinations of the two conditions may cause the outcome. This means that any of the four possible combinations of A and B, not-A and B, A and not-B, or not-A and not-B may lead or not lead to the outcome. For example, an analysis may reveal that if and only if not-A and B appear together, the outcome is present. In the other three combinations, the outcome is not present. For the case of IGO opening, a possible result of the analysis could be that increased transparency on an IGO's decision dimension only occurs when there is both a high demand for external expertise and, at the same time, a high visibility of the IO. This approach thus not only tests the explanatory power of norm and resource based explanations. It also highlights where combining both approaches is necessary. QCA allows for a more detailed analysis and explanation of the outcome than traditional probabilistic methods. In classic regression analysis, for example, the values for A and B would have been added and their middle values would have been used to draw conclusions about when the outcome would most likely be present. QCA, in contrast, does not aim for probabilistic explanations (cf. Ragin 1987).

Next to this respect for multi-causality, QCA is also sensitive for a detailed analysis of the presence of both *necessary* and *sufficient conditions*. Both are important to better understand causal processes. Necessary conditions are those conditions that are always present when the outcome is present. The presence of the outcome implies the presence of a necessary condition. Without the necessary condition, the outcome does not occur. In set-theoretic terms, the cases with the outcome are a subset of the cases with the necessary condition. The last sentence underlines that QCA assumes *asymmetric causality*. Because the outcome is a subset of the necessary condition, there may be cases where the necessary condition is present but the outcome is not (Berg-Schlosser et al. 2008, 9). For example, high unemployment may be present in all occurrences of social unrest and thus be a necessary condition. Cases where high unemployment is present but social unrest does not occur do not violate the necessity relationship. Thus, separate causal analyses for the occurrence and non-occurrence of the outcome are required.

Sufficient conditions, on the other hand, are those conditions whose presence always leads to the outcome. Thus, the sufficient sufficient condition implies the outcome and the sufficient condition is a subset of the outcome. For example, social unrest may be present whenever there is high unemployment, which then is a sufficient condition. However, because cases with unemployment are a subset of all cases with social unrest, there may be cases with social unrest without high unemployment. These cases may then be explained by other sufficient conditions. This is also a strength of QCA, because it allows combinations of individual conditions to be considered as a joint sufficient condition (also cf. Schneider and Wagemann 2012, Ch 3.1, 3.2).

I choose QCA as my methodological approach for the second step because it has some advantages over alternative methods. For example, a structured comparison of cases – e.g. when following a most similar or most different systems design (cf. Gerring 2007, 139f) – would require strong theoretical assumption to decide which cases should be analyzed. Such assumptions are only available in the literature to some degree. For example, Tallberg et al. (2013) only provide those for changes in participation decisions of IGOs and Grigorescu (2015) primarily looks at the normative side of explanations. Thus, I need an open research methodology for my multidimensional concept of organizational openness. Another alternative approach would be to analyze the organizations and to generate inductive assumptions during the research process. QCA however not only allows for re-interpretations of inductive results during re-iterations, but it also provides more control mechanisms and structures for this complex empirical research phase. QCA is designed for a medium number of cases, because it requires a large degree of case knowledge to evaluate the explanatory power of the identified necessary and sufficient conditions. This advice will be followed in this study. I will analyze 70 organization years as cases. This number is too large for less systematic case studies. For the QCA, I will convert the variables in the dataset into set-membership scores, construct truth tables and search for necessary and sufficient conditions (see Appendix C). I will discuss the detailed steps and add further methodological commentary in Chapter 5 when presenting the results of the QCA.

The third step of the study then analyzes interesting combinations of conditions and outcomes that the QCA revealed. For example, if opening on the talk dimension always occurs when the same conditions are present, I look at the cases covered by this mechanism. The in-depth case studies – following the logic of a single case study (cf. e.g. Bennett 2004) – then help to identify causal mechanism of opening. Because QCA works on a higher level of abstraction, only the in-depth case studies allow to explain how opening occurs in the cases. Further, such an analysis may hint at omitted variables and alternative explanations. I will also consider those more systematically in the case studies than during the comparative study.

3.2   SELECTING ORGANIZATIONS

In this study, I chose to analyze the IAEA and OPCW for the following reasons. *First,* there is little empirical knowledge about the openness of both organizations. So far, most studies on organizational openness have mostly covered areas with high participation and transparency like environmental politics (e.g. Nasiritousi and Linnér 2014; Böhmelt 2013; Betsill and Corell 2001) or human rights (e.g. Willetts 2000; Clark, Friedman and Hochstetler 1998; Weiss and Gordenker 1996). While fewer studies are available for economic politics (e.g. Charnovitz 2000; Steffek and Ehling 2008), they are very rare for security politics (e.g. Mayer 2008). My study on both organization thus provides a first detailed analysis of openness and processes of opening up in two organizations in the security sector. My analysis in Chapter 4 thus adds to our empirical knowledge of opening up in organizations that we, so far, know little about.

Second, both organizations are relatively similar and thus allow for a good comparison, also because many factors influencing the workings of organizations are similar. Both organizations are fully fledged intergovernmental organizations with secretariats and formal rules. They thus have a certain amount of independent agency and legal personality. It is thus easier to identify differences in positions on opening up between states and IGO administrations, which may be an important source of variation of organizational openness. Also, the formalized rules makes access to regular forms of communication like annual reports, speeches and conference proceedings easier. Further, full IGOs are more likely to actually have outputs that are politically relevant and are contested in the organizations' environments. Politically relevant output will thus lead to a larger need of legitimacy of these organizations as their performance is more likely to be evaluated by the public. For these reasons, the two IGOs I chose are more suitable for study than less formalized groups of states like the *Wassennaar Arrangement,* or UN conference series like the *Conference on Disarmament.*

In addition, both the IAEA and OPCW are universal membership organizations. At the IAEA, every recognized state can become a member regardless of their nuclear capacities or their standing towards the *Non-Proliferation Treaty.* At the OCPW, member states are those states that are signatories to the *Chemical Weapons Convention.* In fact, both IGOs have nearly achieved universal membership. This is important because there is more potential for contestation of issues like opening between the heterogeneous members than in more selective IGOs with a homogeneous member base. Further, universal membership organizations usually have a wide environment where demands of openness can be formulated. As both the IAEA and OPCW are relatively similar in this regard, variations of organizational cultures are small. Further, both organizations have formal ties to the United Nations and consider themselves to be part of the *United Nations Family organizations,* employing similar accounting, programming and staffing standards.

Third, the case selection of these two relatively similar organizations also has advantages for the analytical efforts of my study. Both cases are interesting because comparative studies of organizational openness have so far shown that IGO in the security field are the least open, compared to other policy areas (Tallberg et al. 2013; Jönsson and Tallberg 2010; Steffek, Kissling and Nanz 2008). Most of these studies are also focused on formal IGOs. My study thus builds on this knowledge of opening up by testing if the existing explanations of opening up also apply to relatively similar organizations in another policy field.

3.3 OPERATIONALIZATION

The following section translates the concepts developed in Chapter 2 into yardsticks that can be applied to the empirical reality. First, I describe how organizational openness is operationalized. Second, I discuss variables derived from resource and norm based explanations of organizational opening. Table 3.1 summarizes the operationalization. Also, I document the construction of my raw data-set in more detail in Appendix A. The proposed operationalization focuses on the variables that are needed for the first, qualitative comparative analysis. Again, here I develop measures of *openness*. I define qualitative thresholds for *opening* when conducting the QCA in Chapter 5.

Table 3.1: Variables and Data

Name	Description	Data
Dependent variable		
Participation Talk	reference to norm of participation in the Annual Report	IAEA Annual Report, 1957-2011; OPCW Annual Report, 1997-2011
Transparency Talk	reference to norm of transparency in the Annual Report	IAEA Annual Report, 1957-2011; OPCW Annual Report, 1997-2011
Participation Decisions	decisions that increase participation	plenary organ resolutions and executive body decisions, references to administrative decisions in the Annual Reports
Transparency Decisions	decisions that increase transparency	plenary organ resolutions and executive body decisions, references to administrative decisions in the Annual Reports
Participation Actions 1	number of NGOs present at annual plenary organ meetings	official lists of participants
Participation Actions 2	participative events mentioned in the Annual Reports	IAEA Annual Report, 1957-2011; OPCW Annual Report, 1997-2011
Transparency Actions	Budget available for public information as share of total budget	annual budget reports
Resource based explanations		
Budget Size	Amount of Annual IGO Budget in 2009 USD	annual budgets, US DoC BEA GDP deflator, ECB currency conversion rates
Ineqality of Members	inequality of the IGO members	Gini coefficient of members' real GDP in 2005 constant national prices, Penn World Tables 8.0
Issue Complexity	complexity of the policy field that the organization covers	number and changes of tasks in IAEA Statute and the Chemical Weapons Convention
Norm based explanations		
Media Salience	presence of organization in the global media	total hits in the Lexis Nexis major world news corpus
Media Headline Salience	relative presence of organization in the headlines of the global media	hits in the Lexis Nexis major world news corpus in headlines as share of total hits
Democratic Members	proportion of democratic members of the whole organization	COW-IGO for membership data, Polity IV
Governance Depth	authority of the IGO	qualitative assessment of changes in the IGOs' authority
Open Governance Norm	presence of the norm of open governance in the general public discourse	Google books n-grams of key terms of the concept of "global democracy"

3.3.1   OUTCOME VARIABLES: ORGANIZATIONAL OPENNESS

As described above, the concept of organizational openness describes institutional output on three dimensions. Organizations are open when they refer to participation or transparency in their talk, when they make decisions on openness, or when they are participative and transparent in their day-to-day activities. How do I empirically analyze this IGO output?

I will identify relevant *talk* by looking at forms of political communication, i.e. primarily at annual reports. This form of organizational talk is important because what organizations say about themselves publicly aims at responding to or creating demands in the environment. Talk will be labeled as open if the organization makes a statement that indicates a commitment to *(i)* include non-state actors in their actions and *(ii)* be transparent. To illustrate, in its annual report for 1958-59, the IAEA highlights that "[i]ncreasing emphasis has been given to liaison work with national and international non-governmental organizations [...]" (GC(3)/74, p. 56).[2] It thus refers to participation as an important aspect of its work. Similarly, in its Annual Report for the year 2000, the OPCW underlines the need for "[t]ransparent and clear procedures for both the review of posts and the internal classification and promotion of staff members" (C-VI/5, 55), thus binding itself to the norm of transparency in its talk.

Methodologically, I include all annual reports of the IGOs in my analysis. I first scan the annual reports for the following search terms and their orthographic alternatives:

• non-governmental	• participation	• disclosure
• NGO	• participate	• public information
• stakeholders	• consultation	• outreach
• civil society	• consult	• website
• open	• transparent	• internet
• openness	• transparency	

The search terms return a number of relevant paragraphs which I subsequently coded qualitatively if they included relevant forms of organizational opening talk.[3] For the qualitative coding, I follow standard procedures of qualitative content analysis with a minimalist code-book (cf. e.g. Mayring 2010).

Next, I look for relevant *decisions* by looking at institutional rules. They are explicit provisions in written form, formally arrived at by decisions. Therefore, I look for rules and rule changes made by the plenary policy organ and by the executive policy organ in their official documents. In

---

[2]Throughout this study, I refer to official documents of the organizations with their official document numbers. Most of the documents are available in the electronic document archives of the IAEA and OPCW.

[3]Again, for a detailed discussion on how to retrieve and process the qualitative codings, see the data appendix (Appendix A).

addition, I look for more administrative rules in the Annual Reports. Here low-level decisions, like new public information or outreach strategies, are often discussed and justified. Relevant rules for this analysis deal with *(i)* facilitating participation of non-state actors in institutional processes (consultative and/or participative) and *(ii)* addressing the transparency of institutional processes. For example, at the OPCW, in 2000, NGOs at the annual Conference of the States Parties get access to official documents, slightly increasing their participation opportunities. As another example, in 1995, the IAEA decided to distribute its official documents directly to the public via its website, thus increasing transparency. Methodologically, I collect all rule changes and create comparative lists of changes for each organization. Rule changes are discussed in detail in the individual case chapters and compared in the QCA chapter.

Finally, *action* is what IGOs do in their operational fields (e.g. industry inspections, disarmament negotiations). These activities may be governed by decision and talk, but need not necessarily be so. I reconstruct actions of organizations from their activity reports. Open activities can be identified when they *(i)* are including non-state actors, and when they are *(ii)* committed to transparent procedures.

For *participation action*, I introduce two measures. First, I collect the number of NGOs represented at the annual plenary meeting. At the OPCW and IAEA, the plenary organs are the highest policy making organs. Therefore, non-state actor presence at these venues is of major importance when assessing openness. At the plenary meetings, NGOs and their representatives have the opportunity to lobby a number of state delegations and administrative staff. Further, they have the chance to influence decision making processes or sponsor resolutions, working papers and other relevant documents (for a similar discussion, see e.g. Tallberg et al. 2013). I measure the participation of NGOs at these meetings with the help of the official lists of participants. These lists provide an overview of the officially accredited non-state actors and are thus a good representation of the general phenomenon of non-state participation. However, they do not represent more informal forms of participation, as e.g. the inclusion of non-state actors in state delegations or the semi-official participation of NGO representatives as individual observers or media representatives.

Second, I create the measure of participation events. Those are events like workshops, seminars, expert meetings or consultative group meetings where the organization invites non-state actors to participate in its activities. These events have a diffuse influence on the decision-making of the organization. For example, expert meetings or groups of consultants may be very influential in setting agendas or for drafting organizational guidelines or standards. Weaker forms of participation, such as training events or workshops, may have less direct influence on organizational policies. Still, they are moments where the organizations open themselves and exchange information with their environments and thus contribute to an organization's openness. Methodologically, I collect participation events by scanning the annual reports for the following key words and their orthographic alternatives:

- workshop
- training
- event
- seminar
- group

- meeting
- course
- forum
- exercise
- Board

- advisory
- project
- committee
- program
- panel

- symposia
- consultant
- network

Next, I check the results for relevance. The resulting list of participation events then represents a filtered list of all such events. Their inclusion in the annual reports marks them as especially important for the organizations' administrations.

In a next step, I measure *transparency actions* with the share of the budget that the organizations spend for public information. This budget includes costs for publications, outreach events, public data-bases and websites. Although international organizations are restricted in their budgetary decisions and dependent on member state financing, they have some choice in how many resources they contribute to reaching out to their environments. The share of the budget that is spent for transparency thus reflects a political decision of the IGO about how it spends its resources. Increases over time in the proportions of the resources attributed to transparency thus hint at a general growth of importance of transparency for the organization. I take the data for this measure from the organizations' official budgets. Here, public information budgets are usually part of the general administrative budgets. Further, the organizations over time also create distinct divisions for information dissemination and outreach to the general public. As these budgetary attributes are different for each organization, they will be discussed in more detail in the individual case chapters and in the data appendix.

3.3.2 EXPLANATORY VARIABLES

In the following subsections, I will discuss operationalizations of the independent variables that will be of relevance for the comparative analysis. The operationalization discusses rather general concepts that will need to be tweaked for the individual IGOs. Therefore, each case section in chapter 4 will briefly discuss which sources were used and if the general operationalization needed to be adjusted minimally.

VARIABLES DERIVED FROM RESOURCE BASED EXPLANATIONS

Hypothesis 1 posits that organizations with few resources are more likely to open up. To measure the resources of the IGO, I collect its budget data. IGO budgets are usually available as public documents. Often, there are different kinds of budgets for organizations, e.g. when funds or special institutions have separate funding sources. I primarily collect aggregate budget data of the IGOs' active, general budget. For comparability and to remove inflation effects, two steps of data transformation are necessary. First, all budget data is converted to current US Dollar. This is necessary for the IAEA after 2006, when IAEA budgeting has switched from USD to Euro. Here, I use the European Central Bank's data on historical currency conversion rates (http://sdw.ecb.europa.eu/, bilateral annual exchange rates) to convert EUR to USD. For the OPCW, in addition, I need currency conversion rates from Netherlands Gulden to USD for the time from 1997-1999. Here, I use data from the Netherlands' National Bank for conversion rates (http://www.statistics.dnb.nl/). Second, to remove inflation effects and to make the budgets comparable over time, I convert the historical USD to constant 2009 USD with the help of the US Department of Commerce's Bureau of Economic Analysis GDP deflator data (http://www.bea.gov/, Table 1.1.9). The collected and transformed data then helps to identify budgetary crises, i.e. phases with budget decreases, which may cause an increased need for non-state resources and transparency.

The second hypothesis states that IGOs with unequal membership are more open. I collect data on changes in the equality of member states by looking at the Gini coefficient of the member's historical GDP data from the Penn World Table 8.0 data-set (www.ggdc.net/pwt, Output-side real GDP at current PPPs). The Gini-Coefficient normalizes the "average absolute difference between all pairs of incomes in the population" (Cowell 2000, 112). The higher the coefficient, the higher the inequality of the member states. A value of 0 represents total equality (e.g. all states have the same GDP) while a value of 1 represent total inequality (e.g. one state has all the income). I construct annual membership data from the information that the IGOs provide on their websites. I then create the annual Gini-Coefficient of GDP inequality of the IGO's membership. This inequality measure is based on economic inequality, which I also understand as a proxy for inequality in state power.

To measure issue complexity (Hypothesis 3), I collect data that allows an interpretation of the nature of the IGO's policy area. As a first cut, I assess and track changes in the organizations' statutory tasks. Such tasks are written expressions of the general purpose and planned functions of an intergovernmental organization. Here, the assumption is that organizations with more statutory tasks need to handle more complexity as they are active in more issue areas. This measure does not adequately capture changes in complexity in a specific statutory task. For example, my operationalization tells me that the IAEA is tasked with non-proliferation inspections since its foundation. However, I have no objective data to qualify if these inspections have become more complex over time. The same is true for most of the other statutory tasks like technical assistance, or supporting scientific research. In general, I assume that there is growing complexity in individual statutory tasks over time, but that this growth is equal in both the IAEA and the OPCW. The main task of both IGOs, inspections, have certainly become more demanding over time as the amount of inspection sites has grown but also as the inspected technologies have developed. Yet, it is hard to tell on a quantitative scale to which degree the IAEA's nuclear inspections have become more complex than the OPCW's chemical inspections. For this study, I assume that both activities have grown equally in their complexity. Relevant changes between both IGOs thus only occur when an organization gets new statutory tasks. This simplified operationalization of complexity only works for this study because of the large similarities between both IGOs.

VARIABLES DERIVED FROM NORM BASED EXPLANATIONS

The norm based explanations are covered with a number of variables, too. First, to operationalize Hypothesis 4 on the visibility of IGOs, I run an analysis of media salience of the IGOs in global media data. I use the *Lexis-Nexis* `major world newspapers` corpus and collect the number of total annual hits in each part of newspaper articles for each IGO. Thus, hits stand for individual articles that mention the intergovernmental organization. The corpus includes only English language quality newspapers from around the world. Reliable data is only available since the late 1970s. Further, data for the 1970s is limited to one source, *The Washington Post*. The media corpus grows over time, potentially causing issues for the comparison over time. However, the growing number of available sources in later years does not have strong effects on the overall development of the trends of media salience of the IGOs under analysis. Hits from The Washington Post and the whole corpus significantly and highly correlate (IAEA: 0.94, OPCW: 0.99). Media salience is relatively low for both organizations and driven by specific events that are reported in all newspapers. Consequently, it does not matter that much which measure for media salience is chosen for the analysis. I chose all hits in the corpus over hits in the Washington Post.

The second measure for media visibility is headline visibility. Here, I use the ratio of hits in the newspaper corpus in article headlines to the total hits. Thus, the measure provides information about which proportion of the news articles put a special focus on the organization. I assume that articles that mention the IGO in the headline section have a larger impact on the legitimacy mechanism of media visibility. Also, headlines visibility and general visibility only weakly correlate (0.32). Thus, a separate causal analysis is necessary.

Next, I test Hypothesis 5 and check if the amount of democratic member states influences opening. I collect annual data on the share of democracies that are members of the organization. Again, I use the IGOs' websites to get the annual membership status of states. Further, I use *Polity IV* data (`http://systemicpeace.org/polity/polity4.htm`) to get information on the democratic quality of member states. The authors of the data-set assess the competitiveness of political participation, the openness and competitiveness of executive recruitment and the constraints on the chief executive (Marshall, Jaggers and Gurr 2014, p. 14). Further, they propose that states with Polity IV democracy scores higher than 6 can be considered to be "full democracies". In consequence, I calculate the annual share of member states with a Polity score higher than 6 to evaluate the overall democratic quality of the IGOs' membership.

Also, I provide a qualitative measure of IGO governance depth to operationalize Hypothesis 6. This measure is based on secondary literature and my assessment of changes in the authority of IGOs. This evaluation is based on the changes in effects that IGO actions have on their member states. For example, the IAEA's governance depth has changed in 1970 when the NPT entered into force and made the Agency a large-scale inspection agency which it would not be without obligatory NPT safeguards. Here, authority has risen because of the Agency's grown impact on national sovereignty: although states still need to allow Agency inspections by signing protocols with the IAEA, once they have, they give up some portions of their national authority over nuclear facilities.

Finally, I account for the general presence of an open governance norm in the public discourse, as posited by Hypothesis 7, by analyzing the *Google Books Corpus* (`http://www.culturomics.org/`). It comprises 361 billion English words in more than 5 million books, mainly made available by university libraries. Further, it includes all 1- to 5-grams that occur at least 40 times in the corpus (cf. Michel et al. 2011). To grasp the concept of open and participative governance, I searched for the following keywords: `democratic deficit`, `participatory governance` and `global democracy`. The frequencies for these 2-grams are than added together into a single indicator for the norm of open governance. (cf. for a similar usage of this indicator Tallberg et al. 2013). While no combination of keywords can perfectly measure the ambiguous meanings of global norms, the increased usage of such terms however suggests that relevant ideas become important in various contexts and discourses.

4   *The Opening of Security IGOs*

In this chapter, I present the openness and processes of opening up of the IAEA and OPCW. This chapter is the first step in the three-step study design and is focused on the *description* of opening up and variation in the explanatory conditions. I will discuss each organization individually and illustrate instances of opening in each organization. Further, I show change in the organizations' environments that could have caused increasing participation or transparency. Thus, this section presents and discusses the data that I will use for the comparative analysis, the second step, in the next chapter (for a detailed discussion of the data, see Appendix A). The sections below can thus be read as descriptive case studies of the two organizations. Uncovering causal links and generalizing over both IGOs will be in the task of Chapter 5.

In summary, my discussion of the two organizations under analysis illustrates that there are a number of interesting instances of opening up (see Table 4.1). First, at both IGOs, talk about openness is present since the 1990s. Both IGOs commonly refer to the ideas of participation and transparency since that time and thus often acknowledge that those principles are of relevance for the organization. Further, in both organizations, the normative content of transparency and participation references become more demanding over time. For participation, over time, a wider range of actors beyond experts gets acknowledged as important for the work of the organizations. Similarly, for transparency, the idea of direct information provision to the public, as opposed to member states or selected actors, becomes stronger in the talk of the organizations. As the discussion below will illustrate, this is not only cheap talk. Instead, both organizations also open up on their decision and action dimensions.

Table 4.1: Openness of Security Organizations and Changes in Explanatory Conditions

		IAEA	OPCW
Participation	*T*	talk in early years, silence in 1970s and 1980s, increased and diversified participation talk since 1990	constant amount of participation talk
	D	formalized accreditation system abandoned in 1960s, ad-hoc system, formalized in 1975, no changes since then	formalized ad-hoc system, slight increases in NGO participation rights in mid 2000s
	A	high participation of NGOs in 1950s, 1960s, 1990s, 2000s	slightly increased NGO participation since late 2000s
		high number of participation events in 1980s	slightly rising numbers of participation events since mid 2000s
Transparency	*T*	transparency talk since mid 1990s	constant amount of participation talk
	D	decisions toward more transparency since late 1980s	decisions towards more transparency since 2000s
	A	high spending for transparency in 1950s, 1960s, and 2000s	increased transparency spending since mid 2000s
res. expl.	*H1*	budget restraints in 1980s and 1990s	budgetary crisis in early 2000s
	H2	high inequality, increasing since 1990s	high inequality, increasing over time
	H3	no change in statutory tasks	no changes in statutory tasks
norm expl.	*H4*	very strong growth of media visibility in 1990s and 2000s	weak visibility in the media
	H5	majority of democratic members since 1990s	majority of democratic members since early 2000s
	H6	increase in authority in 1970 with NPT, increase in authority since 1990s due to special inspections	no change in authority
	H7	presence of norm of open governance since 1990s	

Changes in openness decisions, however, are less strong for participation. High-level rules that are regulating non-state participation at formal IGO meetings change only rarely. Neither of both IGOs currently apply a formal accreditation mechanism for non-state actors. Instead, more or less formalized ad-hoc systems for non-state participation are in place. However, administrative rules about transparency change more frequently. At both IGOs, there is a gradual movement to more organizational transparency towards the general public since the 1990s. This is notable in areas like public information strategies and the provision of documents and reports to the public.

Third, opening up on the action dimension is also strong. Both IGOs increasingly spend money for transparency since the mid 2000s. This occurs at the same time when talk about transparency also increases. Especially with the wider use of the Internet, both organizations spend more resources on providing information about themselves and their policy fields directly to the general public. Regarding participation, the representation of non-state actors is limited compared to larger IGOs but slowly growing over time. In recent years, at both IGOs, there is a notable growth in the number of non-state representatives that are present at their annual policy-making conference. Similarly, the IAEA and OPCW become more participative in their day-to-day activities. Increasing numbers of participation events have increased chances for non-state influence since the 1980s at the IAEA and since the mid 2000s at the OPCW.

Overall, both the IAEA and OPCW are more open today than they were at their creation. The cases thus show that organizational openness also matters in the security sector. Further, at both IGOs, openness increases incrementally. As the discussion below will show, there are no surprisingly strong or fast changes in the openness of the IAEA or the OPCW. Also, to a large degree, most of the change appears to be driven by endogenous factors. Increasing transparency and participation are thus not caused by large-scale demands from the organization's environments or other external shocks. This further suggests that most of the time, both IGOs are in the *maintaining legitimacy* mode when it comes to opening up. This will be discussed in more detail in the case study chapters.

Next, this chapter looks at variation in the explanatory conditions. For the resource based explanations, there are instances of budget shortages at both IGOs. In the OPCW, there even was a budget crisis in the early 2000s, potentially increasing demands for more openness. At both IGOs, inequality between member states is high and slightly increasing since the 1990s. Information asymmetries are thus a likely driver for openness. Regarding complexity, there are no changes in the statutory tasks of the organizations. The IAEA has more statutory tasks than the OPCW, so its openness should be higher. Also, there is a general growth in the complexity of individual tasks of the organizations. However, as there is no measured variation over time, I will exclude Hypothesis 3 from the analysis in the second step.

I also find variation for the norm-based explanations. Visibility in the global media changes dramatically for the IAEA. In the 1990s and 2000s, it becomes increasingly visible to a wide audience. There should thus be effects on the openness of the IAEA due to risen legitimacy challenges from the global public. The OPCW, on the other hand, remains largely invisible from 1997 until 2011. There is also variation in the democratic composition of the organizations' members. At the IAEA, democracies are in a majority since the 1990s, at the OPCW since the 2000s. Effects of democratic socialization should therefore influence opening decisions in both organizations. Further, both IGOs have a considerable level of political authority due to their strong inspection mandates. Only at the IAEA, authority rises over time due to NPT inspections and special inspections under UN Security Council mandates. For both IGOs, legitimacy challenges are thus likely, possibly triggering opening up. Finally, the norm of open governance is present in the global discourse since the 1990s. It should therefore provide an important external normative reference frame for evaluating the appropriateness and quality of governance at the OPCW and IAEA. In summary, the following chapter thus not only shows that the organizations have opened up, but that there is variation in the explanatory variables. Without this variation, the qualitative comparative analysis in Chapter 5 would fail to provide insights on possible explanations of opening up.

4.1   THE INTERNATIONAL ATOMIC ENERGY AGENCY

In the following paragraphs, I will first provide an overview of the IAEA by presenting its main *functions, activities*, its *organizational set-up, important events* and an overview of salient *political conflicts*. Second, I discuss the Agency's openness. Finally, I will describe important changes in the Agency's environment which may explain increased transparency and participation.

4.1.1   THE HISTORY, FUNCTIONS AND DEVELOPMENT OF THE IAEA

FUNCTIONS AND ACTIVITIES

The IAEA is an international organization in the UN system. It is is responsible for peaceful applications of nuclear technology. The IAEA is a universal membership organization with currently 161 member states. The membership includes most states with a significant nuclear industry despite North Korea, which withdrew membership in 1994. Today, 30 of the IAEA members have an active nuclear energy program. The IAEA headquarters are located in Vienna and it currently employs around 2.300 people. The Agency has a founding myth, created by US President Dwight D. Eisenhower in his *Atoms for Peace* speech before the United Nations General Assembly in

December 1953. Realizing the vast destructive potential of nuclear weapons, he called for the pooling of nuclear technology for peaceful uses under an international authority (on the history of the IAEA see e.g. Bechhoefer 1959; IAEA 1977; Baradei and International Atomic Energy Agency 2007; Scheinman 1987; Fischer and IAEA 1997; Schriefer, Sandtner and Rudischhauser 2007; Olwell 2008). Its 1956 *Statute* sees the Agency's main objectives as follows:

> "The Agency shall seek to accelerate and enlarge the contribution of atomic energy to peace, health and prosperity throughout the world. It shall ensure, so far as it is able, that assistance provided by it or at its request or under its supervision or control is not used in such a way as to further any military purpose" (IAEA 1956, Art. II).

Consequently, the Agency understands its mandate as based on three pillars: *(i) technology*, i.e. the transfer of peaceful nuclear applications like nuclear medicine or food irradiation to all member states, *(ii) safety*, which is the provision and review of safety standards for nuclear technology, most prominently for nuclear power and *(iii) verification*, i.e. safeguarding the peaceful nature of nuclear facilities in non-nuclear weapon states. The IAEA thus works on a variety of issues, spanning from development work over the development of safety standards to on-the-ground inspections of national nuclear facilities. This broad range of activities leads to a high demand for expertise, a relatively high visibility in the global media and to contacts with a number of different expert communities.

The relationship of the Agency and its experts is quite special. First, the Agency has numerous committees, special advisory bodies and expert councils that advise it in its daily activities. Second, experts are also often rotating into the Agency staff for a limited time. It is not unusual that, e.g. directors of national research institutions or ministries take positions at the Agency and return to their former jobs after some years of international service. Also, delegations to the Agency's General Conference are often headed not by diplomats but by officials from energy or technology ministries. Further, the elected General Conference presidents often had a professional training in science and have worked at national research institutions. This leads to close connections and exchange of expertise between the Agency and its "community."[4]

How can the IAEA's output be described? It comprises activities in the areas of *science, nuclear energy, nuclear safety,* and *nuclear inspections.* The

---

[4]This sense of community is actively promoted by the Agency. Cf. e.g. an image video that the Agency produced for its 56th General Conference in 2012, stating that the IAEA was a place for "[diplomatic] consensus building, knowledge sharing, peer-to-peer networking", http://vimeo.com/49908778.

Agency is a place where knowledge is collected, organized and created. This scientific function of the IAEA is deeply embedded in its Statute (1956). Article III, A1 empowers the Agency to "encourage and assist research on, and development and practical application of, atomic energy for peaceful uses throughout the world" and Art III, A2 mandates the IAEA to "foster the exchange of scientific and technical information on peaceful uses of atomic energy". Consequently, over the years, the Agency has developed a number of instruments to serve the scientific community and to promote the advancement of nuclear science:

- *Coordinated Research Projects* (CRP) are a main instrument to finance research on nuclear technologies and to get in contact with individual scientists. The IAEA was one of the first organizations in the UN system to organize and finance research projects (cf. Göthel, Voigt and Burkart 2007). CRPs usually focus on a specific topic (e.g. from the areas of cancer therapy, animal health, water, nuclear energy) and bring together researchers from national institutions that conduct the research in cooperation. Today, the Agency hosts over 100 active CRPs with an annual budget of about 7 million EUR.[5]

- *The International Nuclear Information System* (INIS) is a collection of nuclear research. It became operational in the 1970s and was first a collection of microfiche with a companion index, distributed to collaborating national research institutions. Later, it was one of the first data-bases that became accessible online for member-states. Here, the IAEA was a forerunner in the UN system and also became an expert of electronic data-bases (cf. e.g. the extensive holdings of the IAEA's Archives: IAEA Archives 1970; 1975*c*; 1977; 1975*b;a*) Today, INIS is still one of the largest databases on nuclear science, including a vast collection of published and grey literature and it is openly accessible via the Internet since 2009.

- *Scientific Conferences* were a large field of activity in the Agency's early years. It organized large-scale conferences, helped with the management of others' conferences and was a publisher and distributor of proceedings of conferences (cf. IAEA 1977). With the help of its *Scientific Advisory Committee*, the IAEA e.g. co-organized the *International Conferences on the Peaceful Uses of Atomic Energy* with the United Nations, which were major scientific events, bringing together thousands of researchers (cf. Scheinman 1987, chap. 3). Here, the Agency acted as an important networking agent that assisted scientists, in times of the Cold War, from both blocks and enabled an exchange of information (IAEA 1997, 289f).

---

[5] See http://cra.iaea.org/cra/index.html.

- *Expert bodies* were always an important part of the Agency work. Over the years, the Agency has created a number of expert commissions and advisory bodies, manned by scientists and national administrators. There are expert bodies on safeguards, inspection technologies, and technical cooperation. Further, the General Conference often mandates the Agency to set-up ad-hoc groups of experts on relevant issues. Usually, the expert bodies present reports that are than considered by the Agency administration and policy-making organs. Overall, those bodies are important institutionalized forms of non-state participation that provide the Agency with expert advise and scientific knowledge.
- *Publications* are another kind of scientific activity. The Agency has published and distributed vast amounts of information. It runs a large number of publication series, ranging from technical standards, safety assessments to the TECDOCs, a collection of technical documents with relation to the Agency's work. Most publications used to be made available at low prices to member states and individuals. Today, they can be downloaded for free on the Agency's website, thus lowering financial barriers for nuclear research.

Since its early years until the 1980s, the Agency was widely perceived as an international promoter of nuclear energy. Nuclear energy takes a special position under the wide range of possible peaceful nuclear applications. It was regarded as the most advanced and most fruitful technology, enabling safe and cheap electricity for the growing world economy. Dangers of the technology, both for the environment and the people, are recognized. Yet, the calculated risks, especially during the 1960s-1980s, were seen as minimal and manageable through safety standards, training and strong oversight. The promotion of nuclear energy is deeply embedded into to Agency Statute (IAEA 1956, Art. II), indicating the euphoria for this nuclear application at the time of the Agency's foundation. Also, a so far not realized mechanism, the Agency was mandated to act as an international supplier of fission materials, so that nuclear enrichment and the production of nuclear fuel would stay in the hand of a few countries, minimizing risks of proliferation (IAEA 1956, Art IX). Yet, this function only slowly begins to take shape with the establishment of a fuel bank for low enriched Uranium in Kazakhstan in 2015. Further, the Agency runs a number of programs to promote nuclear energy (cf. also Doub and Dukert 1975, 757f):

- *State networks*, in particularly *INPRO* ("International Project on Innovative Nuclear Reactors and Fuel Cycles", founded in 2000), are established to bring states together that exchange information on nuclear power production and to develop new approaches to energy security. Here, the IAEA's working assumption is that nuclear power and "[t]he production of this energy at a reasonable cost, without environmental damage and in a safe and secure manner, will be one of this century's most challenging undertakings" (IAEA 2013, 3). Before INPRO, there have been other formats that encouraged member state cooperation on nuclear energy programs.

- *Information Systems and Databases* are an important part of nuclear power promotion. The Agency collects large amounts of information on reactor designs and national nuclear programs. This information is a valuable source for states that think about developing their own nuclear programs.

Further, the IAEA is the main international body responsible to assure safe and secure usages and applications of nuclear technologies, ranging from nuclear power to nuclear medicine and other techniques. The safety functions of the Agency have become more important since the first large scale nuclear accidents in *Three Mile Island* (1979) and *Chernobyl* (1986). Since the late 1980s, the Agency has been perceived and has described itself with the language of safety (cf. Scheinman 1987, Ch. 3). Further, the Agency is very active and finances many activities to fulfill its statutory function to establish "standards of safety for protection of health and minimization of danger to life and property (including such standards for labour conditions)" (IAEA 1956, Art III A6):

- *Safety standards* are among the most important documents that the Agency develops. They cover a very wide range of nuclear technologies: power plants, the fuel cycle, nuclear waste, research reactors, transportation and mining as well as medical radiation sources. These standards are usually developed in a long process with input from experts, scientists and national administrators. Per se, IAEA Safety Standards are non-binding, but recognized as minimum standards (cf. Niehaus 2007). Further, they are often converted into national law. Especially for developing states, they are important sources of reference to develop their own legislation.
- *International Conventions* were also developed by the IAEA. After Chernobyl, the international community developed binding legal agreements under the auspices of the IAEA to improve nuclear safety. As of today, there are five conventions, regulating issues like the assistance between states and the early warning in the case of a nuclear accident, physical protection of nuclear materials and on general safety standards for nuclear installations. Those conventions have considerably improved the international safety structure for nuclear technologies and, further, have improved state cooperation in questions of nuclear safety. The IAEA hosts these conventions and has been very influential in developing its rules and wordings.

- *Services for member states* are another core activity of the Agency. It provides a number of different safety services. For example, the IAEA organizes peer reviews of national safety regulations and nuclear facility management. Further, the IAEA assists in the training of safety officials and provides confidential review services of nearly all aspects of nuclear safety to its member states (cf. e.g. Washington 1997). These services are used by many states and they are often applauded by member states in their evaluations of the IAEA.

Finally, the Agency is best-known for its inspection activities. Establishing a nuclear inspection regime was a core intention of the Agency's founders that gave it the competence "[t]o establish and administer safeguards designed to ensure that special fissionable and other materials, services, equipment, facilities, and information [...] are not used in such a way as to further any military purpose" (IAEA 1956, Art. III A5). The importance of inspections was strengthened with the entry into force of the *Nuclear Non-Proliferation Treaty* (NPT) in 1970 which established mandatory inspections for all signatory non-nuclear weapons states.

Yet, there is criticism of the IAEA's effectiveness in assuring non-proliferation, and even more fundamental criticism of the Agency's independence under the key terms of politicization and Western bias. These voices are growingly heard in connection to inspection activities in situations of political crisis (e.g. in Iraq, Iran, North Korea). There are a number of speakers in the Agency's environment that are lamenting a growing politicization of the Agency's work that goes hand in hand with its activities in those situations. The politicization is said to dissolve the old, a-political mode of operation of the Agency. Further, states that are directly concerned with such inspections, e.g. Iran, voice accusation of bias. For them, the Agency has lost its independent character and has become an instrument for powerful nuclear weapon states. But what does the Agency do to prevent nuclear proliferation?

- *Safeguards* are probably the best known activity of the Agency. The IAEA Safeguards System is quite complex because it is based on different agreements between states and the Agency (cf. e.g. Szasz 1970, Ch. 21). Before the NPT, IAEA safeguards were used only sparsely and most of the time to control exports of nuclear technologies, like nuclear power plants that the US exported to India. With the entry into force of the NPT, safeguards became common for all states with nuclear industries and research. Those safeguards are usually based on Agency document INFCIRC/153, which also includes a draft treaty that each state signs with the Agency. These *Comprehensive Safeguards Agreements* grant far reaching rights to Agency inspectors to verify the peaceful nature of all declared and non-declared nuclear activities of a state. However, weaknesses in the system became obvious when the Iraqi clandestine nuclear weapons program was discovered in the early 1990s. Stronger safeguards were needed, that e.g. allowed assessments of nuclear activities outside those facilities that states declared. Those were formalized in 1997 with the *Additional Protocol* under INFCIRC/540. Many states have signed Additional Protocols, but as those are also bilateral agreements between the Agency and states, there is no legal way to force states to sign Additional Protocols (cf. Fischer 2000). Overall, safeguards are widely acclaimed as the most valuable tool of non-proliferation. At the same time, they are heavily contested because they bring the Agency into a position of political power: a negative safeguards assessment may have severe political consequences.

- *Special inspection activities in situations of political crises* are a relatively new activity for the IAEA. In contrast to normal safeguards that are conducted on a routine schedule, the Agency has from time to time been asked to conduct special inspections. A first notable case were the special inspections in Iraq that started in 1991. For the first time, the IAEA was mandated by the United Nations Security Council (S/RES/687) to conduct far reaching inspections to verify the complete destruction of the Iraqi nuclear weapons program. While the Iraq inspections continued for many years, new engagements started. In North Korea, the Agency discovered irregularities with the official declaration of materials and called for deeper inspections. The evolving political crisis lead to North Korea's withdrawal from both the NPT and the IAEA and the expulsion of IAEA inspectors. Later, the Agency took over an important verification role for the USA-PRK *Agreed Framework* of 1994. Around the same time, the IAEA was asked to supervise the dismantling of the South African nuclear weapons program. Ten years later, starting in 2003, the Agency was involved in the dismantling of the Libyan nuclear program which also revealed information about the dimensions of a nuclear black market that the Agency was not aware of (cf. for a detailed overview Wing and Simpson 2013). Further, since 2003, IAEA inspections in Iran have become an issue of international politics when the Director-General reported on a number of outstanding issues with inspecting its nuclear program. The various *action plans* and *Board Resolutions* have been backed by UNSC resolutions, asking Iran to cooperate with the IAEA, thus giving the Agency's Iran policy an important political backing. Overall, these inspections during political crises have increased the Agency's media presence and raised state and non-state demands for information.

ORGANIZATIONAL SET-UP

When looking at the organizational set-up, the Agency's highest policy-making organ is the *General Conference* (GC), where all member states meet annually to decide on matters related to the Agency. Thus, the GC is the universal organ with equal representation of all member-states. However, much of the Agency's business is organized by the *Board of Governors*, consisting of currently 35 member states. The members of the Board are elected according to principles of regional representation and the status of the development of their national nuclear industries. De facto, there has been little substantial change in the Board's composition: a number of European and North American countries have quasi-permanent seats, due to the size of their nuclear industry. Further, there is no participatory procedure to determine the "most advanced" countries qualifying for Board Membership, a situation that has often been criticized by Agency member-states.

IMPORTANT HISTORICAL DEVELOPMENTS

Over the years, there have been a number of events in the IAEA's environment that have caused challenges for the IAEA's work and for its public perception. In its early years, there was little public attention for the IAEA and its specialized activities outside its own community of experts and state officials. Today, the Agency has grown into a political actor with lots of media attention (see below, e.g. Figure 4.9) and a number of conflicts between its members. The following points in time illustrate this transformation (also see e.g. Findlay 2012):

1970 With the entry into force of the NPT, the Agency saw an increase in its safeguarding activities. With obligatory inspections for non-nuclear weapon states, the safeguards budget began to increase, raising questions of the appropriate balance between the Agency's verification and technology pillars (see below, e.g. Figure 4.6).

1986 The Chernobyl accident caused increased interest in nuclear safety and calls for a new role of the Agency as the international institution that creates strong safety standards. At the same time, there was growing skepticism of the Agency's active promotion of nuclear energy. Also, more spending for nuclear safety increased demands from developing member states for a renewed focus on the developmental aspects of the IAEA Statute. Also, non-state actors began to ask whether the Agency, with its close connections to the nuclear industry and experts, was the right institution to develop independent safety standards.

1990s and later The 1990s marked the beginning of the politicization of the IAEA's work. When the IAEA was taking over special inspections, like in Iraq in 1991, its impact on international security politics became more visible to its audiences. Instruments, such as submitting possible proliferator countries to the United Nations Security Council (IAEA 1956, Art. III B4) or *Special Inspections* (IAEA INFCIRC/153) were used more often, causing deeper impacts for the concerned countries. The enhanced authority of the Agency has lead to various forms of criticism from the environment, ranging from accusations of a pro-Western bias to the manipulative release of safeguards results to prevent sanctions or escalations of political conflicts.

POLITICAL CONFLICTS

As these events suggest, there are two main political conflicts that strongly influence the IAEA's work. First, the *growing politicization*, caused by growing organizational authority and the Agency's larger impact on international security politics, has created a number of conflicts within the Agency's membership. Second, the main question about the right *balance of statutory functions* has been important since the entry into force of the NPT and the resulting growing expenses for nuclear safeguards. Safeguards are costly and bind resources which the Agency could use for technical assistance work. Further, there is a strong imbalance in the Agency's membership with regard to which states cause most safeguards costs. Mainly, most of safeguards costs are caused by inspections of nuclear power plants. The 30 states with active reactors[6] are mostly Western states. Thus, the majority of the Agency's member states contribute to the Safeguards budget without ever being subject to safeguards, themselves.

4.1.2   IAEA PARTICIPATION

As I have discussed above, the Agency is a relevant organization in the international security infrastructure, mainly through its safeguards and special inspections. Further, it has some impact on the technological development of its member states and on the advancement of nuclear sciences. This puts the Agency into two different policy fields with different expectations for openness. In the security field, as discussed above, little opening is to be expected. Due to its activities in the development field, however, opening would be less surprising. As I show below, the Agency is in fact relatively open.

PARTICIPATION TALK

First, there are some interesting developments in the way how the IAEA *talks* about participation. I track changes in the organizations' talk by looking at

---

[6]See e.g. http://www.iaea.org/pris/.

references to ideas and concepts in their annual reports (AR). The Director-General prepares the AR for the annual General Conference. The Annual Reports are available in the Agency's online General Conference archives (see e.g. `http://iaea.org/About/Policy/GC/GC55/`). I read all ARs that the Agency has issued from 1957 until 2011. The AR of a specific year is usually published a month before the GC of the following year. In recent years, the AR covers the Agency's activities for the previous calendar year. Earlier reports covered the time from July to June. I will refer to the documents by their IAEA document number.

The Agency's AR is a good source because it is the annual document that the Agency produces to report on its activities to its members, but also to the UNGA and the broader public. The ARs are official Agency documents, their production is required by the Agency's Statute (IAEA 1956, Art VI, J). Over the years, their appearance has changed from a very technical document to a report with, since 1997, many pictures, explanatory boxes and statistics. This indicates that the Agency tries to target a wider audience than only its member states. Nevertheless, the style remains very neutral and emotional language, like naming persons, criticizing or applauding actions, or using decorative adjectives, is very rare. Even in its 50th anniversary AR (GC(51)/5), there is no larger emotional appraisal of the organization and its work. The same is true for the description of important events like the Fukushima incident in March 2011 or the Chernobyl Accident in 1986. Here, the IAEA e.g. states that "[t]he most important event in 1986 in the nuclear power field was the Chernobyl accident." Yet, the

> "overall effects of this accident on the nuclear power programmes of Member States have yet to be seen. It produced an expected immediate upsurge in public and political opposition to nuclear power in many countries, but it did not cause the cancellation of any nuclear power programmes" (GC(31)/800: 7).

The usual texts in the AR describe activities that the Agency has funded or run on its own. These presentations usually state that a certain project was funded, that the project members have met several times and, as an output, documents, standards or data-sets were published. Overall, through the AR, the Agency presents itself as a technical organization that evaluates political and technical issues with a professional distance.

Figure 4.1 illustrates the number of references to the idea of participation in the Agency's AR. It is notable that there have been a number of references to participation in the early years and, as expected, also in the recent decade. For many years, however, the Agency is silent about participation. What issues are discussed when the Agency refers to participation?

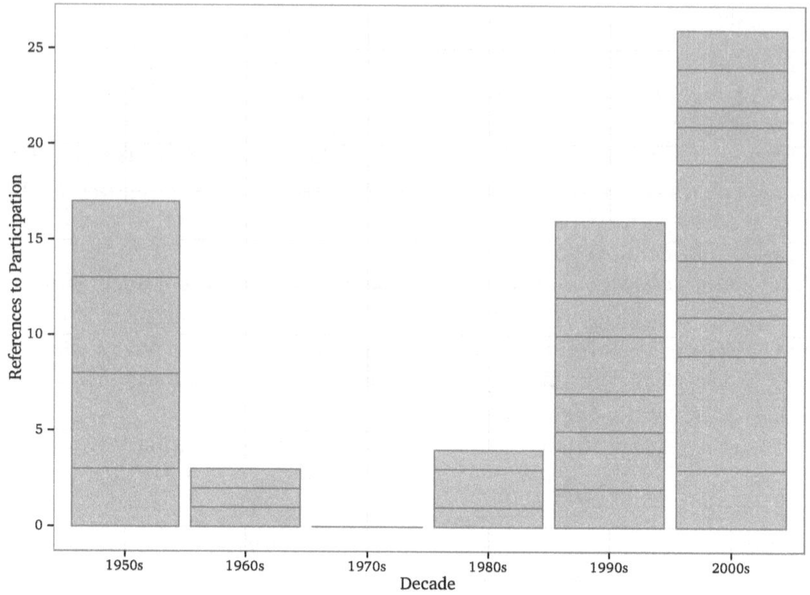

Figure 4.1: Participation Talk in the IAEA Annual Reports

In the early years, participation of non-state actors was regarded as a necessary step to build up the Agency's know how and to establish an international community of experts on nuclear technologies. This is highlighted in many of the early Annual Reports:

> "Increasing emphasis has been given to liaison work with national and international non-governmental organizations which in many countries play an important part in the shaping of public opinion and provide good channels for the distribution of information" (GC(3)/74, p. 56).

> "It has therefore proved necessary to maintain informal contacts with these bodies so as to avoid duplication of activities or to enable the Agency to draw upon the scientific services which they can offer" (GC(3)/74, p. 22).

Next to scientific NGOs, the Agency also underlines its cooperation with organizations that are active in the field of electric energy, which also includes a number of other intergovernmental organizations. Further, there is an emphasis on the representation of workers and employers active in the nuclear industries:

> "All such organizations having consultative status with the Agency
> are now being kept informed of the Agency's activities of interest
> to them, and with their help, knowledge is being spread about
> the Agency's work. In cases where the interest of the organi-
> zation in the Agency's work is particularly direct, for instance,
> in the case of non-governmental organizations concerned with
> science, technology and the economics of electric power pro-
> duction such as ICSU, ICRU, ICRP, ISO, WPC and UNIPEDE,
> relations with the Agency have been close. Closer relations
> are also expected with non-governmental organizations repre-
> senting trade unions and thus interested in the problems of
> radiation protection, such as ICFTU and IFCTU, commercial
> or co-operative economic interests, such as ICC and ICA and
> transportation matters, such as IUIN. WFUNA has helped to
> make the Agency's work familiar to the public and the United
> Nations Associations in various parts of the world" (GC(4)/114,
> p. 14).

Thus, overall, the Agency describes a beneficial exchange and cooperation
with non-governmental organizations:

> "The Agency has continued to receive valuable help from several
> of these bodies, particularly in preparing and implementing its
> recommendations on radiation protection and safety, and third
> party liability, in planning and developing its technical programs
> – for instance, by participation in the Agency's panels – and in
> publicizing its work" (GC(5)/ 154, p. 8).

In addition, there is some reporting on the formal accreditation process
that NGOs need to undergo. Again, statements are often linked to the idea
of building contacts with non-governmental organizations in order to get
information and establish channels for information exchange:

> "The group of organizations thus accorded consultative status
> include a large number of those whose work is of special in-
> terest to the Agency. Nevertheless, certain non-governmental
> organizations working on aspects of the peaceful uses of atomic
> energy, or the services of which can be of value to the Agency
> have not yet found it possible to apply for consultative status"
> (GC(3)/74, p. 22).

In more recent years, issues discussed under the participation label
become more diverse. For example, since the late 1980s, the representation
of women, both in the Agency staff and as participants in Agency programs
and projects, became an important issue:

> "The role of women in development has been receiving increas-
> ing attention in the governing bodies of the United Nations sys-
> tem. Accordingly, and in recognition of the contribution women
> can make to development efforts, the Secretariat has, for a num-
> ber of years, been monitoring the participation of women in
> Agency technical co-operation programmes" (GC(31)/800, p.
> 18).

Also, there is growing concern about the Agency's public perception, especially the one in the global news media. As a consequence, the Agency
begins to host "Public Information Fora." These events are planned as participatory meetings where the Agency can exchange its views on nuclear issues
with the media and provide the media and other non-state actors with their
interpretations on questions like nuclear energy, security and safety.

> "Additionally, the first Public Information Forum was staged
> in Vienna at the time of the General Conference session. This
> initiative brought together over 80 media representatives, gov-
> ernment information officials and industry specialists from 35
> Member States for a broad review of nuclear information prob-
> lems and strategies" (GC(35)/953, p. 146).

Further, direct communication with the public and increasing outreach and
participation becomes an important goal of the Agency strategy since the
late 1990s:

> "The third part of the reform process was a review of the role
> and management of public information and the Agency's out-
> reach to civil society, particularly the nuclear, arms control and
> development communities and the media, using the most mod-
> ern and effective tools. Development of a new strategy was
> started" (GOV/1999/28, p. 14).

> "The Director General approved a new public information and
> outreach policy. This policy is intended to enhance the Agency's
> interaction with opinion leaders, the media and civil society,
> reaching out to both traditional and nontraditional partners, for
> instance among nongovernmental organizations and the private
> sector" (GC(44)/4, p. 102).

Another issue that becomes important under the participation label is the
inclusion of communities effected by the Agency's work. For example, the
Agency promises that "[c]lose collaboration with interested international
organizations and those representing consumers, the food industry and

trade will be sought" (GC(38)/2, p. 63) when developing guidelines for food irradiation. Similarly, the Agency installed an expert panel to provide advice on "current and future options for local participation in the planning, manufacturing, construction, operation and maintenance of nuclear desalination complexes using nuclear energy, both at the level of individual countries and on a regional level" (IAEA 1995).

To sum up, in the IAEA case, there is high participation talk in the years after its foundation. Here, participation talk is basically on the inclusion of experts and the scientific community as well as on the formalities of NGO accreditation. In the 1960s, 1970s and early 1980s, participation is only rarely a topic in IAEA talk. Starting in the late 1980s, participation reappears in the official communication in a more diverse form. Other global discourses, e.g. on the participation of women or of local stakeholders are picked up and become a more common feature of the the IAEA's organizational talk. Overall, there is thus an interesting change over time that needs to be explained.

PARTICIPATION DECISIONS

Next, how have *decisions* of the Agency that relate to participation changed over the years? Overall, there is little change in formal rules: the Preparatory Commission for the IAEA has developed guidelines for NGO participation that were accepted at the first regular General Conference. However, block confrontation made the accreditation of new NGOs nearly impossible so that the Agency turned to a more informal rule that allowed the Director-General to invite interested non-governmental organizations to participate at the GC. Since then, the formal accreditation rules are not applied and participation is regulated by an invitiation-based procedure without formalized rules for the rights of non-state actors.

In more detail, during the Preparatory Commission, the question of non-state participation was made an issue by a number of states. For example, Belgium pushed for the creation of a formal consultative status of non-governmental organizations:

> "The Belgian Government attaches great importance to providing a consultative relationship between the Agency and non-governmental organizations, the work of which is related to that of the International Atomic Energy Agency. [...] The specialized knowledge and experience of such organizations will, in the opinion of the Belgian Government, assist the Agency in its objectives set forth in article II of the Statute" (IAEA/PC/W.26).

Attached to the Belgian proposal, there is a draft resolution that will in later Agency meetings be adopted in large parts as INFCIRC/14, setting the formal NGO accreditation rules of the IAEA. In the discussion around the Belgian draft, a number of related issues were elaborated:

- The Executive Office of the Director General should bear responsibility for NGO coordination and liaison (IAEA/PC/W.33(S)/Add.1, p. 4 and IAEA/PC/W.45(S)/Add.1, p. 5).
- There was discussion about the protection of representatives from NGOs from the prosecution of the Austrian state for statements they had made before Agency meetings (IAEA/PC/OR. 63, p. 10). However, stronger protection rules for NGO representatives, e.g. modeled after the FAO headquarters agreement with the Italian government, where not included in the draft resolution for the first General Conference.
- Finally, seating arrangements for the first GC were discussed, allocating the "second gallery [...] for the remainder of the press, for about twenty-five representatives of non-governmental organizations and for about 200 guests of delegations. The very small number of remaining seats would be open to the public" (IAEA/PC/OR. 65, p. 12).

Overall, however, there was broad consensus on the general idea of non-state participation and the need for the Agency to establish formal relations with non-governmental organizations during the Preparatory Commission. At the first General Conference, held in October 1957, many of the proposed resolutions on non-state participation were adopted. In resolution GC.1(S)/RES/12, the General Conference asks the IAEA Board of Governors "to establish and submit to the General Conference for approval during its second regular session rules for the granting of consultative status to non-governmental organizations." This request is fulfilled during the second General Conference. Here, in resolution GC(II)/RES/20, the Agency sets rules for the consultative status of NGOs. The Annex of GC(II)/RES/20, which is later referred to as INFCIRC/14, takes up many proposals from the Belgian Working Paper, presented during the Preparatory Commission. Again, there was broad consensus, also in the Administrative and Legal Committee that prepared the resolution (GC(II)/57), that the Agency needs regulations for the consultative status of NGOs.

In detail, INFCIRC/14 sets the context of participation. The Agency should allow non-state participation "to enable the Agency to secure expert information or advice [...] and to promote knowledge of the principles and activities of the Agency and [...] to enable organizations which represent important groups whose work is relevant to that of the Agency to express their views" (INFCIRC/14, I/1). Further, it sets the following rights and rules for delegations of non-state actors and develops a number of selection criteria for NGOs:

- Selection criteria for NGOs to be considered for consultative status:

- NGOs should work on issues relevant to the work of the Agency.
- The aims of NGOs should be in line with those of the Agency.
- The NGOs should support the Agency's work
- The NGOs need to be professionally organized and have a good international standing.
- NGOs need to have a regional or global scope. National NGOs may be granted access if necessary and with the approval of their member state.

- Rights of accredited NGOs:

  - NGOs receive the provisional agenda of the GC.
  - NGOs may be represented by an observer and advisors at all public meetings of the General Conference.
  - An NGO observer may be invited to public meetings of the Board of Governors.
  - NGOs may receive selected written member state statements and official Agency documents.
  - NGOs may submit statements to Agency organs, no longer than 2000 words.
  - NGOs may address public IAEA meetings by invitation.

- Facilities made available for accredited NGOs include:

  - access to non-restricted documents
  - access to press statements and documents
  - use of the Agency's library
  - appropriate seating and documents during meetings which the NGO is invited to

- Further, NGOs with consultative status shall also be invited to other Agency meetings like seminars, expert meetings, and symposia.
- Also, accredited NGOs have the opportunity to consult with Agency Secretariat staff after special arrangements.

Institutionally, INFCIRC/14 requests that the Board of Governors sets up a "Committee on Non-Governmental Organizations" that decides about the granting of a consultative status. Further, the Director-General shall provide an NGO liaison officer who acts as the central coordination point between the Agency and all NGOs with consultative status. While the latter office has been quite active since its creation, the Committee soon became a playground of big power politics.

Already a few years after the institutionalization of the consultative status, the question which NGOs shall be granted that status, became politicized.

> "Trouble began in early 1959 when the Board received an application by another international labour organization, the World Federation of Scientific Workers (WFSW), a body that the USA and some other Western countries regarded as a mouthpiece of the extreme Left. [...] After the majority of Governors had rejected the application by the WFSW, the Soviet Union and other Warsaw Pact countries successfully blocked all further grants of consultative status" (Fischer and IAEA 1997, 78).

The accreditation of specific NGOs was already an issue in the third GC, which passed a resolution (GC(III)/RES/47) asking the Board to grant consultative status to the World Federation of Trade Unions (WFTU). A year later, in document GC(IV)/INF/29 which summarizes the Board's deliberations on the issue, block confrontation clearly shows its influence. While Western states like the USA hold that the WFTU "was not, in fact, able to represent the interests of workers or to state an independent, as distinct from a governmental, point of view" (ibid., p. 1), the Governor from the Soviet Union reminds the Board "that the grant of consultative status should [not] be governed by ideological considerations" (ibid., p. 2). The gridlock could not be solved despite a number of diplomatic efforts. As a consequence, by 1961:

> "(i) The Board's Committee on Non-Governmental Organizations, foreseen in the Rules on Consultative Status, has not been re-constituted. (ii) No application from an NGO for consultative status has been considered, even though about half-a-dozen new ones were circulated during 1961-62 as Committee documents. (iii) The Director General has discontinued the annual submission to the General Conference of the list of organizations to which consultative status has been granted, as required by paragraph 13 of the Rules. (iv) The Agency has developed informal relationships with a number of NGOs (e.g., the US Atomic Industrial Forum) to which consultative status had not been granted, and in practice accords them most of the benefits of that status except for formal invitations to the General Conference" (Szasz 1970, 313f).

Thus, "a tacit agreement to abandon the entire procedure for granting such status" (Fischer and IAEA 1997, 78) has been reached that allows the Agency to continue to profit from non-state expertise. This informal arrangement has been formalized in 1975. In document GC(XIX)/546, the Board asks the GC to grant it the right to also invite non-governmental organizations to participate in the General Conference without granting a consultative status. As this formalizes the common practice of the IAEA, there was no substantial discussion during the GC (GC(XIX)/OR.183) or in its Committees (GC(XIX)/COM.5/OR.1) and the Board's proposal was accepted in resolution GC(XIX)/332. Since then, it is now standard procedure that the board invites NGOs to participate in the GC, often after informal requests of NGOs to receive an invitation.

Next to these top-level rules, there has been little change. The Rules of Procedures for the GC and the Board that touch on issues of non-state participation have not been changed (i.e. Rule 32 for the GC and Rule 50 for the Board). Thus, overall, there has been limited change in decisions concerning participation in the IAEA case. A formalized system for granting a consultative status to NGOs has been abandoned for political reasons and has been replaced by an ad hoc system that is primarily governed by informal rules.

Participation Action

How has participation changed in the *actions* of the IAEA? Figure 4.2 shows the first measure for participation action, i.e. the number of NGOs that are represented at the Agency GC each year. Data for the participation of NGOs is taken from the official list of participants for the GC, available online as official GC documents. There are a number of documents missing in the online archive, most of them, except for 2007, could be gathered at the Agency's library in Vienna.

Again, there is an interesting pattern of non-state participation in the General Conference. In the Agency's early years, there appears to be considerably more NGO participation. For example, in the 1960s, there were on average 9 NGOs at each General Conference while in the 1970s there were only 5. The number increases again in the 1980s with about 11 NGOs per GC and 13 in the 1990s. Only since the 2000s does the number increase significantly with on average 20 NGOs. Here, it is especially in the most recent years that NGO participation has sharply increased. Compared to other areas of global governance, non-state participation at the IAEA is relatively low. For example, at the 2011 Durban meeting of the UN Framework Convention on Climate Change, 665 non-governmental organizations were present (FCCC/CP/2011/INF.3). At the World Trade Organization, 235 NGOs attended the 2011 Ministerial Meeting (WT/MIN(11)/INF/6). At the UNHCR's 2011 Annual Consultations with Non-Governmental Organizations, participants from 212 NGOs were present (UNHCR 2011). However, these are also relatively well-known IGOs with high visibility in the global news media.

When looking at other facets of the data, it becomes visible that there is indeed an increased interest in the Agency's work. Figure 4.2 includes a black line which represents the number of new NGOs, i.e. of organizations

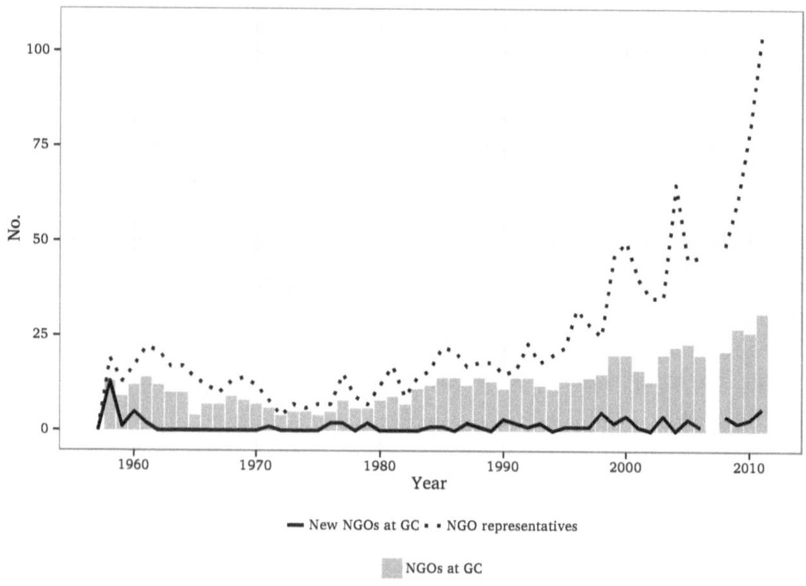

Figure 4.2: Participation of NGOs in IAEA General Conference

that have been invited to the GC for the first time. Despite the spike at the second GC in 1958, a considerable number of new NGOs have started to frequent the GC since the 1990s. Another trend, the increasing number of official NGO representatives, represented by a dotted line in Figure 4.2, points in a similar direction. Until the 1990s, there were on average about 19 officially accredited NGO representatives at each GC. Since then, the number has risen to 35, where the GC of 2011 shows a maximum value of over 100 NGO representatives.

Yet, who are the NGOs that go to the IAEA GC? In the early years, it is especially social issues, represented through professional and worker associations, and topics like business and science that the NGOs stand for. In later years, there is a growing representation of organizations standing for (nuclear) energy. Further, topics like development were strong in the late 1970s and early 1980s, yet lost importance since then. Similarly, representatives of the communication and transportation industries seem to have lost their interest in the work of the IAEA over the last decade. Next to the topics already discussed, issues like peace and international law are constantly represented at the IAEA General Conference. Overall, the represented interests are quite diverse. However, there appears to be some dominance of pro-nuclear organizations. NGOs that are outspoken anti-nuclear are not represented at the GC. This is not too surprising, given that the formal accreditation criteria require NGOs to be supportive of the IAEA's main goals.

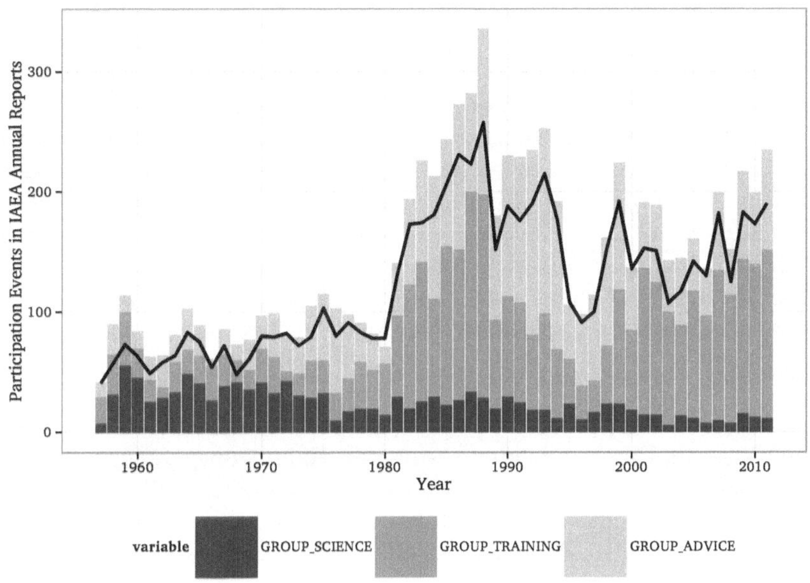

Figure 4.3: Participation Events in IAEA Annual Report by Amount (line) and Type (bars)

Figure 4.3 shows the results for the second measurement for participation action, i.e. *participation events* taken from the Agency's Annual Report. The total amount of participation events is represented by the black line. Again, participation events are participative actions like expert meetings, research meetings or training workshops that let "outsiders" participate in the work of the Agency and where information from the participants flows back to the Agency, possibly influencing IAEA decisions and practices. The data show a large increase in participation events in the 1980s. In the Agency's first two decades, the Annual Reports present on average of 84 participation events. During the 1980s, this amount more than doubles to 192 events per year on average. In the most recent decades, there are on average 147 events per year.

The bars in figure 4.3 group the participation events. Here, it is visible that scientific events like symposia and Agency organized panels were a

very important type of participatory events in the Agency's early years.[7]
Since the 1980s and especially in the 2000s, training events like regional or
national courses are the largest share of participation events. In the 1990s,
however, many events fall into the advice category. Here, the Agency installs
expert panels, standing advisory groups and similar institutions that provide
external expert information to the Agency. Those events are hosted on a
number of issues, ranging from safeguards to more technical issues like food
irradiation or nuclear water desalination.

Overall, since the 1980s, there is thus an increase in Agency participation
events. Yet, opposed to the general trend towards more, but moderate,
participation in the GC, which also increased during the 1980s, there is no
continuous trend towards more participation. To the opposite, especially in
the mid 1990s, the Agency reports less participatory events in its Annual
Reports. Further, in recent years, there is no strong growth in participation,
rather a stabilization of participation events.

4.1.3   IAEA Transparency

What are the developments of IAEA openness on the transparency dimension? Overall, there is also increasing talk about transparency, there are
a number of decisions that increase transparency, and finally, the Agency
becomes more transparent in its day to day activities. Again, at least on
the action dimension, there are surprisingly high levels of openness in the
Agency's early years.

Transparency Talk

First, Figure 4.4 shows the amount of references to the norm of transparency
in the Agency's Annual Report. As the graph indicates, only in the mid 1990s
did the IAEA start to refer to transparency as an important organizational
principle. Further, references to transparency are strong in some years. Yet,
also in the mid 2000s, transparency is not always an issue in the Annual
Report. Overall, this raises questions about the strength of the rhetorical
commitment of the IAEA towards transparency.

When looking at the transparency statements in more detail, there are
two types of references to transparency. First, the Agency begins to accept
transparency as an important principle that others need to respect, e.g. when
discussing ways of improving and reforming its own safeguards system, when
demanding state cooperation, or when describing optimal qualities of the
international non-proliferation regime.

---

[7]The grouping of the participation events is achieved with the help of search-terms. For some
participation events, multiple search-terms may apply. Therefore, the bars in Figure 4.3 are
often larger than the black line, representing the total number of participation events. A
detailed discussion of the methodology used to group the codings is available in the data
appendix (B).

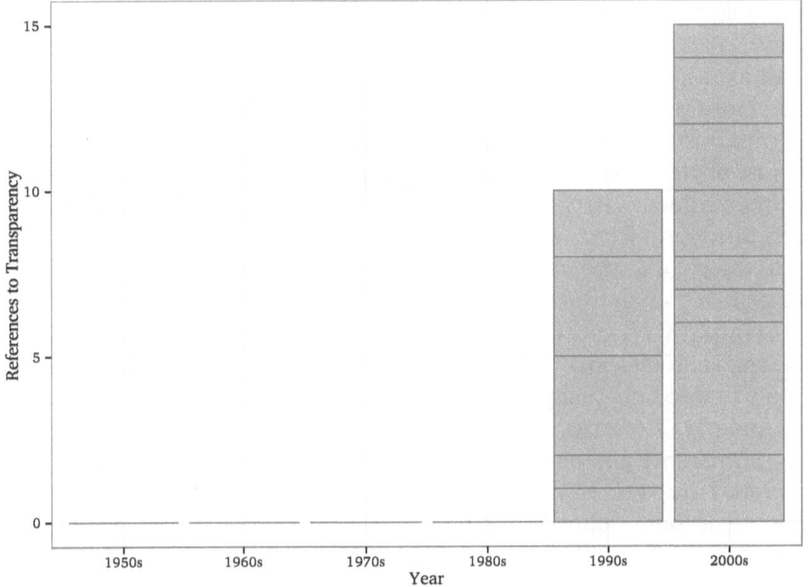

Figure 4.4: Transparency Talk in the IAEA Annual Reports

"These recommendations focused on a safeguards system characterized by greater transparency and openness (i.e. broader inspector access) and by the implementation of new technical measures designed to enhance the Agency's ability to provide assurances regarding the absence of undeclared nuclear activities in States with comprehensive safeguards agreements" (GC(38)/2, p. 143).

"Moreover, the Conference agreed that there should be more transparency on the part of the nuclear weapon States with regard to their capabilities, as well as a diminishing role for nuclear weapons in security policies" (GC(45)/4, p. 11).

"Public demands for reassurance on safety issues, with calls for greater transparency and accountability, are being widely voiced in many countries. The need, therefore, for a more effective and transparent international safety regime continues to be a high priority" (GC(46)/2, p. 8).

Those statements, while not directly linking transparency to the Agency, are relevant because they ascribe transparency to the non-proliferation system. The IAEA understands itself as an integral part of that system. Therefore, when demanding more safeguards transparency from states, the Agency also implies that this will enable it to more transparently report about its inspections results. Similarly, when asking nuclear weapons states to be more transparent, the Agency sees itself as the body through which relevant information should flow. The same is true for the safety issues in the last of the three quotes. The Agency sees itself as the main forum of the international safety regime and thus acknowledges transparency as an important norm for its work.

In the second type of statements, the Agency more directly links itself to transparency as an evaluative norm of the performance of an organization. For example, it accepts that it should "present the results from comparative assessment studies in a more transparent manner so they can be used more readily in decision making processes and communicated to the media and the public" (GC(40)/8, p. 5). Similarly, the Agency commits "to increase the transparency and objectivity of the selection process" (GC(42)/5, p. 62) of its staff and underlines that its reformed management system "will also improve accountability, bring greater transparency and improve internal control of the Agency's financial and procurement operations" (GC(53)/7, p. 16).

In general, however, rhetorical commitments towards organizational transparency, also compared to other international organizations, remain weak. Especially in one of the core functions of the Agency, i.e. safeguards, Agency rhetoric is based on principles like confidentiality and secrecy. This is not too surprising. Detailed public safeguards or security reports would reveal possibly dangerous information on nuclear installations.[8]

TRANSPARENCY DECISIONS

When looking at the *decision* dimension, the Agency has increasingly passed new regulations that improve public access to Agency resources and information. Table 4.2 lists these decisions. The source are the Annual Reports, which have proved to be the best source to gather information on decisions below the level of general conference resolutions.

In the Agency's early years and until the late 1980s, there was little attention to organizational transparency. Rather, the general policy was to channel information about the Agency and its activities through its member states. When there were spikes in public attention, e.g. when the Non-Proliferation Treaty entered into force, the Agency rather reacted to information demands from the general public and news media. After the

---

[8]Also, in the *Vienna International Centre*, the building that houses the IAEA headquarters, access to the offices of the safeguards department requires additional security clearance while the offices of e.g. the research or public information divisions are accessible to everyone with a UN grounds pass.

Table 4.2: IAEA Transparency Decisions

Year	Transparency-relevant Decision	Source
1957 - 1985	base-line policy: mainly reactive outreach to media, partially during phases of little public demand for IAEA transparency	GC(03)/73, p. 35
1986 - 1987	issuing IAEA newsbriefs	GC(31)/800, p. 72
1989	IAEA Highlights publication	GC(34)/915, p. 140
1990 - 1992	new PR policy: e.g. with media seminars	GC(35)/953, p. 146
1993 - 1994	Launch of IAEA website	GC(38)/2, p. 193
1995	distribution of electronic official documents through website to public	GC(40)/8, p. 52
1996 - 1997	partial de-classification of GOV documents	GC(41)/8, p. 53
1998 - 1999	new PR strategy: outreach to non-traditional actors	GC(44)/4, p. 102
2000 - 2001	new TC policy: increase transparency	GC(45)/4, p. 14
2002 - 2006	new PR strategy: pro-active and distribution of Agency publications for free	GC(47)/2, p. 9
2007 - 2009	New PR strategy: increase outreach to development community	GC(52)/9, p. 79
2010	Using social media	GC(55)/2, p. 94

Chernobyl accident, general media visibility of the Agency was rising (see below) and the IAEA recognized the need to proactively work with the public. In the late 1980s, this was e.g. done by issuing special newsbriefs that contained information on the Agency's work and on general developments in nuclear technologies and industries. Here, the focus was on improving media capacities and knowledge on nuclear technologies and their peaceful applications. One additional measure was e.g. the organization of media seminars for developing countries, where journalists were invited and briefed on current nuclear developments.

With the development of the Internet as a global source of information, the Agency also began to provide information to the general public directly. For example, official Agency documents were made available and a mechanism for the de-classification of Board of Governors documents

(e.g. safeguards reports, security assessments) was established. As a next
step, since the late 1990s, the Agency developed new public relations and
technical cooperation strategies, aiming at reaching new publics. These
include non-governmental organizations, especially those from the development community. Together with a strategy for increased transparency of
the Agency's technical cooperation work, the efforts aimed at establishing a
strong public perception of the Agency as a development actor, as opposed
to the IAEA's dominating public perception as a "nuclear watchdog." Finally,
the Agency also made all its publications available for free on its website
– an important service for scientists and political analysts, especially from
developing member states – and increased its social media presence, thus
providing a direct information channel to individuals.

Overall, changes on the decision dimension thus illustrate how the
Agency has increased openness on the transparency dimension. Today, most
of the Agency's documents are easily available. Also, the Agency provides
vast information on its development and scientific work on its website. Only
in the area of safeguards, the general public needs to rely on informal sources
to get more detailed safeguards assessments. Further, as I will discuss in
more detail below, the timing of the transparency-increasing decisions hints
at the influence of external demands for information from the Agency. It is
not surprising that the Agency changed its media strategy after it became
overwhelmed with information demands after the Chernobyl accident. Also,
with the increasing politicization of the Agency's work, it increased its efforts
to be a transparent international organization.

TRANSPARENCY ACTION

Yet, how do the Agency's decisions translate into its day to day transparency
and thus the *action* dimension of transparency? Figure 4.5 shows the development of the share of the budget which the Agency spends for public
information. Budget data is taken from the official IAEA annual budgets,
as reported by the Secretariat to the General Conference. From 1957 to
1970, the data includes all costs for the distribution of information like
publications and public relations documents. In 1971, a separate division of
information was created. From 1973 until 1979, this division became part
of the Office of External Relations. For this time period, I took an average of
45 percent as the budget spent for public information. In 1980, a separate
public information division was re-established. Since 2002, this division
became a part of the Agency's Information Support Services. Data for 1997
is missing. Also, for the most recent decade, I added the budget spent for
Internet and Communication Technologies which covers costs for the Agency
website and numerous public data-bases as those are important providers
of information about the Agency.

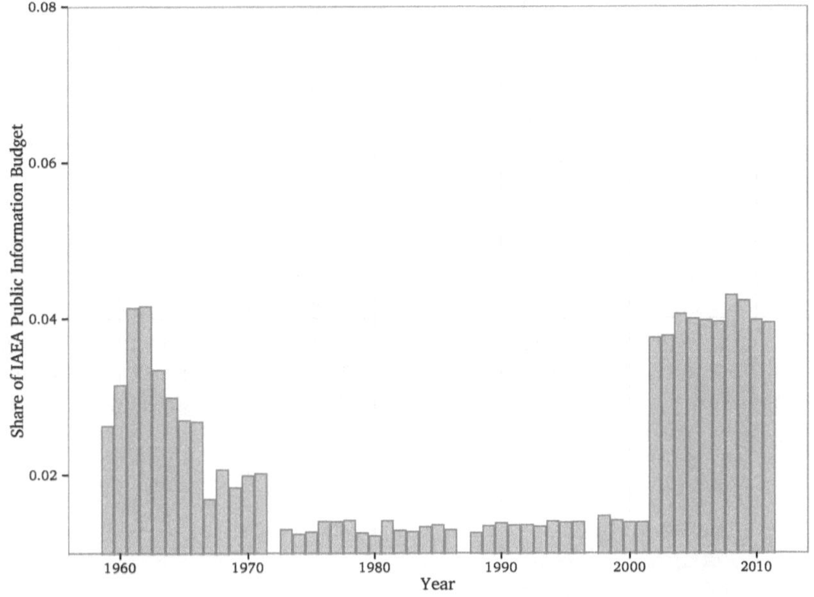

Figure 4.5: Share of IAEA Public Information Budget of Total Budget

When looking at the developments over time, there is a notable u-shaped curve that describes the Agency's relative expenditures for public information. Since its foundation until the early 1970s, on average 2.7 percent of the Agency's budget was spent to produce information products and to distribute them, most of the time to member states and their national nuclear institutions. From the mid 1970s until the 1990s, however, this share sank to 1.3 percent on average. Only with the large scale expansion of electronic and internet-based distribution, the share rose again to 3.8 percent. As I will discuss below (see Figure 4.6), the general budget of the IAEA is continuously increasing over time. The pattern of the public information budget thus cannot be explained by substantial budget changes. Rather, during the times of the low transparency budget, there appears to have been a political consensus in the organization that the public presentation of the organization did not require a larger share of its growing budget. Thus, similarly to the developments on the participation dimension, the Agency's actions were more transparent in its early years and in recent years than during the 1970s, 1980s and 1990s.

4.1.4 CHANGES IN THE AGENCY'S ENVIRONMENT: NORM AND RESOURCE BASED CONDITIONS

As I discuss in detail in Chapter 2, a number of resource and norm based hypotheses of organizational opening need to be assessed. Following the operationalization of these hypotheses, as discussed in Chapter 3, I present the data for the IAEA in the following paragraphs. The data shows how the Agency's environment has changed over the years. Overall, there is a significant increase of Agency resources over time, notable in the steady increase of its general budget. Yet, there is a slight increase in the inequality of the Agency's membership and no change in the complexity of its operational field. When considering the norm based environmental variables, there is a notable increase in the Agency's public visibility, its share of democratic member states and a general trend towards a global discourse, attentive to ideas of global democratic governance.

RESOURCE BASED CONDITIONS

First, I present the data for the resourse-based conditions. A first indicator, the *IAEA Budget*, checks whether there have been phases in IAEA history, where operational resources were scarce and where, so the hypothesis, there was an increased need for the resources that non-state actors can provide. Figure 4.6 represents the development of the Agency's budget, expressed in constant 2009 USD. The bars show that there is a general growth of the Agency's budget. Today, the Agency spends about 430 million USD. The steep increase in the budget from 2005 (302 million USD) to 2006 (359 million USD) is caused by the Agency changing its budgeting to Euro. Data for 1997 is missing. The development of the Agency's regular budget, it needs to be noted, is determined by the dominant doctrine of *zero growth*, i.e. the position of a number of mostly Western states to limit the growth of IGO budgets: increases in budgets should not exceed the adjustments required by inflation (cf. e.g. Taylor 1991). This highlights that each growth in the budget and especially funding for new activities or new posts are the outcome of an intense political process. While the Agency asks for more resources to fulfill its tasks, member states are rather unwilling to approve new funding and instead often ask to further rationalize the budget instead of approving new funds.

When looking at the development over time, there was nevertheless a steady increase in the budget from 1957 to 1971. Then, with the entry into force of the Non-Proliferation Treaty and a resulting increase in safeguards costs, the budget has risen considerably. In the late 1980s, the global USD crisis, caused by a large-scale depreciation of the USD vis-à-vis the Austrian Schilling lead to a real decrease in the Agency's budget. Similarly, the budget of the IAEA did not grow significantly in the 1990s. However, a veritable budget crises, as in the case of the OPCW, could be prevented.

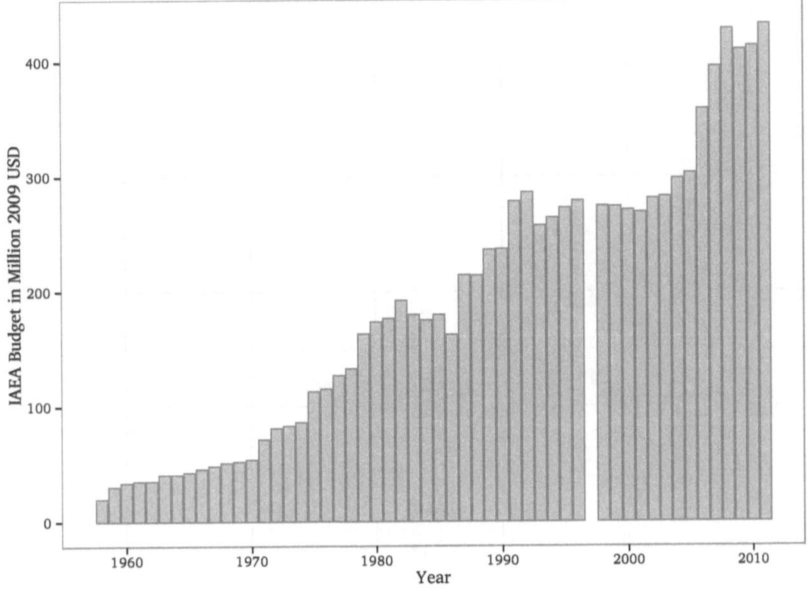

Figure 4.6: IAEA Total budget in 2009 USD

Consequently, there are some periods of time where the Agency faces a reduction in its budget. Therefore, during these times, demands for external expertise are rising. This fits well with the increase of participation events in the 1980s. While the Agency's budget was shrinking, it was increasingly seeking external advice on its activities.

Figure 4.7 shows the different kinds of expenditures that the Agency has spent its budget for. As expected, staff costs are the highest expenses. Until the 1980s, they accounted for about 60 percent of the Agency's budget. After that time, the share diminished, indicating that a staff shortage could trigger increased demands for external expertise. More interestingly, the graph also shows the large increase of safeguards related costs over the years. During the 1970s, when the NPT was already in force, about 20 percent of the Agency's budget was used for safeguards. Until the mid 1980s, this share has about doubled. Since then, however, the share has remained relatively stable. Further, the budget share spent on technical assistance has not kept up with the development of the safeguards budget. The bars in the plot represent the sum of targeted voluntary contributions from the *Technical Cooperation Fund* and regular budget expenditures for technical assistance. During the late 1960s and early 1970s, technical assistance projects attributed to large parts to the overall budget. Since the late 1980s, the share of assistance work has also stabilized at around the same share

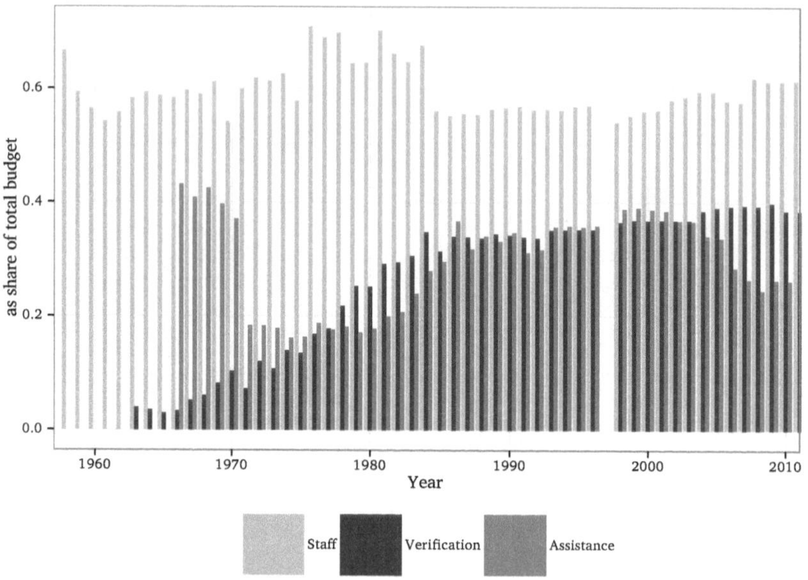

Figure 4.7: IAEA Budget by Expenditure

of the budget spent for verification. For opening up, we would thus expect
to find a high demand for external expertise during the 1970s and 1980s
when activities under the verification and promotion pillar expanded.

Second, I collect data on *membership inequality*. I calculate the Gini
coefficient of inequality based on the GDP data of individual member states.
Figure 4.8 shows the data for the IAEA. Data availability is limited for
historical GDP data. For example, in 1957, the IAEA has 56 member states.
Yet, GDP data is only available for 38 states. The data improves over time.
Thus, the change in Figure 4.8 needs to be interpreted carefully. Overall,
there is slightly increasing economic inequality in the Agency's membership.
In the 1970s, the average Gini-Coefficient is 0.78, in the 2000s, inequality has
risen to 0.81, with 1 marking maximum inequality. Due to the diverse and
universal membership of the Agency, the inequality structures do not change
dramatically over the years. Rich Northern states and poorer Southern states
have been Agency members since its early years. The accession of new states
during times of de-colonialization and the end of the Soviet Union have thus
led to only small changes in the existent structures of inequality. The growth
in inequality since the 1990s thus rather is an effect of growing economic
imbalances and unequal distributions of wealth in the global system of states.
Inequality thus is likely to have a more indirect influence on IAEA openness.

As it increases information asymmetries between member states, it can be regarded as a plausible cause for the general trend towards openness of the IAEA since the 1990s.

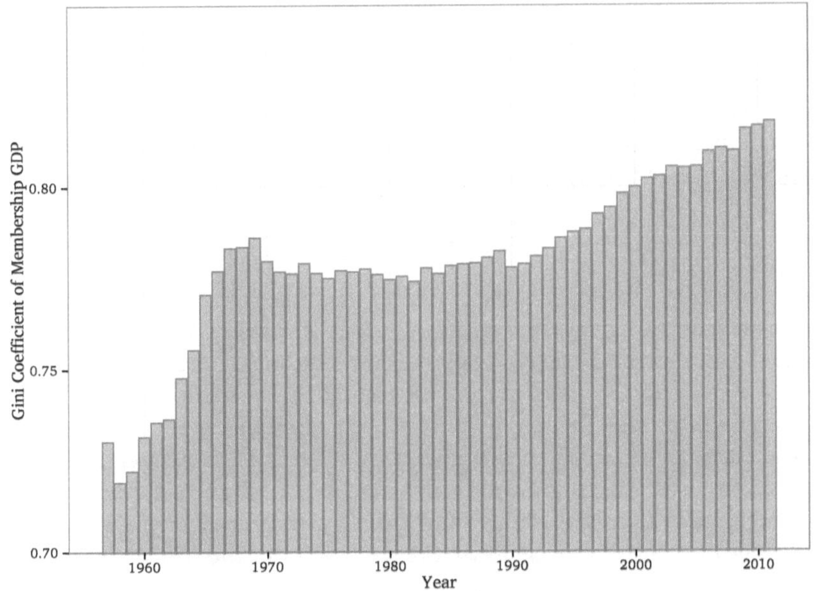

Figure 4.8: Inequality of IAEA Membership, based on Gini-Coefficient of GDP

Finally, I measure the third resource based condition, *complexity* by looking at changes of the tasks described in the mandates of international organizations. For the case of the IAEA, there is no variation over time, i.e. the Agency Statute is not changed in order to add or remove a task. Article III of the Statute of the IAEA sets the following functions for the Agency:

1. encourage, assist and conduct research, develop practical applications
2. foster scientific exchange
3. act as intermediary for supply of materials, services, or facilities for states
4. provide nuclear materials, services, equipment and facilities with focus on developing states, i.e. technical assistance
5. establish and administer safeguards
6. develop and apply safety standards

Again, as discussed in the operationalization section of this study, this does not mean that individual activities under the statutory tasks have not become more complex. To the contrary, I assume that they all have become more complex over time. For example, organizing the wealth of scientific knowledge has certainly become more demanding. Similarly, safeguards have become more complex as technologies and the number of safeguarded sites has grown. The same is true for safety related activities. However, developing a quantitative or qualitative scale for evaluating these changes in complexity is beyond the scope of this analysis. Therefore, I expect that the general increase of complexity will cause more opening up. Yet, as there is no clear expansion of statutory tasks, I would only be able to see this change in the detailed case studies.

NORM BASED CONDITIONS

Next, how have the norm based conditions changed over time? First, there are some interesting developments of the IAEA's visibility in the global news media. Data in the *Lexis Nexis* global news corpus is available since the 1970s. Again, as discussed in the operationalization section, the corpus of articles that this selection is drawn from is not constant over time. Especially in the early years, fewer newspapers are available. However, as shown above, the resulting time-line highly correlates with the time-line for the one newspaper that is available during the whole time of observation (The Washington Post). This tells us that reporting about the IAEA in the whole corpus is not very different from reporting in the Washington Post. It is thus safe to assume that missing newspapers in the early years would not have reported significantly different than the Washington Post.

The first graph in Figure 4.9 shows how often the IAEA has been mentioned over the years in the Lexis Nexis Global News Corups. Here, we do witness a large scale change in the Agency's environment. In its first decades of existence, the IAEA was only rarely visible to a wider audience and it was mostly known to an expert community of scientists and politicians. Since the 2000s, however, it has been very visible to larger audience. For example, its involvement in Iraq, North Korea, and Iran has drawn much attention. The peaks of media attention visible in the graph need to be seen in connection with a number of world events with IAEA involvement. Among others, these are the 1986 Chernobyl Accident, North Korea's withdrawal of the NPT and the IAEA in 1994, growing concerns about the Iranian nuclear program and the dismantlement of the Libyan program in 2004, developments in Iran and North Korea in 2007 and again Iran and the Fukushima accident in 2011.

Further, the second graph in Figure 4.9 represents the relative share of articles where the Agency is named in the headline of all hits. This measure thus captures how many of the hits put a large focus on the Agency and its activities. Over the years, this value also shows peaks for certain events,

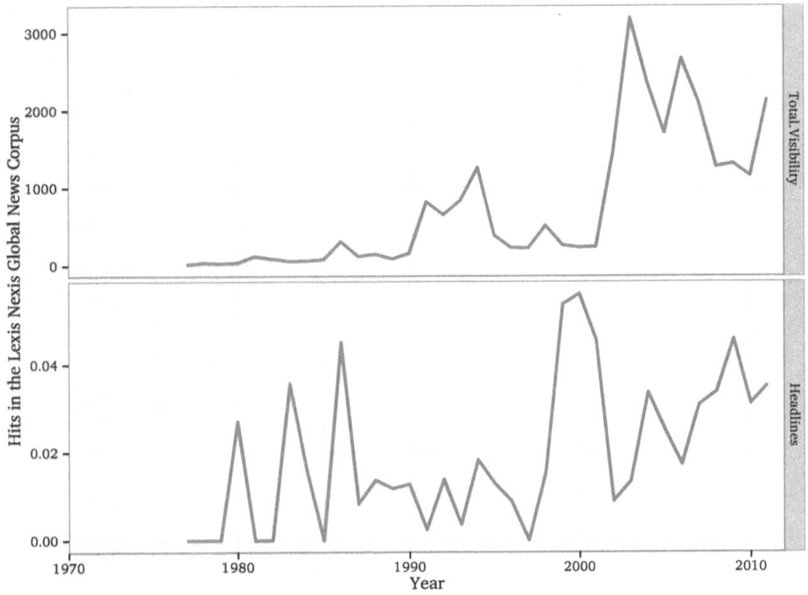

Figure 4.9: Visibility of the IAEA in the Global News Media. Total Visibility and Relative Visibility in Headlines as Share of Total Hits

listed above. The headlines share has risen from an annual average of 1.3 percent until 1999 by the factor of three to 3.1 percent in the 2000s. There is thus some interesting parallel development between visibility and the observed patterns of opening up. Both are strong particularly strong since the 2000s. It is thus likely that visibility, and thus the underlying organizational legitimacy mechanism is a strong explanatory factor for the opening up of the IAEA.

Second, has the *democratic composition of the Agency's membership* changed over time? Here, the assumption is that the more democratic the membership, the more likely an open organization will be. Figure 4.10 plots the share of the Agency's members that qualify as democracies. Data on the democratic quality is not available for all countries, but the overall coverage of countries is good. The plot shows a u-curve, with relatively high shares of democracies in the 1950s, but declining democratic membership until the 1970s. This is probably an effect of new membership by newly de-colonialized countries with lower democratic quality at that time. Since then, Agency member states have become more democratic. For example, in the 1970s, about 30 percent of the member states were democratic. In the last decade, this share has risen to 55 percent. Consequently, the growing

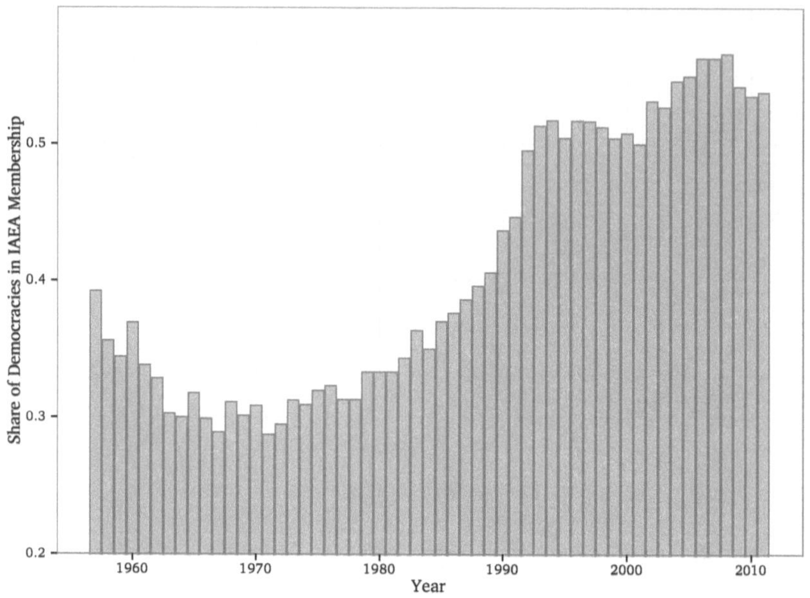

Figure 4.10: Share of Democracies in IAEA Membership

democratization sets a supportive framework for the growing openness of
the IAEA. The democratic composition of the organization thus seems to be
a strong explanation of opening up.

Third, has the Agency's authority and thus its *depth of governance* changed
over time? Here, I propose three qualitative levels of Agency governance
depth over time. The first relevant change for the Agency's impact on its
member states and their citizens came with the entry into force of the
Nuclear Non-Proliferation Treaty in 1970 (cf. e.g. Scheinman 1987, Ch.
5). Due to the obligatory inspections of non-nuclear weapon states that
the treaty prescribes, IAEA inspections have gained importance. Earlier
inspections were based on special agreements, e.g. to monitor a nuclear
weapon free zone or as part of an export treaty of nuclear technology (cf. e.g.
Wing and Simpson 2013). With the subsequent evolution of the safeguards
regime, member states were granting growing rights and powers to Agency
inspectors, opening doors for external review and possible criticism of state
policies.

A second important step that increased the IAEA's authority was the
organization of inspections in Iraq, mandated by the UN Security Council
(S/RES/687) in 1991 (cf. e.g. Harrer 2014). Here, together with other
UN organs, the Agency was tasked to detect all traces of the Iraqi nuclear

program and also to destroy and dismantle installations and material. Since that point in time, the IAEA took over additional inspection tasks in areas of world conflicts, most notably in North Korea, Libya, South Africa, and Iran. Here, the Agency and its inspection reports, which it often addresses directly to the UNSC, thus became an important and politicized actor in security politics. As the inspections before the Iraq war in 2003 illustrate, the Agency's assessments became arguments for states and other international organizations when deciding about the use of force against other states. This new kind of responsibility constitutes a new and increased quality of IAEA authority and depth of governance. Consequently, public contestation and thus calls for IAEA openness become more likely. Further, increased authority could be an important explanatory factor for the adjustment of participation decisions.

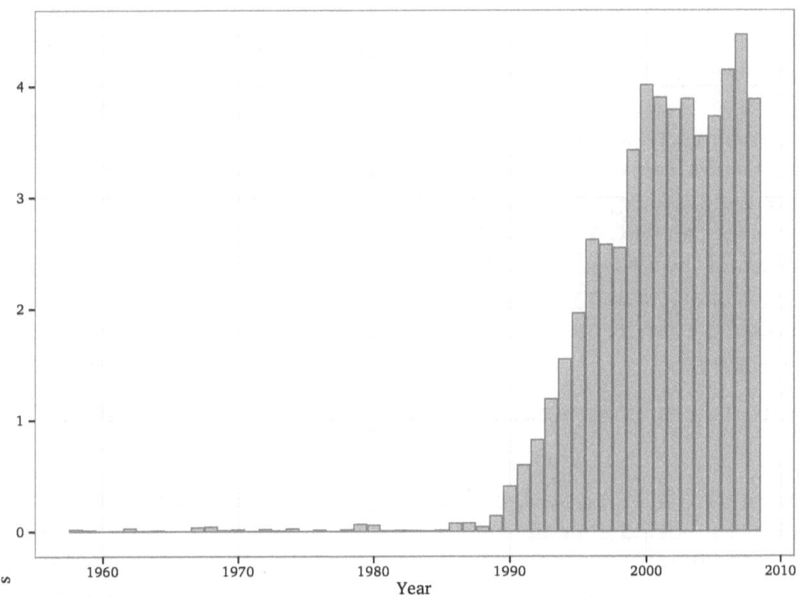

Figure 4.11: Presence of the Norm of Open Governance in Google Books Corpus

Finally, my analytical framework assumes that the general *presence of a norm of open governance* in the global context is an important condition for organizational opening. Figure 4.11 shows the development of this norm from 1967 until 2008. The data is based on the occurrence of key terms of that norm in the English-language Google Books corpus. Data is only available until 2008. Nevertheless, the graph shows the impressive growth of terms like global democracy and participatory governance over time. Since the 1990s, the usage of these terms in the corpus raises exponentially and reaches a high level in the 2000s. Thus, the open governance norm appears to be very present in the late 1990s and 2000s. Consequently, it also is a potentially powerful explanation for the observed patterns of IAEA opening up.

4.2 The Organization for the Prohibition of Chemical Weapons

In the case of the Organization for the Prohibition of Chemical Weapons (OPCW), there are also a number of instances of opening in the organization's history. Further, there are a lot of developments that remind of the IAEA's process of opening, despite the much younger history of the organization. On the action dimension, there is a trend towards more participation and transparency since the organization's creation. On the decision dimension, there is some change for official participation rules and a number of decisions that increase transparency. Finally, on the talk dimension, like in the IAEA case, rhetorical references to the values of participation and transparency have increased significantly since the 2000s. In the following paragraphs, I present the OPCW's main *functions*, *activities*, its *organizational set-up*, *important events* and an overview of salient *political conflicts*. Second, I discuss changes in organizational openness. Finally, I describe changes in the OPCW's environment which may explain increased transparency and participation.

4.2.1 The History, Functions and Development of the OPCW

Functions and Activities

The Organization for the Prohibition of Chemical Weapons (OPCW), some say, was modeled after the IAEA in many ways (cf. e.g. Dorn 1993). Like the IAEA, the OPCW is an independent international organization with close relations to the United Nations. The OPCW aims for universal membership and currently has 190 member states (S/1131/2013). Thus, most states have joined the organization. So far, Israel and Myanmar, as well as Angola, Egypt, North Korea and South Sudan are no member states. The OPCW is headquartered in The Hague and has a staff of about 500 people. It has a budget of about 73 Mio. EUR. The OPCW is deeply embedded in the international chemical weapons regime, based on the *Chemical Weapons Convention* (CWC). The CWC, an expression of the chemical weapons taboo, was negotiated in the context of the *United Nations Conference on Disarmament*. First ideas of preventing the military use of chemicals date back to the 1899 Hague Convention and the 1925 Geneva Protocol. Compared to e.g. the regulation of biological (BWC of 1972) or nuclear weapons (NPT of 1968), however, it took some time for the international community to agree on a regime that verifies the destruction and non-proliferation of chemical weapons (for a detailed comparison with the biological weapons regime, cf. e.g. Enia and Fields 2014). The text of the CWC was opened for signature in early 1993, entering into force on 29 April 1997 after the 65th state deposited its instruments of ratification, thus also formally establishing the OPCW (cf. e.g. Kenyon 2007b).

The organization's legal basis is the CWC. Article VIII includes provisions for an intergovernmental organization, responsible for the implementation of the universal ban of chemical weapons and the verification of non-proliferation of chemicals for military purposes. The OPCW's main tasks and objectives are thus directly bound to those of the CWC:

> "The States Parties to this Convention hereby establish the Organization for the Prohibition of Chemical Weapons to achieve the object and purpose of this Convention, to ensure the implementation of its provisions, including those for international verification of compliance with it, and to provide a forum for consultation and cooperation among States Parties" (CWC 1994, Art. VIII, A1).

The OPCW has translated this mandate into three main fields of activities: *(i)* the destruction of existing chemical weapons stockpiles in its member states, *(ii)* inspections of its members' chemical industries to prevent the production of new chemical weapons, and *(iii)* technical cooperation and assistance. For many years, the OPCW was mainly occupied with the practical destruction of chemical weapons, a task nearly completed in the states with the largest stockpiles (see below). Overall, the destruction of chemical weapons stockpiles has progressed slower than expected. Nevertheless, as of 2012, 78 per cent of all declared chemical weapons were destroyed under OPCW surveilance (OPCW 2013, 1). The second task, i.e. inspecting chemical industry sites to verify that dual use chemicals are only produced for peaceful purposes, is especially challenging. In 2012, a total of 4.898 industry sites that are subject to inspections were declared to the OPCW. However, in 2012, of those only 219 were visited by OPCW inspectors (OPCW 2013, 9). In theory, this leads to a time frame of 25 years for each site to be inspected at least once. This gap between inspection obligations and inspection capacities hints at some short-comings in the CWC regime.

Like the IAEA during its early years, the OPCW is not very present in the global media and there is little public attention to its routine inspection tasks. Also, the slow growth in its annual budget (see below, Figure 4.17) indicates that it has not been a very central organization for its member states, neither (cf. e.g. Kelle 2004; Mathews 2002). Other international organizations, like the IAEA, have acquired more budgetary means over the years. For the OPCW, however, member states seem to be reluctant to finance new tasks and thus to substantially expand OPCW activities. This is a challenge for the OPCW and its Secretariat. Further, there are a number of additional challenges and developments that the OPCW and its member states need to face in the next years (cf. e.g. Trapp 2012; OPCW 2011*b*). Most prominently, the main task of its mandate, i.e. the destruction of chemical weapons, will be completed in the near future and the organization needs to re-invent its purpose and shift its focus on other areas. Also, its inclusion in the political conflict in Syria (Trapp 2014) and the Nobel Peace Award of 2013 have, at least for a certain period of time, raised the prominence of the organization. This may lead to growing politicization of the OPCW's work and thus to increased needs of organizational legitimacy management.

What is the main output of the OPCW and what does it do to achieve its statutory goals? As discussed above, there are basically three fields of activities. First, the *verification of the destruction of chemical weapons and of chemical weapons production sites* is one of the main tasks of the OPCW and governed by Articles III, IV and V of the CWC (for a general overview of the work of the PrepCom on developing the implementation rules of the CWC Articles III, IV and V, see Manley 2007*a*). This strong and direct disarmament goal is a special feature of the OPCW, which is the only international organization directly involved in disarmament (Dunworth 2008, 121).

Under Article III, OPCW member states are obliged to declare all stockpiles of chemical weapons on their territory and to develop plans for their destruction. The CWC defines chemical weapons as *(i)* toxic chemicals and precursors that are used for military purposes, *(ii)* munitions that are equipped with such chemicals and *(iii)* equipment that is directly related to the usage of such equipment (CWC 1994, Art. II, 1). The CWC thus has a very open definition of chemical weapons. The *general purpose criterion* included in Art. II, 1a comprises all chemicals that were present at the time of the CWC's negotiation but also all those that would be developed in the future, as long as they are used for weapons purposes (cf. Robinson 1996, 81). To deal with the legacies of World War I and II chemical weapons, two further categories of chemical weapons are introduced in the CWC: *old chemical weapons* and *abandoned chemical weapons*. The first group includes weapons produced before 1925 or weapons manufactured between 1925 and 1946 if they are in such state of deterioration, that they cannot be used as weapons anymore. The second group are weapons produced after 1925 that a state has left on the territory of another state (CWC 1994, Art. II, 1). Currently, six OPCW member states have declared the possession of chemical weapons: Albania, India, Libya, Russia, the United States, and another non-disclosed state who has requested confidentiality. Further, Iraq is currently in the process of declaring and assessing remnants of chemical weapons on its territory (OPCW 2013, 4).

What does the CWC demand from states to do with their chemical weapons? Article III and the supplementary *Verification Annex* demands states to declare all chemical weapons to the OPCW. The declaration needs to be very detailed, including specifications about the chemicals used, about storage facilities, about destruction sites, and a detailed plan for their destruction (cf. for details e.g. Manley 2007a). The Verification Annex sets detailed deadlines for the destruction of weapons. The most deadly chemical weapons need to be destroyed 10 years after the entry into force of the CWC. The Annex also sets intermediate deadlines to ascertain that states are on a good track towards total destruction.[9] As the figures above indicate, this destruction deadline could not be upheld by all possessor states. While the destruction of weapons in Albania and India are completed, Libya, the USA and Russia have applied for extensions of their destruction deadlines (OPCW 2013, 1).

The OPCW permanently verifies the complete and safe destruction of chemical weapons at the destruction facilities in its member states. OPCW inspections are also regulated by the Verification Annex. The OPCW shall quickly verify the declared numbers of chemical weapons at storage facilities and also conduct first inspections of destruction facilities between 90 and 120 days after the CWC's entry into force. The basis for the destruction inspections are detailed site declarations, submitted by the possessor states. For old and abandoned weapons, comparable rules apply. The Verification Annex also demands that the OPCW verifies the initial state declaration of these weapons. Old weapons may than be destroyed as toxic waste, according to national legislation. Abandoned weapons that are still functional need to be destroyed like conventionally declared weapons stockpiles.

During the inspections, the OPCW staff uses methods of inventory control to ascertain that all declared weapons are safely destroyed. For example, in 2012, 115 weapons related inspections were conducted, amounting to about 8.500 inspector days (OPCW 2013, 4). The verification activities are conducted by an inspectorate that is mostly part of the full staff of the OPCW. Inspectors are regularly trained and need to stick to strict confidentiality rules. In general, the professionalization of the inspectorate was an important concern of member states, but also of the chemical industry, fearing the

---

[9]In detail, the Verification Annex sets four phases for the destruction of chemical weapons: Phase 1, i.e. 3 years after entry into force (EIF), 1 percent of weapons need to be destroyed. Phase 2, 5 years after EIF, 20 percent destroyed. Phase 3, 7 years after EIF, 45 percent destroyed. Phase 4, 10 years after EIF, 100 percent destroyed (cf. Kelle 2004).

disclosure of crucial state or industry secrets (on role, understanding and training of inspectors, see Manley 2007*b*).

Next to the verification of chemical weapons destruction, *inspections of national chemical industries* is another main task of the OPCW. To control the non-proliferation of chemical weapons and of the chemicals needed to construct those weapons, the CWC, in Article VI, prescribes a regime of industry inspections for certain chemicals (on the negotiations of the chemical industry inspection regime, cf. Manley 2007*a*). Next to the general application of the general purpose criterion which includes all potential chemical weapons chemicals, the CWC introduces three groups of especially dangerous chemicals that are often directly or indirectly used for the production of chemical weapons. These groups, or *Schedules*, are included in the CWC's *Annex on Chemicals*. The schedules were negotiated during the CWC negotiation process and they determine the inspection obligations of the OPCW and its member states (on their negotiation, see e.g. Feakes 2007). Schedule 1 comprises substances that are usually used for chemical weapons and have little peaceful applications, like sarin, mustard gas, saxitoxin, ricin and their precursors. The Verification Annex (Part VI) forbids states to acquire or transfer those chemicals, except for limited peaceful applications, like medical research. Production sites need to be declared to the OPCW and inspected to verify the declared amount of produced chemicals. As of 31 December 2012, only 28 Schedule 1 facilities have been declared, mostly national research laboratories, indicating the relative irrelevance of Schedule 1 chemicals for the chemical industry. Of those 28 facilities, 11 were inspected in 2012 (OPCW 2013, 9).

Schedule 2 lists highly toxic chemicals with a high risk of chemical weapons use that may also have a number of legitimate applications. Schedule 2 includes a number of chemicals that are e.g. used for fertilizers or pesticides. States need to declare each facility that produces a certain amount of Schedule 2 chemicals. If a facility produces more than 10 times the amount of the declaration threshold, the facility is subject to OPCW industry inspections. Here, OPCW inspectors need to verify the declared amounts of chemicals, the absence of Schedule 1 chemicals and the non-diversion of Schedule 2 chemicals for military purposes (Verification Annex, Part VII). In planning its industry inspections, the OPCW shall give preference to Schedule 1 production sites. Further, the frequency of Schedule 2 inspections shall be calculated given the actual proliferation risk and no site shall be inspected more than twice a year. In 2012, a total of 169 Schedule 2 facilities in 39 countries are subject to OPCW inspections. They are mostly located in China, India, Germany and the United States. Of the declared facilities, 42 were inspected in 2012 (OPCW 2013, 9).

Third, Schedule 3 is reserved for those chemicals that have many peaceful uses but are also possible precursors for the production of chemical weapons. Schedule 3 chemicals like carbonyl dichloride, cyanogen chloride, or hydrogen cyanide are produced on a large scale by the chemical industry, e.g. for the production of lubricants, paint thinners or for chemical cleansing agents. The CWC demands that states declare all facilities producing more than 30 tonnes of Schedule 3 chemicals (Verification Annex, Part VIII). The OPCW is obliged to inspect those sites that produce more than 230 tonnes of those chemicals. Again, inspection frequencies shall be calculated weighing proliferation risks and an equitable geographical distribution and there shall be no more than two inspections of the same site per year. As of 2012, 412 Schedule 3 facilities in 35 countries are under OPCW inspections. About a half of the inspected facilities are located in China, others mostly in the United States, India and Japan. Of the 412 sites, 29 were inspected in 2012 (OPCW 2013, 9).

Finally, the Verification Annex (Part IX) prescribes general declaration and verification obligations for so called *Other Chemical Production Facilities* (OCPF), i.e. all industry sites producing more than 200 tonnes of discrete organic chemicals that are not included in the Schedules or more than 30 tonnes of such chemicals containing phosphorus, sulfur or fluorine. On-site inspections are mandatory for sites with an output of more than 200 tonnes of the first kind of chemicals and more than 200 tonnes of the second kind. Again, the frequency of inspections and the prioritizing of inspection sites is subject to an algorithm, weighing proliferation risk and geographical distribution. When looking at quantities, OCPF are the largest group of industry sites under OPCW inspections. In 2012, 4289 of those facilities were subject to OPCW inspections and 137 were inspected in that year (OPCW 2013, 9).

Overall, the industry inspection regime is well accepted by the member states and the international chemical industry. In part, much of that acceptance on the side of the chemical industry is also due to the effective lobbying of chemical industry organizations during the drafting phase of the CWC (cf. for a detailed description Feakes 2007). Overall, the industry inspection regime under the CWC is exceptional in its scope, when compared to other international control regimes. Under IAEA safeguards, for example, a much smaller number of nuclear facilities needs to be inspected. Further, many of those sites under inspection used to be operated by state-led energy enterprises. Thus, the negotiations on chemical industry inspections under the CWC needed to make sure that important industry concerns are reflected in the regime. The alternative, i.e. to abstain from industry inspections, would have strongly limited the non-proliferation impact of the CWC, especially as history, e.g. in Iraq, has shown that the chemical industry has been an important player in developing the Iraqi chemical weapons program.

During the CWC negotiations in the context of the UN Conference on Disarmament, the most important points for industry lobbyists were *(i)* confidentiality with regard to industry practices and intellectual property rights, *(ii)* clear definitions of inspection and declaration procedures, and *(iii)* managing the public perceptions of industry inspections. The last aspect was especially important for a chemical industry which, at that time, had a generally bad image after large-scale accidents in Seveso or Bhopal. Thus, the industry saw a chance in promoting its own image in taking a clear stance against chemical weapons in the 1980s by contributing and supporting the CWC negotiations. During the negotiations, a number of industry lobbyists from North America, Western Europe, Japan and Australia participated and provided important technical input into the diplomatic negotiation process. The lobbying activities climaxed in the September 1989 *Government-Industry Conference against Chemical Weapons* in Canberra with 375 delegates from 66 countries who produced a joint outcome document, calling for a world without CW but with free trade in chemicals. Further, chemical industry lobbyists joined forces with NGOs from the peace sector like SIPRI or Pughwash who organized joint conferences and publications (again, cf. Feakes 2007).

Regarding confidentiality, lobbying successfully helped to implement strict procedures in the CWC for the confidential treatment of state and industry declarations and the results of inspections. The *Confidentiality Annex* to the CWC implements measures like high confidentiality for inspection and declaration documents, high standards for the internal management of information and strict rules for staff members. As Feakes (2007) describes, the industry, for example, feared "clandestine sampling" from OPCW inspectors who would take secret samples at industry sites to sell them on the black market. As a counter-measure, the instruments used for inspections are strictly regulated and many are provided by the inspected member states. Further, the industry representatives were concerned with "rumor damage", caused by leaked information from inspectors during on-site inspections. Here, a strict public affairs and media strategy was seen as a remedy for industry fears (OPCW 1997).

Overall, when looking at the quantitative inspection work by the OPCW, there is thus a certain focus on the inspection of scheduled chemicals as those pose the largest risks for the proliferation of chemical weapons. Further, the OPCW has quite a strong mandate in its inspections. After data collection and declarations by its member states, it checks the accuracy of those declarations and verifies that no hidden activities are conducted, like the side-lining of chemicals for non-peaceful uses. Also, although not a tool used as of today, the OPCW can conduct *challenge inspections*, i.e. inspections demanded by a member state of another member state's facilities. The OPCW thus can be an independent verification actor in inter-state disputes around chemical weapons. However, the strict confidentiality and media guidelines make it hard for the OPCW to supply the public demand for information about chemical weapons non-proliferation. In general, the secrecy invites the risk of losing public support for the CWC regime and the Organization (on this point, also see Robinson 1996), while too much transparency could risk state support.

Finally, *technical cooperation* under Article XI of the CWC is the third large field of activities of the OPCW. Article XI asks the member states not to take the CWC as a pretense to limit activities of chemical research, exchange of information, and trade with chemicals for peaceful purposes. The OPCW's technical cooperation activities start from a basic dilemma: preventing the military use of chemicals but enabling the various benefits of dual-use chemicals. This situation is comparable to the IAEA's technical cooperation activities that also need to deal with potentially harmful materials and technologies. Also, like in the case of the IAEA, the funding and balancing of verification and technical cooperation activities is a major issue of state debates about the OPCW's program and budget (Kenyon and Kisselev 2007). However, compared to the IAEA, the OPCW's mandate is much more narrow. The CWC (1994, Art. VIII, D 38 e) does not set a strong promotion function for the OPCW but mandates the Secretariat to "[p]rovide technical assistance and technical evaluation to States Parties in the implementation of the provisions of this Convention, including evaluation of scheduled and unscheduled chemicals." Consequently, OPCW technical assistance is more geared towards helping states in implementing the CWC provisions than being an international promoter of peaceful chemical applications.

Consequently, the OPCW's main activities in the technical cooperation field are rather limited. The Secretariat is active in the fields of research, training and in providing assistance for chemical emergencies. Many parts of the technical cooperation program are guided by a strategy for the implementation of Article XI (OPCW 2011a). The strategy includes four main areas of activities:

capacity building for the safe use of chemicals This issue includes analyses on states' needs for support by the OPCW to develop strong national practices and training programs for chemical safety. Further, the OPCW supports research in non-toxic substitute chemicals, organizes workshops for best practices on safety, provides analytical training and analytical equipment and encourages direct state support for those activities. The OPCW, for example, implements this with its *Associate Programme*, which started in 2000, and "has provided 297 scientists and engineers from 102 developing countries and countries with economies in transition with both theoretical and practical training in modern production and in management and safety practices in the chemical industry" (OPCW 2013, 15). Further, a number of workshops and seminars are organized annually on topics of safety culture and analytical methods.

promote networking of stakeholders Here, the OPCW acts as a network
hub for the scientific community, NGOs, chemical industry associations
and other regional or international organizations. For example, the
OPCW supports international scientific conferences by funding travel
for scientists from developing countries. Further, the OPCW supports
research projects, either on its own or jointly with the International
Foundation for Science.

enhancing the effectiveness of cooperation programs The organization
should act as a clearing house that effectively channels requests for
assistance to available sources of expertise. Further, the Secretariat
shall consult with member states on their needs and capacities in the
area of technical cooperation. This, for example, is achieved through
informal consultations with member states.

facilitating state participation in the benefits of chemistry Next, the TS
is asked to support the exchange between member states to raise
awareness of the convention and to promote exchange on issues of
implementation. This is done in regular workshops for member state
officials.

ORGANIZATIONAL SET-UP

What are the OPCW's main bodies, tasked with the implementation of
verification and technical assistance? The formal organizational set-up is
described in Article VIII of the CWC. The highest policy-making organ is
the *Conference of the States Parties* (CSP) which meets annually. The CSP is
the OPCW's universal decision-making body with equal voting rights for all
members. Much of the day-to-day business is controlled by the *Executive
Council* (EC). The EC consists of 41 member states. Seats are allocated
according to regional representation and the level of advancement of the
national chemical industry. As opposed to the IAEA, it is the regional groups
that decide about the status of national chemical industries. Nine Seats are
reserved for African states, nine for Asian states, five for Eastern Europe,
seven for Latin America, ten for Western Europe and associated states. One
additional seat rotates between Asia and Latin America. De facto, a number
of states thus have quasi-permanent seats on the EC, due to their large
chemical industry sectors.

In the OPCW case, there are also regular *Review Conferences* of the
CWC that have some influence on the work of the OPCW. Article VIII, B,
22 calls for the CSP to convene in a special form five and ten years after
Entry Into Force and then in five year steps to review the workings of the
Convention and the OPCW. The Review Conferences have been established
to take note of scientific or technological changes that may be a threat to the
purpose of the CWC. There is thus the possibility to adopt new CWC rules,
e.g. in the Annexes, to assure the non-proliferation of chemical weapons

and an effective verification regime. So far, the conferences have provided important input for the work of the OPCW and have given attention to open questions of its work.[10]

IMPORTANT HISTORICAL DEVELOPMENTS

The OPCW is still a relatively young intergovernmental organization. Yet, in its short history, a number of important events have shaped the internal processes of the organization and its external image and perception. According to Barbeschi (2002), there are four distinct phases in the history of the organization:

Infancy (1993-1997) The early years of the organization were dominated by the work of the Preparatory Commission. The Commission was established after the signature of the CWC in Paris and tasked to prepare working procedures and a program for the OPCW, which would be established after entry into force (for a detailed discussion of the Preparatory Commission, see Kenyon 2007a). Work in the Preparatory Commission was less productive than initially expected, also given the uncertain status of US and Russian ratification of the CWC (for an analysis of the US ratification process, see Kubig, Dembinski and Kelle 2000). In detail, during the preparatory phase, it was unclear if and when both states would ratify the CWC. This decision, however, would have large implications for program planning of the OPCW. Still, the preliminary secretariat worked well and helped to establish a first set of committed individuals that took their enthusiasm from the CWC negotiation phase to the new organization.

First Steps (1997-1999) After Entry Into Force and the formal establishment of the OPCW, the secretariat grew quickly to be able to implement the tight inspection schedule laid out in the CWC. Also, during the early years, the CSP needed to decide on a number of open issues which the Commission could not solve. Further, chemical disarmament received less attention from the member states than expected, leading to slow decision-making in both the CSP and EC.

Growing Pains (1999-2002) From 1999 to 2002, two related crises shook the OPCW. First, a large-scale financial crisis in 2001 led to a forced decline in OPCW activities. Second, in April 2002, OPCW's Director-General José Bustani's term was ended by a special CSP. Concerning the financial crisis, there are mainly two factors that contributed to it. The costs for OPCW verification activities are not part of the formal general budget, but are paid directly by the inspected states. In the early 2000s, the OPCW administration was slow in sending

---

[10]On the First Review Conference, see e.g. Kelle (2003), on the Second Review Conference, see e.g. Lak (2009), and on the Third Review Conference, see e.g. Kelle (2013).

invoices to member states, also due to some discussion about which costs exactly should be put on the states' bill. Also, like in other international organizations, states were only slowly paying. In the end, these circumstances caused a considerable hole in the organization's budget, leading to a reduced program in the following years (also see Dunworth 2008; Kelle 2004, 56f). Partially due to the financial crisis, a number of member states, above all the United States, lost confidence in DG Bustani who had been re-elected for a second term in 2001. When the new DG Rogelio Pfirtner was elected in a special CSP in April 2002, many member states, but also a number of staff members where disillusioned about the OPCW. Now, "[t]he image of the Secretariat as perceived by capitals was that the OPCW was just 'another UN organization' – a far cry from its original ideals and one that led to disillusionment and disappointment among many in the Secretariat" (Barbeschi 2002, 53).

Moving toward Adulthood (2002 - early 2010s) In the past decade, the organization has developed some routine as industry inspections have become more common and as the destruction of chemical weapons comes closer to an end. Further, there have been few large-scale political conflicts in the work of the OPCW, so that it could concentrate on the more technical aspects of its mandate. Public attention remained relatively low. Also, there were only limited moves from the member states to give new tasks to a future OPCW after complete chemical disarmament. For example, states were not too enthusiastic to give the OPCW a strong anti-terrorism mandate after 9/11 (see below).

New Challenges (since 2013) In the very recent past, the broad public began to take note of the OPCW when it began to investigate claims of chemical weapons usage in Syria in 2013 and began oversight of the destruction of Syrian chemical weapons under UNSC Resolution 2118 (see Trapp 2014). Also, the award of the Nobel Peace Price in the same year underlined the grown role of the OPCW as a political actor. Compared to cases like the IAEA, however, the growth as a political actor is quite limited. Next to the Syria case, there are currently no other high level political conflicts where chemical weapons are involved and where the OPCW could begin to play a greater role. The main challenge currently lies in finalizing the destruction of existing stockpiles and the re-orientation of the organization towards non-proliferation, especially through industry inspections (see below).

The historical developments and changes in the OPCW's institutional environment lead to a number of challenges for the organization's future. First of all, a number of *changes in science and technology* lead to new challenges for the CWC inspection regime. On the occasion of the Review Conferences, the OPCW asks the scientific community for an assessment of changes in science and the chemical industry that relate to the organization's work (Smallwood et al. 2013; Balali-Mood et al. 2008; Parshall et al. 2002). The recommendations usually focus on two core challenges, while on the generally applauding the work of the organization and its conduct of inspections. First, the growing convergence of chemistry and biology, both in science and industry, increases the risk of the development of new products that could be used for chemical weapons. Here, the OPCW needs to increase its efforts to stay knowledgeable of the quick developments. Second, the globalization of research and industry is a challenge for member states that need to implement legislation on chemical safety in line with the CWC. Especially developing and emerging economies need the support of the OPCW in developing legislation. In general, the scientific assessments propose stronger analytical capabilities and more outreach to the scientific and industry communities so that the OPCW can answer the two challenges.

Next to the changes in industry and science, the CWC regime also needs to address growing risks of chemical weapons use in the context of new forms of warfare and globalized terrorism (cf. e.g. Robinson 2008). In both cases, there are not only changing rationales of using chemical agents, e.g. as an indiscriminate weapon of terrorism or use in internal conflicts. Also, there is an increased probability of the usage of non-lethal chemical weapons, e.g. in the form of riot control agents. The regulation of those is another challenge for the OCPW. So far, however, the member states have given little new authority to the OCPW. They have established a working group on questions of chemical terrorism and asked the Secretariat to elaborate on its role in counter-terrorism. Yet, it appears that the OPCW is to remain a central knowledge hub and will not become more active "on the ground" (see Tucker 2012).

Finally, the biggest challenge relates to the end of the verification of the destruction of chemical weapons, expected in this decade. The OPCW has installed an advisory group to develop a plan for new focal points of the organizations work after complete chemical weapons destruction (OPCW 2011*b*). This shift in focus is usually framed as a shift from disarmament to non-proliferation. In this regard, the expert panel proposed more work on today's security concerns (i.e. terrorism and incapacitating agents), greater attention for chemical safety and security and an increased focus on OCPFs, where the experts expect higher proliferation risks. For the OPCW, as an organization, the experts demand a stronger self-understanding as a transparent and open knowledge-based organization that needs to reach out to civil society, science and industry (also see Trapp 2012).

POLITICAL CONFLICTS

To conclude the description of the OPCW's history, functions and developments, I discuss two *prevailing conflicts in the organization* that have been discussed by its members for a long time. First, like in the case of the IAEA, there is continuing debate about the balance of verification and technical cooperation activities. Second, there is some concern about the general effectiveness of the OPCW's industry inspection regime.

When looking at the budget for cooperation activities, it has slightly grown over the years (see below, Figure 4.18). Still, a number of developing member states continue to ask for greater OCPW efforts to assist with the development of the chemical industry in developing member states (cf. Kelle 2004). An important issue in this matter is the work of the *Australia Group*, an informal group of states with a large chemical industry sector that agree on a number of measures to stop the proliferation of chemical and biological weapons with tight export regulations. The Group first convened in 1985 in reaction to the discovery of the Iraqi chemical weapons program. Since then, there is a debate among OPCW members whether the group circumvents the OPCW and the CWC provisions by setting export standards in a non-inclusive matter, thus hindering free trade and development (for a detailed discussion, see e.g. Seevaratnam 2006). Larger projects with regard to exchange in technologies were blocked because of this conflict. Consequently, the OPCW had to limit its cooperation programs to scientific exchanges. Only since 2000, there is a separate division in the Technical Secretariat, responsible for international cooperation activities. Since then, the impact of cooperation projects has increased, e.g. when the OPCW began to host training workshops. Still, as the debate around the new strategy for the implementation of Article XI indicates (OPCW 2011a), the conflict is not yet solved (also see Trapp 2007).

Second, there is much debate about the effectiveness of the OPCW as an organization and about its inspections regime (cf. on these issues Kelle 2004). First of all, there is slower than expected progress in the destruction of chemical weapons. While in practice a task that the possessor states are responsible for, the continuing extension of destruction deadlines decreases general trust in the CWC regime. Second, the creation of state legislation in accordance to the OPCW is an important aspect of the CWC. Without proper national laws to control the chemical industry, states cannot credibly report and declare their activities under the CWC. In 2012, only 89 of the 188 member states had fully functioning national legislation in place (OPCW 2013, 17). Consequently, there is some skepticism on the side of the state parties about the declarations of some other states.

Similarly, as already reported above, the OPCW faces a very large amount of declared chemical industry sites. Especially OCPF are a challenge. With low inspection rates and even lower re-inspection probabilities for once inspected sites, there is the thread of waning credibility of the whole OPCW inspection regime. Finally, there are continued calls by outside observers for the OPCW to become more receptive to the demands of the scientific and NGO communities. As discussed above, more outreach to different communities is often demanded. Further, NGOs and others often tried to put topics like non-lethal chemical weapons on the OPCW's agenda but their efforts were deferred (Kelle 2004, 236).

4.2.2 OPCW PARTICIPATION

How open is the OPCW? As described above, a number of design features and purposes that the organization was created for call for high participation of experts and scientists. On the other hand, the limited mandate in communicating with the public lead to rather low levels of expected transparency. Still, as the next sections will demonstrate, there is some change on both dimensions since the establishment of the OPCW in 1997.

PARTICIPATION TALK

First, there is little change in the quantity of references to participation in the OPCW's *talk*. However, the communicated meaning of participation has become more open in the OPCW's Annual Report. Again, the main source for evaluating openness talk is the organizations' annual report. The OPCW issues its AR each year at the CSP. The annual reports are available in the OPCW's online CSP archives (see http://www.opcw.org/ documents-reports/conference-states-parties/). Like the IAEA, at the CSP, the Secretariat presents the AR for the preceding year. I included all Annual Reports from 1997 until 2011 in my analysis and I will refer to them using their official document number.

The OPCW annual reports present the work of the organization in its various fields of activities and also report on the progress of chemical weapons disarmament in its member states. Thus, the AR is a good source as it presents the whole work of the ogranization in the reported year. Further, the production of an Annual Report is required under the CWC (Art. VIII, C 32) and it is the main source of information for the public and OPCW member states. Like in the case of the IAEA, the tone and language of the AR is very formal and technical. For example, when celebrating the 10th anniversary of the OPCW, the tone remains neutral, highlighting that the organization continues making "further progress in each area of the activities it pursues under the Convention: chemical disarmament, non-proliferation, assistance and protection, and international cooperation" (C-13/4, 1).

However, the form and presentation of the reports has remained relatively constant over the years. There is no strong trend towards including more boxes, graphs or photographs. This indicates that the main anticipated readers of the AR have not changed much over the years. Also, the structure of the reports change little. First, the report informs about the status of OPCW inspections and the progress in chemical weapons disarmament. Next, there are activity reports for the individual constitutional organs of the OPCW. The overall tone of the texts present the OPCW as an a-political and technical organization. On average, the AR has a length of about 80 pages.

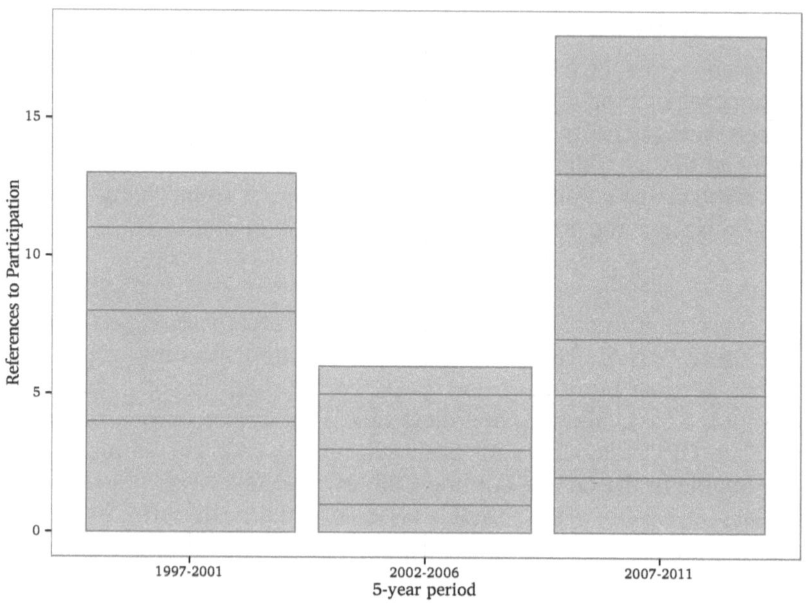

Figure 4.12: Participation Talk in the OPCW Annual Reports

Figure 4.12 shows a mixed image of references to ideas of participation in the OPCW's ARs. The graph groups the years into 5-year periods for easier comparison. There is only one year (2005), where no references are made. Further, especially in the early years and in the most recent years, talk about participation was more present than in the other time periods. Regarding the frequency of talk per year, the numbers are comparable to those of the IAEA. In the 1990s, there were on average 2.6 instances of participation talk. In the 2000s, however, this number decreased slightly to 2.4. On average, there is thus no trend towards more participation talk in the OPCW case. Rather, talk is constant for many years and extraordinary high instances of organizational talk about participation is present in the years after the OPCW's foundation and in the most recent years.

Is there change in the issues that the OPCW addresses when talking participation? In the early years, participation talk emerged around topics like the participation of scientists and the participation of specialists in special courses offered by the OPCW. Also, the inclusion of experts in the creation of OPCW products like information packages or online information was discussed (see e.g. C-V/5, 33). Further, there was talk about possible ways of including NGOs and business associations in the work of the OPCW. The following citations underline the broader understanding of channeled participation with the goal of information and expertise gathering that the OPCW had at that time:

> "During the Third Session of the Conference several NGO representatives attended a roundtable discussion on the role which NGOs could play in increasing public awareness and understanding of the Convention. The participation of appropriate NGOs in the activities of the Organisation enhanced public support for the principles enshrined in the Convention, and encouraged a closer working relationship between some NGOs and the OPCW" (C-IV/5, 37).

> "Working relationships with NGOs are pursued when the goals of their campaigns and the OPCW's efforts to promote universality and to increase awareness of the OPCW are complementary. That cooperation has been pursued in workshops, as well as in the sharing of press contacts and the development of a database of legislative measures relevant to the implementation of the Convention and to chemical weapons destruction efforts. NGOs are also capable of contacting a much wider audience than the OPCW could hope to reach on its own. The OPCW can then distribute its message more effectively, while saving resources" (C-VI/5, 47).

In more recent years, this description of participation has changed and became more open to participation without direct functional benefits for the OPCW, while retaining the old baseline understanding of participation. Since the mid 2000s, the OPCW begins to use a stakeholder language, "including the governments of States Parties and Signatory States, industry associations, civil society, international organisations and the media" as their key partners (C-12/6, 24). Similarly, in 2008, the OPCW Secretariat "initiated the development of a long-term strategy to address the relationship between the OPCW and the many stakeholders of the Convention" (C-14/4, 28).

In the same year, "[t]he OPCW participated in the first-ever 'Open Day' for the general public in cooperation with the municipality of The Hague. Group visits to the Secretariat and presentations for diplomats, students, and members of the public were organised on a regular basis" (C-14/4, 24). While also increasing transparency, these measures are also embedded in "new initiatives taken to strengthen public outreach" C-15/4, 26). Similarly, "the Director-General addressed public forums in Istanbul, The Hague,

Vienna, and Washington DC and published commentaries on Convention-related issues in prominent newspapers" (ibid.). The OPCW thus started a more direct approach of engagement with its environment by engaging more directly with the public and enlarging its understanding of participation.

PARTICIPATION DECISIONS

On the *decision dimension*, there are no large-scale changes in the participation rules. Already at the stage of the Preparatory Commission, member states saw the need to establish rules for the participation of non-governmental organizations. However, as with many issues, no formal rules were set. The Committee for the Preparation of the First CSP discussed NGO participation and provided a recommendation to the CSP for NGO participation (PC-XVI/FS/1/Rev.1). In the committee decision, it is underlined that NGOs will need to show their relevance with regard to CWC issues. Further, the selection of invited NGOs shall be based on "an organization's technical, financial and academic activities" (ibid, 1). Also, the committee proposed a number of rights and limits of NGO participation that were later used as a guideline by the CSP (see below). In its final report, the Preparatory Commission proposed, that all NGOs that have applied to attend the first CSP, will be allowed to attend while highlighting that "the Conference will have final responsibility for the modalities governing NGOs" (PC-XVI/37). There was thus no consensus for creating permanent accreditation rules and a regulated status for NGOs at the Preparatory Commission.

The first CSP in 1997 followed the PrepCom proposal and admitted a number of NGOs and industry representatives to the conference. Further, in the Rules of Procedures for the CSP, it made modest references to non-state participation:

> "Representatives of non-governmental organisations may attend the plenary sessions of the Conference, and participate in the activities of review conferences, in accordance with such rules or guidelines as the Conference has approved" (C-I/3/Rev. 2, Rule 33).

Subsequently, the CSP has decided at the beginning of each session about which NGOs shall be granted participation rights. Compared to the IAEA, there is thus a much lower level of codification of participation rules. In the first participation decision, the CSP grants the following rights to non-state participants (C-I/DEC.1):

- There shall be no financial support for attendance.
- The Conference invites NGOs to attend public meetings of the plenary sessions only.

- NGO participants shall be issued name tags.
- There shall be no NGO placards at the conference tables.
- NGOs do not have the right to address meetings.
- NGOs may put literature outside at designated places outside the conference rooms.

These rules change only little over time. In 2000, non-state participants additionally receive access to official documents that are listed in the official CSP agenda and are distributed during the CSP (C-V/DEC.3). Further, since the 8th Session in 2003, the rules on financial support, NGO placards and the right to address meetings are no longer mentioned (C-8/DEC.2). This last step appears to be a slight upgrade in non-state participants rights. However, as there are no verbal records available, it is hard to assess the impact of this rule change. Nevertheless, the change in the practice of annual rule formulation for NGO participation indicates a slight increase of participation rights and thus in openness decisions.

Regarding participation at the EC, Rule 50 posits that

> "The Council may, on a case by case basis, invite any non-governmental organisation or any individual to be represented at or to attend a meeting of the Council if the consideration of a particular agenda item at the meeting so requires" (C-I/DEC.72, 11).

Again, the lack of verbal records make it hard to qualify the de-facto level of participation in the Executive Council over time. Thus, overall, like at the IAEA, NGOs have passive participation rights at the OPCW and there is no large-scale reform of NGO participation rules until 2011.

PARTICIPATION ACTION

How has participation changed on the OPCW's *action* dimension? Participation of non-state actors at the CSP has been relatively stable since its foundation with a very moderate increase in participation since the late 2000s. The bars in Figure 4.13 show the number of NGOs that participated in each CSP since 1997. The data is taken from the official CSP lists of participants.[11] For the OPCW's first 5 years, there are on average 12 NGOs present per year. In the past ten years, this rises to an average of 13 and the maximum number of NGOs that were present is 28, as opposed to a maximum of 24 at the first CSP in 1997.

Participation action is also relatively stable when looking at the dotted line in Figure 4.13, representing the number of individual NGO representatives. Here, there is also a similar trend, with lots of stability and a moderate

---

[11] When not available online, I obtained the List of Participants from the Documents and Media Sections of the OPCW upon request.

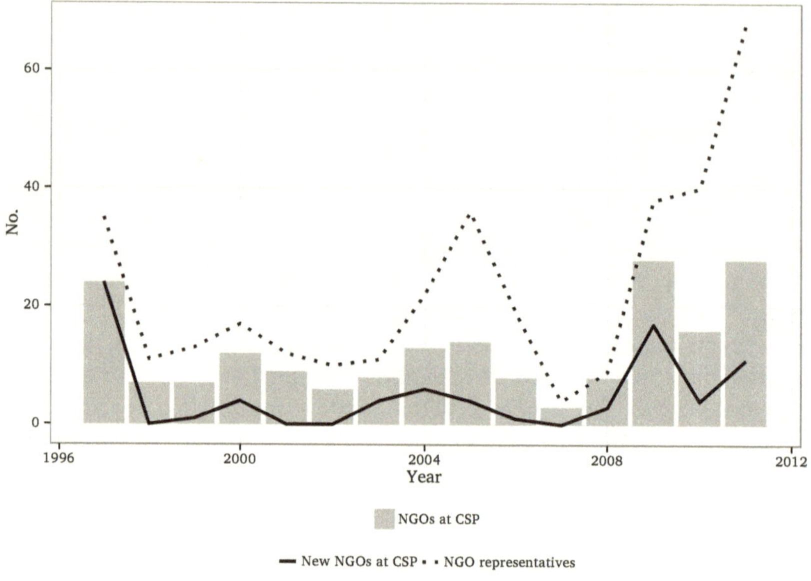

Figure 4.13: Participation of NGOs in OPCW CSP

growth of NGO representatives in the late 2000s. The mean number of NGO representatives in the first five years is 17. In the past ten years, this has risen to 25 with a peak of 68 in 2011. Further, the black line in Figure 4.13 shows a certain volatility in the NGOs that are represented. There are some peak years where new NGOs are coming to the OPCW CSP. In particular, this is the case around 2004 and again in 2009, highlighting the moderate growth of NGO participation around that time.

Which NGOs participate at the CSP? Despite the volatility in numbers, there is relative stability in the types of NGOs that come to The Hague and in the issues they represent. First, there are a number of research institutions and researchers that are registered for the conference. Their focus is thus rather on policy analysis and advice. Next, there are usually a number of chemical industry associations represented. However, compared to their strong lobbying in the early negotiation phase of the CWC, they do not seem to chose the CSP as a main venue to make their interests heard. One would thus have expected more chemical industry participation, given the large impact that OPCW inspections have on their daily activities. Finally, the third group of NGOs are those working on human rights. Often, their work focus is on the care for victims of chemical weapons use, but also on broader questions like the environment and world peace.

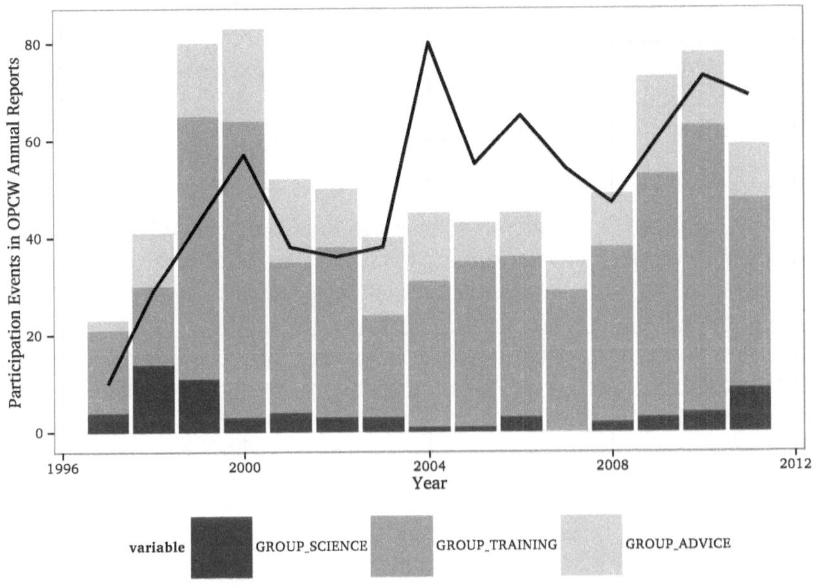

Figure 4.14: Participation Events in OPCW Annual Report by Amount (line) and Type (bars)

Figure 4.14 presents data for the second measure of participation action, i.e. participation events. The black line in the figure indicates a rising trend of participation events, like expert meetings, training or other forms of exchange between the OPCW and its environment, reported in the Annual Reports. In the first five years of OPCW activities, there are on average 35 participation events per year. In the past decade, this number rises to an average of 58.

The bars in Figure 4.14 show that there are only minimal shifts in the kind of participation events that the OPCW offers (for a discussion of the data, see Appendix B). Seminars, panels and symposia, all labeled under the science group, were more important in the early years and become more important, again, since 2008. The majority of events, however, are grouped under the training category. Here, the OPCW organizes workshops, training events and courses for member state officials, scientists and other stakeholders. The share of those events have remained relatively stable over time. The same is true for the group of advisory events, containing meetings of experts, networks of experts and advisory group events.

Thus, overall, on the action dimension, there is only a moderate over-arching trend towards more participation. First, NGO participation in the highest policy making organ, the CSP, has remained relatively stable over most of the years, but there is slightly increasing participation since 2009. Second, the number of participation events, i.e. direct exchanges of information between the OPCW and its environment, have moderately increased over the years. Here, it its especially exchange under the label of training, that has driven change over the years.

4.2.3   OPCW TRANSPARENCY

How has the OPCW's output on the transparency dimension changed? When looking at references to transparency, these are constant over time. There are no large changes, but transparency has always been part of the OPCW's discurse in some specific contexts. Further, decisions that increase transparency are observable, despite the general focus on secrecy and confidentiality, written into the CWC. Finally, on the action dimension there is an increased use of resources for transparency.

TRANSPARENCY TALK

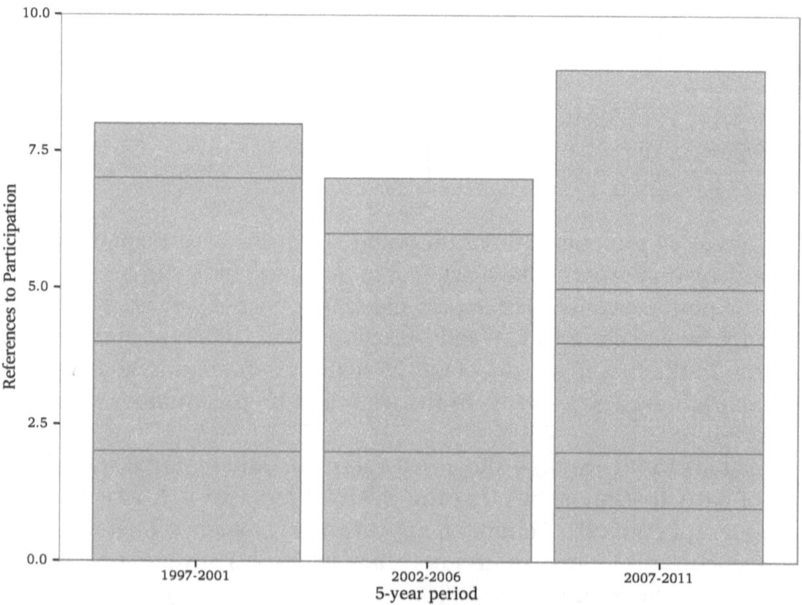

Figure 4.15: Transparency Talk in the OPCW Annual Reports

When *speaking* about transparency, the OPCW, like other international organizations, commits itself to improve its processes so that its decision-making will be more open in the future and more accessible for the broad public. Figure 4.15 illustrates the number of references to practices and ideas of transparency in the OPCW's annual reports. There is only little variance in the use of transparency talk. In the 3 five year periods since the OPCW's foundation, only in 2000 and in 2001, it did not make reference to transparency in its AR. Further, there is no larger trend towards increasing reference to transparency over time. Over the years, there are on average 1.6 instances of transparency talk per year.

Which issues does the OPCW discuss in the context of transparency? In the early years, transparency was important to increase general knowledge about the organization, the CWC and the broad issue of chemical weapons destruction and non-proliferation. At that time, this goal is usually achieved by intensifying publications and the general provision of information to the public and special audiences. For example, in 1998, the organization highlights the importance of providing accessible information:

> "In order to support the external activities of the Organisation and to increase understanding of its objectives, work in the area of publications was considerably diversified and enhanced, amongst other things through the production of two new external publications: a brochure entitled Chemical Disarmament - Basic Facts, and a magazine called OPCW Images. Basic Facts, which provides an easily accessible explanation of the Convention and the operational aspects of the OPCW, targeted a broad audience base" (CIV/5, 37).

Similarly, the idea of accessible information about the organization is discussed with relation to the OPCW library and internet site. Another context where transparency is evoked is the internal organization of the OPCW. For example, "[t]ransparent and clear procedures for both the review of posts and the internal classification and promotion of staff members needed to be concluded and implemented" (C-VI/5, 55) at the high time of the financial and political crisis of the OPCW. Similarly, "the up-grading of staff members through changes of appointment and the provision of new functional titles needs to be based on a transparent, fair and competitive process" (C-7/3, 35). Further, the principle of transparency is mentioned in the process of setting the OPCW budget and program (see e.g. C-9/5, 21).

As expected, there is thus less commitment to strong transparency in the OPCW's talk, especially in decision making procedures or in the assessments of state progress in chemical weapons destruction. Only recently has the CSP asked the Secretariat to assure greater transparency in this respect, while again extending destruction deadlines for member states (cf. C-17/4, 4).

Transparency Decisions

For transparency *decisions*, I see a similar development towards step-by-step increases of transparency as in the IAEA. Table 4.3 shows the most relevant decisions, as mentioned in the OPCW AR. At the outset of the organization, its public relations and publications activities were targeted primarily towards its member states. OPCW publications and the website were supposed to provide information to the member states. This narrow focus became wider in the following years, increasing openness for wider audiences. First, with the establishment of a library, the expert community was targeted. Later, at least since 1999, the focus was on the general public, too. This change was backed up by an expanded "public-outreach effort" (C-9/5, 19) in 2003, aiming for wide geographical reach, and a new public diplomacy strategy in 2011 (internal document, see reference in S/1215/2014).

The initial *OPCW Media and Public Affairs Policy* (C-I/DEC.55) is currently being revised (S/1215/2014). However, already the first version sets the goal to

> "assist the news media and the general public in understanding the tasks and the activities of the Organisation. It shall promote the image of the OPCW as an accessible international organisation which provides balanced, timely and objective information. It will not be overly promotional and active, but will avoid being merely reactive" (C-I/DEC.55, 3).

In this context, "[t]he OPCW will endeavour to be as open and accessible as possible in providing factual information on its activities and shall conduct an effective Public Affairs Programme with respect to the news media and the general public" (ibid.). The Annex of the strategy also includes a list of areas that the Technical Secretariat (TS) shall provide information about, including points on chemical weapons and their destruction, the CWC, and the chemical industry. The new strategy that is currently under development will give the TS a more active mandate in promoting the achievements of the OPCW and the CWC.

Overall, there is thus some development towards increasing transparency. Interestingly, though, compared to the IAEA, this development has started at a relatively low level and a slow pace. Compared to the IAEA at the same time, the OPCW was more closed in its early years. Only in most recent years were decisions taken to increase transparency.

Transparency Action

Finally, how transparent is the OPCW on the *action* dimension? Figure 4.16 represents the share of the public information budget of the OPCW. The budget data is taken from the official budgets, published annually as CSP documents (e.g. C-16/DEC.12). I add the budgets for the external relations and information systems programs to create the indicator. As already described in the operationalization in Chapter 3.3, the relative

Table 4.3: OPCW Transparency Decisions

Year	Transparency-relevant Decision	Source
1997	starting level, with website and publications, yet targeted primarily towards the Member States	C-II/2/Rev.2, p. 9
1998	increasing publications output, aiming at broader audiences and starting library	CIV/5, p. 37
1999	re-worked website policy: now also targeted at general public	C-V/5, p. 39
2000	expansion of Website. "Synthesis" Journal available online for free, course material for national authorities available online	C-VI/5, p. 48
2002	new publications targeted at general public: OPCW Profiles, "Basic Facts" re-issue, Brochures on Basic Information	C-8/5, p. 29f
2003	outreach strategy aiming at broader geographical reach, launch of new publications: "OPCW Regional Series", "Chemical Disarmament Quarterly"	C-9/5, p. 19
2008	participation in "Open Day", i.e. opening its doors to the public for one day, increased outreach to research institutions, website with more official documents	C-14/4, p. 24
2010	starting social media activities, development of a new "Public Diplomacy Strategy" and Task Force, first steps of live reporting of OPCW events.	C-16/4, p. 26

budget data stands for political decisions of an IGO. While the overall budget is largely defined and controlled by its member states, IGO administrations have some leeway in distributing the money internally in the program development phase of the annual or biannual budgeting. The share of the budget that the IGO spends for transparency measures is thus only partially a direct function of its general budget. In times of tight budgets, there are political decisions taken which programs receive less money and which ones grow.

Compared to the IAEA, the OPCW decides to spend on average 6.6 percent of its annual budget to communicate with its environment. For the IAEA, that average is only 2.2 percent. Over time, the share of the public information budget increases slightly. In the OPCW's first 5 years, the

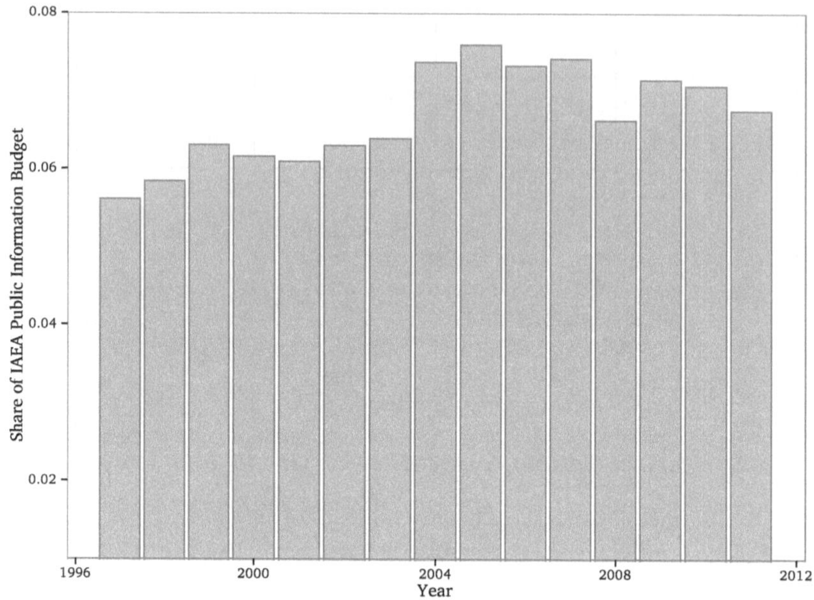

Figure 4.16: Share of OPCW Public Information Budget of Total Budget

annual average is at 6 percent. In the last decade, this share has risen to about 7 percent. There is thus a slight increase in the transparency action of the OPCW since the mid 2000s. The overall importance of transparency action also is visible in the early 2000s. As discussed above, and shown below, despite the budget crisis, the relative budget only slightly decreases. Further, when the general budget is back to its pre-crisis amount in 2004, the organization decides to increase the budget for public information even more. The budget share in 2004 is higher than the pre-crisis share in 1997. This underlines the slight increase in transparency action in the mid 2000s.

4.2.4   CHANGES IN THE OPCW'S ENVIRONMENT: NORM AND RESOURCE BASED CONDITIONS

Overall, there is less variation in the environmental variables for the OPCW compared to the IAEA. Given the much shorter history of the former IO, this is not too surprising. Still, the previous paragraphs identified some changes in the organization's openness that need to be explained. In the following sections, I thus discuss the changes in the conditions identified by the explanatory model. In summary, there is an increase in the OPCW's budget and slightly growing inequality. When looking at the norm based mechanisms, the OPCW is rarely visible in the global news media and the share of democratic member states only increases slightly.

RESOURCE BASED CONDITIONS

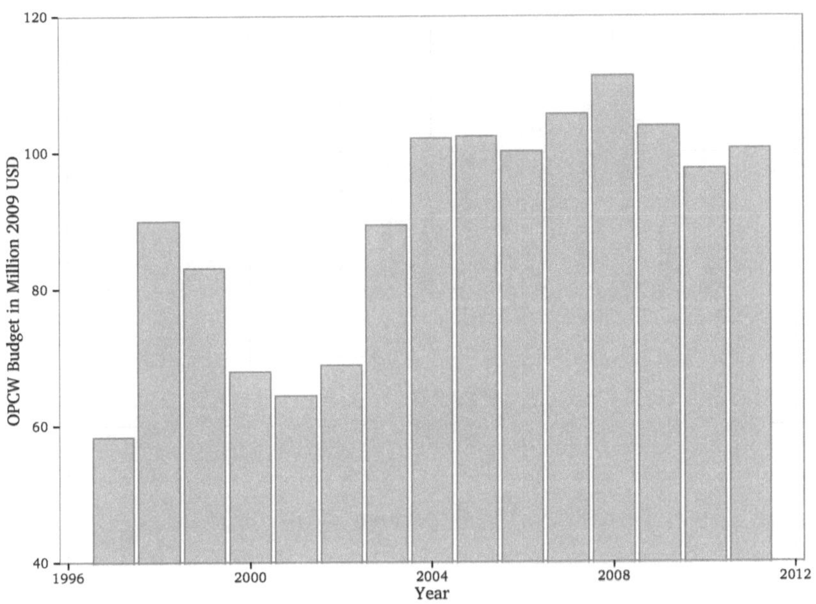

Figure 4.17: OPCW Total budget in 2009 USD

First, the *OPCW budget* has increased over time. Figure 4.17 illustrates the variance of the OPCW budget in 2009 USD over time. In the first 5 years, the average annual budget was about 72 million USD. In the last decade, the budget has risen by 30 percent to an average of 98 million USD. Also, the graph shows the large impact of the OPCW's financial crisis in the early 2000s. From 1999 to 2000, the budget decreased by nearly 20 percent, recovering to early numbers only after three years of crisis. Also, in the late 2000s, there is a less dramatic decrease in the operational budget of the OPCW.

As discussed in more detail above, the financial crisis was caused by management problems at the OPCW and a weak payment morale by member states. Figure 4.18 illustrates that the crisis especially had an impact on the verification budget. In the 2000 and 2001 budgets, total and relative expenditures for inspections and the inspectorate decrease. Such a financial crisis, according to the resource based mechanism, should lead to an increased need for external expertise and thus openness.

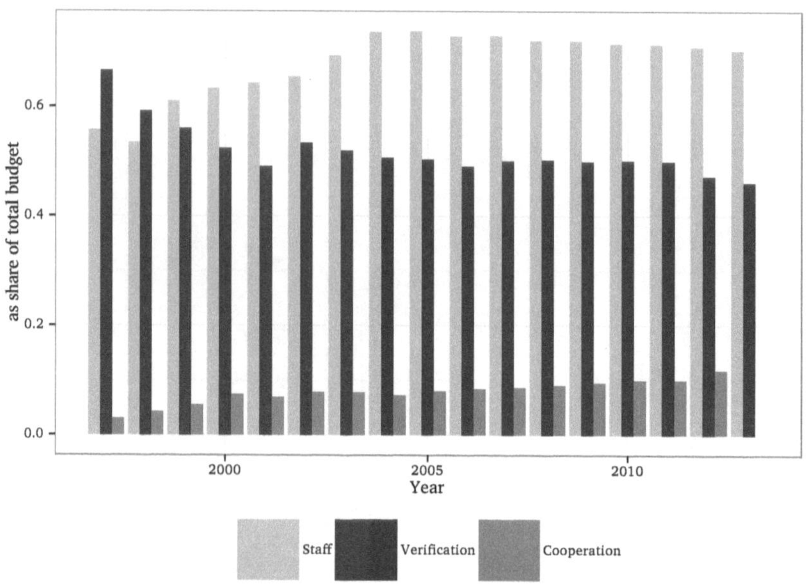

Figure 4.18: OPCW Budget by Expenditure

Also, Figure 4.18 shows the general development of the staff costs and expenditures for cooperation activities. Staff costs are steadily increasing until the mid 2000s, peaking in 2004 and 2005 at almost three quarters of the regular budget. Further, the low share of the OPCW budget for technical assistance is notable, underlining the concerns that many developing member states have with the balance of the organization's activities. Since 1997, on average, the OPCW has spent 52 percent of its budget on verification activities, but only 8 percent on technical assistance. Like in the IAEA case, there is also a *Voluntary Fund For Assistance* for states to finance assistance projects. However, the figures in the graph already include the voluntary contributions of member states to the Fund. In the past decade, the regular budget for assistance amounted to an annual average of 5.3 million EUR. In the same time, there were on average 1.2 million EUR contributed voluntarily per year. The voluntary contributions are thus a relatively small amount.

Finally, as in the IAEA, debates about the budget often underline the importance of a *zero growth budget*. Since 2005, many budget negotiation were driven by the idea of only increasing the budget as required by inflation (see e.g. C-13/4, 2). Overall, there is thus little leeway on the side of the administration to start new large-scale programs. Thus, cheap external expertise and information input, especially for the verification activities, is much needed. Consequently, the resource based explanation fits well with the observable, yet limited, growth of participation and transparency action in the OPCW since the mid 2000s.

Next, how has the economic *inequality* of the OPCW's member states changed over the years? Figure 4.19 shows the Gini-Coefficient for the membership's GDP data. There is only a weak increase over time of already high inequality. On the one hand, this is caused by the late accession of a number of small and developing countries with weak economic performance. On the other hand, growing inequality of OPCW members also reflects the global trends of rising inequality in the global system of states. In the last decade, the average annual Gini-Coefficient of economic inequality is 0.83 and thus slightly higher than at the IAEA. Consequently, the overall high level of membership inequality can indirectly explain the general need for openness.

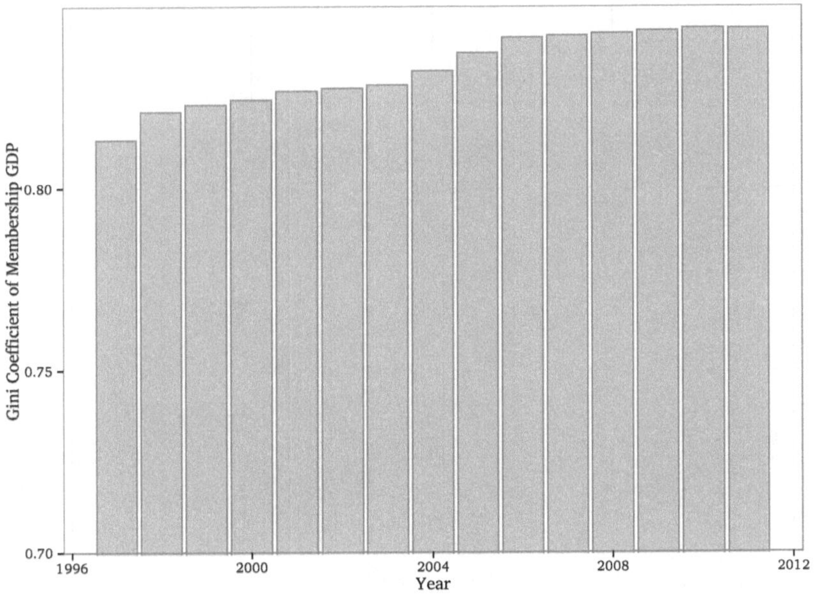

Figure 4.19: Inequality of OPCW Membership, based on Gini-Coefficient of GDP

Finally, there are also no changes in the *complexity* of the OPCW's policy field, measured as changes in statutory tasks. Complexity can thus only explain differences between the IAEA and the OPCW. The CWC sets the following statutory functions for the OPCW:

1. implementation and verification of chemical weapons destruction (Art. VIII)
2. assistance and protection against chemical weapons (Art X)
3. economic and technical development (Art XI)

Compared to the IAEA, the OPCW's field of action is thus comparatively less complex because the organization has no strong promotion function. The IAEA is mandated to support nuclear developments and invest in nuclear research and applications. The OPCW's development function is much weaker. It is, e.g. only mandated to enable free exchange of information and free trade in the chemical industry, but not responsible for developing chemical industry applications for developing countries. In this regard, one would expect less openness at the OPCW, compared to the IAEA because less input is needed for the development work. Again, this does not mean that the activities under e.g. the verification task have not become more demanding for the OPCW. Similarly to the IAEA, the number of sites and the technologies that need to be inspected has grown. Thus, an overall growth of openness due to the need for expertise is likely.

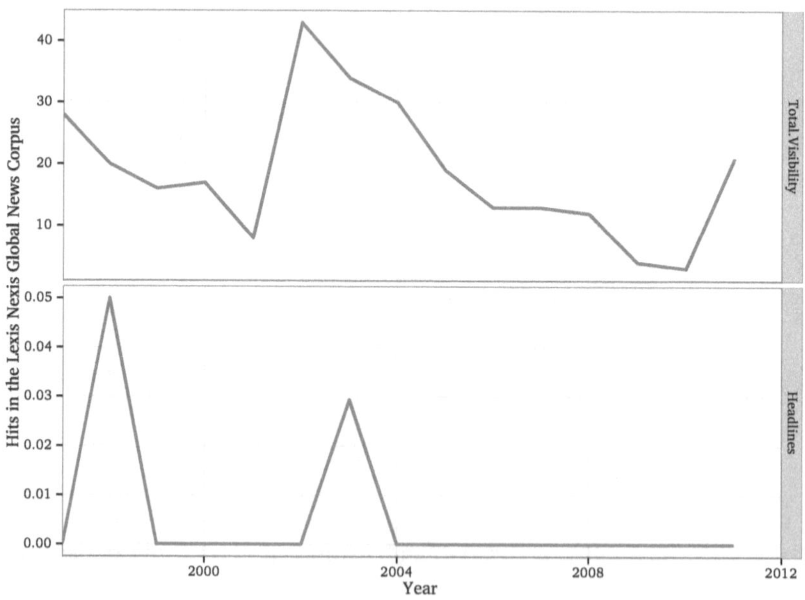

Figure 4.20: Visibility of the OPCW in the Global News Media. Total Visibility and Relative Visibility in Headlines as Share of Total Hits

NORM BASED CONDITIONS

Are there more changes in the variables derived from norm based explanations? First, are there changes in the *visibility* of the OPCW in the global
news media? The first graph in Figure 4.20 shows number of articles per
year that mention the OPCW. Compared to the IAEA, the visibility is very
low. On average, there are 18.7 articles per year on the OPCW. For the same
time, the IAEA is mentioned in about 1.400 articles per year. There is one
peak in visibility in 2002, when DG Bustani was removed from office (see
above). Next to this, the OPCW is from time to time cited or mentioned
in relation to its chemical weapons destruction work. Industry inspections
are a nearly invisible topic. The low visibility is underlined by the second
graph in Figure 4.20: the OPCW is hardly ever mentioned in the headlines
of newspaper articles. In 1998, there is one article about the OPCW and the
status of the North Korean chemical weapons program. Another article in
2003 discusses the employment of a Korean national as OPCW adviser. Both
articles appeared in Korean newspapers. Overall, the general public thus
seems to be little informed about the OPCW during the time under analysis.
A strong causal link between media visibility and increased opening is thus
unlikely for the OPCW.

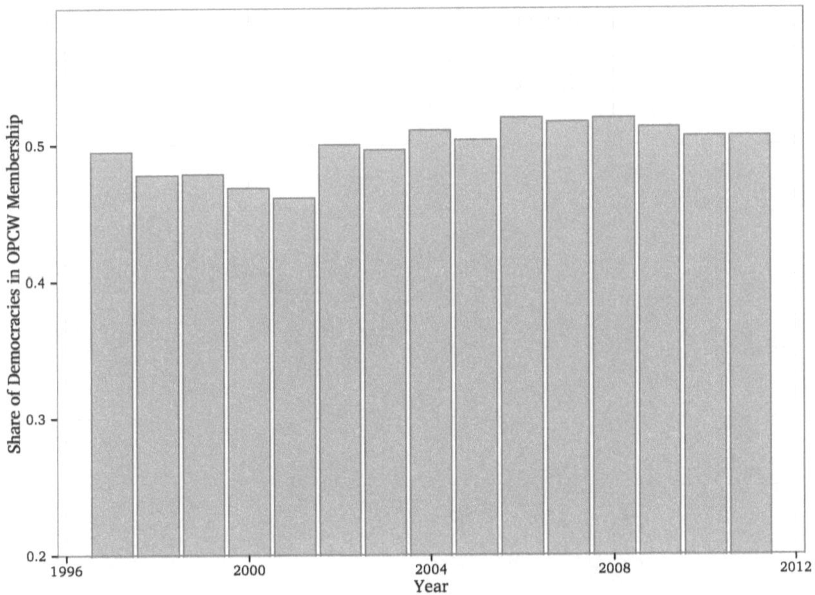

Figure 4.21: Share of Democracies in OPCW Membership

Second, has the OPCW membership become more *democratic*? Figure 4.21 shows the share of members per year that score higher than 6 in the Polity IV index of democracies. There is little change over time, but in general, the OPCW has a high share of democratic members. From 1997 until around 2001, the share of democratic members decreases, probably caused by the accession of numerous less democratic states in the OPCW's early years of existence. Since the mid 2000s, however, more than 50 percent of the members are democracies. Thus, it is likely to expect some influence of norm-socialization on the OPCW's openness. The constant presence of participation and transparency talk, for example, could be caused by the constantly high share of democratic members.

Third, there are no large scale changes in the *governance depth* of the OPCW. The relative policy impact that the organization has on its member states has remained constant over time. Industry and weapons inspections are the activities which contribute most to the general authority of the OPCW. Their mandate has not changed much over the time of analysis. The same is true for political inspection mandates. The oversight of the destruction of chemical weapons in 2013 is a first instance of political inspections under a Security Council Resolution (S/RES/2118). However, this time is not included in the time horizon of my analysis. Before, the OPCW was only mentioned once in a Security Council Resolution in 2011, when the situation in Libya was discussed (S/RES/2017). However, the resolution did not extend the already existing mandate of the OPCW. Thus, the general authority level of the OPCW as laid out in the CWC did not change from 1997 until 2011.

5 *Organizational Opening – A QCA*

In the previous chapter, I discussed processes of organizational opening of the IAEA and OPCW. Further, I presented data on explanatory variables which I derived from the theoretical framework. The analysis showed a number of interesting instances of opening on the output dimensions of talk, decision, and action. Yet, the previous chapter was mainly descriptive. In this chapter, the focus will be on explaining opening up. With the help of QCA as a methodology, I look at combinations of the explanatory conditions to explain organizational opening. As a result, I will present causal mechanisms that explain opening talk, decisions, and action in the IAEA and OPCW.

As described in the methods chapter, I will use *Qualitative Comparative Analysis* (QCA) to compare the combinations of conditions in my data and to draw conclusions about the causal determinants of organizational opening. A first important step in a QCA analysis is the translation of the raw data into membership scores. Second, I will look at necessary and sufficient conditions of organizational opening and thus present causal explanations of the phenomenon. In the final section of the chapter, I discuss the findings and select cases for the more detailed descriptions in Chapter 6.

5.1 Translating the Findings into QCA Language

QCA operates on *sets*. For each case and variable, a decisions needs to be made to what extent a case is a member of a set or not. Take for example the democratic membership variable. At which point do I qualify the share of democratic members to be high enough to have a possible causal influence on the opening of an IGO? Is a share of 50 percent of democracies influential, or does a share of 30 percent have the same causal influence on organizational opening? To make this decision, a process of *set calibration* is necessary. The calibration "has to be based on theoretical knowledge and empirical evidence. Obvious facts, accepted social scientific knowledge, and the researchers' own data collection process all inform the calibration process" (Schneider and Wagemann 2012, 41). During calibration, qualitative *thresholds* need to be set that determine when a case belongs to a set and when it does not.

For this analysis, I apply a *crisp set* methodology. Consequently, set membership scores are either 0 or 1. I chose a crisp set approach because it fits the data and the hypotheses that I am interested in well.[12] In this step of the analysis, I am interested in significant changes in either the openness, i.e. opening, or the environmental conditions of the IGOs. This notion of significant change can be captured with crisp sets. I thus need to define clear qualitative thresholds for change in the openness of IGOs on the various dimensions of the outcome. Values of 1 indicate full set membership, i.e. that significant change, or opening, has occurred, or that a certain environmental variable is present. The independent variables, or *conditions* in QCA language, also need to be calibrated by transparently discussing qualitative thresholds.

Set calibration is a step in the QCA that is often criticized: it is a crucial step in the process, greatly influencing the results and robustness of the analysis. For example, Krogslund, Choi and Poertner (2015) show that even minimal alterations in the setting of thresholds may have a large impact on the conclusions drawn from QCA. Further, there is a high danger of confirmation bias in QCA designs. In particular, there is the danger that unrelated conditions that only spuriously correlate with the outcome variables are considered as necessary or sufficient conditions in a QCA analysis. Similarly, Lucas and Szatrowski (2014) show, next to other problems, the difficulties that QCA sometimes has in eliminating non-causal factors from the analyses' results. Also, they highlight problems with generalizability of QCA results as they are very dependent on the cases selected for analysis.

In the next sections, I document my process of set calibration. To respond to the criticism, I try to be precise and transparent in my description of the calibration steps. Further, I justify my calibrations on theoretical and empirical grounds. Also, I only include conditions in the QCA analysis that I identified from the theoretical literature on organizational opening, thus reducing the risk of confirmation bias, caused by spurious correlation. In addition, I try to be careful in interpreting the results, knowing of the pitfalls of confirmation bias, spurious correlation and generalizability. Despite these limitations, QCA still is my method of choice, as discussed above, because it allows a systematic, transparent and comparative analysis of the IAEA and OPCW. Further, it is a well suited methodology for assessing the interactions of competing or complementary causal explanations.

5.1.1   CALIBRATING THE OUTCOME VARIABLES

In my data, there are 6 outcome variables: talk, decision, and participation on the dimensions of participation and transparency. I will calibrate the talk variables first, the decision variables second, and the participation outcomes third.

---

[12] I also ran several fuzzy set analyses on the data. The results, given some variation in the methods of set calibration, did not reveal any substantially different results. For the sake of a clear presentation and a clear set calibration, I decided to present the results of the crisp set analysis, only. An overview of the fuzzy-set analysis is available in the electronic appendix.

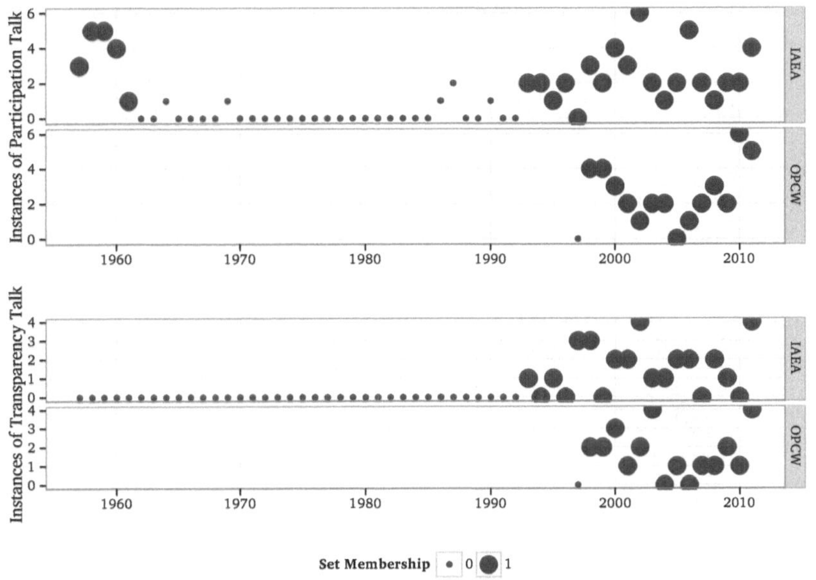

Figure 5.1: Calibrating Talk

CALIBRATING TALK

Figure 5.1 shows the development of participation and transparency talk in the IAEA and OPCW. I define the thresholds for belonging to the set *openning talk* as those years where, first, talk is present for at least three years in a row. For example, participation talk of the IAEA from 1957 to 1961 is included in the set. The instances of talk in 1986 and 1987 are not in the set because there are only 2 consecutive years of talk. At the same time, I include those periods that have a maximum of one year without an instance of relevant talk. Thus, a year without a reference to participation is included in the set if there were references in the year before and after. For example, this applies to IAEA participation talk in 1997. This accounts for a certain continuity in organizational talk: simply because a reference, to e.g. participation, has not been made in a single year does not mean that participation as such was of no importance. Thus, this calibration acknowledges historical continuity in organizational talk, understanding it as a mode of discourse production that changes slowly and is based on routine and organizational culture. Therefore, the result of the calibration are continuous phases of talk. Further, this calibration acknowledges the error potential during the process of data collection, like missing a crucial statement in an organization's talk, e.g. because of confusing wordings or formulations. This source of error is more likely for individual years than for a number of consecutive years.

When looking at the data, there are some years with exceptionally high values of participation or transparency talk. However, I do not include this differentiation in the calibration. My calibration understands opening talk as a contingent phenomenon. What is most important is the fact that an organization continuously talks about openness and thus opens up on the talk dimension. Whether it talks two or five times a year is less important. The set *openness talk* thus has the following levels:

0 for years without talk or for singular instances of talk
1 for years with opening talk:

- Participation Talk. IAEA: 1957-1961, 1993-2011. OPCW: 1998-2011.
- Transparency Talk. IAEA: 1993-2011. OPCW: 1998-2011.

To explain further, the IAEA's talk is open from 1957 until 1961. Then, talk closes again until in 1993, talk opens up again. For the OPCW, talk has opened up in 1998.

CALIBRATING DECISIONS

When looking at the data for participation decisions, there is not much change in both organizations. Both organizations have made decisions on the rights and rules for NGO attendance early in their organizational history and have introduced only minimal changes since then. Thus, assigning high membership values for the whole period of time would be misleading. Instead, I try to capture and explain the instances of change. Therefore, I will assign the membership score 1 only to the years where minimal change was introduced. In addition, I will assign the same value for the 3 preceding years, because I assume that change in organizational rules needs to be prepared over time.

Choosing a four-year period is a general approximation of the duration that IGO decisions take to be prepared. For example, an IGO may be subject to public criticism in 1995. During the year, the IGO secretariat tries to respond to criticism but notices that it needs new measures to respond adequately. During 1996, there could be intensive consultations between the secretariat and member states to e.g. create a system for accrediting NGOs. A proposal is made at the 1996 Annual Conference, but a decision cannot be reached. Only during 1997 can a consensus on the consultative status be found and successfully passes as a Conference resolution in 1998. For the analysis, it is thus also the environmental conditions of the preceding years that influence the decision in a certain year. This calibration resembles the use of a negative lag in regression analyses.

For the IAEA, I include the 1975 decision of the GC that formalizes the ad-hoc rules for NGO participation by invitation of the DG. For the OPCW, I include the decisions in 2000 to allow NGO access to official CSP documents and the decision in 2003 that gives NGOs the possibility to address OPCW meetings and have placards to identify them (see Chapter 4 for a detailed discussion of these instances of change). Thus, the set *participation decisions* has the following two levels:

0 for years without participation decisions
1 for years with participation decisions and the 3 preceding years

  - IAEA: 1972-1975. OPCW: 1997-2003.

For transparency decisions, there is more variance over time and a more visible increase of transparency-enabling decisions. However, the challenge is to develop a calibration that makes both IAEA and OPCW decisions comparable. Therefore, I propose the following qualitative thresholds for the set *transparency decisions* (also see the discussion to Tables 4.2 and 4.3):

0 Transparency decisions focusing on providing information to member states or other international organizations.
0 Transparency decisions focusing on providing information to the media.

  - IAEA: 1986-1992, OPCW: 1998.

1 Transparency decisions mainly focus on providing information to the general public.

  - IAEA: 1993-1999. OPCW: 1999-2007.

1 Transparency decisions explicitly focus on "increasing transparency" of the organization.

  - IAEA: 2000-2011. OPCW 2010-2011.

The first threshold marks a shift in transparency decisions because a greater audience than member states is targeted. For example, in 1986, the IAEA began to issue Newsbriefs that had the goal to inform the global media about important developments in the nuclear sciences, technologies and the IAEA itself. Similarly, in 1998, the OPCW began to target the media and specialized audiences with a streamlined publications portfolio. However, during this time, the rules are not yet part of the transparency decision set, because information is still spread through the media filter and is not provided to the public directly.

This changes when, at the second threshold, the organizations began to focus on the general public as a target audience. At that time, they did no longer rely only on the media for information distribution but addressed interested audiences directly. As the quality of transparency rules is already quite high, I include the cases in the set. In the case of the IAEA, information provision is e.g. discussed when it launches its website with the goal to reach a broad audience. At the OPCW, a redesign of the website with the goal to make it more accessible and informative for the general public was launched in 1998.

Finally, the last level comprises those decisions that acknowledge the general importance of transparency as a principle of the organization. As this is the highest quality threshold for transparency decisions, I also assign a set membership score of 1. In the IAEA, this becomes obvious, for example, in the new technical cooperation strategy that makes transparency of internal processes a major objective. At the OPCW, with the launch of a new "Public Diplomacy Strategy", transparency becomes a main organizational goal.

CALIBRATING ACTION

Next, for calibrating the action dimension, I look at NGO participation at the annual policy-making conferences first. Figure 5.2 shows the development over time. Here, the numbers of NGOs are comparable between the organizations. The maximum number of registered NGOs at the IAEA is 31, for the OPCW it is 28 NGOs. Also, there have been NGOs present at the conferences since the beginning of both IAEA and OPCW. Therefore, as in the case of participation decisions, the goal of the calibration is to identify and classify significant changes. I create a set of *high NGO participation* in which all years are members if there is change towards more NGO participation. I use deviations in the mean of annual NGO participation as a tool to identify the phases. In the case of the IAEA, there are two particular phases. The first ranges from 1958 to 1964. Here, the mean number of NGOs is 11. In the following years, the amount falls to 8. At the end of the period, 1964, participation declined by more than half from 10 NGOs to 4 NGOs. During the second range from 1991 to 2011, the annual mean rises to 18. For the OPCW, the first phase of high participation is from 1997 until 2000 (mean of 13), the second from 2009 to 2011 (mean rising from 9 to 26).

Similarly, I create a set for the number of NGO representatives at the annual conferences. Full membership in the set *high NGO representatives* is attributed when there is a strong trend towards a higher number of NGO representatives. For the IAEA, this is the case since 2008, when individual participation is rising very quickly. Similarly, the same applies to the OPCW. Here, participation has risen to an exceptionally high number since 2009.

A similar calibration logic applies to participation events. They are also present during the whole time of analysis. However, also given its much higher budget, the IAEA organizes much more participation events than the OPCW. Consequently, membership in the set *high participation events* is given to years that belong to the top 25 percent of years with

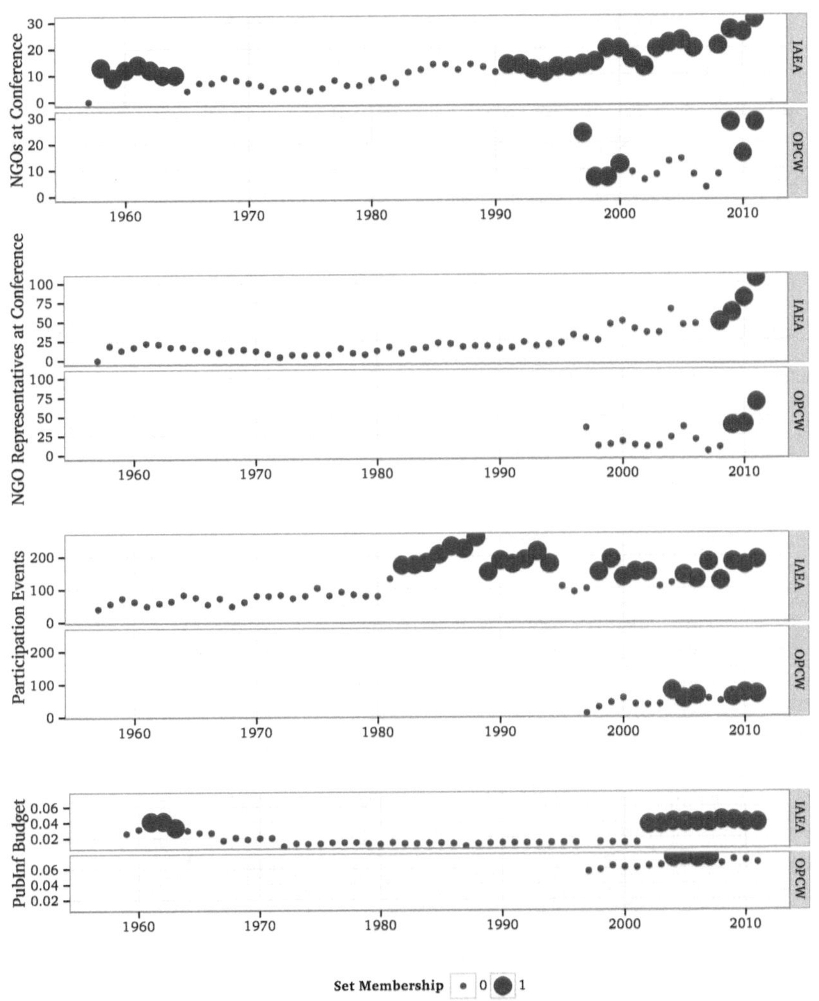

Figure 5.2: Calibrating Action

high participation events of each organization.[13] This measure is thus relative to the maximum amount of participation events that each individual organization has organized. I include additional individual years in the set if they fall between those years with full membership to respect historical continuity. Also, I add years at the beginning or end of those phases if the increase or decrease of participation events is not significant enough to justify a different set score.

Finally, I will treat transparency action, i.e. the share of the public information budget, in a similar manner. The information budgets are not directly comparable between the organizations as different accounting methods and tasks are grouped under the public information budgets. I will thus assign membership to the set *high transparency action* according to relative increases in the organization's budget. Again, the qualitative anchor will be the fourth quartile.[14] The superset *increased openness action*, i.e. the set comprising all openness action sets, thus has the following levels:

0 for years with usual participation action

1 for years with high levels of participation action:

- NGO Participation. IAEA: 1958-1964, 1991-2011. OPCW: 1997-2000, 2009-2011.
- NGO Representatives. IAEA: 2008:2011. OPCW: 2009:2011
- Participation Events. IAEA: 1982-1994, 1998-2002, 2005-2011. OPCW: 2004-2006, 2009-2011.
- Transparency action. IAEA: 1961-1963, 2002-2011. OPCW: 2004-2007.

Note that the high NGO representatives set is a subset of the high NGO participation set. As both sets capture different understandings of opening, it is useful to include both in the analysis. It is possible that the superset cannot be explained by the QCA while a good explanation can be formulated for the subset. Thus, I will test if the number of NGOs or the number of NGO representatives can be explained better with the help of the conditions.

To summarize, I have calibrated the outcome variables so that membership in the talk set shows that in a year, the organization started to continuously talk about participation or transparency. Further, membership in the set for participation decision shows that the organization is in a phase that climaxes in improving participation rules for NGOs. Membership in the transparency decision set illustrates that the IGO has acknowledged that information should be provided to the public directly. Finally, membership

---

[13]The fourth quartiles start at 175 for the IAEA and at 62.5 for the OPCW.

[14]The fourth quartile of the IAEA PI budget share starts at 3.2 percent, for the OPCW at 7.2 percent.

in the action sets is reserved for instances of exceptionally high NGO participation, participation events or a high share of the public information budget. The sets thus summarize phases where the IGOs opened up. Table 5.1 summarizes the set-membership scores.

Table 5.1: Openness Crisp Set

cases	TALK.Part	TALK.Trans	DEC.Part	DEC.Trans	ACT.Part.1	ACT.Part.2	ACT.Part.4
IAEA1957	1	0	0	0	0	0	0
IAEA1958	1	0	0	0	1	0	0
IAEA1959	1	0	0	0	1	0	0
IAEA1960	1	0	0	0	1	0	0
IAEA1961	1	0	0	0	1	0	0
IAEA1962	0	0	0	0	1	0	0
IAEA1963	0	0	0	0	1	0	0
IAEA1964	0	0	0	0	1	0	0
IAEA1965	0	0	0	0	0	0	0
IAEA1966	0	0	0	0	0	0	0
IAEA1967	0	0	0	0	0	0	0
IAEA1968	0	0	0	0	0	0	0
IAEA1969	0	0	0	0	0	0	0
IAEA1970	0	0	0	0	0	0	0
IAEA1971	0	0	0	0	0	0	0
IAEA1972	0	0	1	0	0	0	0
IAEA1973	0	0	1	0	0	0	0
IAEA1974	0	0	1	0	0	0	0
IAEA1975	0	0	1	0	0	0	0
IAEA1976	0	0	0	0	0	0	0
IAEA1977	0	0	0	0	0	0	0
IAEA1978	0	0	0	0	0	0	0
IAEA1979	0	0	0	0	0	0	0
IAEA1980	0	0	0	0	0	0	0
IAEA1981	0	0	0	0	0	0	0
IAEA1982	0	0	0	0	0	0	1
IAEA1983	0	0	0	0	0	0	1
IAEA1984	0	0	0	0	0	0	1
IAEA1985	0	0	0	0	0	0	1
IAEA1986	0	0	0	0	0	0	1
IAEA1987	0	0	0	0	0	0	1
IAEA1988	0	0	0	0	0	0	1
IAEA1989	0	0	0	0	0	0	1
IAEA1990	0	0	0	0	0	0	1
IAEA1991	0	0	0	0	1	0	1
IAEA1992	0	0	0	0	1	0	1
IAEA1993	1	1	0	1	1	0	1
IAEA1994	1	1	0	1	1	0	1
IAEA1995	1	1	0	1	1	0	0
IAEA1996	1	1	0	1	1	0	0
IAEA1997	1	1	0	1	1	0	0

IAEA1998	1	1	0	1	1	0	1
IAEA1999	1	1	0	1	1	0	1
IAEA2000	1	1	0	1	1	0	1
IAEA2001	1	1	0	1	1	0	1
IAEA2002	1	1	0	1	1	0	1
IAEA2003	1	1	0	1	1	0	0
IAEA2004	1	1	0	1	1	0	0
IAEA2005	1	1	0	1	1	0	1
IAEA2006	1	1	0	1	1	0	1
IAEA2007	1	1	0	1	1	0	1
IAEA2008	1	1	0	1	1	1	1
IAEA2009	1	1	0	1	1	1	1
IAEA2010	1	1	0	1	1	1	1
IAEA2011	1	1	0	1	1	1	1
OPCW1997	0	0	1	0	1	0	0
OPCW1998	1	1	1	0	1	0	0
OPCW1999	1	1	1	1	1	0	0
OPCW2000	1	1	1	1	1	0	0
OPCW2001	1	1	1	1	0	0	0
OPCW2002	1	1	1	1	0	0	0
OPCW2003	1	1	1	1	0	0	0
OPCW2004	1	1	0	1	0	0	1
OPCW2005	1	1	0	1	0	0	1
OPCW2006	1	1	0	1	0	0	1
OPCW2007	1	1	0	1	0	0	0
OPCW2008	1	1	0	1	0	0	0
OPCW2009	1	1	0	1	1	1	1
OPCW2010	1	1	0	1	1	1	1
OPCW2011	1	1	0	1	1	1	1

5.1.2 CALIBRATING THE CONDITIONS

Next, I calibrate the conditions, or variables that should explain the outcome. I discuss the resource based conditions first, the norm based conditions second.

RESOURCE BASED CONDITIONS

The first condition to be calibrated is the organizations' budget. Figure 5.3 summarizes the calibration. For the budget variable, I am primarily interested in the effects of resource shortages that would lead to an increased need for external expertise and set incentives for increasing transparency. Thus, the set *budget crisis* describes those years in the organizations' life where the budget decreased and where, consequently, resource constraints on the organization were exceptionally high. In addition, I include the years following the budget decrease until the amount of the budget before the crisis was reached, again. For the IAEA, there are two such phases. During the first, in 1983, the budget decreased from 191 million (2009) USD to 179 million USD. It took until 1986 to recover. The same happend from 1993 until 2001. Similarly, in the OPCW case, there was the major budget

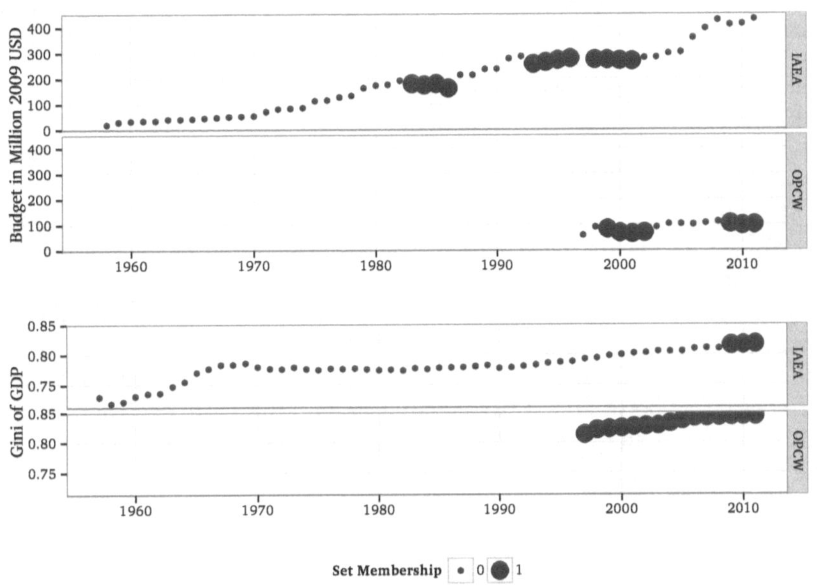

Figure 5.3: Calibrating Resource based Conditions

crisis from 1999 until 2002, with an initial budget decrease of 18 percent from 1999 to 2000. A less dramatic budget decrease occurred again from 2009 to 2011. The set *budget crisis* thus consists of the following levels:

0 for years with growing budgets
1 for years with decreasing budget, or with a budget crisis and recovery

● IAEA: 1983–1986, 1993–2001. OPCW: 1999–2002, 2009–2011.

Next, I create a set for the economic inequality of the organizations' members. As described above, I operationalized inequality as the annual Gini-Coefficient of the members' GDP. As already noted, there is no large scale change in the inequality structure of the OPCW. In the case of the IAEA, there is more change over time, given the longer life of the organization. I construct the set *high inequality* by assigning membership to those years where the Gini-Coefficient is above 0.81. This threshold represents the beginning of the fourth quartile of the inequality data. The minimal changes in the measure do not allow for a more fine-grained differentiation. Causal mechanisms that involve inequality thus need to be interpreted carefully in the QCA. The set includes the IAEA from 2009 until 2010 and all OPCW years. The set thus reflects that the OPCW's membership is more unequal than the one of the IAEA. I construct the set *high inequality* with the following levels:

0 for years with standard inequality
1 for years with increased inequality

- IAEA: 2009-2011. OPCW: 1997-2011

Finally, the set *complexity* can simply be defined as attributing membership for all IAEA years. The complexity variable is constant for the individual organizations over time because they did not receive any additional statutory tasks. Overall, the IAEA is active in more issues areas than the OPCW. Therefore, it can be expected that the Agency is in general more open than the OPCW. Thus, the complexity set holds no relevant information despite differentiating between the two organizations. I therefore exclude the condition from the analyses in the following sections. Table 5.2 summarizes the set memberships of the resource based conditions.

Table 5.2: Resource Based Crisp Set

cases	RB.Budget	RB.Inequality	RB.Complexity
IAEA1957	0	0	1
IAEA1958	0	0	1
IAEA1959	0	0	1
IAEA1960	0	0	1
IAEA1961	0	0	1
IAEA1962	0	0	1
IAEA1963	0	0	1
IAEA1964	0	0	1
IAEA1965	0	0	1
IAEA1966	0	0	1
IAEA1967	0	0	1
IAEA1968	0	0	1
IAEA1969	0	0	1
IAEA1970	0	0	1
IAEA1971	0	0	1
IAEA1972	0	0	1
IAEA1973	0	0	1
IAEA1974	0	0	1
IAEA1975	0	0	1
IAEA1976	0	0	1
IAEA1977	0	0	1
IAEA1978	0	0	1
IAEA1979	0	0	1
IAEA1980	0	0	1
IAEA1981	0	0	1

IAEA1982	0	0	1
IAEA1983	1	0	1
IAEA1984	1	0	1
IAEA1985	1	0	1
IAEA1986	1	0	1
IAEA1987	0	0	1
IAEA1988	0	0	1
IAEA1989	0	0	1
IAEA1990	0	0	1
IAEA1991	0	0	1
IAEA1992	0	0	1
IAEA1993	1	0	1
IAEA1994	1	0	1
IAEA1995	1	0	1
IAEA1996	1	0	1
IAEA1997	1	0	1
IAEA1998	1	0	1
IAEA1999	1	0	1
IAEA2000	1	0	1
IAEA2001	1	0	1
IAEA2002	0	0	1
IAEA2003	0	0	1
IAEA2004	0	0	1
IAEA2005	0	0	1
IAEA2006	0	0	1
IAEA2007	0	0	1
IAEA2008	0	0	1
IAEA2009	0	1	1
IAEA2010	0	1	1
IAEA2011	0	1	1
OPCW1997	0	1	0
OPCW1998	0	1	0
OPCW1999	1	1	0
OPCW2000	1	1	0
OPCW2001	1	1	0
OPCW2002	1	1	0
OPCW2003	0	1	0
OPCW2004	0	1	0
OPCW2005	0	1	0
OPCW2006	0	1	0
OPCW2007	0	1	0
OPCW2008	0	1	0
OPCW2009	1	1	0
OPCW2010	1	1	0
OPCW2011	1	1	0

NORM BASED CONDITIONS

For the norm based conditions, I first discuss the conditions related to media
visibility. Again, the challenge for the calibration of the general visibility is
to compare the two cases adequately. Figure 5.4 shows the large difference
in the number of overall media visibility. The maximum annual visibility for
the IAEA is at 3193 articles per year. For the OPCW, this number is 43. For

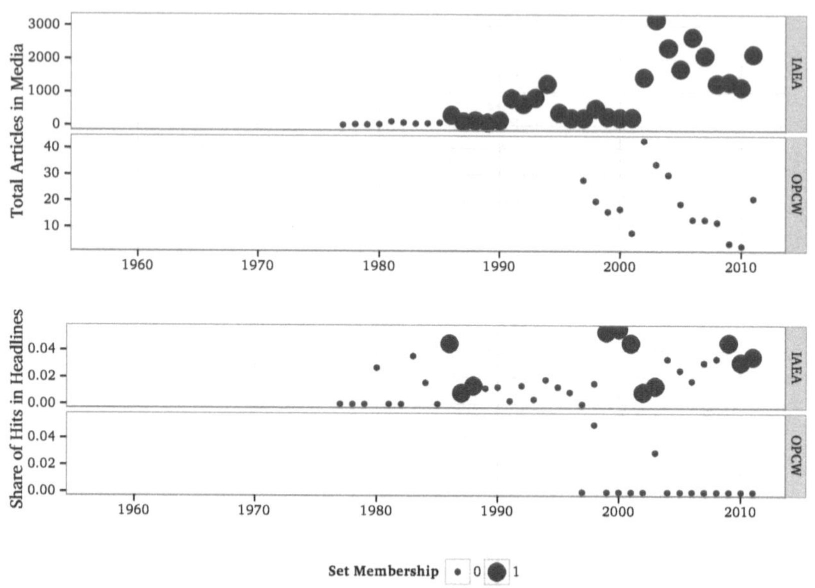

Figure 5.4: Calibrating Media Visibility

overall visibility, I propose a calibration that does not use relative measures because the set *high media visibility* is supposed to show whether there is a global debate in the media about the organization, possibly leading to increased public contestation and demands for openness. I assume that this is the case when there are at least 100 articles per year for a period of at least 2 years. Again, I also include years when the previous and following years are assigned membership for reasons of continuity. I used the same procedure for the talk set. It is justified to add single deviant years because the assumed causal effects of media visibility do not significantly change from year to year. Reactions to legitimacy challenges are more persistent. There are also phases in time where there is an exceptional increase in media reporting. This is the case in the IAEA from 1991 to 1994, where reporting increased by the factor 6. Similar strong increases in IAEA media visibility happened from 2002-2007 and in 2011. Those especially high incidents will be analyzed in the case-study part. Therefore, the set has the following levels:

0 for years with low or no visibility

1 for years with high or exceptional visibility

- ● IAEA: 1986-2011

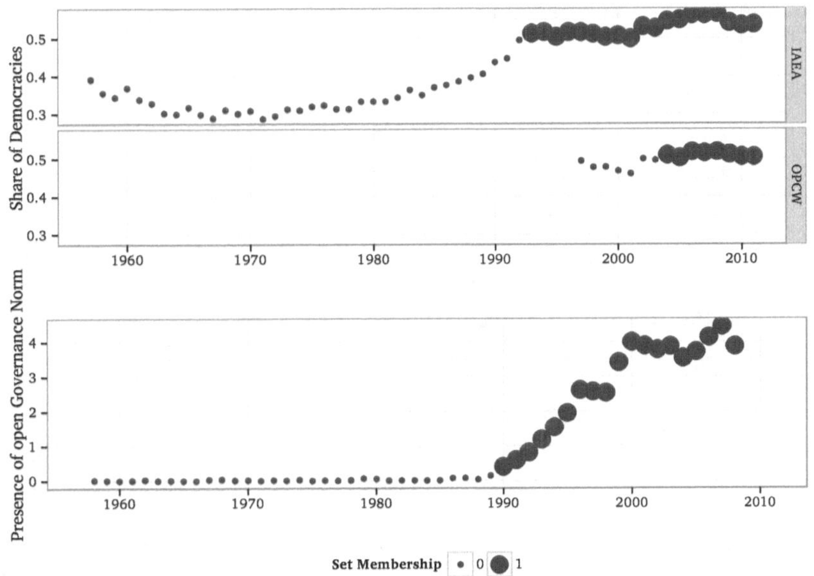

Figure 5.5: Calibrating Democratic Membership and the Presence of the Open Governance Norm

For the headlines visibility variable, I construct a set that illustrates times with focused attention on the IGO. Being mentioned in the headlines of articles is a more direct way of interaction with the global media and the global public. The headlines visibility measure thus potentially is a more exact measure for possible legitimacy crises of organizations, which are also made public to a wider audience. The data in Figure 5.4 shows the number of headline appearances in relation to all articles mentioning the organization in that year. Membership in the set *high headline visibility* is only attributed to those cases with an exceptionally high share of headlines. For the IAEA, there is especially high headline visibility in 1986 (Chernobyl), from 1999-2001 and in 2009 (both relating to political inspection activities). I include the 2 following years in the set because change in IGOs and reactions to external criticism may be slow. Selecting only the years with extraordinarily high visibility also avoids too much parallelism with the general visibility set. Further, I do not include the OPCW in the set, as the maximum number of headlines in real numbers is too low (2 headlines from 1997 to 2011). The headline visibility set is a subset of the high visibility set. It should still be included in the analysis nevertheless because it could be a more powerful explanation than general media visibility. The set is thus constructed as follows:

- 0 for years without exceptional headline visibility
- 1 for years with exceptional headline visibility

  - IAEA: 1986-1988, 1999-2003, 2009-2011

Next, I also define the set *governance depth* with a focus on change. As discussed above, there is no considerable change in the authority and governance depth of the OPCW. For the IAEA, there have been two steps that increased the Agency's authority. In the years 1970-1990, because of the Entry Into Force of the NPT and the increased importance of NPT inspections, IAEA authority has increased. However, full membership is assigned to the years 1991-2011 when political inspections of the IAEA began. At that time, the effects of the norm based legitimacy mechanism are most likely to be causally relevant, given the growing politicization of the organization during this time of risen international authority.

Finally, Figure 5.5 shows the data for the democratic membership and open governance norm variables. Looking at democratic membership first, I create a set *democratic IO* for the years with a high share of democratic member states. Like when creating the inequality set, I choose a numeric threshold for set membership. I assume that an IGO has high democratic membership when at least 50 percent of its members continuously qualify as democratic. Consequently, the IAEA is a member in this set from 1993-2011, the OPCW since 2004. For the open governance norm, the data is equal for both IAEA and OPCW. The graph shows a first phase, where the norm is emerging and where references to it are growing (1990-1995). These years thus already belong to the set *presence of open governance norm*. In the years since 1996, the growth in the data is less pronounced. I thus assume that the norm has spread and I thus also assign set membership to the years 1996-2011. Table 5.3 summarizes the set memberships of the norm based conditions.

Table 5.3: Norm Based Crisp Set

cases	NB.visibility.all	NB.visibility.hl	NB.gov.depth	NB.dem.mem
IAEA1957	0	0	0	0
IAEA1958	0	0	0	0
IAEA1959	0	0	0	0
IAEA1960	0	0	0	0
IAEA1961	0	0	0	0

IAEA1962	0	0	0	0
IAEA1963	0	0	0	0
IAEA1964	0	0	0	0
IAEA1965	0	0	0	0
IAEA1966	0	0	0	0
IAEA1967	0	0	0	0
IAEA1968	0	0	0	0
IAEA1969	0	0	0	0
IAEA1970	0	0	0	0
IAEA1971	0	0	0	0
IAEA1972	0	0	0	0
IAEA1973	0	0	0	0
IAEA1974	0	0	0	0
IAEA1975	0	0	0	0
IAEA1976	0	0	0	0
IAEA1977	0	0	0	0
IAEA1978	0	0	0	0
IAEA1979	0	0	0	0
IAEA1980	0	0	0	0
IAEA1981	0	0	0	0
IAEA1982	0	0	0	0
IAEA1983	0	0	0	0
IAEA1984	0	0	0	0
IAEA1985	0	0	0	0
IAEA1986	1	1	0	0
IAEA1987	1	1	0	0
IAEA1988	1	1	0	0
IAEA1989	1	0	0	0
IAEA1990	1	0	0	0
IAEA1991	1	0	1	0
IAEA1992	1	0	1	0
IAEA1993	1	0	1	1
IAEA1994	1	0	1	1
IAEA1995	1	0	1	1
IAEA1996	1	0	1	1
IAEA1997	1	0	1	1
IAEA1998	1	0	1	1
IAEA1999	1	1	1	1
IAEA2000	1	1	1	1
IAEA2001	1	1	1	1
IAEA2002	1	1	1	1
IAEA2003	1	1	1	1
IAEA2004	1	0	1	1
IAEA2005	1	0	1	1
IAEA2006	1	0	1	1
IAEA2007	1	0	1	1
IAEA2008	1	0	1	1
IAEA2009	1	1	1	1
IAEA2010	1	1	1	1
IAEA2011	1	1	1	1
OPCW1997	0	0	0	0
OPCW1998	0	0	0	0
OPCW1999	0	0	0	0
OPCW2000	0	0	0	0

OPCW2001	0	0	0	0
OPCW2002	0	0	0	0
OPCW2003	0	0	0	0
OPCW2004	0	0	0	1
OPCW2005	0	0	0	1
OPCW2006	0	0	0	1
OPCW2007	0	0	0	1
OPCW2008	0	0	0	1
OPCW2009	0	0	0	1
OPCW2010	0	0	0	1
OPCW2011	0	0	0	1

5.1.3 Summary: Patterns of Opening Up over Time

Figure 5.6 shows the changes in the openness of both the OPCW and IAEA. Comparing the trends of openness on the various dimensions, there are three particularly relevant observations:

1. Since the 1990s, both the IAEA and the OPCW increasingly talk about participation and transparency.
2. Transparency talk and transparency decisions are not de-coupled, they occur and grow around the same time in both organizations.
3. The action dimension of organizational opening is loosely coupled to the talk and decision dimensions.

First of all, the close connection and parallel movement of talk about openness in both organizations is an important finding. When ignoring the early participation talk of the IAEA, it is in the 1990s that talk about participation and transparency begins in both organizations. Since this time, references to the ideas of participation and transparency are common in the public discourses of both organizations. As discussed above, the meanings of participation and transparency that are transported in the IGOs' talk are also expanding, slowly getting closer to the democratic ideal of open and participative governance. Overall, this is a less expected phenomenon for two organizations that are active in the field of security. Here, normative references to participative governance are in concurrence with other security-related norms like confidentiality.

Second, and underlining the importance of the first finding, transparency talk appears to be more than "cheap talk." Starting in the late 1980s and getting stronger in the 1990s, transparency decisions continuously improve as more transparency is provided to a wider audience. This is closely coupled with talk about transparency. There thus appears to be a true commitment of the IGOs to not only accept a norm of transparent governance on the rhetoric level, but also to commit itself through rules to a transparent way of work. Again, this highlights that transparency as a principle of IGO governance appears to become more important in the security sector.

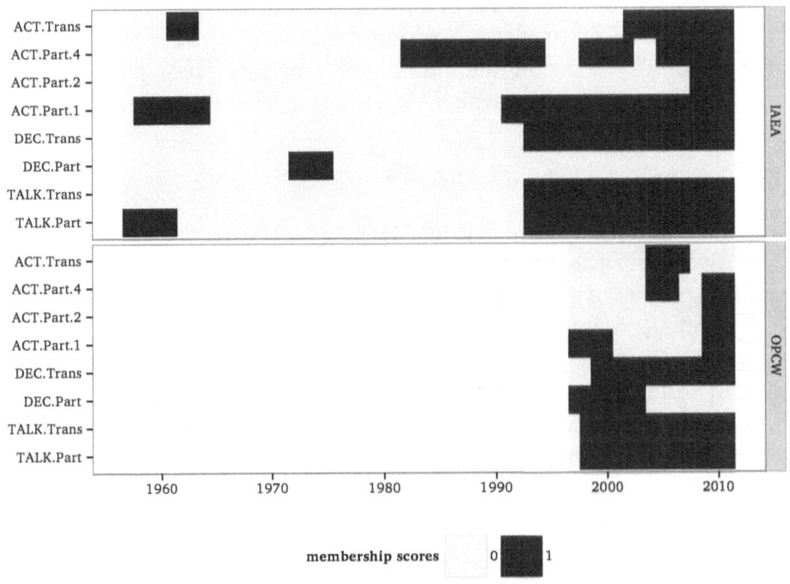

Figure 5.6: Changes in IAEA and OPCW Openness Sets

Third, however, the relatively loose coupling of the action dimension somewhat limits the enthusiasm for participation and transparency. For participation action, it is NGO participation at the annual policy-making conference that is most strongly connected to participation talk. Especially in the IAEA case, periods with high NGO participation are also those periods with lots of talk about participation. However, this is less so for the OPCW. Here, NGO participation varies more strongly despite constant levels of talk. Further, participation events, i.e. participative activities organized by the IGOs, are very loosely coupled to talk or decision. They thus also seem to follow a different causal logic. For example, in the IAEA, participation events were very important in the 1980s, a time with little talk and no decisions about participation.

Similarly, for transparency action, I observe only loose coupling. In the IAEA case, the highest level of transparency action is reached in the early 2000s. Yet, transparency talk and decisions have already been strong in the early 1990s. There thus seems to be an implementation gap of ten years until the IAEA fully implemented its rhetoric and rule-based commitments to full transparency. A similar pattern is visible for the OPCW. Since 1998, there has been strong talk about transparency and decisions for more transparency were made since the same time. However, the highest transparency budget is only implemented a few years later in the mid 2000s. Further, the once achieved level of transparency action decreases in the late 2000s, thus widening the gap between talk, decision and action. These phenomena ask for a specific explanations, which I try to provide in the following section.

5.2 What QCA tells us about Opening

In this section, I discuss the findings of the qualitative comparative analyses. When discussing the findings of the analyses, I also explain some QCA terminology, analytical assumptions and procedures. Table 5.4 summarizes the key findings of my analysis. My outcome *organizational opening* is multi-dimensional. Therefore, I run separate QCA analyses for individual outcome variables. Thus, I do not look for one single explanation of organizational opening, but for detailed explanations of each dimension of organizational openness. This reflects my multi-dimensional concept of organizational openness. In the following sections, I only present those QCA analyses that produced meaningful results.[15]

Table 5.4: Summary of QCA Analyses

Outcome	Type	Explanations
Talk[a]	Nec.	presence of open governance norm
	Suff.	IAEA: norm based mechanism combining visibility, authority and democratic membership
		OPCW: resource based inequality mechanism
Decision[b]	Nec.	presence of open governance norm
	Suff.	IAEA: norm based mechanism, combining visibility, authority and democratic membership
		OPCW: resource based inequality mechanism
Participation Action[c]	Suff.	IAEA: visibility mechanism, budget crisis mechanism for participation events
		OPCW: inequality mechanism
Transparency Action[d]	Nec.	high share of democratic members or the presence of the open governance norm

[a] The solution does not cover the IAEA from 1957-1961 and the OPCW in 1997.
[b] The solution does not cover the IAEA from 1972-1975.
[c] The solution does not cover the OPCW 1997-2000, OPCW 2003, OPCW2007-2008, and the IAEA 1958-1964.
[d] The solutions do not cover the IAEA from 1961-1963.

In summary, I find that participation is particularly well explained by resource based conditions. Transparency, on the other hand, appears to be driven more by the norm based conditions. In more detail, I *first* find strong set-relationships for organizational talk about participation and transparency.

---

[15] For reproduction material of the analyses and QCAs of individual outcomes not presented here, see Appendix C.

The empirical data of both phenomena are relatively similar. For both kinds of openness talk, the presence of the norm of open governance is a strong necessary condition. Without a strong norm of open governance, the OPCW and IAEA do not refer to transparency or participation in their organizational talk. Further, there appear to be specific causal pathways towards talk about openness for each IO. For the IAEA, I find a particularly strong sufficient path towards talk that combines the assumptions of the norm based explanations. For the IAEA, the co-occurrence of high visibility, high authority and a high share of democratic members sufficiently causes talk about participation or transparency. This is a consistent pattern for most of the organization years. Only the early years of the IAEA are an exception. I will discuss this *norm based mechanism* in more detail in a case study (see Chapter 6.1). For the OPCW, I find stronger influence of a *first resource based mechanism* that builds on inequality, which I also discuss in a separate case study (see Chapter 6.2). Overall, the norm based explanations are thus very powerful in explaining openness talk.

Second, when looking at the decision dimension, similar causal relations are present. As discussed above, talk and decisions, especially for transparency, are closely coupled. Consequently, to a large extent, the same mechanism that explain talk about openness also explain openness decisions. Again, the presence of the norm of open governance is an overarching, necessary condition for increasing participation action. Also, change in the IAEA is driven by a norm based mechanism, change in the OPCW by inequality. Overall, this highlights the different organizational contexts in which different configurations of conditions lead to the same outcomes.

Third, there is a more complex image for openness on the action dimension. For participation action, I cannot identify an overarching necessary condition. Yet, there are again different sufficient pathways towards participation action for each organization. For the IAEA, it is high media visibility that causes participation. When the IAEA was not yet very visible, it was resource constraints that lead to a functional demand for external expertise. This demand was then answered by increased numbers of participation events. I discuss this *second resource based mechanism* in another case study (see Chapter 6.3). The OPCW and changes in its participation action are less well explained by my framework. Yet, the analysis suggests that, again, budgetary constraints and inequality are the main drivers of change in the OPCW. Finally, when looking at transparency action, more gaps in our analytical understanding of organizational opening become apparent. Here, I could identify the presence of the open governance norm and a high share of democratic member states as necessary for increased action. However, both conditions also occur in many organization years without causing increased transparency action.

5.2.1   TALK: THE POWER OF NORMS AND INEQUALITY

What explains increasing talk about transparency and participation in detail? The next step of a QCA to get to the answer after the calibration of the sets is the creation of a *truth table*. A complete truth tables list all possible configurations of the explanatory conditions and the outcome. It is thus an important tool to order the theoretical and empirical complexity of comparative case studies. In a truth table, each of these combinations occupies one row. The number of possible rows exponentially grows with the number of conditions. The total number of possible combinations is given by 2^n, where n stands for the number of conditions. Often, not all theoretically possible combinations are realized in the empirical data. In the following sections, I thus only present those combinations that I observed in the data.

Table 5.5 shows the truth table for the outcome *openness talk*. I created this variable by combining the transparency and participation talk variables with the OR operation. Openness talk is thus present when, in a given year, the IGO has made references to either transparency or participation. I chose to combine the variable because there is much parallelism in both kinds of talk.[16]

The first columns in the truth table show the values for the explanatory variables. OUT stands for the outcome, i.e. for openness talk in this case. The values for the outcome are easy to translate from the underlying crisp set values of 0 or 1 if all underlying empirical cases in the row share membership in the outcome. This is, however, not always the case. There may be contradictory cases. In crisp set QCA, *true contradictory cases* can occur when one of the cases with a certain configuration of conditions belongs to the set (1) and another one with the same does not (0). In such a case, the same configuration of explanatory conditions leads to the outcome in some cases, but fails to cause the outcome in others.

To objectively make a decision about the treatment of contradictory cases, the *consistency measure* is used as a parameter of fit.[17] The incl column in the table reports the result of a consistency test of the row in the outcome. Consistency for sufficient conditions is defined as $\frac{\text{cases with outcome and conditions present}}{\text{cases with conditions present}}$ (Schneider and Wagemann 2012, 124). The closer the value is to 1, the

---

[16] Further, separate QCA analyses of both outcomes reveal similar results. Please see the QCA appendix for more details.

[17] The PRI (proportional reduction in consistency) measure that is also included in the truth table is an alternative parameter of fit. It controls for the consistency of the conditions in the outcome as well the non-outcome. If both consistency values are high, a truth table row would both sufficiently cause the outcome and the opposite of the outcome and thus lead to erroneous interpretations. It is defined as $\frac{\sum min(X,Y)-\sum min(X,Y,\sim Y)}{\sum min(X)-\sum min(X,Y,\sim Y)}$ with X standing for the condition and Y for the outcome (Schneider and Wagemann 2012, 242). The higher the value, the less the condition is sufficient for both Y and $\sim Y$.

Table 5.5: Truth Table: Openness Talk

RB.BUDGET	RB.INEQUALITY	NB.VISIBILITY.ALL	NB.VISIBILITY.HL	NB.GOVDEPTH	NB.DEM.MEM	NB.OG.NORM	OUT	n	incl	PRI	cases
0	0	1	0	1	1	1	1	5	1	1	IAEA2004, IAEA2005, IAEA2006, IAEA2007, IAEA2008
0	0	1	1	1	1	1	1	2	1	1	IAEA2002, IAEA2003
0	1	0	0	0	1	1	1	5	1	1	OPCW2004, OPCW2005, OPCW2006, OPCW2007, OPCW2008
0	1	1	1	1	1	1	1	3	1	1	IAEA2009, IAEA2010, IAEA2011
1	0	1	0	1	1	1	1	6	1	1	IAEA1993, IAEA1994, IAEA1995, IAEA1996, IAEA1997, IAEA1998
1	0	1	1	1	1	1	1	3	1	1	IAEA1999, IAEA2000, IAEA2001
1	1	0	0	0	0	1	1	4	1	1	OPCW1999, OPCW2000, OPCW2001, OPCW2002
1	1	0	0	0	1	1	1	3	1	1	OPCW2009, OPCW2010, OPCW2011
0	1	0	0	0	0	1	0	3	0.667	0.667	OPCW1997, OPCW1998, OPCW2003
0	0	0	0	0	0	0	0	26	0.192	0.192	IAEA1957, IAEA1958, IAEA1959, IAEA1960, IAEA1961, IAEA1962, IAEA1963, IAEA1964, IAEA1965, IAEA1966, IAEA1967, IAEA1968, IAEA1969, IAEA1970, IAEA1971, IAEA1972, IAEA1973, IAEA1974, IAEA1975, IAEA1976, IAEA1977, IAEA1978, IAEA1979, IAEA1980, IAEA1981, IAEA1982
0	0	1	0	0	0	0	0	1	0	0	IAEA1989
0	0	1	0	0	0	1	0	1	0	0	IAEA1990
0	0	1	0	1	0	1	0	2	0	0	IAEA1991, IAEA1992
0	0	1	1	0	0	0	0	2	0	0	IAEA1987, IAEA1988
1	0	0	0	0	0	0	0	3	0	0	IAEA1983, IAEA1984, IAEA1985
1	0	1	1	0	0	0	0	1	0	0	IAEA1986

Note: Inclusion cut: 1.

more "sufficient" the row is. A cut-off threshold for the consistency value needs to be set by the researcher. Setting the cut-off threshold needs to be justified on the basis of the empirical cases. Usually, the literature suggests that consistency cut-offs below 0.75 should not be used because the results of the analysis could include too many contradictory cases.

For the analysis of openness talk, I chose a consistency threshold of 1. In particular, this excludes two rows in the truth table for openness talk. Row number 9 has a consistency value of 0.667 and the configuration of conditions covers three cases (OPCW1997, 1998, 2003). The row has a low coverage value because there is no openness talk in the OPCW in 1997, but there is talk in the OPCW in 1998 and 2003 under the same configuration of explanatory conditions. Similarly, in row 10, there is talk in the IAEA from 1957-1961, but no talk under the same configuration from 1962 until 1982. My explanations of openness talk thus excludes those deviant instances of talk.

The exclusion of these contradictory cases does not have too strong theoretical implications. As discussed in more detail in Chapter 4.1, early participation talk in the IAEA is very functional and directed towards the participation and creation of expert communities. In its early talk, the Agency describes how it interacts with non-state actors to profit from their resources. Overall, this talk constitutes a special kind of talk that was necessary during setting up the organization. This also explains why this form of participation talk no longer appears after 1961 when the basic mechanisms of expert consultations were settled in the organization. Thus, the excluded case is not really a deviant case of organizational opening but a case that describes the initial state of participation talk of the IAEA. It is therefore not captured by variance in the variables because other variables would be necessary to describe the phenomenon of initial openness talk, as opposed to changes of organizational opening on the talk dimension.[18]

Consequently, the truth table does not cover all observed instances of talk, but only the following majority of cases. The cases are grouped together given their underlying configuration of explanatory conditions:

- `IAEA1993:1998`
- `IAEA1999:2001`
- `IAEA2002:2003`
- `IAEA2004:2008`
- `IAEA2009:2011`
- `OPCW1999:2002`
- `OPCW2004:2008`
- `OPCW2009:2011`

What does the truth table tell us about the occurrences of openness talk? First, in the IAEA case, early participation and transparency talk from 1993 until 1998 occurred in an environment of a slight budget crisis, high media visibility, high IAEA authority, a high share of democratic member states and with an emerging norm of open governance. Openness talk continued from 1999 until 2001 under the same conditions, but with higher media attention, as captured by the headline visibility variable. In the next time period from 2002 until 2008, talk remained present despite an improved financial situation and reduced headline visibility. Finally, for the last period from 2009 until 2011, participation or transparency talk was also present while there was a change towards more inequality in the Agency's membership.

For the OPCW, openness talk started in 1999 when there was high membership inequality, a strong norm of open governance, and a budget crisis. From 2004 until 2008, talk about participation or transparency continued in a context without resource constraints but with increased

---

[18] At this point in the research process, one could also return to the concept-building or calibration phase to exclude contradictory cases on theoretical grounds. However, I chose to transparently discuss contradictory cases and examine them if they indeed strongly challenge the assumptions of the model. As a result, the discovery of contradictory cases invites the researcher and the reader to discuss concepts, operationalizations, calibrations and theoretical assumptions.

democratic membership. Finally, from 2009 until 2011, when in addition resource constraints grew again, openness talk continued.

This description of the truth table rows already helps to understand the causal complexity by ordering the empirical material. To systematize this process of comparative reasoning, QCA provides a procedure of formalized analysis of the truth table. The next step in the QCA is to look for *necessary conditions* of the outcome. As noted above, in QCA's set-logic, the outcome set Y is a subset of the necessary set X. Thus, X is a necessary condition of Y if X is present whenever Y is present. The presence of X when Y is not present does not contradict the necessity assumption.

Methodologically, one needs to check the truth table for conditions that are present at all instances of the outcome. Again, parameters of fit are helpful to decide about the status of candidate necessary conditions. First, I use the consistency measure for necessary conditions as an important indicator. It is defined as $\frac{\text{cases with outcome and conditions present}}{\text{cases with outcome present}}$ (Schneider and Wagemann 2012, 140). It can thus be interpreted as the share of cases with the outcome and the candidate necessary condition in all cases where the outcome is present. The values of consistency should be high. Further, a test for contradictory cases needs to be conducted. For necessary conditions, a contradictory case has a score of 0 in the necessary set while at the same time having a score of 1 in the outcome set. In such a case, the outcome is present but the candidate necessary condition is not, thus violating the assumption of necessity.

As a second measure for the relevance of necessary conditions, I use the coverage of necessary conditions. Schneider and Wagemann (2012, 144) define coverage as $\frac{\text{cases with outcome and conditions present}}{\text{cases with conditions present}}$. The coverage value of a necessary condition thus shows how relevant the necessary condition is. The value should be high. Low values indicate at trivial necessary conditions. Trivial conditions are close to constants in the data and are thus present in a large share of cases. Such a condition would risk to produce contradictory outcomes, especially because it would be necessary for both the outcome and its negation.

For openness talk, I identified the presence of the open governance norms as a necessary condition:[19]

	incl	PRI	cov.r
NB.OG.NORM	0.868	0.868	0.892

As above, the early years of the IAEA contradict the necessity assumption and are deviant cases. However, I still consider the presence of the open governance norm a necessary condition because it applies to the majority

---

[19]Again, for more details and analytical plots, please see Appendix C.

of instances of participation or transparency talk. Alternative explanations need to be discussed for the early participation talk of the IAEA. Because of those contradictory cases, the consistency value (`incl` in the table above) of the necessary condition is not perfect.[20] Further, the coverage value (`cov.r` in the table above) is not 1 as there are some non-contradictory cases where the norm of open governance is already present, but where the organizations have not yet started talking about the values of participation or transparency (IAEA 1990-1992, OPCW 1997).[21]

Thus, except for the contradictory cases, the IAEA and OPCW talk about participation or transparency in an environment with a strong norm of open governance. The finding underlines a main assumption of norm based explanations. A strong norm of transparent and participatory governance in the environment of IGOs is necessary for the IGOs to pick up this norm to either strategically respond to demands or to speak as an organization socialized to the norm. Yet, the results also show that this effect is not instantaneous. Some time seems to be necessary for the IGOs to respond to the norm. The IAEA in the early 1990s did not immediately pick up the notions of transparency or participation in its talk. Similarly, the OPCW's first Annual Report does not include openness talk. Thus, some organizational learning or norm adaptation seems to be necessary. After this phase, however, the normative mechanism appears to be strong.

The QCA does not stop with the identification of necessary conditions. Its strength is in searching for sets of sufficient conditions. Here, configurations of conditions become more important, underlining that not only single conditions, but specific combinations of conditions can be causally important. In this final step of a QCA analysis, the truth table is reduced in order to identify those sets of sufficient conditions. Again, in QCA logic, the sufficient condition X is a subset of the outcome Y. Conditions are assumed to be sufficient when they are always present when the outcome is also present. This understanding of sufficiency allows the presence of the outcome without the sufficient condition as the latter is a subset of the former. Technically, sufficient conditions are identified in the truth table by either including or not including *logical remainders*, i.e. those rows in the truth table that have not been observed empirically. An algorithm that uses set-algebra, the Quine-McCluskey algorithm, logically minimizes the configurations to identify relations of sufficiency. The results are candidates for sufficient conditions.

---

[20] To illustrate, the inclusion value is calculated as follows: $\frac{\text{cases with TALK and NB.OG.NORM}}{\text{cases with TALK}} = \frac{33}{38} = 0.868$. Thus, 5 cases violate the necessity relationship.

[21] To illustrate, the coverage value is calculated as follows: $\frac{\text{cases with TALK and NB.OG.NORM}}{\text{cases with NB.OG.NORM}} = \frac{33}{37} = 0.892$. Thus, there are 4 cases where the norm of open governance is strong but the organization has not committed itself to openness.

In my QCAs, I present the solution formulas for the *conservative solution*, the *intermediate solution* and the *parsimonious solution*. For the conservative solution, logical remainders are not used at all. Only the rows that occur in the empirical material are reduced. For the intermediate solution, only those remainders are included that do not conflict the underlying theoretical assumptions about the causal effects of the conditions. For example, in my analysis, I do expect all conditions to individually be capable of causing openness. It would thus be contradictory to include remainders in the minimization algorithm that e.g. assume that the presence of all conditions does not lead to the outcome. Finally, the parsimonious solution uses all remainders to reduce the complexity of the conservative solution. The advantage of the parsimonious solution is that it is often easier to interpret than the conservative solution.

I present all solutions for reasons of transparency. For the interpretation, I will focus on the intermediate solutions. In the QCA literature, there is some discussion about the best ways to handle logical remainders (again, see the discussion in Schneider and Wagemann 2012). Especially for QCA operating with time-series data, there is no clear guideline about the inclusion of logical remainders. Opposed to a special translation of time-series data (see Caren and Panofsky 2005), I chose to run a normal QCA analysis while justifying the logical remainder inclusion (cf. Thiem 2011).

Finally, parameters of fit are needed to make a decision on the quality of the candidate sufficient conditions. Next to the consistency of sufficient conditions discussed above when introducing truth tables, I use the coverage of sufficient conditions as an additional measure. It is defined as $\frac{\text{cases with outcome and conditions present}}{\text{cases with outcome present}}$ (Schneider and Wagemann 2012, 130). It can be interpreted as the share of cases with the outcome that are explained by the sufficient condition. The parameters of fit are identical for the different kinds of solution formulas as the conservative, intermediate and parsimonious solutions do not alter the assumptions about the empirical outcomes in the truth table. Thus, all three formulas consistently describe the truth table.

For openness talk, I identified the following sufficient conditions:

Solution	Formula	incl.	PRI	cov
conservative	rb.inequality * NB.VISIBILITY.ALL * NB.GOV.DEPTH * NB.DEM.MEM OR rb.budget * NB.VISIBILITY.ALL * NB.VISIBILITY.HL * NB.GOV.DEPTH * NB.DEM.MEM OR RB.BUDGET * RB.INEQUALITY * nb.visibility.all * nb.visibility.hl * nb.gov.depth OR RB.INEQUALITY * nb.visibility.all * nb.visibility.hl * nb.gov.depth * NB.DEM.MEM	1.000	1.000	0.816
intermediate	RB.BUDGET * RB.INEQUALITY OR RB.INEQUALITY * NB.DEM.MEM OR NB.VISIBILITY.ALL * NB.GOV.DEPTH * NB.DEM.MEM	1.000	1.000	0.816
parsimonious	NB.DEM.MEM OR RB.BUDGET * RB.INEQUALITY	1.000	1.000	0.816

As discussed above, the conservative solution is very complex and not easy to interpret. I thus focus on the intermediate solution and add the parsimonious solution for reference. For the analysis of sufficient conditions, I excluded the presence of the norm of open governance because it was already identified as a necessary condition. The solution formula RB.BUDGET and RB.INEQUALITY OR RB.INEQUALITY and NB.DEM.MEM OR NB.VISIBILITY.ALL and NB.-GOV.DEPTH and NB.DEM.MEM can be interpreted in the following way. Opening talk occurs when there is

- a budget deficit and high inequality, or
- high inequality and a high share of democratic members, or
- high media visibility and high authority and a high share of democratic members.

The solution covers all cases of participation or transparency talk that made it over the inclusion threshold. Thus, all rows of the truth table are covered by the presented sufficient solution formulas. Each of the three paths, or *prime implicants* in QCA language, lead to increased talk about participation or transparency. While there is equifinality of the three parts of the solution formula, each of the parts covers different cases. Table 5.6 lists the prime implicants separately. The table also includes a number of parameters of fit for the prime implicants. Next to the inclusion/consistency and PRI values discussed above, there are also entries for raw and unique coverage values, as well as a list of cases that the prime implicant covers. The raw coverage value indicates how many percent of all cases the implicant explains. The unique coverage value shows how many of the cases are explained by the specific solution term, only.

At closer inspection, the distribution of the cases in Table 5.6 indicates different causal pathways towards openness talk for both organizations. For

Table 5.6: Openness Talk, Sufficient Prime Implicants

	incl	PRI	cov.r	cov.u	cases
RB.BUDGET * RB.INEQUALITY	1.000	1.000	0.184	0.105	OPCW1999, OPCW2000, OPCW2001, OPCW2002; OPCW2009, OPCW2010, OPCW2011
RB.INEQUALITY * NB.DEM.MEM	1.000	1.000	0.289	0.132	OPCW2004, OPCW2005, OPCW2006, OPCW2007, OPCW2008; IAEA2009, IAEA2010, IAEA2011; OPCW2009, OPCW2010, OPCW2011
NB.VISIBILITY.ALL * NB.GOV.DEPTH * NB.DEM.MEM	1.000	1.000	0.500	0.421	IAEA2004, IAEA2005, IAEA2006, IAEA2007, IAEA2008; IAEA2002, IAEA2003; IAEA2009, IAEA2010, IAEA2011; IAEA1993, IAEA1994, IAEA1995, IAEA1996, IAEA1997, IAEA1998; IAEA1999, IAEA2000, IAEA2001

the IAEA, all cases of participation or transparency talk are explained and covered by the third prime implicant (high visibility and heigh authority and high share of democratic members). Further, the IAEA cases are explained by norm based conditions, only. For the IAEA, openness talk only occurred in situations when the organization was visible in the media, had acquired some political authority and had a high share of democratic members. This indicates that a single factor alone, like a high share of democratic member states, is not sufficient to cause openness talk alone. For the OPCW, another story appears to be true. Here, a more resource based explanation is causally relevant. For the OPCW, openness talk occurs whenever there is high inequality in combination with a budget crisis or a high share of democratic members. This seems to suggest that next to the norm socialization process at work at the IAEA, economic inequality between member states is another driver of organizational openness.

Overall, the causal paths provided by the sufficient condition are in line with theoretical expectations from the norm and resource based literature. There appear to be strong combination effects of normative conditions in the IAEA case. Talk about participation occurs in a context of high media visibility and high IAEA authority. There thus is a critical mass of interlocutors in the organization's environment that may challenge the legitimacy of the organization. In addition, there is a high share of democratic member states that is likely to respond to legitimacy challenges based on democratic values. Further, all this happens at a time with a strong norm of open governance which readily provides a framework of reference for democratic framing of IAEA activities. I will label this finding as the *norm based mechanism.*

Second, the inequality mechanism indicates that states try to overcome the costs of information asymmetries by demanding more transparency and participation of non-state actors. These concerns are then reflected in the organization's talk. I refer to this mechanism as the *first resource based mechanism.* It is interesting to see that this mechanism seems to be at work in the OPCW. The OPCW with its chemical industry inspections and weapon destruction verification is especially vulnerable to information asymmetries. Powerful states are the ones with the largest chemical industries and the largest historic weapons stockpiles. Consequently, the majority of member states that do not have chemical weapons or only have a small chemical industry fear a lack of information on the activities of the organization. Therefore, it is in the interest of these less powerful states to demand independent expert reviews and expert advise, as well as transparency about OPCW procedures and missions. Again, this happens in a context of a global discourse on open governance which also provides normative anchors for state demands for openness.

In summary, openness talk in the OPCW and IAEA thus appears to be a norm driven phenomenon, first. Without a strong norm of open governance present, the organizations (with the exception of the early IAEA) do not start to talk about participation and transparency. This global reference frame of good global governance is thus of importance for the discursive production of the IGOs. Further, a high share of democratic members, high visibility and increased authority to a large part sufficiently explains the occurrence of openness talk in the IAEA. There thus seems to be an effect of norm socialization and public legitimacy challenges on the organization (see 6.1). Finally, the resource based inequality mechanism is capable of explaining high openness talk in the OPCW. As it appears, the fear of information asymmetries also translates into participation and transparency talk despite a relatively low share of democratic members (see 6.2). Norm based approaches alone thus do not explain the whole empirical variance.

5.2.2 DECISIONS: SIMILARITIES CAUSED BY CLOSE COUPLING

What explains openness decisions? I found surprisingly parallel explanations for openness decisions and openness talk. Again, there is a more norm based story for the IAEA and the *norm based mechanism* seems to be at work. Participation or transparency decisions are driven by visibility, democratic members and high authority. For the OPCW, there is again strong inequality between the member states that appears to be a driving factor for transparency or participation decisions, i.e. the *first resource based mechanism*. Also, like in the explanation of talk, the presence of the norm of open governance is a strong necessary condition for openness decisions to occur. Overall, this hints at a strong coupling of openness decisions and talk for the two IGOs under analysis.

Table 5.7: Truth Table: Openness Decisions

RB.BUDGET	RB.INEQUALITY	NB.VISIBILITY.ALL	NB.VISIBILITY.HI	NB.GOVDEPTH	NB.DEM.MEM	NB.OG.NORM	OUT	n	incl	PRI	cases
0	0	1	0	1	1	1	1	5	1	1	IAEA2004, IAEA2005, IAEA2006, IAEA2007, IAEA2008
0	0	1	1	1	1	1	1	2	1	1	IAEA2002, IAEA2003
0	1	0	0	0	0	1	1	3	1	1	OPCW1997, OPCW1998, OPCW2003
0	1	0	0	0	1	1	1	5	1	1	OPCW2004, OPCW2005, OPCW2006, OPCW2007, OPCW2008
0	1	1	1	1	1	1	1	3	1	1	IAEA2009, IAEA2010, IAEA2011
1	0	1	0	1	1	1	1	6	1	1	IAEA1993, IAEA1994, IAEA1995, IAEA1996, IAEA1997, IAEA1998
1	0	1	1	1	1	1	1	3	1	1	IAEA1999, IAEA2000, IAEA2001
1	1	0	0	0	0	1	1	4	1	1	OPCW1999, OPCW2000, OPCW2001, OPCW2002
1	1	0	0	0	1	1	1	3	1	1	OPCW2009, OPCW2010, OPCW2011
0	0	0	0	0	0	0	0	26	0.154	0.154	IAEA1957, IAEA1958, IAEA1959, IAEA1960, IAEA1961, IAEA1962, IAEA1963, IAEA1964, IAEA1965, IAEA1966, IAEA1967, IAEA1968, IAEA1969, IAEA1970, IAEA1971, IAEA1972, IAEA1973, IAEA1974, IAEA1975, IAEA1976, IAEA1977, IAEA1978, IAEA1979, IAEA1980, IAEA1981, IAEA1982
0	0	1	0	0	0	0	0	1	0	0	IAEA1989
0	0	1	0	0	0	1	0	1	0	0	IAEA1990
0	0	1	0	1	0	1	0	2	0	0	IAEA1991, IAEA1992
0	0	1	1	0	0	0	0	2	0	0	IAEA1987, IAEA1988
1	0	0	0	0	0	0	0	3	0	0	IAEA1983, IAEA1984, IAEA1985
1	0	1	1	0	0	0	0	1	0	0	IAEA1986

Note: Inclusion cut: 1.

Table 5.7 is the truth table for the QCA on decisions leading towards more openness. I created the openness decisions outcome by combining the participation and transparency decisions with the OR operator. A 1 thus either stands for increasing participation or transparency decisions.[22] In the

---

[22]As earlier, I also ran separate QCAs for both dimensions. The results for participation decisions alone only had a low coverage. Those for transparency decisions were quite similar to those presented here. Again, please see the QCA appendix for more details.

truth table, there is one row with contradictory cases. It includes the phase of opening decisions in the IAEA that lasted from 1972 to 1975. During this episode of opening, the IAEA General Conference formalized the informal regulation that allows the Director-General to invite interested NGOs to participate in the GC. This change cannot be explained with the conditions under analysis: they do not change in the given period. However, this is not a problem for the analysis of the theories at hand. The change in rules does not change formal participation rights of non-state actors. Those remain the same as before the formal decision. What changes is rather an administrative procedure, but not so much the formal status of NGOs at the IAEA GC (see above). Therefore, the case is not truly contradictory.

As the consistency cutoff threshold, I chose 1 to include only cases with perfect membership in the openness decision set. Further, there are no other rows in the truth table that are close candidates for inclusion in the outcome set. Consequently, the truth table covers the following cases:

- `IAEA1993:1998`
- `IAEA1999:2001`
- `IAEA2002:2003`
- `IAEA2004:2008`
- `IAEA2009:2011`
- `OPCW1997:1998`
- `OPCW1999:2002`
- `OPCW2003`
- `OPCW2004:2008`
- `OPCW2009:2011`

How have the configurations leading to participation or transparency decisions developed over time? For the IAEA, decisions, despite the participation decisions in the 1970s, started in the early 1990s in an environment of resource constraint, high visibility, high authority, a high share of democratic members and under the presence of the open governance norm. Transparency decisions continued to increase in the late 1990s with even more pronounced media visibility. Decreasing headline visibility and an improved budgetary situation had no strong effect on openness decisions in the 2000s. There is thus, in large parts, a parallel development between openness decisions and openness talk. As discussed above, both dimensions appear to be closely coupled.

For the OPCW, we similarly see that decisions begin to increase under high inequality with the norm of open governance present. Openness decisions continue to be made under strong resource constraints in the early 2000s. Finally, an increase, especially in transparency decisions, continues under a growing democratic membership and new budgetary constraints in the mid and late 2000s.

As the discussion of the developments over time suggests, I identified the presence of the norm of open governance as a necessary condition for increasing openness decisions:

	incl	PRI	cov.r
NB.OG.NORM	0.895	0.919	0.919

The presence of the norm of open governance has a high consistency value. As above, only the IAEA decision in 1975 to formalize NGO participation rules contradicts the necessity assumption. For all other 34 cases of openness decisions, however, the necessity assumption holds. Further, there are only 3 cases (IAEA1990:1992) that are not members of the outcome set, where the norm of open governance is already present. Again, this is in line with norm based explanations of organizational opening.

Similarly, I again found strong evidence for norm based mechanisms when looking for sufficient conditions. I identified the following, highly sufficient solution formulas:

Solution	Formula	incl.	PRI	cov
conservative	rb.inequality * NB.VISIBILITY.ALL * NB.GOV.DEPTH * NB.DEM.MEM OR RB.INEQUALITY * nb.visibility.all * nb.visibility.hl * nb.gov.depth OR rb.budget * NB.VISIBILITY.ALL * NB.VISIBILITY.HL * NB.GOV.DEPTH * NB.DEM.MEM	1.000	1.000	0.895
intermediate	RB.INEQUALITY OR NB.VISIBILITY.ALL * NB.GOV.DEPTH * NB.DEM.MEM	1.000	1.000	0.895
parsimonious	NB.DEM.MEM OR RB.INEQUALITY	1.000	1.000	0.895

The intermediate solution `RB.INEQUALITY OR NB.VISIBILITY.ALL * NB.GOV.DEPTH * NB.DEM.MEM` suggests that openness decisions are caused by

- high economic inequality between the member states, or
- high media visibility and high authority and a high share of democratic members.

The solution formulas have perfect consistency, that is, there are no contradictory cases. Coverage is limited because the explanation fails to, as discussed above, account for the participation decision of the IAEA in the 1970s.

A look at the detailed values for the prime implicants of the intermediate solution in Table 5.8 again reveals different causal pathways for both organizations under analysis. The inequality prime implicant explains the participation and transparency decisions of the OPCW. Here, only high inequality sufficiently causes organizational change on the decision dimension. For the IAEA, it is again the *norm based mechanism* that has strong explanatory power. Here, a configuration of the environment where the organization is visible in the media, has high authority and a high share of democratic members appears to be sufficient to cause decisions for more transparency.

With regard to the overarching theoretical expectations, the *first resource based mechanism* seems to work as expected: high inequality increases incentives for member states to push for more open organizations. Also,

Table 5.8: Openness Decisions, Sufficient Prime Implicants

	incl	PRI	cov.r	cov.u	cases
RB.INEQUALITY	1.000	1.000	0.474	0.395	OPCW1997, OPCW1998, OPCW2003; OPCW2004, OPCW2005, OPCW2006, OPCW2007, OPCW2008; IAEA2009, IAEA2010, IAEA2011; OPCW1999, OPCW2000, OPCW2001, OPCW2002; OPCW2009, OPCW2010, OPCW2011
NB.VISIBILITY.ALL * NB.GOV.DEPTH * NB.DEM.MEM	1.000	1.000	0.500	0.421	IAEA2004, IAEA2005, IAEA2006, IAEA2007, IAEA2008; IAEA2002, IAEA2003; IAEA2009, IAEA2010, IAEA2011; IAEA1993, IAEA1994, IAEA1995, IAEA1996, IAEA1997, IAEA1998; IAEA1999, IAEA2000, IAEA2001

as before, the *norm based mechanism* appears to be particularly influential. Again, I will check the plausibility of both mechanisms in more detail in the case-study chapter.

5.2.3 PARTICIPATION ACTION: THE EFFECTS OF MEDIA VISIBILITY AND RESOURCE CONSTRAINTS

What explains openness on the action dimension of IGO output? I first look at the combined participation action for both IGOs. I created the combined variable by combining the participation action variables with the OR operator. The participation action set thus stands for either a high amount of NGOs at the annual conference, a high number of NGO representatives at these conferences, or an exceptionally high number of participation events.[23] Overall, I only found a weak explanation for participation action, covering about 70 percent of the relevant cases. Yet, the analysis shows another interesting pathway to participation action, the *second resource*

---

[23] The QCAs for the individual participation action variables did not reveal any strong explanatory patterns. Please consult the appendix for more details.

based mechanism, that does not rely on the norm of open governance and democratic member states. Instead, there are strong effects of visibility and budgetary constraints that seem to drive participation action.

Table 5.9: Truth Table: Participation Action

RB.BUDGET	RB.INEQUALITY	NB.VISIBILITY.ALL	NB.VISIBILITY.HL	NB.GOVDEPTH	NB.DEM.MEM	NB.OG.NORM	OUT	n	incl	PRI	cases
0	0	1	0	0	0	0	1	1	1	1	IAEA1989
0	0	1	0	0	0	1	1	1	1	1	IAEA1990
0	0	1	0	1	0	1	1	2	1	1	IAEA1991, IAEA1992
0	0	1	0	1	1	1	1	5	1	1	IAEA2004, IAEA2005, IAEA2006, IAEA2007, IAEA2008
0	0	1	1	0	0	0	1	2	1	1	IAEA1987, IAEA1988
0	0	1	1	1	1	1	1	2	1	1	IAEA2002, IAEA2003
0	1	1	1	1	1	1	1	3	1	1	IAEA2009, IAEA2010, IAEA2011
1	0	0	0	0	0	0	1	3	1	1	IAEA1983, IAEA1984, IAEA1985
1	0	1	0	1	1	1	1	6	1	1	IAEA1993, IAEA1994, IAEA1995, IAEA1996, IAEA1997, IAEA1998
1	0	1	1	0	0	0	1	1	1	1	IAEA1986
1	0	1	1	1	1	1	1	3	1	1	IAEA1999, IAEA2000, IAEA2001
1	1	0	0	0	1	1	1	3	1	1	OPCW2009, OPCW2010, OPCW2011
0	1	0	0	0	0	1	0	3	0.667	0.667	OPCW1997, OPCW1998, OPCW2003
0	1	0	0	0	1	1	0	5	0.6	0.6	OPCW2004, OPCW2005, OPCW2006, OPCW2007, OPCW2008
1	1	0	0	0	0	1	0	4	0.5	0.5	OPCW1999, OPCW2000, OPCW2001, OPCW2002
0	0	0	0	0	0	0	0	26	0.308	0.308	IAEA1957, IAEA1958, IAEA1959, IAEA1960, IAEA1961, IAEA1962, IAEA1963, IAEA1964, IAEA1965, IAEA1966, IAEA1967, IAEA1968, IAEA1969, IAEA1970, IAEA1971, IAEA1972, IAEA1973, IAEA1974, IAEA1975, IAEA1976, IAEA1977, IAEA1978, IAEA1979, IAEA1980, IAEA1981, IAEA1982

Note: Inclusion cut: 1.

Table 5.9 is the truth table for the combined participation events. It includes a number of contradictory cases (OPCW1997:1998, OPCW1999, OPCW2000, OPCW2003, OPCW2007:2008, IAEA 1958:1964), where the same configuration of conditions leads to both action and non-action. At closer inspection, there is no row in the truth table with a consistency value of 0. This illustrates that the artificial calibrations of the extraordinary high instances of action I introduced above do not create clear empirical distinctions in the data. However, this is not too severe a problem. The underlying calibration is focused on extraordinary instances of participation. Thus, when setting the consistency threshold to 1, the algorithm identifies only particularly strong and consistent phases of participation action. The contradictory cases are thus no true logical contradictions because the o stands for normal phases of participation action and not for its complete absence. The following cases are covered by the explanation:

- IAEA1983:1985
- IAEA1986
- IAEA1987:1988
- IAEA1989

- IAEA1990
- IAEA1991:1992
- IAEA1993:1998
- IAEA1999:2001

- IAEA2002:2003
- IAEA2004:2008
- IAEA2009:2011
- OPCW2009:2011

Over time, there is the following development for the IAEA. Strong participation action started in the 1980s with strong resource constraints. Since the 1990s, participation action was a constant feature of the IAEA, occurring under the influence of high visibility, and rising authority, inequality, and democratic member states. For the OPCW, the only consistent phase of high participation action can be found in the late 2000s, where all typical environmental conditions for the OPCW are present. In the earlier years of the OPCW, participation action was more volatile and thus cannot be attributed to consistent truth table rows.

A quick look at the truth table also shows that there is no single necessary condition causing participation action. Compared to talk and decisions, participation action has started much earlier, in the 1980s. At that time, the norm of open governance was not yet strong and it thus cannot be necessary for the expansion of IGO participation action. Participation action thus is an important test case for my theoretical framework as it tries to explain developments towards openness in the time before the 1990s.

While no single necessary conditions could be found, I identified the following sufficient solution formulas:

Solution	Formula	incl.	PRI	cov
conservative	rb.inequality * NB.VISIBILITY.ALL * NB.GOV.DEPTH * NB.DEM.MEM * NB.OG.NORM OR rb.budget * NB.VISIBILITY.ALL * NB.VISIBILITY.HL * NB.GOV.DEPTH * NB.DEM.MEM * NB.OG.NORM OR rb.budget * rb.inequality * NB.VISIBILITY.ALL * nb.gov.depth * nb.dem.mem * nb.og.norm OR rb.budget * rb.inequality * NB.VISIBILITY.ALL * nb.visibility.hl * nb.dem.mem * NB.OG.NORM OR rb.budget * rb.inequality * NB.VISIBILITY.ALL * nb.visibility.hl * nb.gov.depth * nb.dem.mem OR rb.budget * rb.inequality * NB.VISIBILITY.ALL * nb.visibility.hl * NB.GOV.DEPTH * NB.OG.NORM OR rb.inequality * NB.VISIBILITY.ALL * NB.VISIBILITY.HL * nb.gov.depth * nb.dem.mem * nb.og.norm OR RB.BUDGET * rb.inequality * nb.visibility.all * nb.visibility.hl * nb.gov.depth * nb.dem.mem * nb.og.norm OR RB.BUDGET * RB.INEQUALITY * nb.visibility.all * nb.visibility.hl * nb.gov.depth * NB.DEM.MEM * NB.OG.NORM	1.000	1.000	0.681
intermediate	NB.VISIBILITY.ALL OR RB.BUDGET * nb.og.norm OR RB.BUDGET * RB.INEQUALITY * NB.DEM.MEM	1.000	1.000	0.681
parsimonious	NB.VISIBILITY.ALL OR RB.BUDGET * NB.DEM.MEM OR RB.BUDGET * nb.og.norm OR RB.BUDGET * rb.inequality	1.000	1.000	0.681

Due to the many contradictory cases in the initial truth table, the coverage values for the sufficient conditions is only at 68 percent. The formulas do not provide explanations for the contradictory cases above. Yet, for the many covered cases, I find that participation action is caused by

- high media visibility, or
- budgetary constraints when the norm of open governance is absent, or
- budget constraints and high inequality and a high share of democratic members.

Table 5.10 includes the prime implicants of the intermediate solution and shows which cases each implicant covers. As in the analyses before, there is again an interesting distribution of the covered cases by organization. First,

Table 5.10: Participation Action, Sufficient Prime Implicants

	incl	PRI	cov.r	cov.u	cases
NB.VISIBILITY.ALL	1.000	1.000	0.553	0.532	IAEA1989; IAEA1990; IAEA1991, IAEA1992; IAEA2004, IAEA2005, IAEA2006, IAEA2007, IAEA2008; IAEA1987, IAEA1988; IAEA2002, IAEA2003; IAEA2009, IAEA2010, IAEA2011; IAEA1993, IAEA1994, IAEA1995, IAEA1996, IAEA1997, IAEA1998; IAEA1986; IAEA1999, IAEA2000, IAEA2001
RB.BUDGET * nb.og.norm	1.000	1.000	0.085	0.064	IAEA1983, IAEA1984, IAEA1985; IAEA1986
RB.BUDGET * RB.INEQUALITY * NB.DEM.MEM	1.000	1.000	0.064	0.064	OPCW2009, OPCW2010, OPCW2011

for the IAEA, there is a long period of time with high participation action when visibility appears to be the only sufficient condition. Since the late 1980s, media visibility drives increasing NGO participation and participation events at the IAEA. This fits norm based explanations of organizational opening: the IGOs need to react to increased visibility and possible sources of criticism from their environments. Allowing more non-state participation, especially at their highest policy-making conference, may thus help the organization in spreading and targeting information and thus actively building its public image and maintaining legitimacy.

In the early 1980s, when the IAEA is only rarely visible in the global news media, another mechanism is influential. From 1983 until 1986, it is participation events that are very strong. They appear to be caused by times of budget constraints. This is well explained by resource based explanations. Especially in times of low organizational resources, inviting external expertise and input is functionally beneficial for the IGOs. Thus, the goal of increasing the number of participation events at that time, despite less monetary resources, seems to be an effort of the IAEA to target external expertise. That this happens in times without a strong normative reference frame of open governance, again underlines a rather functional character of the participation events at that time. In this regard, the nonexistence of the norm of open governance should not be interpreted as a strong causal statement that contradicts the theoretical assumptions of norm based mechanism. Rather, it describes an environmental setting where the norm was not yet present and when, nevertheless, participation could increase due to resource based mechanisms. For a more detailed discussion, see the case study in Chapter 6.3.

Finally, for the OPCW, high participation action from 2009 until 2011 is caused by a configuration of resource constraints, high inequality and a high share of democratic members. During this time, all three participation action variables are present. Thus, various mechanisms may be at work. Resource constraints and high inequality between the member states may increase the need for external expertise and the transparent provision of information of external actors. At the same time, the high share of democratic members may make it more easy for NGOs to get access to the annual Conference of the States Parties to make their voices heard.

Overall, there are thus still some gaps in the theoretical framework for the explanation of participation action. While a norm driven visibility mechanism and a resource driven budget constraint mechanism seem to be at work at various points in time, 30 percent of the cases of participation action are still unexplained. This invites a more thorough analysis of participation action.

5.2.4 TRANSPARENCY ACTION: WEAK NORM BASED INFLUENCE

Finally, is there a strong explanation for increases in transparency action, i.e. extraordinary high shares of the public information budget? I found some evidence that a high share of democratic members or the presence of the norm of open governance is necessary for high transparency action.

Table 5.11 shows the truth table that summarizes the configurations of conditions leading to increased public information budgets. There are some contradictory cases. First, the OPCW in 2008 does not belong to the high transparency action set. However, I chose to set the consistency cutoff to 0.8 to include the time period of the OPCW from 2004 until 2008 as a case of high transparency action. It is the only row that contains cases with high action from the OPCW. Therefore, excluding it from the analysis would strongly limit the interpretation of the QCA. Further, the year 2008 borders on a phase of years with high transparency action. Therefore, it is not truly logically contradicting. In addition, there is high participation action in the IAEA from 1961 until 1963. These are also deviant cases, which are not covered by the explanation. The table thus covers the following phases of a high public information budget:

- IAEA2002:2003
- IAEA2004:2008
- IAEA2009:2011
- OPCW2004:2008

For the OPCW, a high public information budget share is present in an environment defined by high inequality, a high share of democratic members and the presence of the norm of open governance. For the IAEA in the 2000s,

Table 5.11: Truth Table: Transparency Action

RB.BUDGET	RB.INEQUALITY	NB.VISIBILITY.ALL	NB.VISIBILITY.HL	NB.GOVDEPTH	NB.DEM.MEM	NB.OG.NORM	OUT	n	incl	PRI	cases
0	0	1	0	1	1	1	1	5	1	1	IAEA2004, IAEA2005, IAEA2006, IAEA2007, IAEA2008
0	0	1	1	1	1	1	1	2	1	1	IAEA2002, IAEA2003
0	1	1	1	1	1	1	1	3	1	1	IAEA2009, IAEA2010, IAEA2011
0	1	0	0	0	1	1	1	5	0.8	0.8	OPCW2004, OPCW2005, OPCW2006, OPCW2007, OPCW2008
0	0	0	0	0	0	0	0	26	0.115	0.115	IAEA1957, IAEA1958, IAEA1959, IAEA1960, IAEA1961, IAEA1962, IAEA1963, IAEA1964, IAEA1965, IAEA1966, IAEA1967, IAEA1968, IAEA1969, IAEA1970, IAEA1971, IAEA1972, IAEA1973, IAEA1974, IAEA1975, IAEA1976, IAEA1977, IAEA1978, IAEA1979, IAEA1980, IAEA1981, IAEA1982
0	0	1	0	0	0	0	0	1	0	0	IAEA1989
0	0	1	0	0	0	1	0	1	0	0	IAEA1990
0	0	1	0	1	0	1	0	2	0	0	IAEA1991, IAEA1992
0	0	1	1	0	0	0	0	2	0	0	IAEA1987, IAEA1988
0	1	0	0	0	0	1	0	3	0	0	OPCW1997, OPCW1998, OPCW2003
1	0	0	0	0	0	0	0	3	0	0	IAEA1983, IAEA1984, IAEA1985
1	0	1	0	1	1	1	0	6	0	0	IAEA1993, IAEA1994, IAEA1995, IAEA1996, IAEA1997, IAEA1998
1	0	1	1	0	0	0	0	1	0	0	IAEA1986
1	0	1	1	1	1	1	0	3	0	0	IAEA1999, IAEA2000, IAEA2001
1	1	0	0	0	0	1	0	4	0	0	OPCW1999, OPCW2000, OPCW2001, OPCW2002
1	1	0	0	0	1	1	0	3	0	0	OPCW2009, OPCW2010, OPCW2011

Note: Inclusion cut: 0.8.

the same is true. In addition, transparency action occurs when there is high authority, and high media visibility.

The truth table suggests, that there are two necessary conditions. The presence of the norm of open governance or a high share of democratic member states is necessary that states invest a higher share of IGO budgets in public information:

	incl	PRI	cov.r
NB.OG.NORM	0.824	0.378	0.378
NB.DEM.MEM	0.824	0.519	0.519

Yet, the high transparency action in the IAEA from 1961 until 1963 contradicts both assumptions of necessity. Another explanation needs to be found for this period of time. Note in addition that the coverage values of both conditions are quite low. This indicates the risk of a trivial necessary condition. In other words, there are a number of cases with low transparency action where the share of democratic members or the presence of the open governance norm are high.[24] For example, this is the case for the IAEA in the 1990s. Both conditions are present but expenditures for transparency do not increase significantly. Similarly, in the OPCW from 2009 until 2011, one would also expect some effect of the necessary conditions on the transparency budget.

Overall, both necessary conditions fit norm based expectations. However, they need to be explored in more detail to determine possible scope conditions. The analysis for sufficient conditions did not reveal any of those. Further, there are no solutions for sufficiency that have good parameters of fit. There are thus some gaps in the theoretical explanations of increased transparency action.

5.3 Summary: The Power of Norm and Resource based Explanations

After having described organizational opening in the previous chapter, in this chapter, I have turned to the second step in the research approach. How can organizational opening up be explained and how do both resource and norm based logics hold up to the empirical test? As discussed quickly above, both approaches are needed to explain the observed empirical variance in full. However, some explanatory factors are more influential and thus better predictors of organizational opening (see Figure 5.7). When looking at the resource based conditions, it has to be noted that complexity is the first variable shown to be irrelevant for the comparative analysis. As discussed above, given the data, complexity can be understood as a constant background process that however does not help to explain differences between the IAEA and OPCW. Second, budgetary constraints have shown to be influential to some extent. The assumed mechanism, that IGOs with limited resources rely on external actors for service provision, seems to fit well with the explanation of participation action. Here, for example in the case of the IAEA in the 1980s, there are increased participation events in times of budget constraints. Also, and third, inequality appears to be a driving force of organizational opening up at the OPCW. I identified strong causal links for this case. Here, inequality drives talk about participation and transparency, as well as openness decisions and participation action.

The norm based conditions are particularly strong necessary conditions for organizational opening. It is especially the presence of the open governance norm that is a major enabler for the large-scale occurrence of openness

---

[24]Yet, when analyzing the necessity relations of both conditions and the negated outcome, consistency and coverage values are also low (democratic members: 0.245, 0.481; open governance norm: 0.434, 0.622). Therefore, both conditions may have low explanatory power, but they are not necessary for non-transparency action.

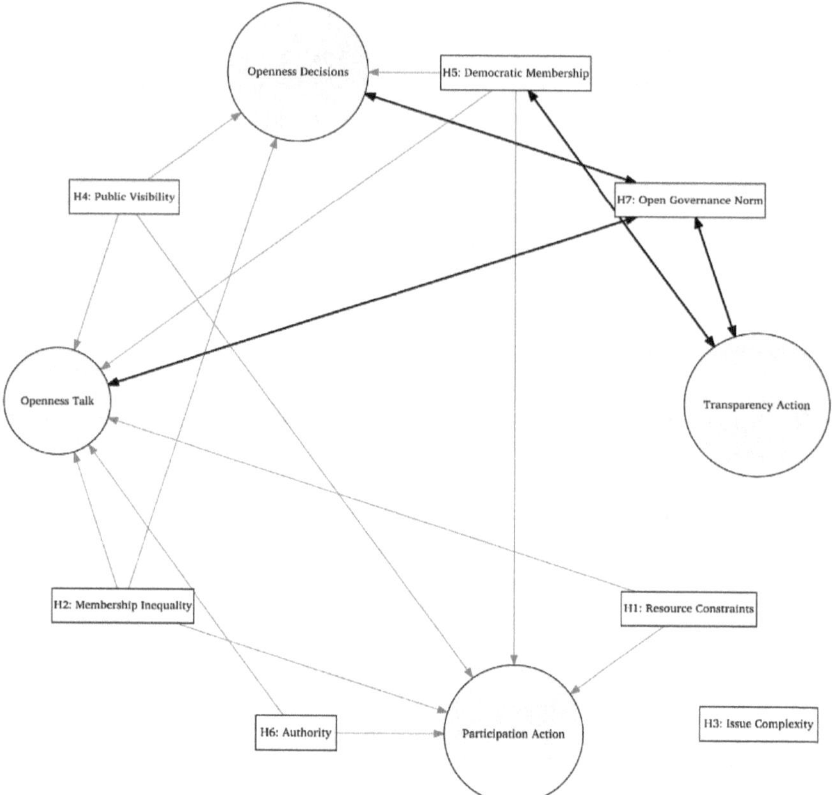

Figure 5.7: Causal Pathways towards Organizational Opening (Black Lines: Necessary Conditions)

talk and participation or transparency decisions. Like democratic membership, it is also a weak necessary condition for increasing transparency action. Next to these necessity relations, the norm based conditions also form strong relations of sufficiency with the outcome sets. First, the co-occurrence of high visibility, authority and a high share of democratic members is sufficient for openness talk and decisions in the IAEA. Further, high visibility explains strong participation action for the same organization.

Overall, I thus find slightly stronger support for the norm based conditions. However, there are a number of contradictory cases that the analytical framework so far cannot explain. Further, the three main causal mechanisms discovered by the QCA strongly suggest that the causal powers stipulated by theory are indeed at work in the organizations. However, a detailed and rich description of these mechanisms that also checks their plausibility still needs to be developed. This is the goal of the next chapter.

5.3.1 SELECTING CASES FOR THE CASE STUDIES

Before concluding the QCA analysis, I need to decide which of the mechanisms and which cases that I identified in this chapter should be analyzed in more detail in the following case-study chapter. I chose the following cases for closer analysis:

- Illustrating the *norm based mechanism*, sufficiently causing participation and transparency talk as well as openness decisions in the IAEA, I will sketch relevant developments in this organization from 1992 until 2011.
- Examining the *first resource based mechanism*, I will take a closer look at the OPCW from 1997 until 2011 and its moves towards more openness talk, decision and action.
- To explain participation action in the IAEA, I will describe the effects of media visibility and budget constraints, and thus of the *second resource based mechanism*, on the increase in participation events and NGO participation at the annual General Conference.

6   *Case Studies on Organizational Opening and Causal Mechanisms*

In the last empirical chapter of this study, the final step in the three step study design, I check the plausibility of the causal mechanisms that the QCA identified. The QCA helped with ordering and with comparing the various interactions of the conditions and their effects on organizational opening. The resulting causal mechanisms, however, are still relatively abstract and need to be elaborated. This is done in the three following case studies. They are based on a deeper look at the material used for the QCA. In addition, new sources are used where available. The case studies try not only to confirm the identified mechanisms but also to check for possible alternative explanations and other interactions of the explanatory variables.

In the first case study, I look at the norm based mechanism that leads to transparency talk and decisions at the IAEA. The case study reveals a more nuanced causal mechanism of organizational opening on the transparency dimension. In the IAEA, risen authority and high media visibility have lead to a rising number of legitimacy challenges for the organization. Those are communicated in the media, but also picked up by the rising share of democratic member states. The Secretariat replies to both demands for transparency by increasing its transparency on the decision dimension and by linking its organizational discourse to transparency as a principle of good global governance. Overall, the norm based explanations are thus powerful in explaining IAEA transparency. The same is true for the OPCW. Here, the case studies shows how inequality between member states, a resource based mechanism, interacts with the norm of open governance and causes increased transparency decisions and talk of the OPCW's Technical Secretariat. In detail, the OPCW members voice functional demands for transparency to reduce information asymmetries in the regime. The Secretariat only partially translates those demands and rather refers to the broader, norm based notion of transparency in its discourse and decisions. Overall, there is thus strong evidence for the overarching power of norm based explanations for increasing transparency in international security organizations.

Looking at participation, the results are less clear. In the OPCW case study, there is some evidence that links participation to the reduction of inequality and thus to a resource based explanation. For the IAEA, the same seems to be the case. Here, the QCA identified a strong effect of media visibility on participation since the 1990s. However, the case study shows that media visibility does not translate into participation for representational purposes, as the norm based explanations suggest. Rather, I find evidence that the IAEA strategically invites those non-state actors to participate that help the Agency to promote its organizational self-understanding as an a-political and technical organization. Similarly, for the 1980s, I show that the IAEA uses participation events as a tool to reduce costs of information gathering and dissemination. Overall, participation in international security organizations thus seems to be driven by a resource based logic, underlining the functional benefits of selective non-state participation. Including non-state actors to give under-represented groups a voice in the organizations is rare and not the main driver of the organizational opening on the participation dimension.

6.1 TRANSPARENCY TALK AND DECISIONS IN THE IAEA: NORMS AND THE QUEST FOR LEGITIMACY

In this first section, I examine the norm based mechanism that leads to increased transparency talk and decisions in the IAEA. I focus on transparency here, because most of the explained cases in the QCA are either transparency talk (which is mostly parallel to participation talk) or transparency decisions. I will focus on the IAEA's participation decision in another section, below. The QCA for transparency talk and decisions showed that the presence of the norm of open governance is necessary for talk and decisions to occur. Further, the presence of high visibility and high authority and a high share of democratic members is jointly sufficient for increased openness talk and decisions. How does this norm based mechanism work in detail and is it plausible when looking at the data more closely?

The IAEA case illustrates, as I will show below, that transparency talk and decisions are indeed caused by the following norm based mechanism (see Figure 6.1). First, enhanced authority and visibility have caused a growing number of legitimacy challenges for the IAEA. As the IAEA has begun to take over more political inspection tasks, its work became more politicized. This increased politicization is also mirrored in the media and causes a number of legitimation challenges for the Agency. Second, these challenges are then picked up by the IAEA Secretariat. It responds to the increased media interest by making itself more accessible and by providing more information about itself and its work to a larger group of audiences. Also, from its member states, it picks up demands for more transparency in various fields of its activities. In its talk, it acknowledges transparency as an important value and promises to be transparent to counter legitimacy challenges of biased and politicized inspections and promotion activities. Further, this

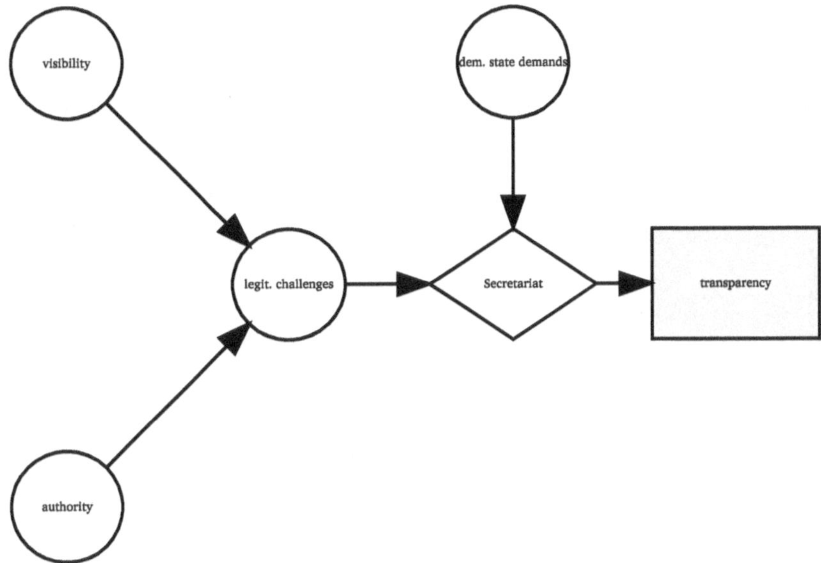

Figure 6.1: The Norm based Mechanism causing Transparency Talk and Decisions

case study illustrates the large impact that an IGO administration has on opening up. In addition, it shows how the bureaucracy uses transparency as a means to maintain its pragmatic legitimacy, built on independence and expertise.

6.1.1 INCREASED VISIBILITY AND AUTHORITY TRIGGER LEGITIMACY CHALLENGES

When taking a closer look at the IAEA in the global media, the following points are important for the interpretation of the causal mechanism. First, the media often cites the IAEA as a source of information. There is thus a focus on its reports and assessments. The work it does on the ground, i.e. inspections and development assistance are only rarely described in detail. Of those two, the Agency's work in the development sector is nearly invisible in the media I analyzed. Further, direct criticism of the IAEA, its officers and procedures is only rarely voiced. There is thus little direct pressure from the global news media on the organization. Also, there are only very few direct calls for more transparency in the media.[25] Overall, there is thus no direct

---

[25]I read all articles in the Lexis-Nexis `major world newspapers` corpus where the the IAEA with the keywords `IAEA, International Atomic Energy Agency, UN watchdog, atomic watchdog` appeared to-

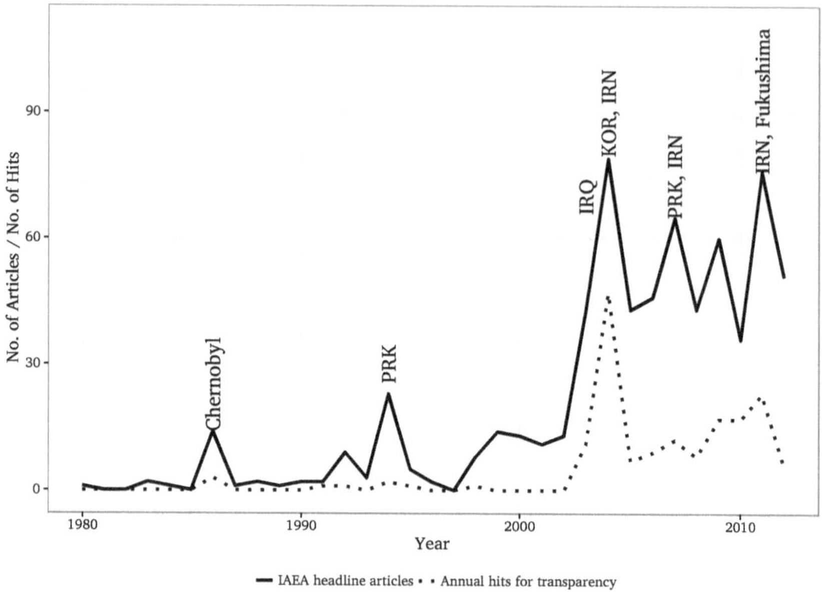

Figure 6.2: Transparency Search Terms in the IAEA Headline Articles and Political Crises

channel from the media to a concerned public and back to the organization where demands for transparency are voiced. I do not conclude that there are no demands at all, but they are not very visible to a broad audience. Such demands may thus rather be channeled through less visible expert consultations or member-state demands.

However, what is remarkable about the media presence of the IAEA is that reporting about the Agency is largely driven by the political crises it is involved in. Figure 6.2 shows the line for the annual number of articles that mention the IAEA in their headlines in the Lexis-Nexis major world newspapers corpus. The graph shows a number of peaks that closely correlate with the involvement of the IAEA in political inspections. During theses crisis situations, references to transparency (the dotted line in the figure) are made in a number of forms, with direct requests for IAEA transparency being a rare case:

1986 The Agency is often cited in its function as the international organization that took a lead role in assessing the causes of the Chernobyl

gether with the keywords transparency, transparent, public information in an article. Of the 1.076 resulting articles (1977-2012), only 10 made mild demands for IAEA transparency.

accident of that year. In the media, concerns about the general safety of nuclear applications are voiced. A number of commentators see the IAEA in a role to increase its work in the safety field, especially by designing stronger safety standards and developing tools for their implementation. Regarding transparency, there are major concerns of the member states about the slow disclosure of information of the USSR. As a result, the IAEA is seen as the international organization that can render disclosures more easy for states by providing fora or mechanisms for information about nuclear accidents (cf. e.g. Dobbs 1986). The IAEA is thus seen as a promoter of transparency.

1994 In 1994, the conflict on the North Korean nuclear program escalated. North Korea (PRK) withdrew from the IAEA and claimed it would no longer adhere to the NPT. As a consequence, Agency inspectors were expelled from the country and monitoring equipment was removed. Also, the IAEA took the lead role in verifying the nuclear freeze that was negotiated later in this year between PRK and USA. Often, the articles call for PRK to allow inspections by the IAEA and describe the IAEA inspection activities in PRK. Here, the IAEA becomes an instrument of nuclear transparency, as it is supposed to provide unbiased on-the-grounds information on nuclear programs of its member states (cf. e.g. Coll 1994). In this respect, it builds on the functions it took over after the Chernobyl accident which gave the issue of nuclear transparency a much higher rating on the international agenda.

2003 This perception of the IAEA as a provider of transparent information is also central during the inspections in Iraq, culminating in the UN Security Council discussions of 2003, when the US failed to negotiate a resolution for the use of military force (see e.g. Ryan 2014). In the debate, the IAEA and many of its member states demanded full transparency and disclosure of nuclear information from Iraq. However, there was also some criticism of the IAEA and UNSCOM inspections. Mostly voiced in the US media, there was some skepticism about the effectiveness of IAEA safeguards in Iraq (see e.g. The Washington Times 2003; Traub 2004). Given the relatively weak tools and legal rights of IAEA inspections in the 1990s, there was the fear that they could not create assurance for the international community that there was indeed no nuclear program.

2004-2011 Since the 2000s, media reporting about the IAEA is dominated by the atomic conflict with Iran. The media discusses many Agency reports and assessments on the nature of the Iranian nuclear program. As during the Iraq inspections, the IAEA is presented as the international organization that should neutrally assess the program. Consequently, many states demand Iran to cooperate with the IAEA and allow inspections. The IAEA itself also demands full transparency of Iran in order to make a complete and convincing evaluation of the peaceful nature of the nuclear activities in the country. Over the years, however, there is also growing skepticism about the way the IAEA, and its Director-General M. ElBaradei, handles the Iran issue. Some comments, especially from the US and Israel argue that the IAEA is too lenient on Iran and that Iran uses the IAEA and its inspections process to win time to develop a nuclear weapons capability (see Daily News 2009; Akbarzadeh 2006; Glick 2007). Here, the role of the IAEA as an agent of transparency is questioned. However, in the overall media, this appears to be a minority position.

Finally, during 2011, the IAEA was actively involved in reporting on the nuclear accidents at Fukushima. It published reports and data on radiation levels and possible causes of the accident. Also, it was demanding more transparency from the Japanese government on the effects of the nuclear accident. As before, there is no large scale criticism of the role of the IAEA in this political crisis. However, there are a few reports that criticize the IAEA for doing too little during the crisis in terms of public information. As a rare example of direct transparency requests, an article in *The Australian* (Atkins 2011) criticizes this by claiming that "[t]he only way to combat misinformation is with information and on that score the IAEA has failed".

In general, the growing reporting about political conflicts and the IAEA's involvement has thus only rarely led to more direct demands for transparency. However, the media image of the Agency as a quasi-political actor has changed the perception of the IAEA. By reporting about the critical role that the Agency and its inspection system plays in assuring non-proliferation and peaceful conflict settlement, the Agency has become strongly politicized. This politicization is picked up by a number of member states and it is criticized in the media, especially by those that are parties to the conflicts with IAEA involvement. For example, Iran has begun to question the Agency's independence and claimed that it may be biased in its assessments of the Iranian nuclear program. An article in the *South China Morning Post* summarizes the typical replies of the Iranian government on new IAEA inspection reports pretty well:

> "For Iran and other signatories of the nuclear Non-Proliferation Treaty, that means unfettered inspections and monitoring of facilities. But these have been only partly allowed by Tehran, leaving more questions than answers. The response to the report has been, as always, bombastic – reiterations of a legitimate right to a nuclear programme, that the IAEA's work is politically motivated and that the US should live up to its NPT obligations

by scrapping its atomic arsenal. Resolve to comply with provisions, not rhetoric and finger-pointing, are what critics want to see" (South China Morning Post 2011, 16).

The politicization of the Agency's work goes hand in hand with its increased authority. As described above, the largest increase in international authority came with the Agency's mandate under the United Nations Security Council to inspect and dismantle the Iraqi nuclear program in 1991. Before, inspections under the NPT, usually regulated by INFCIRC/153 type country agreements, IAEA inspections were more like the work of an accountant, checking the information provided by member states. After the Iraq experiences and the newly developed inspections under the Additional Protocol (INFCIRC/540), IAEA inspections could take the form of more thorough investigations. Consequently, IAEA inspections became more intrusive and also more dangerous for states with undeclared activities. With the addition of UNSC involvement and UNSC mandated inspections, the IAEA assessments also have significant implications for the use of force by the international community. The weight of an IAEA report on a country thus became higher. Before 1991, an inconclusive safeguards assessment meant little more than accounting errors on the side of member states. After that, a negative report could imply serious threats to non-proliferation and thus to international peace. The most prominent example are the Iran inspections. IAEA reports about the Iranian nuclear program have become highly politicized and very sensible for political interpretations. Thus, increased authority has transformed the Agency's inspection work from an accountant to a "watchdog."

Over the years, this politicization and the shift in activities has created a number of challenges of the pragmatic legitimacy of the IAEA that it needs to respond to. The challenges are co-constituted by high media visibility, transporting the inspections work and its possible political implications to a wider audience. In detail, there are two particular legitimation challenges:

1. The *effectiveness of inspections* becomes much more important in the politicized IAEA. Member states and the international community need to be able to trust that Agency inspections indeed are capable of detecting non-declared military-use programs. As discussed early, this was often not the case under INFCIRC/153 safeguards. As a consequence, trust in the IAEA fell and new mechanisms, like the Additional Protocol, were developed. Still, trust in assessments is limited in situations were states do not grant such far reaching inspection rights to the Agency. This is part of the dilemma in Iran. It has not signed an Additional Protocol and IAEA assessments are thus limited.

2. Further, the *independence of inspections and assessments* has become
    challenged by a growing number of states. This is also a result of
    the growing politicization and authority of the IAEA safeguards in-
    spections. Some member-states criticize that the IAEA is driven by
    Western interests and that its assessments, e.g. of the Iranian nuclear
    program are biased. There are statements of the Iranian government
    in the media arguing that the Agency "illegally insisted on politicising
    the Iranian nation's nuclear case" (Balogh 2007), that the IAEA is "a
    front for nuclear-capable members to protect their existing technology
    while preventing other nations – such as Iran – from developing the
    same technology for peaceful purposes" (Fitzpatrick 2006), and that
    the IAEA is "kowtowing to Washington" (The Globe and Mail 2004).
    This even translates into fears of espionage. For example, during the
    Iraq inspections of the early 2000s, the Iraqui deputy prime minister
    "wanted a more transparent system to ensure that inspectors could
    not double up as spies for the US" (Watt, MacAskill and Engel 2002).

To sum up, the risen IAEA authority and politicization have created
legitimacy concerns for the organization. With a growing impact of their
decisions and inspections on global politics, the IAEA's independence and
effectiveness was questioned. Also driven by heightened public visibility,
these legitimacy challenges need to be answered by the IAEA. Transparency,
as an important element of the global norm of open governance, is a likely
norm that the Agency will use in its replies. Because it is seen as an agent
of state transparency and demands transparency from the states it inspects,
the Agency is vulnerable to the charge of being intransparent itself. As I
show in the next section, the Agency prevents this by actively promoting
transparency and by increasing public access.

6.1.2 TRANSPARENCY DEMANDS BY MEMBER STATES

How do member states refer to the value of transparency when they talk
about the IAEA? Figure 6.3 shows the salience of transparency and related
issues in the debates of IAEA member states at the annual General Conference.[26] The data is taken from the official verbal records of the IAEA GC.
Most of the statements are made during the general debate of the Agency's
annual report. Here, states usually describe their cooperation with the IAEA
in the last years and, sometimes, make statements about the policies and
the development of the IAEA. The bars clearly show that transparency has
become important for the member states in the mid 1980s and that references to the concept have dramatically increased since the 1990s. From

---

[26]The TRANSPARENCY group includes the search term transparen*, the group DISCLOSURE the term disc-
los* and the group PUBLIC.INFO the terms public information, information exchange, disseminate
information, information center, provide information, information campaign.

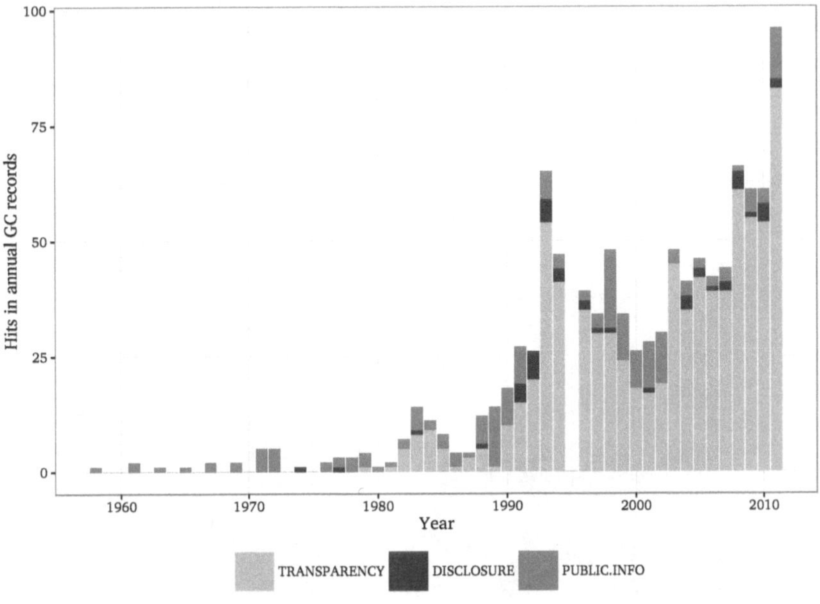

Figure 6.3: Transparency Search Terms in the IAEA General Conference Records

the Agency's foundation until 1979, there is on average 1.5 mentions per year. In the 1980s and 1990s, this increases to 20.75 mentions and increases again to 49 mentions on average since the year 2000. There thus seems to be a clearly risen concern about transparency in the institutional discussions of the Agency. Further, the biggest increase in the discussion of transparency happens in the 1990s. Around that time, the Agency also began a significant production of transparency talk and improved its transparency rules.

However, what are the main concerns that the member states have regarding transparency? In the numbers reported above, it becomes clear that transparency as a concept has become more important. Yet, the data does not show if the states discuss transparency with direct relation to the Agency, or if, like in the media, they demand transparency from other member states. To answer this question, I looked at every fourth General Conference debate, starting from 2010, in more detail.[27] In those reports, I identified those

---

[27] A four year interval is a shortcut to getting a manageable corpus size. Also, reading the whole debates for these years provides a better understanding of the general contents and issues that were addressed, as compared to alternative strategies like e.g. reading only statements from selected states. The statements are included in the electronic appendix. I labeled states as democratic when their POLITY IV score of the year that their statement was issues was 7 or above.

statements where the member states made a direct connection between the Agency and the value of transparency. Figure 6.4 gives an overview of the main issues that member states discussed.

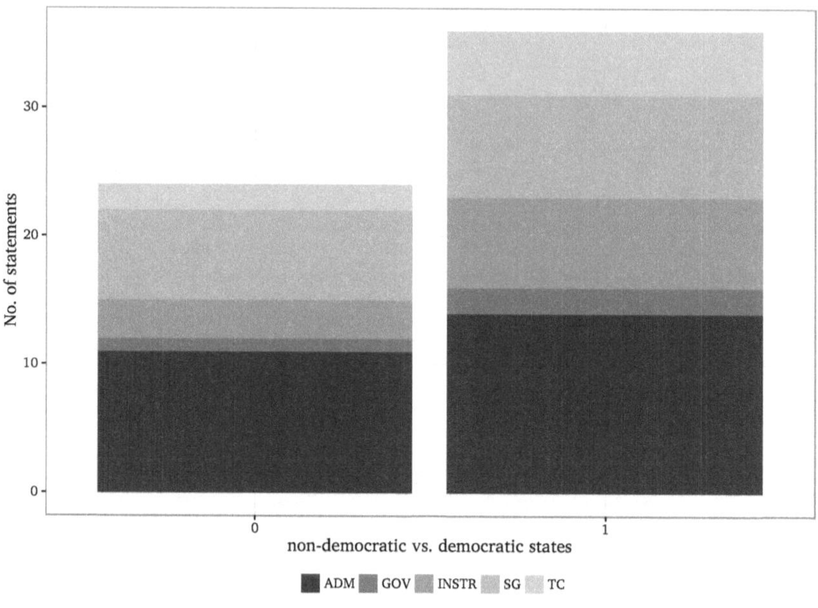

Figure 6.4: Transparency Statements directed at the IAEA in the IAEA General Conference Records 2010, 2006, 2002, 1998, 1994, 1990, 1986, 1982, 1978, 1974, 1970

Further, the graph differentiates between democracies and less democratic states to check if democracies are more active in demanding or promoting transparency in the IAEA. In sum, democracies request transparency from the IAEA more often. However, the differences (37 demands from democracies vs. 23 from non-democracies) are smaller than expected. However, there is some variation concerning the types of references both groups of states make to transparency. The largest group of transparency issues of the member states evolve around the IAEA's administration (ADM). Here, both democracies and non-democracies call for more transparency in the administrative processes of the IAEA, e.g. demanding in general "that the Agency carried out its mandate with independence, objectivity and transparency" (IRQ, GC(54)/OR.4, 28), or that "it was equally incumbent on the Agency to improve the efficiency, efficacy, cost-effectiveness and transparency of its structures and practices" (IRL, GC(54)/OR. 5, 25). Other common issues where states demand more transparency are the "transparency, effectiveness and efficiency in the Agency's management of its financial resources" (DNK, GC(46)/OR.1, 28) and the process of personnel selection, where "more transparent selection criteria would benefit management and would eventually lead to a greater spirit of ownership and participation among member states" (ITA, GC(46)/OR.3, 8). Demanding a more transparent administration often also implies hopes for a more efficient working of the Agency. As the statements above illustrate, transparency is often directly linked to efficiency.

Furthermore, two rather marginal groups of statements deal with the transparency of the Agency's Board of Governors (GOV) and of the technical cooperation program (TC). The former is an issue in the 1990s, where states demand more transparency in the process of selecting and designating new members for the Board (see e.g. the discussion around draft resolution GC(38)/16 in 1994). In the latter, as a subset of the more general demands for administration transparency, the transparency of the technical cooperation program should be improved. On the one hand, there are calls for "making the Agency's technical cooperation policies more transparent" (TUN, GC(26)/ OR.241, 12). On the other hand, "the management and transparency of the programme needed to be improved and brought into line with established United Nations standards" (NLD, GC(54)/OR.5, 16).

For the two remaining groups of transparency demands, the transparency of the safeguards system (SG) and of the general idea of the Agency as an instrument of transparency (INSTR), there are more distinct differences between democratic and non-democratic states. It is those two groups that are, however, most relevant to the legitimacy challenges raised against the IAEA. Regarding safeguards, there is a first larger discussion in the late 1990s about the introduction of the *Additional Protocol*. Here, it is only democracies that invoke transparency when discussing the issue. To those states, there are a number of benefits from the Additional Protocol, which is an improvement that "would bring greater transparency to the nuclear activities of countries" (CHL, GC(42)/OR.4, 31). However, the Agency also needed to assure the states that it would be "open and clear about how safeguards conclusions would be formulated in future on the basis of more qualitative judgments" (ZAF, GC(42)/OR. 2, 21). There was thus some concern about the new, more far reaching inspection rights of the IAEA under the new inspections regime (also see Hirsch 2004). In a way, demanding more transparency from the safeguards system, and thus also increasing state control over it, is also a way of assuring more effective safeguards and also less biased safeguards.

These concerns are picked up by a large number of less democratic states in the 2000s. After the experience of IAEA inspections in Iran, Libya and Iraq, these states reflect on the grown authority and power of IAEA safeguards and demand "universal, transparent and just implementation" (MAR,

GC(50)/OR.4, 12) of the system. Similarly, with regard to the inspections in Iran, Cuba "called on the Secretariat to continue its efforts to foster a climate of understanding, impartiality, confidence and transparency in which a solution could be found once and for all to the safeguards issues under consideration by the Board of Governors and the General Conference" (CUB, GC(54)/OR.6, 5). This is in line with the overall criticism of Agency bias and strong US influence, voiced by a number of non-aligned states. In the same direction, states like Egypt demand the Secretary-General to "disclose all information available to the Secretariat on the nature and scope of Israeli nuclear facilities and activities that would be covered by any comprehensive safeguards agreement concluded with that country" (EGY, GC(54)/OR.9, 13), thus highlighting a perceived misbalance in the treatment of Iran and Israel by the Agency.

The Agency's politicization thus seems to also influence member state demands for IAEA transparency. The statements underline the existence of the two legitimation challenges caused by politicization: independence and effectiveness. This is also visible when looking at the statements that describe the Agency as an instrument of nuclear transparency. The most democratic states usually applaud the Agency's system because it assures transparency in nuclear safety reviews (e.g. AUT, GC(50)/OR.2, 3; NZL, GC(33)/OR.6, 48), in independent analyses, e.g. of the impact of French nuclear tests (CHE, GC(42)/ OR.4, 33), and in promoting transparency in nuclear law in its member states (e.g. NOR, GC(42)/OR.4, 35). Implicitly, they thus also strengthen IAEA legitimacy as an independent and unbiased agent of the international community. Note that these kinds of statements come from both democracies with and without national nuclear power programs. Less democratic states do not applaud this function. If they mention it, they rather criticize it as biased (IRQ, GC(42)/OR.7, 6) or discuss it in passing, when discussing other topics.

As it appears, democracies thus push for more IAEA transparency in the more politicized areas of the IAEA's work, i.e. safeguards and the general promotion of state transparency, for which the IAEA is seen as an instrument. For the member states, transparency as an idea and its practical implications is also a way of shielding the Agency from criticism of bias, and for improving IAEA effectiveness. Also, there are demands for more administrative transparency from all member states. Overall, together with the relatively strong increase of the topic of transparency in all General Conference debates, there is some pressure on the Agency to reply to these state demands and to defuse rising legitimation challenges caused by politicization. As the next section shows, the IAEA indeed picks up a number of those demands in its rhetoric and in its decisions on information provision.

6.1.3 IAEA RESPONSES TO POLITICIZATION AND STATE DEMANDS

As already discussed in Chapter 4.1, the IAEA begins to talk transparency in the 1990s. Also, there is relatively little talk overall, but talk about transparency is a steady feature of the IAEA Annual Reports since then. However, the IAEA only responds to a limited number of the transparency issues identified, above. I showed that member states where primarily concerned with the administrative transparency of the Agency and its function as an instrument of transparency. Further, there was some concern about safeguards transparency. However, the IAEA in its Annual Reports primarily responds by linking transparency to its administrative procedures and to its function as a forum to provide nuclear transparency. By doing so, however, it also responds to some extent to the accusations of political bias and ineffective operations.

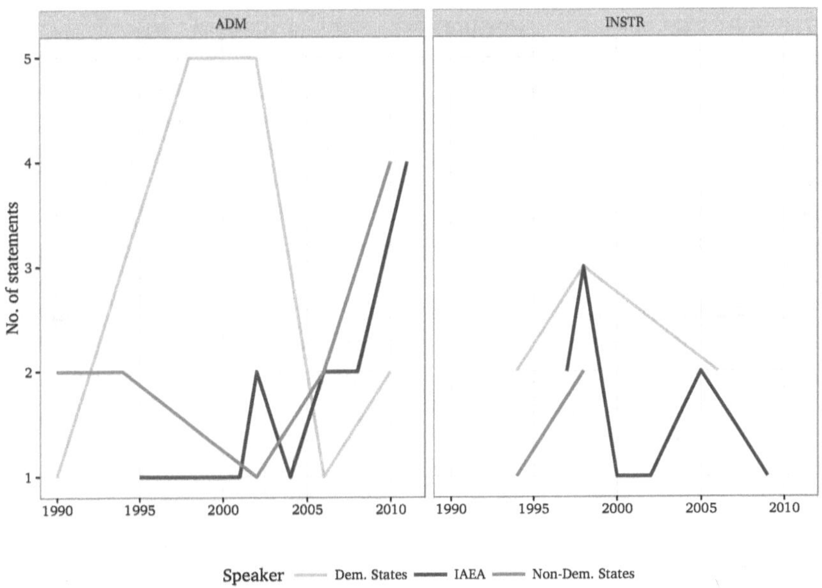

Figure 6.5: Transparency Statements of IAEA and Member States over Time

Figure 6.5 shows the development over time of those transparency statements. Overall, the states make more statements, which is not surprising given the source material: there are over 100 member states that could possibly talk about transparency at the General Conference, but the Agency only issues one Annual Report, limiting the possible references to transparency. Are there effects of democratic member demands on the IAEA's talk? The data show that there is some parallelism in the demands of member states and the IAEA talk.

First, looking at administrative transparency, the Secretariat seems to require some time to respond to state demands. States begin to discuss the transparency of the Agency's administration in the early 1990s. Issues like transparent staff selection, budgeting and programming are important requests from both democratic and non-democratic member states. However, the IAEA only begins to respond in the mid 1990s. This is puzzling because, as the plot in the first panel suggests, the IAEA seems to respond stronger to calls for administration transparency from non-democracies in the late 2000s. Thus, it seems to be less important if democracies or non-democracies demand transparency. Overall, this speaks for a mechanism driven by the necessary presence of the norm of open governance. Given the contents of the norm, transparency in the administration of public goods cannot be denied easily by the IAEA. It thus appears to be irrelevant which member states demands transparency. On the level of talk, the Agency needs to reply to those demands, because a justification of intransparency of the administration appears to be unlikely under the broader normative framework.

Regarding demands for the IAEA as a transparency instrument, the graph is more in line with the theoretical expectations. It is the democratic members that demand the IAEA to assure transparency through its activities. Also, the IAEA replies in a timely manner to those requests and starts to highlight its contributions to the transparency of national nuclear programs, nuclear safety and nuclear regulations. By doing so, the Agency also tries to counter the legitimacy challenge of biased operation, when underlining its goal to provide general transparency to all member states and to the whole international community. Of course, there is also some influence of the presence of the norm of open governance, which can be assumed to be another main driver for nation states to demand transparency about nuclear programs and nuclear safety mechanisms from other states. Also, these particular demands are closely connected to the increased authority of the IAEA. As discussed above, the risen political power of the IAEA is closely connected to its capability to assure unbiased and correct assessments of suspected national nuclear programs. As the data shows, this is also an important issue for democracies at the IAEA.

Finally, how do the changes in transparency rules of the IAEA fit the picture? Table 4.2 in Chapter 4 lists the main changes in transparency rules. From 1986 until 1998, changes in transparency mainly had the goal to respond to the increasing media interest in the work of the IAEA. After Chernobyl, the focus of the rules was on providing information to the press on the safety of nuclear applications. In the words of the Agency, "[t]he Chernobyl accident greatly increased interest in the activities of the Agency and hence contacts between the Agency and news media all over the world" (GC(31)/800, 72). As a response "the Agency distributed information material (brochures, pamphlets and press releases) in response to more than 2000 requests for information from the public. All brochures and leaflets on nuclear safety were updated, and two new brochures were distributed [...]" (ibid.). Later, with growing political inspection activities, the IAEA responded to even larger interest in its work, and reflecting its grown impact, by introducing media seminars, and by beginning to distribute official documents to the public and establishing de-classification procedures for GOV documents.

Next to the media visibility driven changes in public relation rules, the IAEA also responded to more detailed demands. For example, the new media strategy from 1998 included the goal "to enhance the Agency's interaction with opinion leaders, the media and civil society, reaching out to both traditional and non-traditional partners, for instance among non-governmental organizations and the private sector" (GC(44)/4, 102). This is likely a reaction to the changed reporting and perception of the Agency. Reaching out to specialized media outlets is no longer the only goal. The political implications of its deepened inspections required closer contact to civil society and "opinion leaders," also to promote an image of an open and independent organization.

There are also responses to transparency demands in the less politicized fields. For example, in 2000, the programming process of the Agency, which also relates to the technical cooperation program, was changed to a "results based methodology." "The advantages of this approach include: increased transparency; greater participation of Member States in programming, leading to better identification of their needs; better priority setting; and improved evaluation of performance"(GC(45)/4, 14). This change in the management process directly picks up state concerns about management transparency and relates, as discussed above, to the overal requirements of a strong norm of open governance. Again, and this time with a more direct focus on the technical cooperation program, in 2007, a new public relations strategy "aims to provide information on and raise awareness of the work of the technical cooperation programme and to build support for activities at the national and regional levels" (GC(52)/9, 79). Part of the goal of this strategy is to be more pro-active and transparent about the IAEA's development work. As an IAEA official put it during the 2012 General Confernce, the Agency was largely misrepresented in the media, only being portrayed as a political actor whereas its important development work was nearly invisible to the public.[28] In this respect, transparency and outreach aim at showing the other achievements of the Agency outside the politicized field of safeguards inspections, where its legitimacy is challenged.

In summary, both the IAEA's transparency talk and action thus appear to be influenced by member state demands and the effects of grown authority and politicization. Despite the lack of transparency demands from the media,

---

[28]Interview and observation of the author.

the increased attention the Agency receives is translated into more open media and outreach policies. These also help in defusing the legitimation challenges that have risen out of increased authority and politicization. In addition, since the 1990s, this process happens with a strong norm of open governance in the background. It provides scripts of appropriate modes of governance that include transparency. This has effects on member state demands. They increasingly link overarching ideas of IAEA functionality and effectiveness to transparency. Also, the IAEA administration, especially when producing talk, is influenced by this normative environment. Given the growing strength of the norm, it becomes harder for the Agency to ignore or defuse the normative pressure towards transparency (see also Grigorescu 2015).

6.1.4 Summary and Alternative Explanations

To conclude, this section shows how the causal mechanism identified by the QCA works in the case of IAEA transparency talk and action. Again, as Figure 6.1 illustrates, visibility and risen authority do not directly influence the Agency's opening up on the talk and decision dimensions. Rather, the configuration stands for the background condition of risen politicization of the IAEA. It is in this context, combined with a global presence of the norm of open governance, that the IAEA begins to talk transparency and decides to increase public access to its information. The influence of democratic members on this process is limited, underlining the power of the bureaucracy. As discussed above, democracies make more transparency demands than less democratic states. However, at least on the talk dimension, the Agency only slowly responds to general demands for more transparent administrative processes. The power of democracies is larger in promoting an image of the IAEA as an instrument of transparency, underlining the IAEA's independence. Democracies see the Agency as an important international body, efficiently creating and sharing information on nuclear applications, security and nuclear non-proliferation. Of course, this function also implies transparency in the governance of the Agency itself. The IAEA responds to these demands, underlining its contribution to those areas of concern and thus also accepting the importance of the value of transparency.

All these events occur around the same time. There is increased media visibility since the Chernobyl Accident in 1986. The IAEA responds with a more open way of communicating with the press. However, visibility again increases drastically in the 1990s. At the same time, the IAEA began more political inspection work. It is also in the 1990s that the politicization of the Agency's work begins to be strong. Democratic member states applaud the IAEA as an instrument of transparency, especially in the political inspection cases. Similarly, less democratic states begin to raise questions about the Agency's effectiveness and independence. The IAEA responds by further opening up and providing access to information, and by reaching out to new audiences like civil society. At the same time, it acknowledges transparency as an important norm for its governance activities.

The norm based mechanism thus works as expected from the theoretical assumptions. One might have expected stronger transparency demands from democracies. However, the sources of my analysis, i.e. General Conference debates, are already a strong filter. It is not implausible that states will be more open regarding their demands for transparency in more closed fora, like the Board of Governors or in private consultations. The same applies to the Agency's responses in its Annual Reports. Here, Agency talk is also filtered and more direct replies to state demands may be formulated at other venues. Nevertheless, it is telling that issues of transparency do show in the sources analyzed here, indicating a not so minor relevance of the issue of openness.

In this section, I only discussed transparency talk and decisions. Regarding participation talk, some interconnections already became visible. For example, the Agency's move to reach out towards new publics also implies rhetoric acknowledgements of cooperation with non-state actors. Thus, it would be implausible to assume a completely different causal mechanism to be at work for participation talk. Strong and diverse rhetoric about participation is also found around the same time in the Agency's annual reports. Further, politicization is likely to also cause demands from various actors to participate in IAEA decision making. Overall, the described norm based mechanism thus clearly shows that the opening up of international organizations in the security sector can be caused by configurations of norm based factors.

Are there alternative explanations for the described process of increasing transparency? Two additional explanations come to mind, that may also contribute. First, world cultural approaches would not be surprised by the high share of demands and replies to transparency of administrative processes. After all, a growing number of public administrations had to adopt the principle of transparency. Similarly, management attitudes like "results-based management" have spread to many international organizations, transporting certain values, like transparency and efficiency, with it. Second, the IAEA's organizational culture may also be quite influential for increasing transparency. Various factors could plausibly influence the IAEA's administrative culture towards transparency. First, there is high rotation of IAEA and other UN System staff. Second, there is also considerable rotation of staff from national institutions like universities or national research facilities that take over posts at the IAEA for a limited time. Further, lots of the local staff has a background in the Austrian public administration sector. All three sources of organizational culture may have also introduced transparency in the IAEA Secretariat as an important value of appropriate global public administration and global governance. In summary, these alternative explanations are worthwhile to explore in more detail. However, they appear to be contributing factors in the causal mechanism described above.

6.2   State Inequality in the OPCW: Driver of Organizational Opening

The QCA revealed that another mechanism, the first resource based mechanism, seems to be at work when looking at the organizational opening of the OPCW. Opposed to the norm based mechanism identified above, resource based variables, especially inequality between member states, are a driving factor of the opening up of the OPCW. This section discusses and illustrates how inequality leads to more openness talk, decisions and participation action. As a reminder, the QCA identified the following causal pathways to organizational opening of the OPCW:

- Opening talk is caused by a budget crisis in combination with high inequality.
- Opening decisions are happening in a context of high inequality.
- Participation action increases when there is a budget crisis and high inequality and a high share of democratic members.

It needs to be noted that the crisp-set score of membership inequality is constant in the OPCW case. The Gini-Coefficient of the members' annual GDP is above 0.81 during the whole period of investigation. Still, the variable helps to identify that there is a separate pathway to opening up when comparing both the IAEA and the OPCW. In the IAEA, there is less economic inequality between the members and the norm based factors like media visibility are much stronger. The OPCW thus helps to illustrate a case of opening up beyond politicization and high authority. Further, all these processes of opening up take place in the context of a strong open governance norm. However, as the OPCW only became operative in 1997, it is not possible to make strong assumptions about possible OPCW developments if the norm was not strong. Nevertheless, the presence of the norm is, as I discuss below, an important reference point. The Secretariat appears to follow the norm when reporting to state demands for transparency. On the following pages, I show that the tasks of the OPCW, the destruction of chemical weapons and the prevention of their proliferation, causes high information inequalities regarding the implementation of the Chemical Weapons Convention between rich and less rich states.

As discussed in more detail in the OPCW chapter (4.2), the organization's task of verifying chemical weapons destruction and verifying peaceful

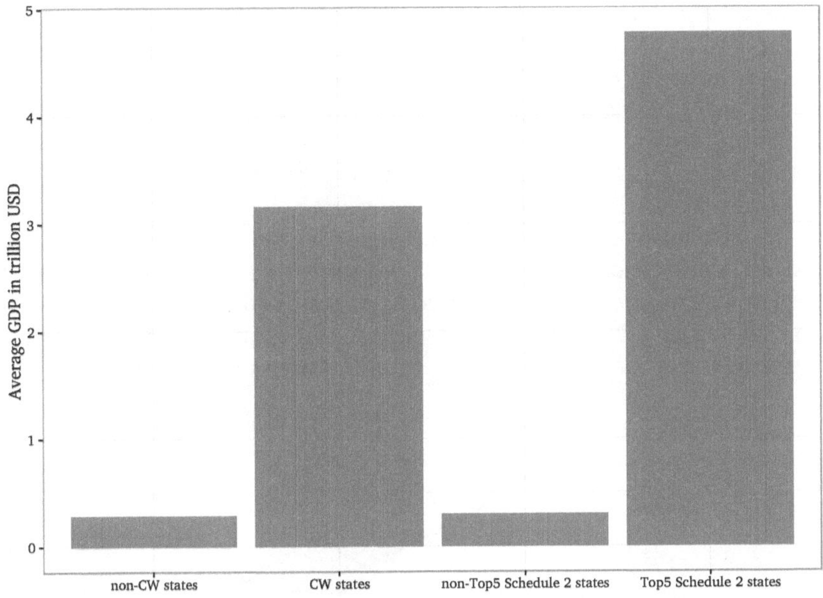

Figure 6.6: Average GDP for CW Possessor States and Non-Possessor States in 1997 and the Top 5 Schedule 2 Facilities States in 2011

chemical industry uses creates high needs for information sharing among the member states. Only if complete destruction can be assured and transparently demonstrated, all member states lose the interest in developing their own chemical arsenal. As the OPCW verifies the destruction of weapons, complete information for member states is even more important than in the case of the IAEA, where existing atomic weapons are exempt from the verification regime. In addition, states have the goal of assuring non-proliferation of chemical weapons and preventing the clandestine production of these weapons. In 2011, of the 188 member states, only 79 have industry facilities that need to be declared and possibly inspected. Thus, the states that do not have a significant chemical industry need to rely on the OPCW's assessments on non-proliferation because they lack experience, and often resources, to identify proliferation risks from others' chemical industries.

Further, the states with the largest remaining arsenals and with the largest chemical industries are large and powerful states. Figure 6.6 illustrates this by comparing the average GDPs for chemical weapons states in 1997 and the average GDPs of the top 5 states with the most declared Schedule 2 facilities in 2011. The average state without chemical weapons had a GDP of 0.29 trillion USD in 1997, while the average chemical weapons possessor state had a GDP of 3.2 trillion USD. The gap is even larger in 2011 for the states with the most Schedule 2 facilities. Their average GDP is at 4.8 trillion USD while the countries with smaller or no chemical industries had an average GDP of 0.3 trillion USD. These are stark contrasts and illustrate the strong need for information from the OPCW for the weaker states. To summarize, there is the potential for strong information asymmetries in two issue areas. First, the non-weapons states have less resources than the weapon states and thus require independent information on weapons destruction. Second, the majority of states has no relevant chemical industry and also has on average less resources than states with a chemical industry. Thus, to be assured of non-proliferation, they need independent information on the peaceful character of the chemical industries in the other states.

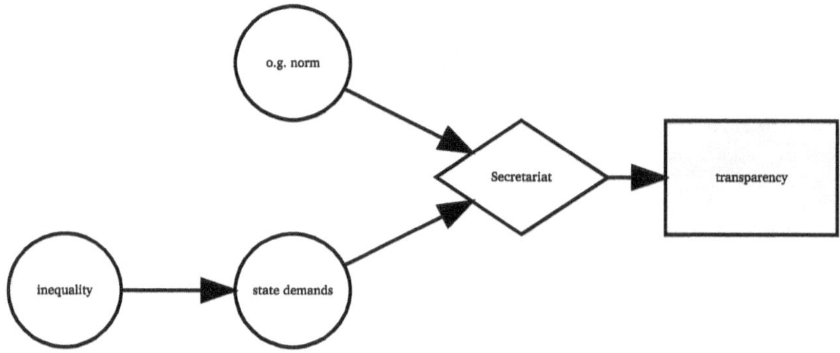

Figure 6.7: OPCW: Inequality Mechanism

There is thus a special interest of small member states to demand transparency about the destruction and inspection activities from the OPCW. Further, this inequality is also more important at the OPCW than at the IAEA because the former has only a very limited technical cooperation program. At the IAEA, most member states have an additional incentive to stay in the Agency for its wide range of development activities. At the OPCW, states gain little from technical cooperation which makes credible assurances on non-proliferation and weapons destruction an even more important task for the OPCW.

On the other hand, the powerful states with weapons and significant chemical industries have a certain interest in protecting crucial information on national security and in protecting their chemical industries from too costly and too intrusive inspections. The OPCW Secretariat thus needs to carefully weigh both sides of the transparency-confidentialty scales to assure that the chemical non-proliferation regime works. In the next section, I discuss how this inequality is made an issue in the member state demands for OPCW transparency. Second, I show that the OPCW responds to these demands only in a limited way. In its talk and decisions, it rather refers to a broader notion of transparency, which is directed at the public and not exclusively at member states (see Figure 6.7). At least in the Annual Reports, opening up thus appears to be rather driven by the global norm of open governance and thus by the emulation of global reference frames than by direct member state demands.

6.2.1 STATE DEMANDS FOR TRANSPARENCY AND OPCW RESPONSES

Compared to the IAEA, there is less data available on member state demands directed at the OPCW. One source are the *Reports of the Sessions of Conference of the States Parties*. These reports are summarizing the main agenda items of each CSP. However, they are consensus documents, discussed and negotiated at the end of each CSP. There is thus little room for individual states to voice their demands and there is little controversy given its consensus nature. Similar reports are available for the CWC review conferences. Those reports are a bit more detailed, but their general character is comparable to the CSP reports. As an additional source, there are limited numbers of *national statements* available. Some of them are distributed as official CSP documents, others are simply uploaded to the OPCW website in their original format. Their availability varies strongly from year to year and they are not reflecting the whole spectrum of member state demands. Nevertheless, they have some additional value, because they provide some unfiltered demands of the member states.

STATE DEMANDS

In general, the different documents allow the reconstruction of two main transparency dimensions of the member state demands. *First,* there is the general claim that the OPCW should be as transparent as possible. This demand concentrates on the core verification tasks of the organization, but also problematizes administrative transparency. However, the states also make it clear that there are strong limits to transparency and that confidentiality is an equally strong value for the OPCW's work. *Second,* the states use the OPCW as a forum to request more transparency from chemical weapons possessor states with regard to their destruction activites. Here, the OPCW is identified as an important organization that can help channel and enforce such demands.

In more detail on the first point, there are a number of state remarks about the general importance of transparency as a principle of the OPCW's work. Already in 1998, "[t]he Conference decided to task the Council to further discuss the issue of transparency, and to prepare a format for reporting information to the Council on the verification activities, including inspection results" (C-III/4, p. 6), underlining a need for open information in the OPCW's work. This is highlighted again and again over the years. For example, in 2006, Pakistan states that it "considers the transparency and confidence building measures of the Convention integral to its credibility" (Pakistan 2006, 6). Overall, states have a clear understanding of the OPCW as an instrument for transparency and of the importance of open information for the functioning of the regime. For example, during the Second CWC Review Conference, they again demand clear reporting of inspection results of the Secretariat "in the interests of transparency and continued assurance of States Parties' compliance" (RC-2/4, p. 13). Next to these broad and general statements, there is also concern for administrative transparency. For example during the financial crisis in 2002, when discussing the need for a streamlined Secretariat, the members underline that "focused efforts to develop and implement more cost-effective procedures and more transparent methods are needed" (C-7/5, p. 8). After the financial crisis, statements of this kind are only made less directly.

Despite asking for more transparency and underlining its important functions, the member states also clearly see the need for a strong role of confidentiality in the OPCW. The Second Review Conference underlines that "[c]onfidence in the OPCW's ability to protect confidential information is thus essential" (RC-2/4, p. 27). Many statements arguing for more transparency explicitly or implicitly bind the demand to some standards of confidentiality. Again, during the Second Review Conference, states vote for "improving OPCW classified verification reporting by providing more information", which however should be "consistent with confidentiality requirements" (RC-2/4, p. 17). In general, demands for confidentiality, and also for better management of the confidential information that states provide to the OPCW, are often made. Yet, the confidentiality system appears to work quite well: the OPCW's Confidentiality Commission, during the time of analysis, had not had to consider state complaints of breaches of confidentiality.

Second, while transparency and confidentiality are conflicting but not irreconcilable issues in the OPCW's work, the special importance of information asymmetries becomes apparent when states discuss chemical weapons destruction. Here, as discussed above, the effects of insufficient information would be largest for non-possessor states. Consequently, on the one hand, there are a number of statements demanding more transparency during weapons destruction. For example, Australia argues that destruction deadlines should only be extended if "predicated on effective management of the destruction process and high levels of international transparency and local security" (Australia 2006, 3). In the same year, there are also a number of demands for establishing a practice of Executive Council visits to destruction sites. As the EC is a state body, this again shows the states' need for credible destruction assurances. Such measures are often accompanied by transparency rhetoric. In this regard, the OPCW is often seen as an intermediary actor, managing state demands – "[w]e hope that possessor states will inform regularly and transparently about progress and difficulties they are facing" (Ukraine 2006, 4) – directed at chemical weapons states. In their statements, at least the USA as one of the largest chemical weapons states also picks up on the grievances of smaller member states. For example in 2009, the US promises that it "will continue to provide the transparency measures necessary to ensure that the Member States of this Organisation have confidence in our domestic efforts" (C-14/NAT.7, p. 6).

In summary, I have shown that transparency demands from member states in the OPCW context are primarily driven by concerns of information asymmetries. There is a large power and resource gap between the possessor states and the largest relevant chemical producer states on the one hand and non-possessor states and states without relevant chemical industries, on the other. Consequently, states see the OPCW as an important instrument to reduce those asymmetries by providing information, especially about chemical weapons destruction. However, confidentiality concerns are also raised to protect national interests.

OPCW RESPONSES

How does the OPCW react to these conflicting interests? The next paragraphs will show that in its public communication, the OPCW responds to the specific state demands only in a limited manner. In its transparency talk and decisions, it presents the general public as the target of transparency. Concrete improvements for member state transparency are only rarely mentioned. Overall, the OPCW secretariat appears to be relatively free in its decision to increase its transparency. On the one hand, this can be interpreted as a sign for the strength of the norm of open governance. Like in the IAEA case, the OPCW Secretariat commits itself to open administrative structures and an open information channel to the public. This is not publicly contested by member states. On the other hand, for the member states, in general, it would be hard to argue against increased openness towards the public while at the same time demanding more transparency for themselves. I would thus argue that there is a consensus among the member states that transparency is an important normative and functional value for the OPCW and that it should be supported, not opposed.

As discussed in more detail in the OPCW chapter (4.2), the OPCW refers to the value of transparency in its talk, it increases its organizational transparency by decisions and it provides increasing resources for public information over time. On the talk dimension, references to transparency are almost exclusively understood in the notion of information provision or the transparency of administrative processes. Further, the OPCW Secretariat understands the challenge to deal with both transparency and confidentiality. However, already in 1997, DG R. Pfirter takes a clear position when addressing the Second CSP, underlining the importance of transparency towards the general public and discounting state interests for confidentiality:

> "One of my most important aims is the development of a culture of transparency for the work of the OPCW. It is true that the Convention itself requires the protection of confidential information, and it is also true that it was this reassurance which allowed such an intrusive verification system to be accepted in the first instance. But the preservation of confidential information in the chemical industry needs to be balanced with the need to be as open and transparent as possible about activities in the military field. I therefore urge you all to strive to overcome the traditional reluctance which has grown up over the years in relation to chemical weapons-related matters and to develop instead a culture of openness on this issue, not only vis-à-vis the OPCW, but also vis-à-vis the outside world at large." (C-II/DG.10, p 4).

Further on this first point, the OPCW underlines its efforts "to increase understanding of its objectives" (C-IV/5, p. 37) and "to assist the general public and the news media to better understand the tasks and the activities of the Organization" (C-V/5, p. 39). This is often done by increasing its publication output, by providing information material for free and by using the OPCW website as a major information hub for the public. On the second point, the OPCW promises to establish "[t]ransparent and clear procedures" (C-VI/5, p. 55) in the administration to become "more transparent and [...] remain accountable to the Member States" (C-9/5, p. 21). This last aspect appears to be an effect of the financial crisis in the early 2000s, where the administrative procedures were criticized and where transparency and accountability are offered as insurances against renewed crises. However, this last point is not made explicit in either the public member state demands or the official OPCW rhetoric output. The OPCW's decisions for increased transparency are also mainly directed towards increasing information towards the public (see Table 4.3). Most decisions concern the publication of new kinds of documents which should reach wider audiences. In comparison, only a few transparency measures for member states are introduced. Those are mainly limited to new information databases (see e.g. C-7/3, p. 26; C-17/4, p. 18), providing scientific and industry information for the members and institutions in the member states.

In summary, there is thus an interesting disconnect between state demands for transparency and the actual transparency responses by the OPCW. The former are concentrating on information asymmetries. The latter resemble more the broad and general adjustments to transparency as a value of the norm of open governance. It is interesting to see that the OPCW Secretariat adheres to this value without explicit demands from the member states or the general public. This points towards an explanation of a general norm based nature, where OPCW members and the Secretariat become socialized with norms of open governance beyond the state. This, however, is closely connected to the general interest of member states for the OPCW to be a tool of transparency for the CW regime to function properly. Both effects seems to interact. Member states demanding transparency from their peers and from the organization they have founded have few good arguments to stop the Secretariat to become more open towards the general public. This is especially the case when measures directed towards the public, like the declassification of documents and the provision of information and publications also is beneficial to increase information about state compliance to the CWC. In sum, there is thus some interesting interaction between both norm and resource based mechanisms of organizational opening. In the OPCW case, the norm based mechanism of norm socialization also works without democratic socialization of the members or large-scale public contestation of the OPCW. The norm can ride piggyback on the more functional transparency needs of the members to reduce information asymmetries.

6.2.2 NON-STATE PARTICIPATION UNDER INEQUALITY AND BUDGETARY CONSTRAINTS

Finally, I discuss some evidence for the third mechanism that the QCA identified for non-state participation in the OPCW. The analysis showed that high participation occurred in times of financial crises under conditions of high inequality. However, as the following paragraphs show, I do not find strong support for this mechanism in the detailed source material for the OPCW. Participation is discussed in a functional understanding by the OPCW. However, member states seem to have weak preferences about this issue, which they hardly ever discuss in the official OPCW discourses. Also, an analysis at the actual non-state participation patterns show no large scale changes of NGO participation during times of budgetary constraints. Overall, the effect of budget crisis and inequality on non-state participation seems to be less direct than the QCA suggested.

Information on transparency demands already was sparse, the situation for non-state participation is worse. There are no statements in the CSP reports discussing the value of non-state participation. Also, in the member state statements, there are only four such statements. Here, states applaud current cooperation between the OPCW and NGOs. Also, illustrated by this statement of the USA, they underline that "[a]nother area which deserves greater attention is strengthening the Organisation's relationship with stakeholders and civil society, including industry and non-governmental organisations" (C-14/NAT.7, p. 4). Overall however, it is not possible to reconstruct strong demands for NGO participation from these spare statements.

When looking at OPCW references to non-state participation in the Annual Reports, the image does not change much. There are a number of statements that report on NGO involvement in OPCW workshops, conferences or other outreach events. Only very few statements provide insights into the possible logic of non-state participation. The few statements that do, underline the functional benefits of NGO participation like being "capable of contacting a much wider audience than the OPCW could hope to reach on its own" (C-VI/5, p. 47). This functional understanding is also highlighted by DG R. Pfirter when addressing the third CSP in 1998:

> "We have to recognise NGOs as a potent force, growing in importance and making positive contributions to national and international disarmament and non-proliferation programmes. There is a clearly identifiable role for the NGOs in the CWC regime. The very diversity of the Convention's range of concerns makes it imperative for us to harness the considerable potential of NGOs to help States to transcend any fears which they may harbour about joining and implementing the Convention. We are already working with a few NGOs, and I look forward to establishing lasting and harmonious relationships with many more. I am sure that the Member States of OPCW will echo my call when I assure NGOs that the OPCW will seek and find appropriate and positive ways of cooperating with them" (C-III/DG.12, p. 7).

These kind of statements suggest that functional concerns play an important role in the OPCW's work with NGOs, but there are no explicit references made that link increasing participation to information asymmetries or budgetary constraints. Consequently, I will next look at the kinds of non-state actors that frequented the CSPs since 1997. I do not find substantial changes, hinting at the assumed explanatory mechanism. There appears to be less participation of political NGOs during the times of budgetary restriction. Yet, it is unclear what drives this effect. On the one hand, it could be the OPCW steering participation in specific directions. On the other hand, it could be a lack of interest of these NGOs at specific times.

Figure 6.8 shows the number of NGO representatives of the four most frequent types of NGOs that have visited the OPCW CSP. The number of NGO representatives is of special interest here, because it reflects the power of NGOs to influence member states at the Conference on the one hand, and the amount of expertise they can provide during the event, on the other. Over the years, NGOs representing chemical industry interests are rare participants of the Conference of the States Parties. This group of NGOs is

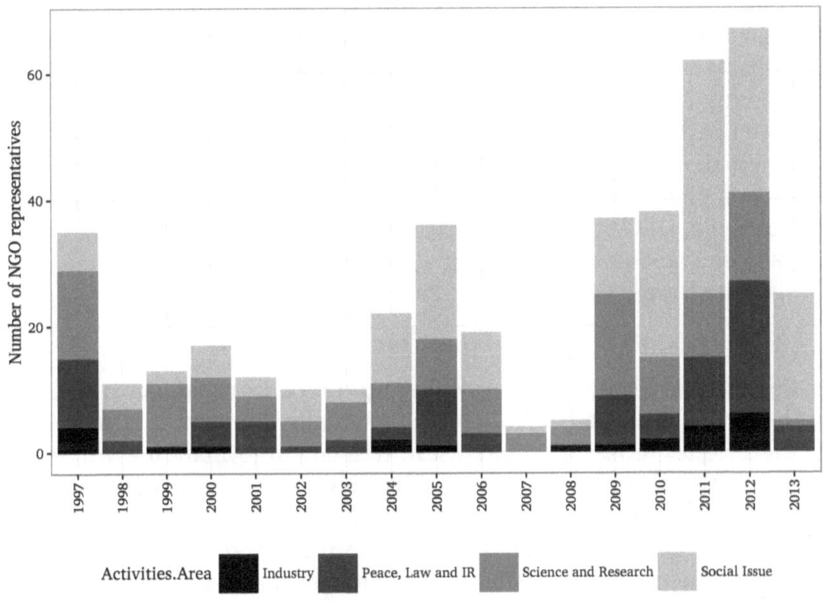

Figure 6.8: OPCW CSP: Number of NGO Representatives by Type of NGO

an important source of information for the OPCW and its members because it can provide important information on industry issues with inspections. Only in the most recent years have they begun to send a larger number of representatives. A second group with valuable input is the `Science and Research` group, including university research institutes on political, chemical and biological sciences. However, the number of these representatives has not changed much over time. The same is true for the advocacy NGOs for most years under analysis. The `Peace, Law and IR` group includes think tanks and associations of political scientists and lawyers that have political goals. Similarly, the `Social Issue` group includes NGOs that also have a political mandate but do not limit their area of activities on chemical weapons issues, only. It is remarkable that during the first financial crisis during the early 2000s, representation of the political advocacy group diminishes. During the second, but less dramatic, time of budgetary constraints during the late 2000s, there also is less participation of the `Peace, Law, and IR` group.

Assigning causal relationships and interpreting these developments, however, is difficult as no detailed documents on the procedures of NGO admittance are available. Under the resource based mechanism, it would make sense for the OPCW to limit participation of advocacy NGOs but not of scientific and research NGOs. However, the sparsely available data does not allow quick conclusions. It could be equally plausible that the advocacy groups chose not to send many representatives to an international organization that currently struggles under shortened resources, especially if initiating cooperation and joint projects is a goal of these NGOs. Overall, NGO participation remains a dimension of the OPCW's organizational openness that requires some additional research and new kinds of sources. There are a number of hints that resource based considerations play a role. For example, OPCW talk about participation is mostly functional. Yet, the sparsity of available data does not allow the formulation of a clear causal mechanism for the OPCW case.

6.2.3 Summary and Alternative Explanations

In this section, I showed that opening up on the transparency dimension of the OPCW is partially driven by the inequality of member states. Weak member states have a high interest in reducing information asymmetries in international organizations to be assured that all states stick to their commitments. In the OCPW, there is particularly large inequality between the chemical weapons possessor states and non-possessors, as well as between the largest chemical industry nations and those that have comparably small or no industries producing scheduled chemicals. In consequence, members often frame issues of transparency as related to information about the destruction of chemical weapons and about chemical industry inspections. While the member states use such a framing, the OPCW Secretariat rather justifies transparency as an important means for reaching out to the wider public, and not only to provide information to its members. This disconnect between outspoken state transparency demands and Secretariat replies hints at the interconnectedness of the norm based and resource based mechanisms of organizational opening in the OPCW case. As states demand transparency for their functional information needs, the Secretariat responds more in line with the norm of open governance, i.e. providing information about itself and its activities to wider audiences. This illustrates that the norm of open governance can also be effective in IGOs without large public visibility and politicization. Further, it illustrates that norm broadening in the implementation of the transparency norm, as described by Grigorescu (2015, 31f), is also happening at the OPCW. Confronted with normative pressure to implement the transparency norm so that it benefits member-states, the OPCW broadens the implementation of transparency to the benefit of a wider audience.

Regarding non-state participation, the image is less clear. There is very little talk about non-state participation and states hardly ever publicly voice demands for more participation. The Secretariat, if it discusses the issue, dresses its rhetoric in the language of functionality, highlighting functional benefits of non-state participation. Clear references to resource constraints or information asymmetries, however, are not made. This seems to suggest that participation is rather driven by resource based mechanisms. However, more recent developments in the OPCW point to the raising power of the norm of open governance. During the Third Review Conference in April 2013, the member states "[e]ncouraged the OPCW to engage in more active involvement and participation of relevant civil society organisations and chemical industry associations in the assistance and protection programmes" (RC-3/3, p. 24). Further, the Conference passed a resolution (RC-3/DEC.2) granting non-state actors more rights when participating at the CSP. The largest change is that a plenary debate is reserved for NGO statements. This is a large improvement for NGOs that can now directly and officially address OPCW member states and make their issues heard. This appears to be driven by the norm based mechanisms also identified for the IAEA. With the award of the Nobel Peace Price in 2013 and the ongoing inspections and destruction activities in Syria, public interest in the OPCW has risen. Granting more participation rights could be a plausible response.

Now, turning to alternative explanations, it is again notions of world culture and organizational culture, like in the IAEA case, that could significantly contribute to the understanding of opening up. For transparency, there is a plausible argument made in world culture approaches that the norm of open governance will eventually spread to a large number of international organizations. The OPCW and IAEA are relatively similar, also, their use of transparency talk is comparable. The same applies for transparency decisions. What is different, however, is the timing of transparency decisions. The IAEA started to adopt transparency rules much earlier. The OPCW is a much younger organization. Nevertheless, it is interesting to note that in 1997, the OPCW did not already start with a set of transparency rules with a comparable content like the IAEA rules. Rather, the turn towards information provision to the general public needed to be developed by the OPCW secretariat in its early years. Here, I argue, an adaption to organizational scripts of good global governance was facilitated by the high demand for transparency of OPCW member states. In the IAEA, this was achieved by increased public attention to the work of the Agency. Regarding organizational culture, it is also plausible that many of the new OPCW staff brought ideas about transparent and participative governance from their earlier assignments. Given that the OPCW is a non-career organization that limits contracts to a period of 7 years, there is constant inflow of trained IGO workers, often from the UN context, which transport United Nations ideas about transparent administration into the OPCW. Again, these two strands of alternatives are rather complementary to the explanations developed above and therefore warrant deeper analysis in separate studies.

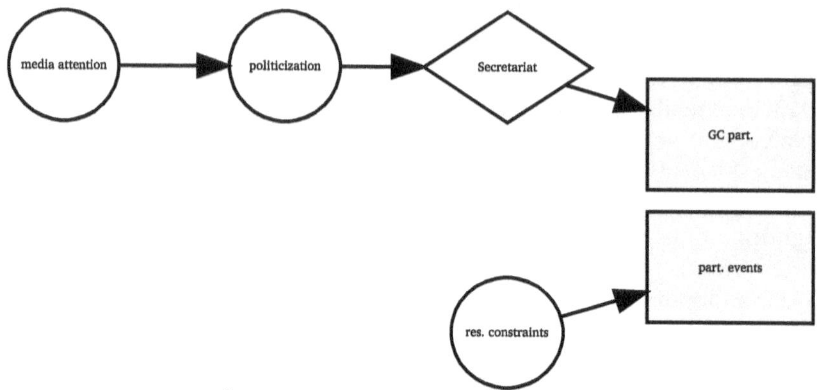

Figure 6.9: IAEA: Resource Driven Participation Mechanism

6.3   MEDIA VISIBILITY, BUDGET CONSTRAINTS AND NGO PARTICIPATION IN THE IAEA

For non-state participation at the IAEA, the QCA identified a second resource based mechanisms: First, NGO participation is expanding during the politicized phase of the IAEA since the 1990s. Here, it is high media visibility that is a sufficient condition for growing NGO participation. Second, for the IAEA during the 1980s when media attention was still low, resource constraints appear to be an important driver of participation events. In this section, I discuss both aspects in more detail. I first show how the IAEA invites NGOs to participate to have some influence over its organizational image that it wants transported by the non-state actors. NGO participation is used more as a tool for image control than for the representation of multiple interests. Second, I show how participation events, especially during the 1980s, helped the IAEA to overcome budget constraints. The Agency invited collaboration with non-state actors in fields where lots of expertise was needed that NGOs could provide at relatively low costs (see Figure 6.9). Overall, both processes show that participation of non-state actors was more often granted due to a functional logic, thus highlighting the power of resource based mechanisms.

6.3.1   NGO PARTICIPATION FOR IMAGE CONTROL

Media visibility appears to be an important driving factor of non-state participation in the case of the IAEA. While there may certainly be increased interest in the work of the IAEA from non-state actors, I highlight that the type of NGOs that are invited to attend the General Conference rather reflects a functional understanding of non-state participation. Further, I show that the Agency, in its strategic documents, understands participation as functional and as a tool for promoting its organizational self-understanding. This is in contrast to the norm based understanding, where participation is understood as a means to increase good democratic governance in international organizations.

How does the IAEA respond and react to the increased media presence it receives since the 1990s? First, the IAEA acknowledges that there has been an increase in media reporting about itself and that this has effects on the organization. For example, in 1991, "[p]ublic information work centred on the need to accommodate the surge in media and public attention on the Agency's Iraq related activities in the wake of the Persian Gulf crisis and United Nations Security Council Resolution 687" (GC(36)/1004, p. 152). Similarly, in 1993, "[p]ublic information work was largely oriented toward meeting the growing level of media and public interest in the Agency's activities. The interest concentrated on the difficulties experienced by safeguards inspection teams in the Democratic People's Republic of Korea and the many related discussions and resolutions of the Board of Governors" (GC(38)/2, p. 191). These kind of statements are present from time to time since the 1990s. For example, again in 2002, "[a]s a result of political developments during 2002, there was a sharp increase in interest in the Agency and its work. While part of this interest was in response to the worldwide discussion of the threat of nuclear and radiological terrorism, developments in Iraq and the DPRK also resulted in wide media coverage of the Agency and its involvement in these issues" (GC(47)/2, p. 9). Again, in 2005, "[g]lobal developments — particularly in the areas of verification and non-proliferation — as well as its own efforts to raise public awareness have transformed the Agency's visibility and public image over the last few years (Fig. 4). In addition, the award of the 2005 Nobel Peace Prize to the Agency greatly increased media interest and attention" (GC(50)/4, p. 10).

As already discussed further above, public attention towards the IAEA has risen since the 1990s, but only for the Agency's work under its verification pillar. It is interesting to note that the Agency reports that highlight growing media attention also try to make clear that the Agency tries to respond to increased media demands for information in a balanced way, i.e. especially highlighting its achievements under its safety and development pillars. For example, in 1991, a series of fact sheets was produced for media training, "covering topics such as nuclear applications in medicine, and energy, electricity and nuclear power" (GC(36)/1004, p. 152), i.e. all issues but verification. Similarly in 1993, "a range of press releases and publications were produced highlighting the Agency's technical co-operation activities" (GC(38)/2, p. 191). Even more directly in 2002, "[t]o meet this increased interest, the Agency adopted a proactive media and communications policy to communicate, on as wide a basis as possible, the Agency's important role under its three pillars of technology, safety and verification" (GC(47)/2, p. 9). In summary, as a response to growing media attention of the Agency's verification activities, the IAEA adjusts its media strategy to highlight its contribution to peaceful nuclear applications in the fields that are not related to verification.

As the Agency tries to develop a self-image of an organization based on a technical-scientific self-understanding, highlighting its achievements in nuclear security and technical development, it tries to partner with non-state actors to achieve this goal. The Agency's strategy documents of that time show that participation of non-state actors was seen as an important tool to transport this particular self-image of the Agency. This goal of non-state contact becomes visible in the Agency's *Medium Term Strategies*, which the IAEA has formulated since 2000 for 5-year periods. In the first strategy paper (IAEA 2000), the IAEA acknowledges that "[c]ivil society is acquiring an increasing role in shaping national and international policy, with the attendant need for enhanced and more open communication between the Agency and civil society" (ibid., 4). As a consequence, the Agency aims at "[d]eveloping new partnerships with private industry and other non-traditional partners while respecting the inter-governmental and non-commercial character of the Agency" (ibid., 18). When reading the Medium Term Strategy, it becomes clear that partnership with civil society and the private sector is primarily sought in relation to the Agency's technology and safety pillars. For example, research institutions are mentioned as a group of non-state actors that the IAEA should increase cooperation with. The second Medium Term Strategy (IAEA 2005) underlines this even further. Instead of aiming for large-scale outreach to civil society, the goal is now to "[e]nhance the impact of the Agency's work through strengthened relationships with Member States, development and funding organizations, scientific and technical institutions and the private sector" (ibid., 21). Scientific and technical institutions are now the main partners for the IAEA. This is in harmony with the goal to "[e]xplain complex, technical subjects clearly to the general public and media " (ibid., 22), where those kinds of organizations can help to provide important resources.

It is apparent the the Agency does not plan to increase cooperation with political NGOs, or think tanks and similar political actors on a larger scale. It does not respond to the increased media interest and politicization of its verification work by planning strategic partnerships with political actors. Instead, it tries to maintain its a-political character and therefore also aims for more technical relationships with non-state actors. This is also highlighted in the Director-General's addresses to the GC. For example in 1999, when discussing the new outreach and public information strategy of the IAEA, he underlines that "[p]art of that effort would focus on establishing a dialogue with private industry groups, nuclear research centres, the arms control and disarmament community and other relevant non-governmental organizations [which] should help the international community to assess objectively the advantages and risks of nuclear science and technology" (GC(43)/OR.1, 13-14).

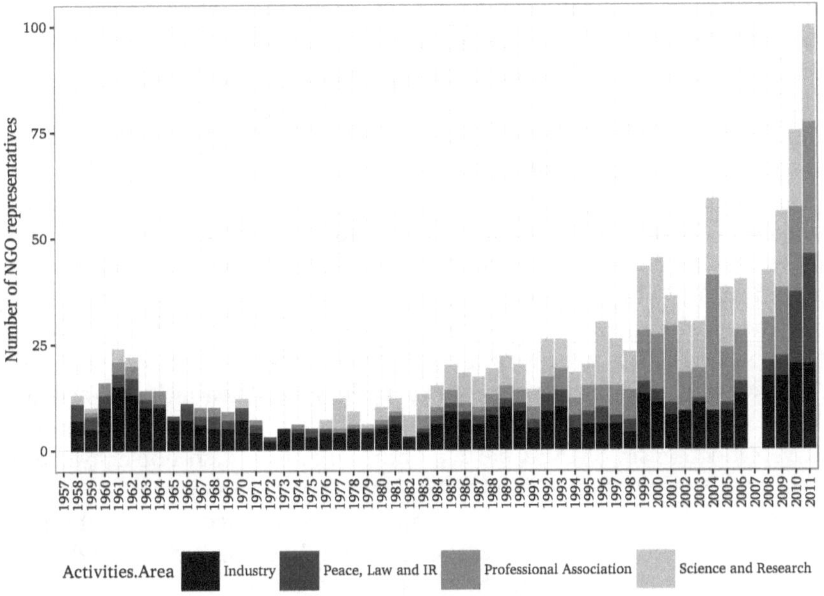

Figure 6.10: IAEA GC: Number of NGO representatives by type of NGO

Is this goal also visible in the actual patterns of non-state participation at the General Conference? Figure 6.10 shows the number of NGO representatives for the four largest groups of NGOs present at the IAEA's GC since 1957. There is missing data for 2007. The graph first shows that industry representatives, mostly from the nuclear industries, are a large group of non-state representatives since the early IAEA GCs. They have been present at all GCs. They were especially numerous during the early 1960s and again since the 2000s. A second group are think tanks and similar organizations that work in the field of Peace, Law and IR. They usually have a political agenda and not only a purely scientific interest. These NGO representatives are also present during most of the GCs, their numbers only rising in the most recent years.

For two other groups, there is a marked increase over time. First, scientific NGOs like chemical science or physical science associations or political science research institutes have increased their presence since the 1980s and again in the 2000s. Similarly, representatives of professional associations, like nuclear workers unions or workers in nuclear irradiation, strongly grow since the 1990s. Both kinds of NGOs are substantial in assisting the IAEA in providing information to more technically oriented audiences. The science and Research group includes large scientific associations of nuclear scientists and only a few political science research institutions. The scientific groups thus help the IAEA in communicating its more complex and technical issues, acting as multipliers of the technical image of the IAEA to the broader public. Similarly, the professional associations are also part of the larger expert community of the IAEA and less interested in talking about political issues at the GC or to their members.

In summary, the patterns of participation and the discourse around it suggests that the IAEA was successful in steering participation. It invited those NGOs to its GCs that help it to promote its image of a technical organization. There is no large scale participation of "true" civil society like chemical weapons victims organizations in the case of the OPCW. The participating NGOs are less interested in the political implications of the Agency's work and thus help to transport the specialized-technical activities of the Agency to their members. Overall, this speaks for a rather resource driven mechanism of IAEA participation. Due to the ad-hoc character of non-state accreditation at the IAEA GC, it is hard to say if there is a strong demand of "true" civil society organizations to participate or if the IAEA prevents or even tries to encourage participation. Answering this detailed empirical question is beyond the scope of this study.

On the talk dimension, there were clear references to global norms of transparency that guided the organization's discourse. For participation, both discourse and practice rather reflect functional demands of the Agency. Therefore, non-state participation in the IAEA should be understood as a strategically used tool. The pattern of participation shows that wide inclusion of different types of non-state actors is not the goal of the IAEA.

6.3.2   Functional Participation under Budget Constraints

Now, I turn to the second mechanism of IAEA participation, i.e. growing participation events under budget constraints. First, I show how patterns of participation action have changed during times with less financial resources during the 1980s. Second, I argue that the pattern is well in line with the overall functional understanding of NGO participation, as discussed above. This section illustrates the working of this particular resource based mechanism, as identified by the QCA.

For the IAEA, I identified two phases of resource constraints. The first ranges from 1983 until 1986 and the second one from 1993 until 2001. Figure 6.11 shows changes in the mean for the given time period for the

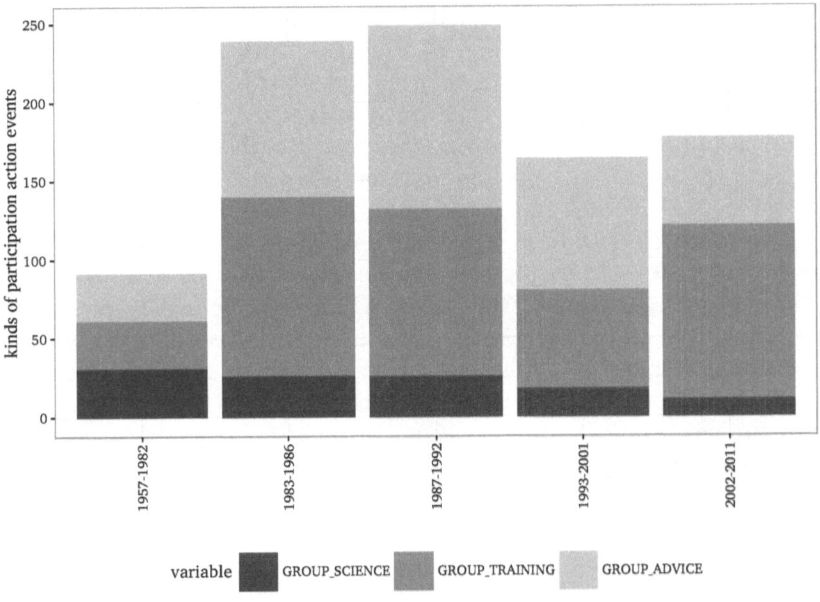

Figure 6.11: IAEA Participation Events during Times of Budgetary Constraints

main types of participation events (Science, Training, Advice) during those times of budgetary constraints (see Appendix B for more details). Changes for the first period of budgetary constraint during the 1980s are particularly interesting because this is the phase where the QCA identified the sufficiency relationship between resource constraints and participation events. Figure 6.11 clearly shows that there is an increase in the average number of participation events in the first phase of budget constraints from 1983 until 1986. As the different colors in the plot show, the increase comes mainly in the form of training events and those events that bring advice to the Agency. It is this last group that fits the expected mechanism well. Here, the Agency invites external expertise to comment, evaluate and adjust its activities, saving resources that would otherwise be required to gather the information on its own. Advice also remains high during the next phase with more stable resources. External advice thus seems to have become an important element of the Agency's participation events. Also, during the next budgetary crisis phase from 1993 until 2001, it is remarkable that while all participation events are reduced, events with an advisory character are now the largest group and are less reduced than training or scientific events. Overall, this suggests that the QCA identified a valid mechanism.

In more detail, under the advice label, there are events like meetings of consultants, of networks and of advisors. During the first budgetary crisis, common events were e.g. consultants meetings for the planning of the Agency's coordinated research programs (GC(28)/713, 27), for the IAEA's activities concerning the nuclear fuel cycle (ibid., 34), consultations on safety reviews (ibid., 39), on plant breeding (ibid., 41), on detection instruments (ibid., 48), on isotope data collection (ibid., 50), and on state nuclear materials accounting (ibid., 65). All these meetings and the many more that were held during this phase clearly have the goal to include external resources into the work of the Agency without having to prepare the knowledge on its own. Further, in the Agency's discourse at that time, this resource based logic also is visible. For example, when addressing the General Conference in 1986, DG Blix noted that "[i]n preparing the programme and budget in the future, it would be necessary to have the advice and comments of Member States attending the General Conference and the views of the many representatives and experts with whom the Secretariat was in touch in its daily work" (GC(29)/OR.269, 48-49).

In summary, there is some evidence for the effect of resource constraints on participation events of the IAEA. As the data shows, the IAEA increasingly uses external experts and consultants during the first phase of resource constraints. They provide expertise and knowledge on the whole range of IAEA activities that would otherwise have to be gathered in-house at higher costs. This is very much in line with the resource based mechanism that the QCA identified to be sufficient for the explanation of early participation in times when the norm based mechanism was not yet functional. Also, for the period from 1993 until 2001, when the norm based mechanism of visibility and politicization was also active, the data show that despite a general decline in participation events, the Secretariat was selective in reducing those events. Those that provide most expertise where cut only minimally as opposed to training events, where there is less direct input of expertise into the organization.

6.3.3   Summary and Alternative Explanations

To summarize, this section has found evidence for patterns of non-state participation at the IAEA that are more driven by resource based mechanisms. Participation at the IAEA General Conference has shown to be driven by selective participation, in line with the Agency's goal to promote itself as a technical and expertise driven organization as an effort to maintain its pragmatic legitimacy. Here, the QCA identified high media visibility to be sufficient for high participation since the 1990s. However, this participation is not universal and is not targeted at providing a democratic participation mechanism for underrepresented interests, as the norm based mechanism suggests. Civil society organizations, representing such interests like environmental issues or equitable development are rare visitors of the IAEA GC.

Instead, most NGOs either have scientific or industry interests. Also, for the early rise in participation events in the 1980s, evidence for the resource based mechanism is found. The Secretariat increasingly engages in expert and advisory arrangements to gather external input on nearly all aspects of its day-to-day work. Overall, as also discussed in the OPCW case above, the resource based explanations of organizational opening seem to capture the patterns in these two security organizations best. Only recently, in the case of the OPCW, there are some indicators that participation is to be understood as something more than resource gathering and may have a value on its own and for increasing the democratic quality of the organizations.

Turning to alternative explanations, in the IAEA case, organizational culture could provide additional insights into the mechanisms of participation. As discussed earlier, the Agency understands itself as a community of nuclear science and application experts. In addition, many of the Agency staff have working experience in national ministries or scientific institutions. Therefore, it is likely that they will look for external experience among their peers. This is especially the case under resource constraints when there are not enough funds for internal assessments. Again, exploring this path with different sources seems promising.

6.4 SUMMARY

With this chapter, I conclude the empirical analysis of organizational opening of the OPCW and IAEA. In the case studies above, I contextualized the working of the causal mechanisms of organizational opening that the QCA in Chapter 5 showed to be important. At the end of the previous chapter, I concluded that there was stronger support for the norm based than for the resource based mechanisms. As the case studies showed, it is now possible to refine this statement. As discussed above, there is some evidence that the norm based mechanisms are particularly powerful in explaining organizational opening on the transparency dimension. Further, resource based mechanisms appear to be strong in explaining participation in the OPCW and IAEA.

The norm based logic fits well with the observed processes of opening up in the IAEA. As I showed, transparency talk and decisions increase as a result of risen politicization of the IAEA's work. The IAEA responds to growing legitimacy challenges of the public and its members by providing more information about itself and its activities. There is some evidence suggesting that the IAEA Secretariat indeed understands transparency as a principle of good governance. Therefore, increasing rhetorical references to transparency and changing rules to create more transparency is a strong response of the IAEA, trying to counter legitimacy challenges from its environment. As the OPCW study shows, the power of the norm of open governance is also present without large-scale politicization of an organization. Here, states open a window of opportunity for the Secretariat when they demand more functional transparency to control compliance in the CWC regime. As states demand more transparency for themselves and from chemical weapons states, they have few arguments to stop the OPCW Secretariat from opening up the organization to the general public, as long as appropriate measures for confidentiality remain in place. Also, the OPCW's transparency talk shows that the Secretariat embraces the transparency components of the norm of open governance despite strong limitations that confidentiality norms put on its activities.

Opening up on the transparency dimension thus sounds promising for proponents of good democratic governance and optimists of global democracy. However, when looking at participation, optimism is limited. As the studies have shown, resource based mechanisms still seem to fit the observed phenomena best. In the IAEA, despite politicization and public contestation, participation remains driven by resource considerations as opposed to ideas of inclusiveness and representation. Since the IAEA of the 1980s, there are clear signs of participation aimed at gathering resources. Participation events are clearly targeted at experts of the nuclear community to overcome resource shortages. The same is true for non-state participation at the General Conference. Despite high public visibility, there are only few representatives of "true" civil society invited. Concerns like the social or environmental impact of the Agency's nuclear promotion activities are rarely represented. The majority of participating NGO representatives come from the IAEA's expert community. This pattern is becoming even stronger with growing politicization in the 1990s. In the OPCW, similar mechanisms seem to be at work during the time of analysis. Only in the most recent years, there is growing evidence for a rising power of the norm of open governance on the dimension of participation. Since the Third CWC Review Conference, the discourse on participation is slightly changing and participation rules are altered, acknowledging a wider role of non-state actors beyond resource gathering. In the concluding chapter, I will contextualize the findings of norm driven transparency and resource driven participation and discuss implications for international politics and our understanding of the phenomenon of the opening up of international organizations.

7   *Conclusions*

In this final chapter, I first summarize the main findings of this study. I discuss both the empirical findings and the status of the hypotheses and mechanisms discussed in my model of organizational opening. Also, I highlight how my findings add to the existing knowledge of organizational opening. I close this study with a short discussion of the implications of organizational opening for the democratic legitimacy of intergovernmental organizations. That section discusses some important normative consequences of the observed practices of organizational opening.

7.1   THE OPENING UP OF THE IAEA AND OPCW. MAIN FINDINGS AND EXPLANATIONS

MAIN EMPIRICAL FINDINGS

Organizational opening is a large-scale phenomenon and this study has shown that it also has an effect on the IAEA and OPCW. Both organizations are not the most likely candidates for opening up. According to Tallberg et al. (2013), the activities of both organizations incur high sovereignty costs. Such costs are a main inhibiting factor for openness. Further, both IGOs are not very central in the public perception of global governance, as the media analysis showed. Demands for opening up and normative democratic pressure from the public (Grigorescu 2015) are thus limited. Nevertheless, in both organizations, there was significant change. Opening especially occurred on the talk and action dimensions. Furthermore, opening up in both organizations is a process of incremental institutional change. At the IAEA and OPCW, there are no large external shocks that have caused sudden organizational opening. Rather, change is continuous and gradually builds on existing rules of the organizations. Thus, opening up is primarily used as a tool to maintain the organizations' pragmatic legitimacy. In the following paragraphs, I quickly summarize the main empirical findings. They are not only a novel contribution to our knowledge about opening up. They also contribute to the empirical knowledge about the IAEA and OPCW.

Starting with the *IAEA*, this study has shown that the Agency has made numerous references to participation and transparency in its talk. In its early years, the organization has talked about participation in a rather functional way. Non-state participation was largely seen as a tool to get expertise and knowledge. In more recent years, participation talk became wider, while remaining functional in its core. It now embraces issues like the inclusion of locals in development projects or the participation of women in the Agency's activities and projects. Transparency became an issue in the Agency's talk after 1990. Topics discussed related to transparency demands for member states and inspections. The administrative procedures of the Agency were discussed, too. Overall, there is thus some movement towards acknowledging participation and transparency as important principles. Most of the talk, however, remains functional. It highlights the benefits that transparency, and especially participation can have for the work of the Agency. References to both ideas as contributing to good and legitimate governance are rare. They occur from time to time since the 1990s.

Next, there is also some change in the transparency and participation decisions of the IAEA. As expected, rule changes on the top organizational level are relatively rare. Regarding the participation of non-state actors, there is only one General Conference decision. In the early 1970s, it formalizes an informal practice of the Director General who invited interested NGOs to the annual conferences. This informal practice became necessary because the formal mechanisms of non-state actor accreditation were defunct due to block confrontations. There is considerably more change when looking at transparency. On the level of operative rules, numerous decisions, e.g. media and outreach strategies, the handling of documents, and targeting publications, have made the IAEA more transparent to the general public over the years. There is, generally speaking, a shift from rules regulating information distribution to member states to a rule-set that aims at providing information to the general public directly.

In addition, on the action dimension of the IAEA, there is considerable organizational opening. Formal non-state participation at the General Conference, the highest policy making body, was already high during the late 1950s and 1960s. The number of non-state actors declines during the 1970s and 1980s and rises again since the 1990s. Further, there is a large-scale expansion in the number of non-state representatives that participate at the General Conference. Their numbers rise from around 25 non-state individuals from 1957 until 1990 to over 100 in 2011. In addition, there is a strong increase since the 1980s in participation events, i.e. IAEA activities with non-state participation like expert groups, workshops and seminars. Looking at transparency action, measured as the share of the Agency's budget spent for outreach and public information, there also is a high share in the early years and since 1990. Overall, participation and transparency have thus increased on all three dimensions of organizational openness.

For the *OPCW*, I identified relatively similar patterns of opening. Looking at talk first, there are also many references to the idea of non-state participation. Like at the IAEA, they are also strong in the early years of the organization. In the early 2000s, participation talk diminishes and resurfaces much stronger in the late 2000s. Again, like at the IAEA, early participation talk was rather functional. It discussed the cooperation with the scientific community and industry associations. Since the mid 2000s, talk changes to include a stakeholder language. It then highlights participation beyond direct resource gains. For both organizations, early participation talk is often about the establishment of formal or informal relationships with relevant non-state actors. Those actors should contribute to furthering the organizations' interests. Since the mid 2000s, in both IGOs, talk gets an additional layer, highlighting benefits of participation like inclusiveness and representation.

There was a high level of transparency talk at the OPCW since its founding years. The topics discussed resemble those talked about at the IAEA. They range from demands for state transparency to binding the organization to the goal of general transparency towards the public. This coincides with the occurrence of transparency talk at the IAEA, which also started in the 1990s, illustrating temporal similarities in transparency talk. Assessing the quality of references to participation and transparency, I argue that the 1990s mark a substantial shift for transparency as a value of good global governance. Both organizations link their internal processes of administration and rule-making to this particular value of organizational openness. For participation, the change occurs later, in the mid 2000s. Here, both IGOs slowly begin to acknowledge that participation is valuable for more than gaining external expertise. The inclusion of previously excluded voices becomes slightly more important. In summary, on the talk dimension, there is thus a visible shift towards values of openness that both IGOs commit to.

Concerning decisions, there is more variance regarding participation at the OPCW. The OPCW has no strict formal rules or a fixed legal status for non-state actors at the annual Conference of the States Parties. Instead, at the opening of each Conference, the member states decide which actors are granted access and which rights non-state participants shall have. This more flexible arrangement allows for more change in participation rules. For example, since 2000, NGOs and others are granted the right to access Conference documents and to identify themselves via placards at meetings. The largest change happened after 2011, when non-state actors got the right to address the Conference at a special plenary session. At the OPCW, there is thus a stronger movement towards participation decisions than at the IAEA. For transparency decisions, both IGOs develop comparable rules for access to information and outreach strategies over the years. Like at the IAEA, the OPCW's transparency decisions strengthen the direct distribution of information to the wider public. Overall, there is strong coupling between the transparency talk and decision dimensions of both IGOs. Again, this highlights that opening up is more than just a rhetorical commitment. Instead, the rhetorical binding of the organizations to the value of transparency is also translated into operational rules.

Finally, on the action dimension of the OPCW, there also is growth of non-state actors participating at the annual conference. Participation is particularly strong in the late 2000s. Like at the IAEA, it is the number of non-state representatives that grows strongest during this period. In the first five years, there were on average 17 non-state individuals at the CSP. In 2011, this number has risen to 68. For both IGOs, the participation patterns indicate that actual participation has become more important. Certainly, there may also be stronger interest from the non-state side in the workings of the IAEA and OPCW. However, as both IGOs have no strict rules on limiting the number of NGOs and representatives, this also hints at a certain interest of the organizations to invite more input from their non-state audiences. Looking at more informal participation, for the OPCW, it is harder to evaluate the trend in participation events. Since its founding years, the Secretariat has mainly organized training events. In addition, the share of advisory groups and scientific input remains relatively stable. Thus, it can be noted that inviting participation on this more informal level has become a common feature of both organizations. Finally, like the IAEA, the OPCW has increased its relative expenditures for outreach and public information. Again, this trend is strongest since the mid 2000s. For the OPCW, it is notable that during the times of financial crisis in the early 2000s, the relative share of the budget spent for transparency does not decrease. Publications, the web-site and other transparency actions thus appear to have a high value for the organization. For both IGOs, the rise of Internet technology, which is now among their primary outlets for information, has increased expenses for transparency. However, the data show that both organizations embrace the new technologies as a means to increase transparency. This is also highlighted in the dedicated Internet and social media strategies that both organizations have developed. Overall, transparency is thus also happening at both IGOs. They do not only talk more about it or pass rules on it, they also invest more money in the distribution of information to the general public.

My empirical findings confirm the findings of previous studies on organizational openness. In congruence with Tallberg et al. (2013), I only find limited change in the formal access rules for non-state participation. Also, the formal rules only allow limited participation in an advisory function. This is expected for IGOs with high sovereignty costs. Also, at both IGOs, rules are not strongly formalized. Further, there is no direct non-state influence on decision-making bodies. However, I add to the knowledge of non-state participation by showing that participation increases stronger on the dimensions that do not require formal rule changes. At both IGOs, talk about participation and participation action increase over time. In particular, participation events and non-state actor representation at the annual IGO conferences are a growing source of possible non-state influence on the two IGOs. Consequently, Tallberg et al. (2013) to some extent underestimate the already impressive change towards open organizations.

My results also link to earlier studies of non-state participation in security organizations. For example, Peter Mayer (2008) shows that security organizations are only likely to allow participation when non-state actors have crucial resources that they can offer. For this reason, for example, NATO stays relatively closed because there is little information that NGOs can provide to this kind of IGO, a military alliance. Security IGOs with a broader mandate like the OSCE, however, have more need of NGO input because their mandates include broader functions, like state democratization and human rights. Here, non-state actors have valuable knowledge. For the IAEA and OPCW, non-state actors provide technical information on nuclear and chemical issues that are valuable for the organizations' inspection tasks. From this perspective, it is not that surprising that non-technical NGOs are much less often participants at both organizations' annual conferences. My results suggest that such a functional bargain influences the whole range of participation talk, decision and action.

Finally, the empirical results also confirm Grigorescu's (2015) argument that non-state participation is often described as a non-democratic value by IGOs and their member states. At both organizations, participation is primarily described as a functional tool. Transparency norms, however, are harder to frame in a non-democratic way. This also becomes visible at the OPCW and IAEA. Both IGOs link transparency not only to a functional understanding of providing information to their audiences but begin to connect it to democratic oversight and accountability. Further, as the OPCW case illustrates, normative pressure with democratic values does not always have to be strongly voiced in the public. Despite lacking public exposure, the OPCW broadens member state demands for internal transparency to general transparency. It does so under the latent pressure of the norm of open governance, prescribing transparency as an important element of appropriate rule-making.

Evaluating the Explanations of Organizational Opening

How can these findings be explained? In the following paragraphs, I discuss the evidence that I found for my model of organizational opening. Its hypotheses are derived from norm and resource based explanations. Again, I show that mechanisms from both literatures are important to understand and explain the patterns of opening up at the IAEA and OPCW. I also highlight that the resource based mechanisms are strong in explaining participation. Transparency, however, is best explained by mechanisms from the norm based literature.

The first resource-driven hypothesis states that organizational opening occurs when an organization has few resources available. This study shows that for the OPCW and IAEA, resource constraints can help to explain patterns of participation. As the case studies have shown in more detail, both organizations increase participation action when resources are scarce. Non-state participation is thus used as a tool to gain expertise in the form of expert groups and other forms of consultation. Also, this increased participation action is closely linked to talk about participation. Thus, at times of budgetary constraints, there is also more talk about the benefits and utilities of non-state participation.

The second resource based hypothesis posits that the more unequal the members of an IGO are, the more likely it is that they will push for opening up to decrease information asymmetries in the organization. The QCA and the case study on the OPCW have shown that inequality indeed has some effect on opening up on the talk dimension. At the OPCW, I found that state inequality, illustrated by the strong economic differences between the chemical weapons states and non-possessors and the strength of the top 5 chemical industries, matters. Weak member states demand transparency from the OPCW and its member states to be able to assess compliance in the CWC regime. The Secretariat takes up these demands and translates them into wider transparency measures at the organizational level. This only happens because of a strong norm of open governance in the public discourse that the bureaucracy can relate to. There is thus combined causality of inequality and global norm change, where the latter is necessary for member state inequality to be effective. For the last resource based hypothesis, the effect of issue area complexity, I did not find evidence in this study. Complexity, understood here as an extensions of the organizations' mandated tasks, does not change. Thus, additional studies are needed with a design were complexity varies stronger between the organizations. Alternatively, studies could focus on developing a measurement of complexity of individual tasks like inspections to effectively grasp change over time.

The first norm based hypothesis argues that increased public visibility of an IGO causes opening. When IGOs are in the eyes of the public, their activities and procedures are under public scrutiny, causing legitimacy challenges that the IGOs need to react to. This mechanism is closely connected to the governance depth hypothesis. Here, the literature argues that legitimacy challenges to organizations also rise when they accumulate more political authority. The decisions and actions of IGOs with high authority have a larger impact on member states and individuals. The environment will thus increasingly demand (democratic) justifications for political authority. I find strong evidence for both hypotheses in the IAEA case. Since the 1990s, the Agency is involved in political inspections, which is also brought up in global news media. As a result, the work of the Agency is becoming politicized and a wide range of legitimacy challenges arise. The IAEA responds to some of these challenges by increasing transparency to maintain its legitimacy. At the OPCW, such a mechanism is not visible because it lacks both growing authority and public visibility.

The next norm based hypothesis states that an increased share of democratic IGO members causes opening. On the one hand, democratic members transport their domestic values to the policy-making processes in IGOs. On the other hand, they need to justify their rule-making in IGOs to their national constituencies, which they can do in democratic terms. Democratic membership appears to be influential when looking at the results of the QCA. Here, it has effects on talk, decisions and participation action and is necessary for transparency action. However, in the case studies, I found less clear evidence. For example at the IAEA, democracies demand transparency from the IAEA only slightly more often than non-democratic states. Also, the Agency responds very slowly to the demands of democracies. Transparency only becomes important in the Agency's discourse when both democracies and non-democracies demand it. Regarding transparency action, a high share of democratic member-states is a necessary condition. In both organizations, an extraordinary high public information budget only passes the budgeting process when democracies are in a majority position in the organization. However, there is little empirical material on the budgeting processes of both OPCW and IAEA to corroborate this finding.

Finally, the last norm based hypothesis is the one that finds the strongest support in the analysis of the OPCW and IAEA. It argues that the presence of a norm of open governance, including values like transparency, accountability, participation, inclusiveness and representation, increases organizational openness. Because the norm prescribes transparency and participation as values for good and appropriate governance, they become important reference frames. Agents in the IGOs, be it state diplomats or members of the bureaucracy, need to refer to the norm, especially when being confronted with related demands from their environments. In the empirical material, I find that the presence of the norm is a necessary condition for openness talk and decisions, and for transparency action. Also, the case studies have shown that the norm has become an important reference point for both organizations when talking and deciding about transparency. There is one exception: the early years of the IAEA. Here, openness was high without a strong open-governance norm. However, as the analysis has shown, participation was rather discussed in functional and resource related terms at that time. Similarly, the patterns of non-state participation then show that participation in the early 1960s meant something different to the IAEA and is far from the normative goal of including underrepresented groups.

In summary, there is thus strong evidence for a norm based explanation of transparency. The case studies and QCA have shown that the norm of open governance is an important frame of reference for the organizations' administrations. Also, a particularly strong norm based mechanism is visible at the IAEA, combining growing authority, visibility and a risen share of democratic member states. Even at the OPCW, that has seen little politicization and media attention, norms matter. As the case study has shown, the demand for equal information in the OPCW has introduced transparency into the organizational discourse. The Secretariat has picked up these demands and has extended them by relying on ideas of good global governance. Participation, on the other hand, still appears to be driven by resource considerations. Participation discourses in both IGOs remain largely functional. Only in more recent years is participation for representation added to the organizations' talk. Also, the patterns of participation show that a resource logic drives the selection of non-state input. For example at the IAEA, participation at the General Conference is mainly limited to the Agency's expert communities. The same is true for participation events, where it is especially advisory events that are maintained despite times of financial crises.

How do these theoretical findings add to the knowledge of previous studies of organizational opening? First, they confirm most of the explanations for non-state participation of Tallberg et al. (2013). Functional demands for non-state expertise is the strongest driver for participation at the OPCW and IAEA. The influence of democratic member states is also only limited in my study. In addition, there appears to be no strong link between democratic state demands for transparency or participation and the IGOs' response. In addition, I implicitly confirm that participation is inhibited by high sovereignty costs. At the OPCW, this point is often highlighted by member states when they underline the need for confidentiality and the sensitive handling of state information. In contrast to Tallberg et al. (2013), I find that the presence of the norm of open governance does have an influence on the non-decision dimensions of participation. Rhetorical references to participation beyond functionality and participation events increase in times when the norm of open governance is strong. In addition, I show that the analytical framework also holds for opening up beyond formal access rules. Resource needs and normative considerations are also influential for openness talk and action. Focusing on transparency, I find support for Grigorescu's (2007) finding that the transparency of IGOs is influenced by the democratic quality of their members.

What do we learn about the specificities of the opening up of intergovernmental *security* organizations? First, the general finding is that openness matters for security organizations, despite high sovereignty costs. Second, openness is constrained by high sovereignty costs. Third, regarding participation, there is only limited access and only specific non-state actors participate. Participation in security organizations is mainly driven by functional demands. In the concepts of Jens Steffek (2013), the dominating *pull factor* is that security IGOs seek non-state expertise. Consequently, their influence is mainly limited to the research and analysis phase of the IGOs' policy cycle. At both the IAEA and OPCW, there is only limited non-state participation in policy implementation. Also, compliance monitoring is only rarely handed over to non-state actors. Further, influence on the agenda setting phase in the IGO policy cycle is rare. Finding conclusions about *pull factors* is harder as I did not systematically study the reasons why non-state actors seek access. A quick look at the kinds of participating NGOs however suggests that they are quite content with their expertise provision function. Finally, transparency has become an important feature of intergovernmental security organizations. At the IAEA and OPCW, increases in transparency appear to be primarily norm-driven. I do not find strong effects of IGO resources or public visibility. Thus, it appears that with the reservation of states' confidentiality requirements, an effective distribution of information about activities, evaluations and policy goals is as important to IGOs in the security as in other fields.

How has the choice of QCA as a methodology influenced the findings of this study? QCA was particularly helpful in managing the explanations for the multi-dimensional concept of organizational opening. Also, it helped to show where explanations for the different dimensions overlap. Further, QCA was important for my development of measures of *change* in openness. The calibration procedure and the related robustness checks highlight the need to develop clear definitions of change of the many variables. Finally, the method was useful in eliminating explanatory variables from the case study analysis. As my discussion in the case study chapter shows, this second step in my research design was essential to make sense of the causal combinations that the QCA identified. As many variables in my data-set covary, the case studies were necessary to check the plausibility of causal relationships by checking for additional evidence from the empirical material. In the end, the three-step research design has produced results with relatively high confidence in the proposed causal mechanisms.

7.2 Organizational Opening and the Democratic Legitimacy of Security IGOs

My empirical findings have normative implications, which I will discuss in the remainder of this concluding chapter. What do we learn about the democratic legitimacy of the IAEA and OPCW from the observed patterns of transparency and non-state participation? First, I discuss implications of increased transparency. Here, I argue that increasing transparency has helped both organizations to manage their legitimacy. More specifically, the increased distribution of information helps them to present themselves as accountable places of governance despite the high levels of confidentiality that they need to uphold. As a result, their democratic credentials have improved. Second, I show how non-state participation at both IGOs is still far from fulfilling its ideal-type democratizing function. Both IGOs use non-state actors instrumentally for their purposes. They understand them as a democratizing force only in a very limited way. Instead, perceptions of non-state actors as suppliers of expert information are dominant. Consequently, there are still large potentials in democratic non-state participation at the OPCW and IAEA.

What are the criteria for evaluating the democratic quality of an IGO with regard to *transparency*? First, for transparency to have a democratic effect, it is important that information is made available in an unfiltered form directly to the general public (see Grigorescu 2003). Thanks to the Internet and IGO investments in using this technology, information is easily accessible for the general public. At the IAEA, next to publications, safety standards, journals and information brochures, nearly all official documents can be searched and downloaded on the Agency's website. Furthermore, since the most recent years, the IAEA is live-streaming the General Conference on the Internet, making it accessible to everyone with a decent Internet connection. However, there are limits for documents of the Board of Governors. The proceedings and other official board documents are only made available to the public upon the Board's decision. As a consequence, many influential Board reports are only available as leaked documents. Otherwise, most of the decision-making procedures of the organization are transparent to the general public. At the OPCW, transparency is even higher. Information material, technical documents and inspection results are available for download. Also, Conference of the States Parties and also Executive Council documents and statements are available. Further, although there are no verbal proceedings of the Conference, some member statements are available. In recent years, the OPCW has also started live-streaming the Conference on YouTube and has archived past Conferences. In this regard, decision-making processes are even more comprehensible than at the IAEA.

From a normative point of view, this level of transparency is quite promising. Transparency is especially important to hold IGOs accountable. IGO decision-making happens in forums far from direct public visibility and contestation. Also, national publics do not only require IGO transparency to control their activities. In addition, IGO transparency is necessary for the control of their own governments that frequently delegate governance tasks to IGOs (Grigorescu 2015, 135f). At both IGOs, transparency appears to fulfill that function quite well. Both organizations document and publish their decision-making processes and report about their activities. Interested individuals thus have the possibility to contest IAEA and OPCW decisions and hold their governments responsible for their policies in those organizations. In summary, IGO transparency thus has a positive effect on the democratic quality of the organizations. As the study has shown, the organizations also actively legitimize themselves by highlighting their transparency. Since the 1990s, both IGOs frequently talk about their public information strategies and present their measures to increase access to information. Considering the only modest demands and criticism based on transparency from their member states, both IGOs appear to have successfully included transparency into their repertoire of legitimacy maintenance.

The normative assessment of non-state participation at the IAEA and OPCW is less enthusiastic. Theorists of democratic participation applaud NGO access when it helps to *(a)* represent ideas and interests that are not adequately represented by state officials, *(b)* create a fair, equal and well informed deliberative process of policy making and *(c)* establish mechanisms of political accountability. This requires a balanced participation of NGOs that indeed speak for underrepresented interests and introduce alternative ideas into political deliberations. Further, non-state actors need to be independent of states to provide additional accountability (see e.g. Bexell, Tallberg and Uhlin 2010; Charnovitz 2003). At the OPCW and IAEA, these criteria are hardly met. As the empirical discussion in this study has shown, non-state participation is very limited. The patterns of participation at the annual conference, for example, show that the majority of represented non-state actors are part of the larger epistemic communities of the organizations. At the IAEA, the General Conference is more of a gathering of like-minded experts on nuclear applications than an open discussion forum on nuclear issues. Critical voices are rare and the largest non-state critics of the IAEA, environmental NGOs, are not represented. At the OPCW, most non-state actors are also closely linked to the chemical industry and non-proliferation community. Here, however, some actors like victims associations and environmental NGOs provide some limited alternative views to the dominant community discourse. The same can be said for research institutions that are participating in both IGOs. They do provide independent analysis of the organizations. Yet, they define their purpose as academic analysis and not advocacy. In summary, representation of underrepresented groups, a strengthening of the deliberative process and accountability are not the main achievements of non-state participation at the OPCW or IAEA. Participation thus hardly democratizes the organizations.

This finding is also supported by the organizations' discourse about non-state participation. At both IGOs, in the majority of cases, participation is framed as a functional tool to gather expertise. This de-democratization of the norm of participation is also visible in other intergovernmental organizations (Grigorescu 2015, 180). Many IGOs frame participation as a mechanism of expert advice. Consequently, they also often highlight why non-state actors are not capable of improving democracy. Here, IGOs echo concerns of representativeness, equal participation opportunities and the accountability of the non-state actors themselves. In this way, they intentionally strip participation of its democratic value. This can also be shown in diplomatic discourses on non-state participation. Diplomats are highly skeptical of the democratic quality of NGOs, too and thus question their democratizing potential (Weise 2015).

At the end of this study, the lessons for better, more democratic global governance are the following: *First,* organizational opening has increased organizational transparency. This has improved chances of more public contestation of IGO policies. Further, it has helped to create more accountability of national governments for their activities in IGOs. Hopes for more democratic governance can thus be put on transparency as a norm of global rule making. Its acceptance in security IGOs shows that IGO resistance to become more transparent will be hard to uphold. *Second,* hopes for strong democratizing effects of non-state actors are low. Certainly, security organizations are not the first place to expect the blossom of democratic participation. Yet, the analysis suggests that the framing of participation as a non-demoratic resource based tool likely also holds for a whole range of intergovernmental organizations. To overcome this hurdle, global civil society needs to overcome its own democratic deficits. This will be crucial to convince IGO administrations and state diplomats of their potential to build more equitable and democratic systems of global governance.

A   Constructing the Raw Dataset

This appendix tries to make the construction of the raw data-set reproducible.
It lists the *R* code that I used to create and transform the data. It also hints at
other data files, e.g. from the qualitative data coding and more detailed data-
sets, e.g. on the participation of NGOs or the budgets of the organizations.
These files are available in the electronic data appendix.

For the analysis, I used the following R packages:[29]

```
library(knitr)
library(XML)
library(dplyr)
library(ineq)
library(reshape2)
library(countrycode)
library(psData)
library(ggplot2)
```

---

[29]Vincent Arel-Bundock (2014). countrycode: Convert country names and country codes. R
package version 0.17. http://CRAN.R-project.org/package=countrycode. David B. Dahl (2014).
xtable: Export tables to LaTeX or HTML. R package version 1.7-4. http://CRAN.R-project.org/
package=xtable. Daróczi, G. (2014). pander: An R Pandoc Writer. R package version 0.5.1,
URL http://cran.r-project.org/package=pander Ingo Feinerer and Kurt Hornik (2014). tm: Text
Mining Package. R package version 0.6. http://CRAN.R-project.org/package=tm. Christopher
Gandrud (2014). psData: A package to download regularlymaintained political science data
sets and make commonly used, but infrequently updated variables based on this data. R package
version 0.1.2. http://CRAN.R-project.org/package=psData. Garrett Grolemund, Hadley Wickham
(2011). Dates and Times Made Easy with lubridate. Journal of Statistical Software, 40(3),
1-25. http://www.jstatsoft.org/v40/i03/. Duncan Temple Lang (2013). XML: Tools for parsing
and generating XML within R and S-Plus.. R package version 3.98-1.1. http://CRAN.R-project.
org/package=XML. Duncan Temple Lang (2013). RCurl: General network (HTTP/FTP/...) client
interface for R. R package version 1.95-4.1. http://CRAN.R-project.org/package=RCurl. Duncan
Temple Lang (2014). RJSONIO: Serialize R objects to JSON, JavaScript Object Notation. R
package version 1.3-0. http://CRAN.R-project.org/package=RJSONIO. Hadley Wickham (2007).
Reshaping Data with the reshape Package. Journal of Statistical Software, 21(12), 1-20. URL
http://www.jstatsoft.org/v21/i12/. H. Wickham. ggplot2: elegant graphics for data analysis.
Springer :New York, 2009. Hadley Wickham and Romain Francois (2014). dplyr: A Grammar
of Data Manipulation. R package version 0.3.0.2. http://CRAN.R-project.org/package=dplyr.
Yihui Xie (2014). knitr: A general-purpose package for dynamic report generation in R. R
package version 1.7. Achim Zeileis (2014). ineq: Measuring Inequality, Concentration, and
Poverty. R package version 0.2-13. http://CRAN.R-project.org/package=ineq.

```
library(RCurl)
library(RJSONIO)
library(pander)
library(xtable)
library(lubridate)
library(tm)
```

A.1   Dependent Variables

First, I collected a number of dependent variables on transparency and
participation in intergovernmental organizations. Below, I will document
how I created the individual variables and how I collected and transformed
the data. In most cases, the same steps are necessary to create the data
for both IAEA and OPCW. If this is not the case, I document the different
procedures.

A.1.1   TALK-Participation

IAEA

- References to norm of participation in the Annual Report
- Source: number of statements in the Annual Report that refer to the
  idea of participation, inclusion and representation of non-state actors
  like NGOs, business groups or experts.
- Data derived from qualitative coding. See the IAEA RQDA file and the
  instructions to export the TALK-Participation codes.

```
#create empty data-set
data <- data.frame(IO=c(rep("IAEA", 55), rep("OPCW", 15)),
                   Year = c(1957:2011, 1997:2011),
                       Decade = c(
                           rep("1950s", 4),
                           rep("1960s", 10),
                           rep("1970s", 10),
                           rep("1980s", 10),
                           rep("1990s", 10),
                           rep("2000s", 10), "2010s",
                           rep("1990s", 4),
                           rep("2000s", 10),
                               "2010s"))


# import codings from RQDA file
## this is commented here, as it breaks the knitr chain
#RQDA::openProject("../data/IAEA.rqda")
#iaea_codings <- RQDA::getCodingTable()
```

```r
#iaea_summary <- iaea_codings %>% group_by(filename, codename)
        #%>% summarise(n = n())
#save(iaea_summary, file = "iaea_summary")
load("../data/iaea_summary")


# filter for relevant codings and add to dataset
iaea_part <- as.data.frame(filter(iaea_summary,
                                  codename == "TALK-Participation"))$n


# replace "missings" with 0 because they are true zeros
data$TALK.Part <- rep(NA, 70)
data$TALK.Part[which(data$IO == "IAEA")] <-
    c(iaea_part[1:5], rep(0, 2),
        iaea_part[6], rep(0, 4),
        iaea_part[7], rep(0, 16),
        iaea_part[8:9], rep(0, 2),
        iaea_part[10], rep(0,2),
        iaea_part[11:14], 0,
        iaea_part[15:28])
```

OPCW

```r
# import my codings data from RQDA
#RQDA::openProject("../data/OPCW.rqda")
#codings <- RQDA::getCodingTable()
#opcw_summary <- codings %>% group_by(filename, codename)
    #%>% summarise(n = n())
#save(opcw_summary, file = "opcw_summary")
load("../data/opcw_summary")


# filter for relevant codings and add to dataset
opcw_part <- as.data.frame(filter(opcw_summary,
                                  codename == "TALK-Participation"))$n


# replace "missings" with 0 because they are true zeros
data$TALK.Part[which(data$IO == "OPCW")] <-
    c(0, opcw_part[1:7], 0,
    opcw_part[8:13])
```

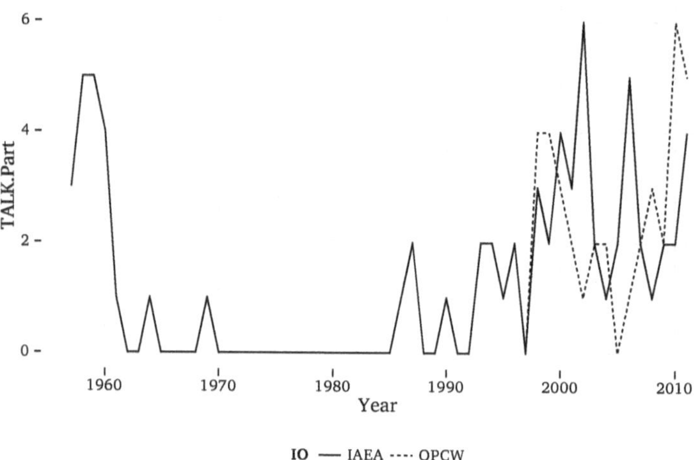

A.1.2   TALK-TRANSPARENCY

IAEA

- References to norm of transparency in the Annual Report
- Source: number of statements in the Annual Report that refer directly to the principle of transparency.
- see IAEA RQDA file and instructions to get TALK-Transparency codings.

```
# filter for relevant codings and add to dataset
iaea_trans <- as.data.frame(filter(iaea_summary,
                     codename == "TALK-Transparency"))$n

data$TALK.Trans <- rep(NA, 70)
data$TALK.Trans[which(data$IO == "IAEA")] <-
    c(rep(0, 36), iaea_trans[1], 0,
        iaea_trans[2], 0, iaea_trans[3:4], 0,
        iaea_trans[5:11], 0, iaea_trans[12:13], 0,
        iaea_trans[14])
```

OPCW

```
# filter for relevant codings and add to dataset
opcw_trans <- as.data.frame(filter(opcw_summary,
                     codename == "TALK-Transparency"))$n

data$TALK.Trans[which(data$IO == "OPCW")] <-
```

```
c(0, opcw_trans[1:6], 0, opcw_trans[7],
    0, opcw_trans[8:12])
```

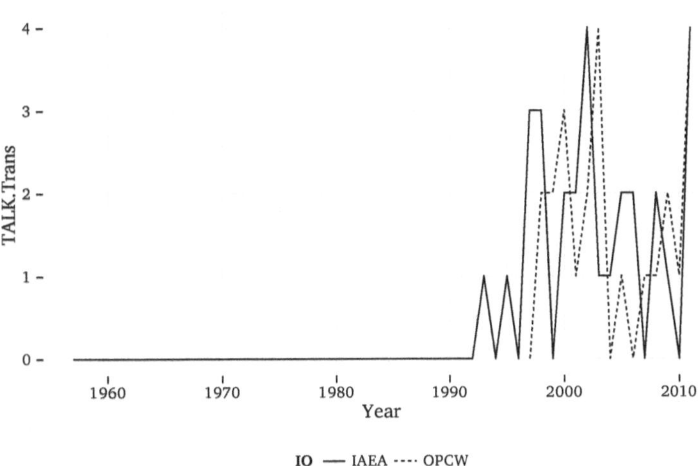

A.1.3 DECISION-PARTICIPATION

IAEA

- Decisions that increase participation
- Source: General Conference resolutions, secondary literature
- 2 Levels:

    - 1: 1957-1974: fixed rules for consultation and participation in GC, yet, not really enacted after 1959
    - 2: 1975-2011: keeping the rules, yet allowing ad-hoc invitations to participate at GC without formal consultative status by GOV.

```
data$DEC.Part <- rep(NA, 70)
data$DEC.Part[which(data$IO == "IAEA")] <-
    c(rep(1, 18), rep(2, 37))
```

OPCW

- 3 levels:

    - 1997-1999: ad-hoc rules for passive participation
    - 2000-2002: plus access to official CSP documents
    - 2003-2011: plus limited rights to address meetings

```
data$DEC.Part[which(data$IO == "OPCW")] <-
    c(rep(1, 3), rep(2, 3), rep(3, 9))
```

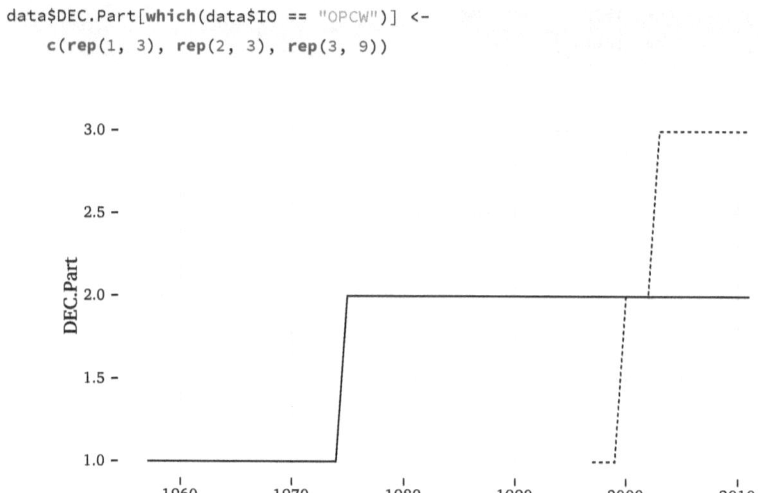

A.1.4   DECISION-TRANSPARENCY

IAEA

- Decisions that increase transparency
- Source: Annual Report, General Conference resolutions and GOV decisions
- From the AR research, I propose the following 12 phases of transparency relevant decisions.

  - 1: base-line policy: mainly reactive outreach to media, partially during phases of little public demand for IAEA transparency
  - 2: issuing IAEA newsbriefs
  - 3: IAEA Highlights publication
  - 4: new PR policy: e.g. with media seminars
  - 5: Launch of IAEA website
  - 6: distribution of electronic official documents through website to public
  - 7: partial de-classification of GOV documents
  - 8: new PR strategy: outreach to non-traditional actors
  - 9: new TC policy: increase transparency
  - 10: new PR strategy: pro-active and distribution of Agency publications for free

- 11: New PR strategy: increase outreach to devlopment community
- 12: Using social media

```
data$DEC.Trans <- rep(NA, 70)
data$DEC.Trans[which(data$IO == "IAEA")] <-
    c(rep(1, 29), rep(2, 3), 3, rep(4, 3),
        5, 5, 6, 7, 7, 8, 8, 9, 9, rep(10, 5),
        11, 11, 11, 12, 12)
```

OPCW

- There are the following levels of increased transparency decisions, taken from the Annual Reports and CoSP-Resolutions

    - 1: 1997: starting level, with website and publications, yet targeted primarily towards the Member States
    - 2: 1998: increasing publications output, aiming at broader audiences and starting library
    - 3: 1999: re-worked website policy: now also targeted at general public
    - 4: 2000: Expansion of Website. "Synthesis" Journal available online for free, course material for national authorities available online
    - 5: 2002: new publications targeted at general public: OPCW Profiles, "Basic Facts" re-issue, Flyers on Basic Information
    - 6: 2003: outreach strategy aiming at broader geographical reach, launch of new publications: "OPCW Regional Series", "Chemical Disarmament Quarterly"
    - 7: 2008: participation in "Open Day", i.e. opening its doors to the public for 1 day, increased outreach to research institutions, website with more official documents
    - 8: 2010: starting social media activities, development of a new "Public Diplomacy Strategy" and Task Force, first steps of live reporting of OPCW events.

```
data$DEC.Trans[which(data$IO == "OPCW")] <-
    c(1, 2, 3, 4, 4, 5, rep(6, 5), 7, 7, 8, 8)
```

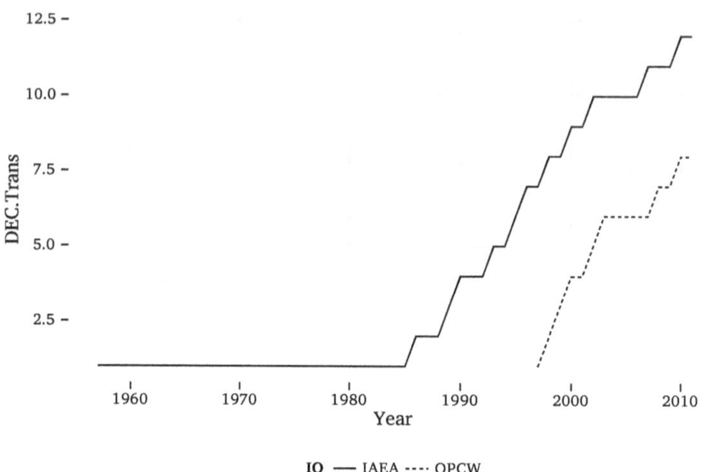

A.1.5   ACTION-PARTICIPATION-GC-NGO-PRESENT

IAEA

- Number of NGOs present at annual General Conference
- Source: Number of Non-Governmental Organizations in official list of delegations

```
# importing my data-set on IAEA GC participation
iaea_gc_ngo <- read.csv('../data/IAEA-GC-NGOs.csv')

data$ACT.Part.1 <- rep(NA, 70)
data$ACT.Part.1[which(data$IO == "IAEA")] <-
    iaea_gc_ngo$NGO.present
```

OPCW

- Number of NGOs present at the annual Session of the Conference of State Parties
- Source: Lists of CSP Participants (from OPCW Documents Office)

```
# importing my data on OPCW participation
opcw_ngo <- read.csv2('../data/OPCW-CSP-NGO.csv')
data$ACT.Part.1[which(data$IO == "OPCW")] <-
    opcw_ngo$SUM.NGOS[1:15]
```

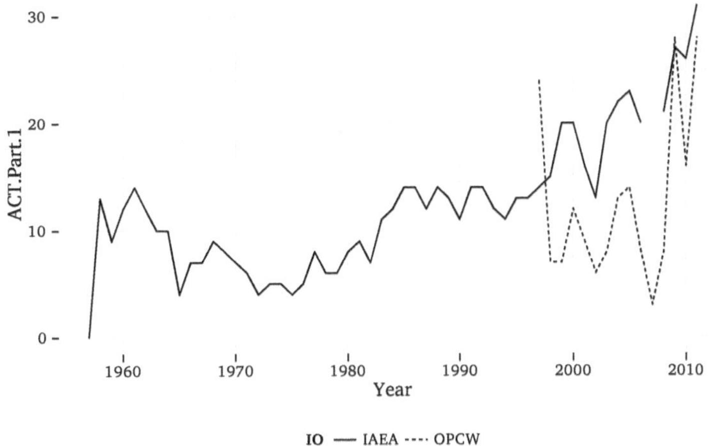

A.1.6   ACTION-PARTICIPATION-GC-NGO-REPRESENTATIVES

IAEA

- Number of NGO representatives at General Conference
- Source: Count of registered representatives of Non-Governmental Organizations in official list of Delegations

```
data$ACT.Part.2 <- rep(NA, 70)
data$ACT.Part.2[which(data$IO == "IAEA")] <-
    iaea_gc_ngo$Representatives.present
```

OPCW

- Source: List of participants

```
data$ACT.Part.2[which(data$IO == "OPCW")] <-
    opcw_ngo$SUM.NGO.REP[1:15]
```

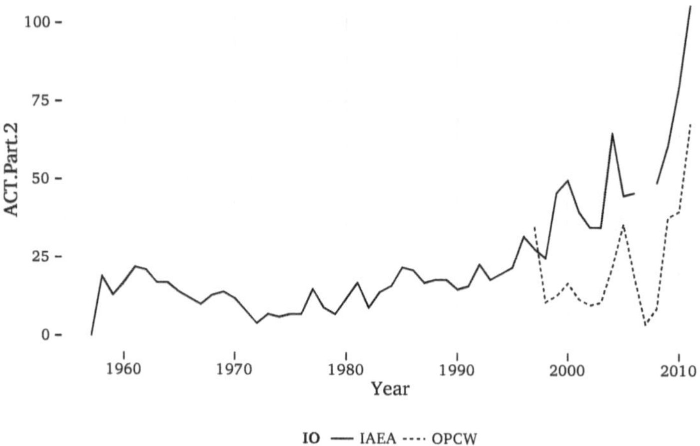

A.1.7   ACTION-PARTICIPATION-GC-NEW-NGO

IAEA

- Number of NGOs that participate at GC for the first time
- Source: List of Non-Governmental Organizations in official list of Delegations

```
data$ACT.Part.3 <- rep(NA, 70)
data$ACT.Part.3[which(data$IO == "IAEA")] <-
    iaea_gc_ngo$Number.of.New.NGO.present
```

How do the different IAEA measures for ACTION-Participation correlate?

```
data %>% filter(IO == "IAEA") %>%
    select(ACT.Part.1, ACT.Part.2, ACT.Part.3) %>%
    cor(use = 'pairwise.complete.obs')
```

```
##           ACT.Part.1 ACT.Part.2 ACT.Part.3
## ACT.Part.1    1.0000     0.9263     0.4353
## ACT.Part.2    0.9263     1.0000     0.3585
## ACT.Part.3    0.4353     0.3585     1.0000
```

So, the amount of NGOs and NGO representatives correlates highly. The presence of new NGOs, however, seems to follow a different trend.

OPCW

```
data$ACT.Part.3[which(data$IO == "OPCW")] <-
  opcw_ngo$NEW.NGOS[1:15]
```

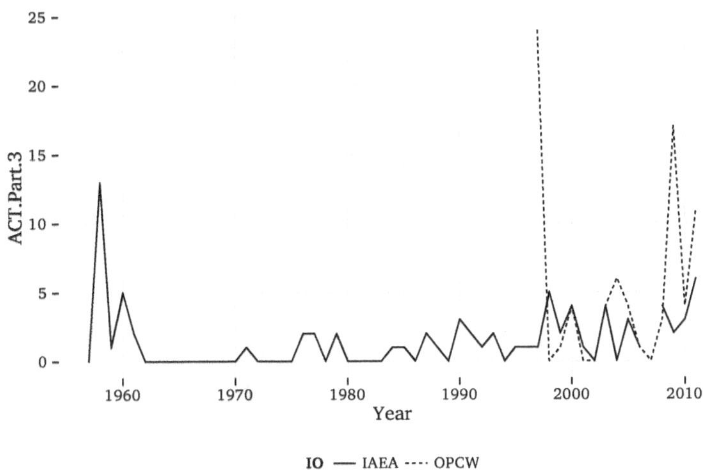

How do the different OPCW measures for ACTION-Participation correlate?

```
data %>% filter(IO == "OPCW") %>%
  select(ACT.Part.1, ACT.Part.2, ACT.Part.3) %>%
    cor(use = 'pairwise.complete.obs')
```

```
##              ACT.Part.1 ACT.Part.2 ACT.Part.3
## ACT.Part.1      1.0000     0.8889     0.8606
## ACT.Part.2      0.8889     1.0000     0.6099
## ACT.Part.3      0.8606     0.6099     1.0000
```

All measures of NGOs and NGO representatives correlate highly. The
presence of new NGOs, however, at the IAEA, seems to follow a different
trend. I will thus use the number of NGOs and NGO representatives for the
analysis.

A.1.8   ACTION-PARTICIPATION-EVENTS

IAEA

- number of participation events (i.e. events with non-state or sub-state
  level participation) that are discussed in the Annual Reports. Counts
  both actual events and more general references to events.
- Source: Annual Report, qualitative codings, guided by the following
  search terms:

```
    -  workshop
    -  training
    -  event
    -  seminar
    -  group
    -  meeting
    -  course
    -  forum
    -  exercise
    -  advisory
    -  panel
    -  symposia
    -  consultant
    -  network
```

```r
# filter for relevant codings and add to dataset
data$ACT.Part.4 <- rep(NA, 70)
data$ACT.Part.4[which(data$IO == "IAEA")] <-
    as.data.frame(filter(iaea_summary, codename == "ACT.Part"))$n
```

OPCW

- number of participation events (i.e. events with non-state or sub-state level participation) that are discussed in the Annual Reports. Counts both actual events and more general references to events.
- Source: Annual Report, qualitative codings, guided by the following search terms:

```
    -  workshop
    -  training
    -  event
    -  seminar
    -  group
    -  course
    -  meeting
    -  forum
    -  exercise
    -  Board
    -  advisory
    -  project
    -  committee
    -  program
```

```r
# filter for relevant codings and add to dataset
data$ACT.Part.4[which(data$IO == "OPCW")] <-
    as.data.frame(filter(opcw_summary, codename == "ACT.Part"))$n[2:16]
```

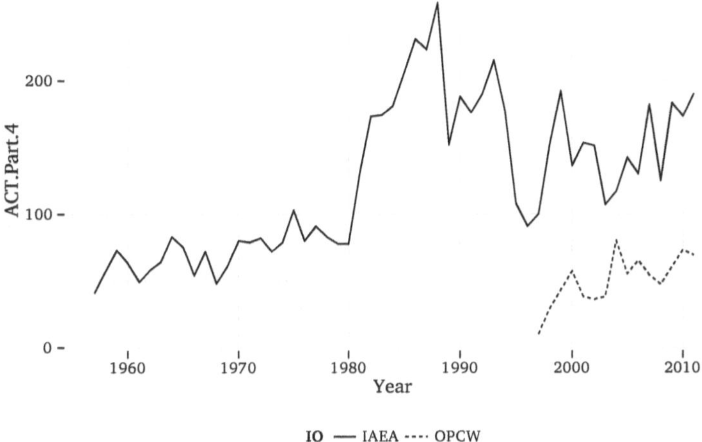

How do the two participation action data correlate?

```
cor(data$ACT.Part.1, data$ACT.Part.4, use = "pairwise.complete.obs")
```

```
## [1] 0.3413084
```

There is only weak correlation, so it matters which of the indicators are chosen as they measure different aspects of participation. I will thus include both in my analysis.

A.1.9 ACTION-TRANSPARENCY-PUBLIC INFORMATION BUDGET

IAEA

- share of the Budget available for public information
- source: annual budget reports (often under Administrative Department, or listed under "distribution of information")
- From 1957 to 1970: costs for distribution of information, 1971-1972: separate division of information, 1973-1979: public information part of office of external relations, budget shows that part of public information on former external relations budget is about 45 percent. I therefore use 45 percent of the 1973-1979 budget for the data row, 1980: separate division of public information, since 2002: under Information support services. Also, additional budget for ICT, I added this to the usual public information costs, as websites etc. provide transparency.
- also see see RB-BudgSize

```
# importing my data-set on IAEA budgets
iaea_budget <- read.csv2('../data/IAEA-BUDGET.csv')
data$ACT.Trans.1 <- rep(NA, 70)
data$ACT.Trans.1[which(data$IO == "IAEA")] <-
    iaea_budget$Public.Information.Budget / iaea_budget$Total.Budget
```

OPCW

- The share of the total budget that the OPCW spends for external
  relations and information systems
- Source: OPCW budgets. Total budgeted expenditures for the *External
  Relations* and *Information Systems* programs.

```
# importing my data-set on OPCW budgets
opcw_budget <- read.csv2('../data/OPCW-BUDGET.csv', dec = '.')
data$ACT.Trans.1[which(data$IO == "OPCW")] <-
    opcw_budget$Public.Information.Budget[1:15] /
    opcw_budget$Total.Budget[1:15]
```

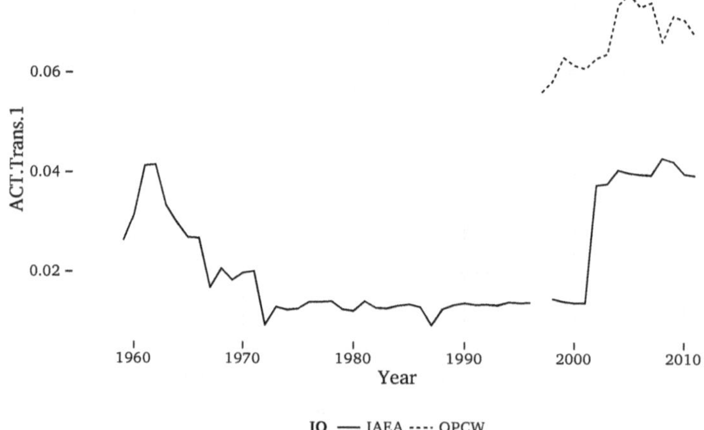

A.2   INDEPENDENT VARIABLES

Next, here is the description of the construction of the independent variables.
RB identifies resource-based mechanisms, NB the norm-based ones.

A.2.1   RB-BUDGSIZE

IAEA

- Annual Budget in 2009 USD
- In years where there were 2 year budgets, I take the data from the updated budgets for each year, if available.
- If available, I give preference to the "Total Operational Regular Budget" (by item of expenditure, total costs) numbers, when available, because this lists staff costs.
- When there are price estimates, I always use the prize estimates for the budgeted year.
- Source: annual budget reports. Note: budgets for year x is discussed and presented in GC x-1
- Source for conversion in 2009 USD: GDP Deflator data, US DoC, BEA, Table 1.1.9
- Source for conversion rates EUR, USD for 2006 - 2012: ECB, statistics data warehouse, averaged standardized measures

```r
# fetch conversion rates from EUR to USD because IAEA changed
# accounting to EUR in 2006
url <- "http://sdw.ecb.europa.eu/browseTable.do?DATASET=0&node=2018794&FREQ
=A&CURRENCY=USD&sfl1=4&sfl3=4&SERIES_KEY=120.EXR.A.USD.EUR.SP00.A"


table <- htmlParse(getURL(url))
table <- readHTMLTable(table)
EUR_USD <- as.data.frame(table[5])
EUR_USD <- arrange(EUR_USD, NULL.V1)
iaea_budget$exchange <- c(rep(1, 49),
        as.numeric(as.character(EUR_USD$NULL.V2[10:15])))


# for conversion to 2009 USD, use GDP deflator, source cannot be
# loaded with R
#url2 <- "http://www.bea.gov/iTable/iTableHtml.cfm?reqid=9&step=3&
#isuri=1&910=x&911=0&903=13&904=1957&905=2011&906=a"
iaea_budget$deflator <- c(16.641,   17.018, 17.254, 17.493, 17.686,
        17.903, 18.105, 18.383, 18.720, 19.246, 19.805, 20.647, 21.663,
        22.805, 23.964, 25.005, 26.366, 28.734, 31.395, 33.119, 35.173,
        37.643, 40.750, 44.425, 48.572, 51.586, 53.623, 55.525, 57.302,
        58.458, 59.949, 62.048, 64.460, 66.845, 69.069, 70.644, 72.325,
        73.865, 75.406, 76.783, 78.096, 78.944, 80.071, 81.891, 83.766,
        85.054, 86.754, 89.132, 91.991, 94.818, 97.335, 99.236, 100.000,
        101.211, 103.199)


# now, calculate IAEA budget in 2009 USD
```

```r
data$RB.Budget.All <- rep(NA, 70)
data$RB.Budget.All[which(data$IO == "IAEA")]   <-
    iaea_budget$exchange * iaea_budget$Total.Budget *
    (100 / iaea_budget$deflator)
```

OPCW

- Total Budget of OPCW in 2009 USD
- Source: Annual Budget Decisions from CoSP

```r
# Need EUR to USD conversion rates and NLG to USD rates for 1997-1999
## NLG to USD rates from Netherlands National Bank, make R recognize
## ',' as decimal point
url5 <- "http://www.statistics.dnb.nl/index.jsp?lang=nl&todo=Koersen&
service=show&data=21&type=y&cur=g&s=1&begin1=1997&end1=1999"
table <- htmlParse(getURL(url5))
table <- readHTMLTable(table)
NLG_USD <- as.data.frame(table[2])
write.csv(NLG_USD[c(1,3)], file = 'nlg_usd.csv')
NLG_USD <- read.csv('nlg_usd.csv', dec = ",")


opcw_budget$exchange <- c(1 / NLG_USD$NULL.1[1:3],
        as.numeric(as.character(EUR_USD$NULL.V2[4:17])))


# as above, convert to 2009 USD, using GDP deflator and add to data-set
opcw_budget$deflator <- c(iaea_budget$deflator[41:55],
        105.002,    106.590)
data$RB.Budget.All[which(data$IO == "OPCW")]   <-
    opcw_budget$exchange[1:15] *
    opcw_budget$Total.Budget[1:15] * (100 / opcw_budget$deflator[1:15])
```

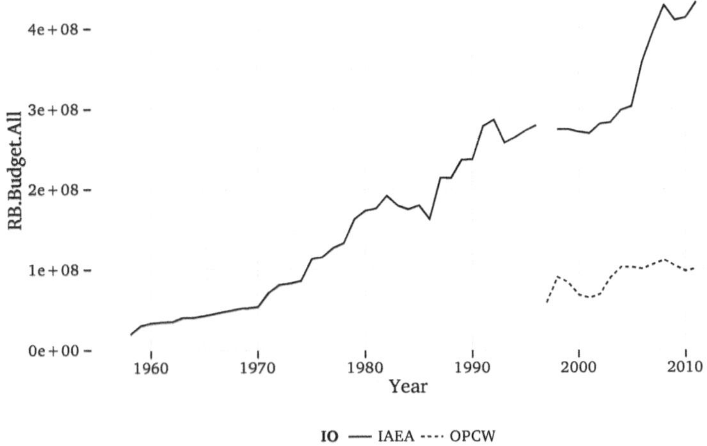

A.2.2   RB-STAFFCOSTS

IAEA

- staff costs as share of total operational budget
- staff costs taken from budget reports, including salaries and general staff costs

- Source: budget reports, see RB-BudSize.

```
data$RB.Budget.Staff <- rep(NA, 70)
data$RB.Budget.Staff[which(data$IO == "IAEA")] <-
    iaea_budget$Staff.Costs / iaea_budget$Total.Budget
```

OPCW

- Staff costs (including salaries and general staff costs) as a share of the total budget.
- Source: OPCW budgets.

```
data$RB.Budget.Staff[which(data$IO == "OPCW")] <-
    opcw_budget$Staff.Costs[1:15] /
    opcw_budget$Total.Budget[1:15]
```

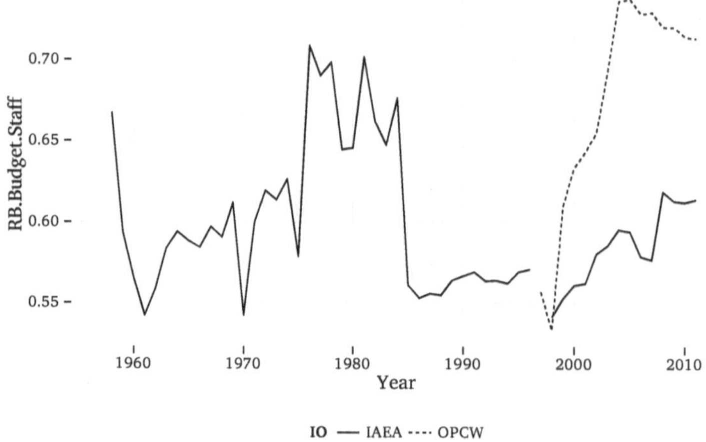

How do the two budget measures correlate?

```
cor(data$RB.Budget.All, data$RB.Budget.Staff,
        use = 'pairwise.complete.obs')
```

```
## [1] -0.2554299
```

There is weak negative correlation, so they rather measure different things.

A.2.3   RB-INEQMEMBERS

IAEA

- Measures the inequality of the member states. I use the Gini Coefficient of the annual GDP data for the members. The higher the coefficient, the more inequal the states are.
- Membership Data taken from the IAEA Website
- source: Penn World Tables 8.0, Real GDP at constant 2005 national prices (in mil. 2005US$) for states that are available.
- Limited data resources limit the interpretation of the results. Calculated inequality will probably be smaller than actual one.

```
# I take the IAEA membership data from the Agency's website.
# For reasons of reproducibility, I take an archived version
url_iaea = "https://web.archive.org/web/20140125141116/http://www.iaea
.org/About/Policy/MemberStates/"
```

```r
table <- htmlParse(getURL(url_iaea))
table <- readHTMLList(table)

table_iaea <- table[[6]]
table_iaea <-   data.frame(matrix(unlist(table_iaea), nrow=45, byrow=T))
colnames(table_iaea) <- "data"
table_iaea$data <- as.character(table_iaea$data)
# add empty cell for 2010 and add missing years
table_iaea[41,] <- "2010: none"
table_iaea[46,] <- "1971: none"
table_iaea[47,] <- "1975: none"
table_iaea[48,] <- "1978: none"
table_iaea[49,] <- "1979: none"
table_iaea[50,] <- "1980: none"
table_iaea[51,] <- "1981: none"
table_iaea[52,] <- "1982: none"
table_iaea[53,] <- "1985: none"
table_iaea[54,] <- "1987: none"
table_iaea[55,] <- "1988: none"
table_iaea[56,] <- "1989: none"
table_iaea[57,] <- "1990: none"
table_iaea[58,] <- "1991: none"

# tidy the data
table_iaea <- colsplit(table_iaea$data, ": ", c("year", "countries"))
table_iaea <- arrange(table_iaea, year)
countries_iaea <- list()
for (i in seq(along = table_iaea$year)) {
countries_iaea[i] <- strsplit(as.list(table_iaea$countries)[[i]], ", ")
  }

countries_iaea <- melt(countries_iaea)
countries_iaea$Year <- countries_iaea$L1 + 1956
countries_iaea$L1 <- NULL
countries_iaea <- filter(countries_iaea, Year < 2012)
countries_iaea <- filter(countries_iaea, value != "none")

write.csv(countries_iaea, file="iaea_members.csv")

# convert table into country-year format
# see for reference:
# http://stackoverflow.com/questions/5425584/creating-new-
#variable-and-new-data-rows-for-country-conflict-year-observations
countries_iaea$end.date <- rep(2011, length(countries_iaea$YEAR))

library(plyr)
```

```r
members_iaea <- ddply(countries_iaea, .(value), function(x){
    data.frame(
        #country=x$Member.State,
        Year=seq(x$YEAR, x$end.date)
        #accession=x$accession
        #yrend=x$end
    )
}
)
detach("package:plyr", unload=TRUE)


# join gdp and membership data
# first, add country code to cow data with countrycodes-package
members_iaea$isoc <-
    countrycode(members_iaea$value,
                            origin="country.name",
                            destination="iso3c", warn=T)


# get Penn World Tables data for all states, Real GDP at constant
# 2005 national prices, downloaded as csv from url below
# url2 <- "http://citaotest01.housing.rug.nl/FebPwt/Dmn/AggregateXs.mvc/
# PivotShow#"
penn_gdp <- read.csv('../data/PENN-GDP.csv')


# join / merge
iaea_ineq <- merge(x = members_iaea, y = penn_gdp,
                                by.x = c("isoc", "Year"),
                                by.y = c("RegionCode", "YearCode"))


# those stats are not in the merged data set
# because GDP data is missing
setdiff(unique(members_iaea$isoc), unique(iaea_ineq$isoc))


##  [1] "AFG" "DZA" "CUB" "ERI" "HTI" "VAT" "LBY" "LIE" "MHL" "MCO" "MMR"
## [12] "NIC" NA    "PLW" "SYC" "YUG" "TON" "ARE"


# calculate Gini per year
iaea_ineq2 <- iaea_ineq %>% group_by(Year) %>%
    summarise(members = n(), gini = ineq(AggValue),
                        mean = mean(AggValue))


data$RB.Inequality <- rep(NA, 70)
data$RB.Inequality[which(data$IO == "IAEA")] <-
    iaea_ineq2$gini
```

OPCW

```r
# I take data from membership table off OPCW website
url_opcw = "https://web.archive.org/web/20140108120526/http://www.opcw.org/
about-opcw/member-states/"


table <- htmlParse(getURL(url_opcw))
table <- readHTMLTable(table)

table_opcw <- as.data.frame(table[[4]])
table_opcw$accession <- year(dmy(table_opcw$"Entry into Force"))
table_opcw$Member.State <- as.character(table_opcw$"Member State")

table_opcw <-
    table_opcw %>% select(accession, Member.State) %>% arrange(accession)

write.csv(table_opcw, file="opcw_members.csv")

# convert table into country-year format
# see for reference:
# http://stackoverflow.com/questions/5425584/creating-new-variable-and-new-
#   data-rows-for-country-conflict-year-observations
table_opcw$end.date <- rep(2011, length(table_opcw$accession))

library(plyr)
members_opcw <- ddply(table_opcw, .(Member.State), function(x){
    data.frame(
        #country=x$Member.State,
        Year=seq(x$accession, x$end.date)
        #accession=x$accession
        #yrend=x$end
        )
    }
)
detach("package:plyr", unload=TRUE)

# join gdp and membership data
# first, add country code to cow data with countrycodes-package
members_opcw$isoc <-  countrycode(members_opcw$Member.State,
        origin="country.name", destination="iso3c", warn=T)


# join / merge
opcw_ineq <- merge(x = members_opcw, y = penn_gdp,
        by.x = c("isoc", "Year"), by.y = c("RegionCode", "YearCode"))
```

```r
# those stats are not in the merged data set
# because GDP data is missing
setdiff(unique(members_opcw$isoc), unique(opcw_ineq$isoc))


## [1] "AFG" "DZA" "AND" "COK" "CUB" "ERI" "GUY" "HTI" "VAT" "KIR" "LBY"
## [12] "LIE" "MHL" "FSM" "MCO" "NRU" "NIC" "NIU" "PLW" "PNG" "WSM" "SMR"
## [23] NA    "SYC" "SLB" "SOM" "TLS" "TON" "TUV" "ARE" "VUT"


# calculate Gini per year
opcw_ineq2 <- opcw_ineq %>% group_by(Year) %>%
    summarise(members = n(), gini = ineq(AggValue),
    mean = mean(AggValue))


data$RB.Inequality[which(data$IO == "OPCW")] <-
    opcw_ineq2$gini
```


A.2.4 RB-COMPLEXITY

IAEA

- Measures the complexity of the policy field that the organization covers.
- I create a qualitative variable. I quantify the number of activities that the organizations' statutes say the organizations have. I assume that the more tasks the organization has to fulfill, the more complex its operations are.

- The IAEA statute (Art III) lists the following tasks

    1. encourage, assist and conduct research, develop practical applications foster scientific exchange
    2. act as intermediary for supply of materials, services, or facilities for states
    3. provide nuclear materials, services, equipment and facilities with focus on developing states, i.e. technical assistance
    4. establish and administer safeguards
    5. develop and apply safety standards

```r
data$RB.Complexity <- rep(NA, 70)
data$RB.Complexity[which(data$IO == "IAEA")] <-
    c(rep(5, 55))
```

OPCW

- The CWC, which is also the founding document of the OPCW, lists the following tasks for the OPCW:

    1. implementation and verification of chemical weapons destruction (Art. VIII)
    2. assistance and protection against chemical weapons (Art X)
    3. economic and technical development (Art XI)

```r
data$RB.Complexity[which(data$IO == "OPCW")] <-
    c(rep(3, 15))
```

A.2.5 NB-PRESS SALIENCE

IAEA

- Shows how visible the organization is in the global press.
- source: hits in the "major world news" corpus of Lexis Nexis

First, I show that there are no effects of the larger corpus size and that the reporting of total numbers is a good indicator for visibility.

```r
# import my IAEA Lexis-Nexis data
iaea_media <- read.csv2("../data/IAEA-MEDIA.csv")
cor(iaea_media$All.Hits, iaea_media$All.WashPost,
        use = 'pairwise.complete.obs')
```

```
## [1] 0.9360839
```

There is high correlation (0.936) between `All Media Hits` and those in the `Washington Post` only. Thus, the higher number of sources in the corpus in later years does not significantly change the amount of media attention, when compared to one source alone.

```
data$NB.visibility.1 <- rep(NA, 70)
data$NB.visibility.1[which(data$IO == "IAEA")] <-
    iaea_media$All.Hits[1:55]
```

OPCW

- see above

```
# import my OPCW Lexis-Nexis data
opcw_media <- read.csv2("../data/OPCW-MEDIA.csv")
cor(opcw_media$AllHits, opcw_media$WashPost,
        use = 'pairwise.complete.obs')
```

```
## [1] 0.9953661
```

Also for the OPCW, there is high correlation (0.995) between `All Media Hits` and those in the `Washington Post` only.

```
data$NB.visibility.1[which(data$IO == "OPCW")] <-
    opcw_media$AllHits[1:15]
```

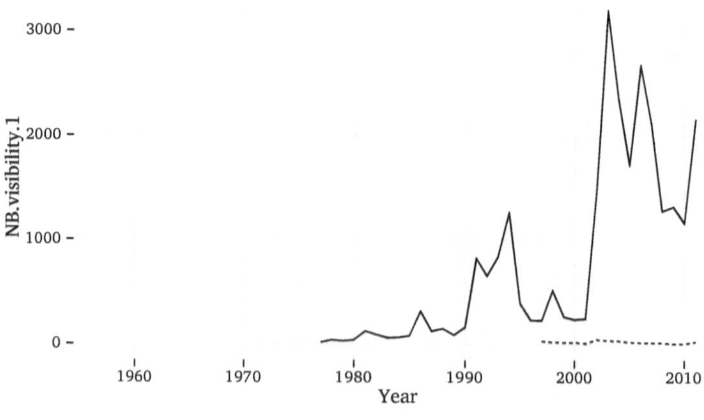

A.2.6 NB-PRESS HEADLINE

IAEA

- Media salience in the headlines of articles
- Data as a share of headlines per total hits for comparability and to know when the organization is only cited and when there's a focused article on the IO.
- Source: hits in the headlines of the "major world news" corpus of Lexis Nexis

```
data$NB.visibility.2 <- rep(NA, 70)
data$NB.visibility.2[which(data$IO == "IAEA")] <-
    iaea_media$Headlines[1:55] /
    iaea_media$All.Hits[1:55]
```

OPCW

```
data$NB.visibility.2[which(data$IO == "OPCW")] <-
    opcw_media$Headlines[1:15] /
    opcw_media$AllHits[1:15]
```

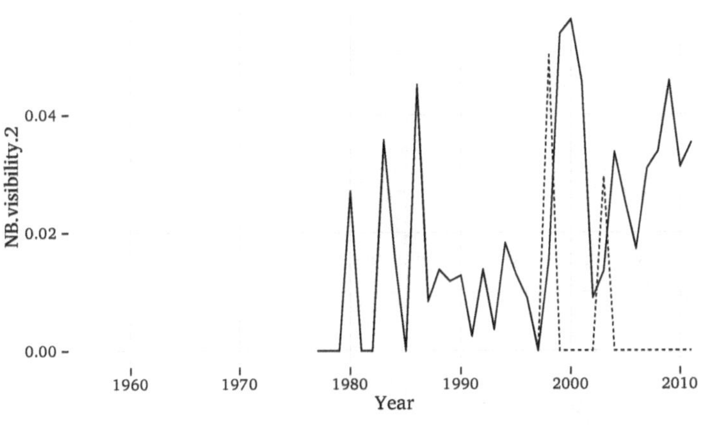

How do the visibility measures correlate?

```
cor(data[17:18], use = 'pairwise.complete.obs')
```

```
##               NB.visibility.1 NB.visibility.2
## NB.visibility.1      1.0000000       0.3189018
```

```
## NB.visibility.2         0.3189018        1.0000000
##
```

There is low correlation between the variables. I will thus consider the headlines variable separately.

A.2.7   NB-DEMOCRATIC MEMBERS

IAEA

- Provides the annual proportion of democratic members (Polity IV, `polity2` $>= 7$) of the whole organization.
- Source: Democracy values from POLITY IV dataset, membership data from organizations' websites.

```r
# get Polity IV values with psData package, data available
polity4 <-
    PolityGet(url = "http://www.systemicpeace.org/inscr/p4v2012.sav",
    OutCountryID = "iso3c")
```

```
## 663 duplicated values were created when standardising the country ID with iso3c.
## 637 observations dropped based on missing values of the standardised ID variable.
```

```r
polity <- polity4[c(1,6,12)]
```

```r
## merge with IAEA member data
iaea_polity <- merge(x = members_iaea, y = polity,
        by.x = c("isoc", "Year"), by.y = c("iso3c", "year"))
```

```r
# dropped observations, due to missing data in polityIV
setdiff(unique(members_iaea$isoc), unique(iaea_polity$isoc))
```

```
##  [1] "BLZ" "VAT" "ISL" "LIE" "MLT" "MHL" "MCO" NA      "PLW" "SYC" "YUG"
## [12] "TON" "ARE"
```

```r
# calculate share of states with polity2 >6 and other indicators
iaea_demmem <- iaea_polity %>% group_by(Year) %>%
    summarise(n = n(),
    mean_polity = mean(polity2, na.rm = T),
    n_democratic = sum(polity2 > 6, na.rm = T))
iaea_demmem$dem_share <- iaea_demmem$n_democratic / iaea_demmem$n
```

```r
data$NB.dem.mem <- rep(NA, 70)
data$NB.dem.mem[which(data$IO == "IAEA")] <-
    iaea_demmem$dem_share
```

OPCW

```
## merge polity with OPCW member data
opcw_polity <- merge(x = members_opcw, y = polity,
        by.x = c("isoc", "Year"), by.y = c("iso3c", "year"))


# dropped observations, due to missing data in polityIV
setdiff(unique(members_iaea$isoc), unique(iaea_polity$isoc))


##  [1] "BLZ" "VAT" "ISL" "LIE" "MLT" "MHL" "MCO" NA     "PLW" "SYC" "YUG"
## [12] "TON" "ARE"


# calculate share of states with polity2 >6 and other indicators
opcw_demmem <- opcw_polity %>% group_by(Year) %>%
    summarise(n = n(),
    mean_polity = mean(polity2, na.rm = T),
    n_democratic = sum(polity2 > 6, na.rm = T))
opcw_demmem$dem_share <- opcw_demmem$n_democratic / opcw_demmem$n

data$NB.dem.mem[which(data$IO == "OPCW")] <-
    opcw_demmem$dem_share[1:15]
```

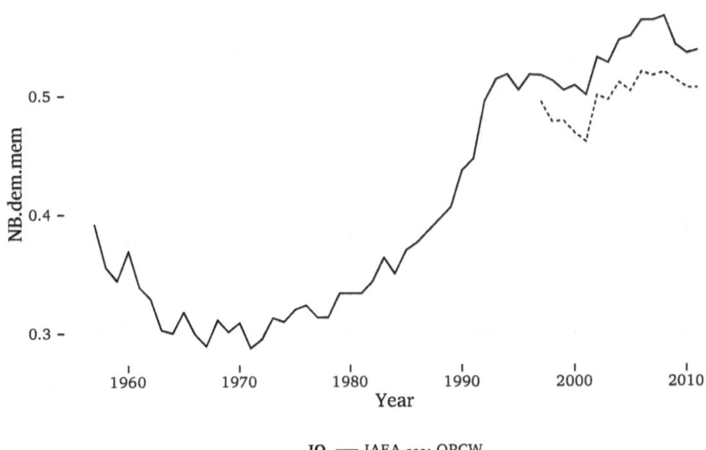

A.2.8   NB-GOVERNANCE DEPTH

IAEA

- The authority of the IGO

- I will use the following qualitative factor levels to describe growing governance depth of the IAEA:

  - 1957 - 1969: business as usual
  - 1970 - 1990: NPT inspections
  - 1991 - 2011: contribution to political conflicts

```
data$NB.gov.depth <- rep(NA, 70)
data$NB.gov.depth[which(data$IO == "IAEA")] <-
    c(rep(1, 13), rep(2, 21), rep(3, 21))
```

OPCW

- The literature does not suggest any larger changes in the governance depth of the OPCW. The SYR inspections may be such an instance, but the event is outside of my time of analysis.

```
data$NB.gov.depth[which(data$IO == "OPCW")] <-
    rep(1, 15)
```

A.2.9 NB-OPEN GOVERNANCE NORM

IAEA

- The presence of the norm of open governance in the general public discourse, expressed as percentages of n-grams, multiplied by 10 Millions (to scale up to other variables).
- Source: google books n-grams (http://books.google.com/ngrams/), 1945-2008: keywords: democratic deficit, participatory governance, global democracy
- Sum of percentages into one single indicator of open governance norm presence.

```
# get json data from n-grams site
url3 <-  "https://books.google.com/ngrams/graph?content=democratic+deficit%2
Cparticipatory+governance%2Cglobal+democracy&case_insensitive=on&year_start
=1957&year_end=2008&corpus=15&smoothing=0&share=&direct_url=t4%3B%2
Cdemocratic%20deficit%3B%2Cc0%3B%2Cs0%3B%3Bdemocratic%20deficit%3B%2Cc0%3B%3B
Democratic%20Deficit%3B%2Cc0%3B%3BDemocratic%20deficit%3B%2Cc0%3B.t4%3B
%2Cparticipatory%20governance%3B%2Cc0%3B%2Cs0%3B%3Bparticipatory%20
governance%3B%2Cc0%3B%3BParticipatory%20Governance%3B%2Cc0%3B%3B
Participatory%20governance%3B%2Cc0%3B.t4%3B%2Cglobal%20democracy%3B
%2Cc0%3B%2Cs0%3B%3Bglobal%20democracy%3B%2Cc0%3B%3BGlobal%20
Democracy%3B%2Cc0%3B%3BGlobal%20democracy%3B%2Cc0%3B%3BGLOBAL
%20DEMOCRACY%3B%2Cc0"
```

```r
ngram <- htmlParse(getURL(url3))
ngram2 <- xpathSApply(ngram, "//script", xmlValue)[8]

# clean up and convert to data table
ngram2 <- gsub(pattern="\n  var data = ", x=ngram2,
                      replacement = "")
ngram2 <- gsub(pattern=
        ";\n  if (data.length > 0) {\n    ngrams.drawD3Chart(data, 1957,
         2008, 1.0, \"main\");\n  }\n",
        x=ngram2, replacement = "", fixed=T)
write(ngram2, file='ngram2')


ngram3 <- fromJSON('ngram2')
dem_def <- unlist(ngram3[[1]], use.names = F)
part_gov <- unlist(ngram3[[2]], use.names = F)
global_dem <- unlist(ngram3[[3]], use.names = F)


# create data-frame and add years, first rows are junk,
# add missing values
open_gov_norm <- data.frame(democratic.deficit = dem_def,
        participative.governance = part_gov,
        global.democracy = global_dem)
open_gov_norm[56, ] <- c(NA, NA, NA)
open_gov_norm[57, ] <- c(NA, NA, NA)
open_gov_norm$year <- 1955:2011


# add values of all three search terms and
# add to data-set
open_gov_norm$ogn <-
    as.numeric(as.character(open_gov_norm$democratic.deficit)) +
    as.numeric(as.character(open_gov_norm$participative.governance)) +
    as.numeric(as.character(open_gov_norm$global.democracy))


# multiply with 10 Million and add to data table
data$NB.og.norm <- rep(NA, 70)
data$NB.og.norm[which(data$IO == "IAEA")] <-
    10000000 * open_gov_norm$ogn[3:57]
```

OPCW

- The same data as for the IAEA.

```r
data$NB.og.norm[which(data$IO == "OPCW")] <-
    10000000 * open_gov_norm$ogn[43:57]
```

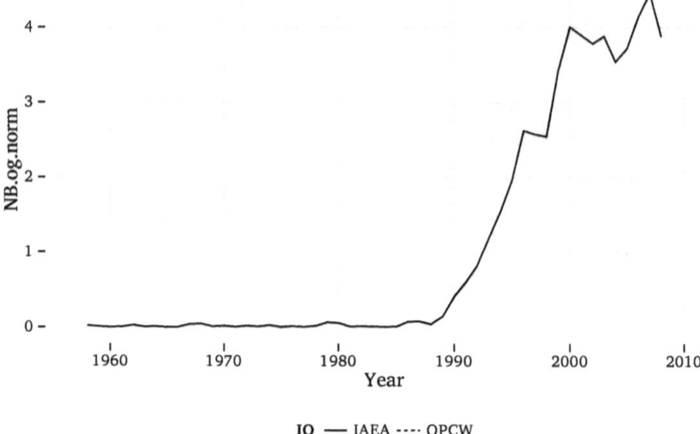
NB.og.norm
4
3
2
1
0
1960
1970
1980
1990
2000
2010
Year
IO — IAEA ···· OPCW

A.3 RAW DATA

A.3.1 DEPENDENT VARIABLES

IO	Year	Decade	TALK.Part	TALK.Trans	DEC.Part	DEC.Trans	ACT.Part.1	ACT.Part.2	ACT.Part.3	ACT.Part.4
IAEA	1957	1950s	3	0	1	1	0	0	0	41
IAEA	1958	1950s	5	0	1	1	13	19	13	57
IAEA	1959	1950s	5	0	1	1	9	13	1	73
IAEA	1960	1950s	4	0	1	1	12	17	5	63
IAEA	1961	1960s	1	0	1	1	14	22	2	49
IAEA	1962	1960s	0	0	1	1	12	21	0	58
IAEA	1963	1960s	0	0	1	1	10	17	0	64
IAEA	1964	1960s	1	0	1	1	10	17	0	83
IAEA	1965	1960s	0	0	1	1	4	14	0	75
IAEA	1966	1960s	0	0	1	1	7	12	0	54
IAEA	1967	1960s	0	0	1	1	7	10	0	72
IAEA	1968	1960s	0	0	1	1	9	13	0	48
IAEA	1969	1960s	1	0	1	1	8	14	0	61
IAEA	1970	1960s	0	0	1	1	7	12	0	80
IAEA	1971	1970s	0	0	1	1	6	8	1	79
IAEA	1972	1970s	0	0	1	1	4	4	0	82
IAEA	1973	1970s	0	0	1	1	5	7	0	72
IAEA	1974	1970s	0	0	1	1	5	6	0	79
IAEA	1975	1970s	0	0	2	1	4	7	0	103
IAEA	1976	1970s	0	0	2	1	5	7	2	80
IAEA	1977	1970s	0	0	2	1	8	15	2	91
IAEA	1978	1970s	0	0	2	1	6	9	0	83
IAEA	1979	1970s	0	0	2	1	6	7	2	78
IAEA	1980	1970s	0	0	2	1	8	12	0	78
IAEA	1981	1980s	0	0	2	1	9	17	0	131
IAEA	1982	1980s	0	0	2	1	7	9	0	173
IAEA	1983	1980s	0	0	2	1	11	14	0	174
IAEA	1984	1980s	0	0	2	1	12	16	1	181
IAEA	1985	1980s	0	0	2	1	14	22	1	206
IAEA	1986	1980s	1	0	2	2	14	21	0	231
IAEA	1987	1980s	2	0	2	2	12	17	2	223
IAEA	1988	1980s	0	0	2	2	14	18	1	258
IAEA	1989	1980s	0	0	2	3	13	18	0	152
IAEA	1990	1980s	1	0	2	4	11	15	3	188
IAEA	1991	1990s	0	0	2	4	14	16	2	176
IAEA	1992	1990s	0	0	2	4	14	23	1	190
IAEA	1993	1990s	2	1	2	5	12	18	2	215
IAEA	1994	1990s	2	0	2	5	11	20	0	177

IAEA	1995	1990s	1	1	2	6	13	22	1	108
IAEA	1996	1990s	2	0	2	7	13	32	1	91
IAEA	1997	1990s	0	3	2	7	14	28	1	100
IAEA	1998	1990s	3	3	2	8	15	25	5	152
IAEA	1999	1990s	2	0	2	8	20	46	2	192
IAEA	2000	1990s	4	2	2	9	20	50	4	136
IAEA	2001	2000s	3	2	2	9	16	40	1	153
IAEA	2002	2000s	6	4	2	10	13	35	0	151
IAEA	2003	2000s	2	1	2	10	20	35	4	107
IAEA	2004	2000s	1	1	2	10	22	65	0	117
IAEA	2005	2000s	2	2	2	10	23	45	3	142
IAEA	2006	2000s	5	2	2	10	20	46	1	130
IAEA	2007	2000s	2	0	2	11				182
IAEA	2008	2000s	1	2	2	11	21	49	4	125
IAEA	2009	2000s	2	1	2	11	27	61	2	183
IAEA	2010	2000s	2	0	2	12	26	80	3	173
IAEA	2011	2010s	4	4	2	12	31	106	6	190
OPCW	1997	1990s	0	0	1	1	16			10
OPCW	1998	1990s	4	2	1	2	12			29
OPCW	1999	1990s	4	2	1	3	8			43
OPCW	2000	1990s	3	3	2	4	16			57
OPCW	2001	2000s	2	1	2	4	8			38
OPCW	2002	2000s	1	2	2	5	6			36
OPCW	2003	2000s	2	4	3	6	11			38
OPCW	2004	2000s	2	0	3	6	13			80
OPCW	2005	2000s	0	1	3	6	14			55
OPCW	2006	2000s	1	0	3	6	10			65
OPCW	2007	2000s	2	1	3	6	4			54
OPCW	2008	2000s	3	1	3	7	7			47
OPCW	2009	2000s	2	2	3	7	30			60
OPCW	2010	2000s	6	1	3	8	20			73
OPCW	2011	2010s	5	4	3	8	29			69

A.3.2 Independent Variables

IO	Year	ACT.Trans.1	RB.Budget.All	RB.Budget.Staff	RB.Inequality	RB.Complexity	NB.visibility.1	NB.visibility.2	NB.demands.part	NB.demands.trans	NB.dem.mem
IAEA	1957				1	5					0
IAEA	1958		19643906	1	1	5					0
IAEA	1959	0	30282833	1	1	5					0
IAEA	1960	0	33401932	1	1	5					0
IAEA	1961	0	34875042	1	1	5					0
IAEA	1962	0	34971792	1	1	5					0
IAEA	1963	0	40527479	1	1	5					0
IAEA	1964	0	40496655	1	1	5					0
IAEA	1965	0	42403846	1	1	5					0
IAEA	1966	0	45432817	1	1	5					0
IAEA	1967	0	47924766	1	1	5					0
IAEA	1968	0	50743449	1	1	5					0
IAEA	1969	0	51936482	1	1	5					0
IAEA	1970	0	53716290	1	1	5					0
IAEA	1971	0	71060758	1	1	5					0
IAEA	1972	0	81087782	1	1	5					0
IAEA	1973	0	82940150	1	1	5					0
IAEA	1974	0	85866917	1	1	5					0
IAEA	1975	0	112998885	1	1	5					0
IAEA	1976	0	115414113	1	1	5					0
IAEA	1977	0	126961021	1	1	5	15	0	1	1	0
IAEA	1978	0	132917143	1	1	5	38	0	0	0	0
IAEA	1979	0	163096933	1	1	5	29	0	3	0	0
IAEA	1980	0	173384356	1	1	5	37	0	3	0	0
IAEA	1981	0	176262044	1	1	5	122	0	1	3	0
IAEA	1982	0	191891211	1	1	5	86	0	20	1	0
IAEA	1983	0	179805307	1	1	5	56	0	6	1	0
IAEA	1984	0	174863575	1	1	5	63	0	4	0	0
IAEA	1985	0	179669121	1	1	5	79	0	3	0	0
IAEA	1986	0	162468781	1	1	5	311	0	8	3	0
IAEA	1987	0	214111995	1	1	5	120	0	2	1	0
IAEA	1988	0	213765150	1	1	5	146	0	4	1	0
IAEA	1989	0	236306236	1	1	5	85	0	5	1	0
IAEA	1990	0	236888324	1	1	5	157	0	3	1	0
IAEA	1991	0	278165313	1	1	5	821	0	10	6	0
IAEA	1992	0	285960591	1	1	5	653	0	14	11	0
IAEA	1993	0	257204286	1	1	5	839	0	13	8	1
IAEA	1994	0	264019495	1	1	5	1261	0	23	27	1
IAEA	1995	0	272547277	1	1	5	388	0	11	11	1
IAEA	1996	0	278824740	1	1	5	226	0	6	2	1
IAEA	1997			1	1	5	224	0	8	2	1
IAEA	1998	0	274212100	1	1	5	515	0	12	17	1
IAEA	1999	0	273868192	1	1	5	261	0	16	9	1
IAEA	2000	0	270747701	1	1	5	232	0	9	6	1
IAEA	2001	0	268716424	1	1	5	242	0	10	6	0
IAEA	2002	0	280654643	1	1	5	1457	0	22	29	1
IAEA	2003	0	282450377	1	1	5	3193	0	69	147	1
IAEA	2004	0	298093838	1	1	5	2350	0	43	128	1
IAEA	2005	0	302772010	1	1	5	1708	0	39	75	1
IAEA	2006	0	358599085	1	1	5	2668	0	61	98	1
IAEA	2007	0	395530792	1	1	5	2108	0	53	120	1
IAEA	2008	0	428080792	1	1	5	1272	0	37	57	1
IAEA	2009	0	409779207	1	1	5	1312	0	34	56	1
IAEA	2010	0	413233754	1	1	5	1156	0	64	89	1
IAEA	2011	0	432173522	1	1	5	2153	0	72	98	1
OPCW	1997	0	58287598	1	1	3	28	0	4	1	0
OPCW	1998	0	89962409	1	1	3	20	0	0	0	0
OPCW	1999	0	83083319	1	1	3	16	0	2	1	0
OPCW	2000	0	67939339	1	1	3	17	0	3	1	0
OPCW	2001	0	64405022	1	1	3	8	0	1	0	0
OPCW	2002	0	68854453	1	1	3	43	0	0	1	0
OPCW	2003	0	89400405	1	1	3	34	0	0	4	0

OPCW	2004	0	102090721	1	1	3	30	0	0	1	1
OPCW	2005	0	102371047	1	1	3	19	0	0	1	1
OPCW	2006	0	100129976	1	1	3	13	0	0	0	1
OPCW	2007	0	105638046	1	1	3	13	0	0	2	1
OPCW	2008	0	111197398	1	1	3	12	0	0	0	1
OPCW	2009	0	103912042	1	1	3	4	0	0	0	1
OPCW	2010	0	97589994	1	1	3	3	0	1	0	1
OPCW	2011	0	100561644	1	1	3	21	0	0	3	1

B *Classifying Participation Events*

This appendix illustrates the grouping of the participation events data. Methodologically, I use a simple keyword search on all codings of a year. The original coding data can be retrieved by opening the `IAEA.rqda` and `OPCW.rqda` files with the `RQDA` software package.[30]

For the keyword classification, I extracted all `ACT.Part` codings from the files and copied them to text files for each year. The search is thus only performed on those parts of texts of the Annual Reports that I coded qualitatively as relevant statements about participation events.

The following packages were used for the analysis[31]:

```
library(tm)
library(slam)
library(dplyr)
library(ggplot2)
library(reshape2)
library(xtable)
```

IAEA

In the first step I create a corpus from the annual codings and pre-process the texts to remove stopwords, punctuation and upper case letters. Next, I create a document term matrix, which includes the frequency of each term in each document. The matrix is then used to extract relevant search terms.

---

[30]HUANG, Ronggui. (2014). RQDA: R-based Qualitative Data Analysis. R package version 0.2-7. URL http://rqda.r-forge.r-project.org/.

[31] David B. Dahl (2014). xtable: Export tables to LaTeX or HTML. R package version 1.7-4. http://CRAN.R-project.org/package=xtable. Ingo Feinerer and Kurt Hornik (2014). tm: Text Mining Package. R package version 0.6. http://CRAN.R-project.org/package=tm. Kurt Hornik, David Meyer and Christian Buchta (2014). slam: Sparse Lightweight Arrays and Matrices. R package version 0.1-32. http://CRAN.R-project.org/package=slam. Hadley Wickham and Romain Francois (2014). dplyr: A Grammar of Data Manipulation. R package version 0.3.0.2. http://CRAN.R-project.org/package=dplyr. Hadley Wickham (2009) ggplot2: elegant graphics for data analysis. Springer New York, 2009. Hadley Wickham (2007). Reshaping Data with the reshape Package. Journal of Statistical Software, 21(12), 1-2.

```r
corpus <- Corpus(DirSource("../data/corpora/iaea-part-events/",
           encoding="UTF-8"), readerControl=list(language="en"))
corpusVars <- data.frame(var1=factor(rep("", length(corpus))),
           row.names=names(corpus))
dtmCorpus <- corpus
dtmCorpus <- tm_map(dtmCorpus, content_transformer(tolower))
dtmCorpus <- tm_map(dtmCorpus, content_transformer(function(x)
           gsub("(["\n]|[[:punct:]]|[[:space:]]|[[:cntrl:]])+",
               " ", x)))
dtmCorpus <- tm_map(dtmCorpus, removeNumbers)
dtm <- DocumentTermMatrix(dtmCorpus, control=list(tolower=FALSE,
               wordLengths=c(2, Inf)))
rm(dtmCorpus)
dictionary <- data.frame(row.names=colnames(dtm),
             "Occurrences"=col_sums(dtm),
             "Stopword"=ifelse(colnames(dtm) %in% stopwords("en"),
             "Stopword", ""),   stringsAsFactors=FALSE)
dtm <- dtm[, !colnames(dtm) %in% stopwords("en")]
attr(dtm, "dictionary") <- dictionary
rm(dictionary)
meta(corpus, type="corpus", tag="language") <-
    attr(dtm, "language") <- "en"
meta(corpus, type="corpus", tag="processing") <-
    attr(dtm, "processing") <- c(lowercase=TRUE, punctuation=TRUE,
                  digits=TRUE, stopwords=TRUE, stemming=FALSE,
                  customStemming=FALSE, twitter=FALSE,
                  removeHashtags=NA, removeNames=NA)
corpus


## «VCorpus (documents: 55, metadata (corpus/indexed): 2/0)»


dtm


## «DocumentTermMatrix (documents: 55, terms: 7986)»
## Non-/sparse entries: 48860/390370
## Sparsity          : 89%
## Maximal term length: 26
## Weighting          : term frequency (tf)
```

In the second step, I first collect all search terms that still may have
different orthography. Second, I group them together according to the
overarching topics of Science, Training, and Advice.

```r
terms <- as.data.frame(as.matrix(dtm))
terms$Year <- 1957:2011

## combine relevant terms
terms$WORKSHOP <- terms$workshop + terms$workshops +
    terms$workshopsí
terms$SEMINAR <- terms$seminar + terms$seminarí +
    terms$seminars +terms$seminarsã
terms$TRAINING <- terms$training + terms$trainingí
terms$MEETING <- terms$meeting + terms$meetingís +
    terms$meetings
terms$COURSE <- terms$course + terms$courses
terms$PANEL <- terms$panel + terms$panelonthe +
    terms$panels
terms$CONSULTANT <- terms$consultant +
    terms$consultants
terms$SYMPOSIA <- terms$symposia + terms$symposium
terms$NETWORK <- terms$network + terms$networki +
    terms$networkís + terms$networks
terms$ADVISOR <- terms$advisor + terms$advisory

## create term categories
terms$GROUP_SCIENCE <- terms$SEMINAR + terms$PANEL +
    terms$SYMPOSIA
terms$GROUP_TRAINING <- terms$TRAINING + terms$COURSE +
    terms$WORKSHOP
terms$GROUP_ADVICE <- terms$MEETING + terms$CONSULTANT +
    terms$NETWORK + terms$ADVISOR


write.csv(terms, file = "coding_terms.csv")


terms2 <- terms %>% select(Year, WORKSHOP, SEMINAR, TRAINING,
                   MEETING, COURSE, PANEL, CONSULTANT, SYMPOSIA,
                   NETWORK, GROUP_SCIENCE, GROUP_TRAINING,
                   GROUP_ADVICE)
write.csv(terms2, file = "coding_terms2.csv")
```

Year	WORKSHOP	SEMINAR	TRAINING	MEETING	COURSE	PANEL	CONSULTANT	SYMPOSIA	NETWORK	GROUP_SCIENCE	GROUP_TRAINING	GROUP_ADVICE
1957	0	3	22	4	0	3	5	2	0	8	22	12

1958	0	8	19	17	14	12	1	12	0	32	33	25
1959	1	5	18	14	25	39	0	12	0	56	44	14
1960	0	2	12	11	12	29	1	15	0	46	24	14
1961	0	7	8	15	10	9	3	10	0	26	18	19
1962	0	4	6	20	3	15	4	10	0	29	9	26
1963	0	1	15	21	10	23	1	10	0	34	25	22
1964	0	4	13	26	7	29	1	16	0	49	20	34
1965	0	8	14	19	9	20	4	13	0	41	23	25
1966	0	1	17	5	12	12	0	14	0	27	29	5
1967	0	3	15	17	12	21	3	15	0	39	27	20
1968	0	3	9	8	9	23	5	16	0	42	18	13
1969	0	2	8	18	8	22	7	12	0	36	16	25
1970	0	7	15	23	13	21	2	14	0	42	28	27
1971	1	6	17	25	12	17	9	10	0	33	30	36
1972	1	4	4	23	3	22	5	17	0	43	8	28
1973	3	5	8	28	7	11	1	15	0	31	18	30
1974	3	7	18	26	10	7	4	15	1	29	31	45
1975	2	12	17	24	8	1	7	20	2	33	27	55
1976	5	5	9	40	9	0	7	5	4	10	23	70
1977	3	5	11	29	13	0	5	13	2	18	27	53
1978	7	7	19	19	13	0	4	13	1	20	39	32
1979	6	7	16	19	10	1	1	12	2	20	32	30
1980	3	8	22	8	17	0	1	7	2	15	42	14
1981	8	17	33	25	26	0	11	13	1	30	67	44
1982	14	10	45	41	44	0	13	10	1	20	103	71
1983	14	18	61	48	41	2	13	6	5	26	116	84
1984	2	15	41	58	38	1	17	14	8	30	81	102
1985	20	11	65	46	47	0	18	12	5	23	132	89
1986	20	14	60	69	45	1	26	12	5	27	125	121
1987	38	18	75	46	53	1	11	15	4	34	166	82
1988	26	17	86	90	57	1	21	11	5	29	169	138
1989	10	5	43	61	21	1	3	14	0	20	74	86
1990	11	13	52	79	20	1	10	16	6	30	83	117
1991	14	9	45	78	24	2	17	14	2	25	83	121
1992	14	5	36	107	12	1	22	13	9	19	62	154
1993	15	8	43	105	22	2	20	9	2	19	80	154
1994	10	5	37	86	10	1	17	6	3	12	57	123
1995	7	12	23	36	7	0	0	12	2	24	37	45
1996	2	6	20	32	6	0	2	5	6	11	28	59
1997	3	3	17	39	6	1	2	13	5	17	26	71
1998	15	10	24	63	9	0	5	14	6	24	48	90
1999	28	8	43	70	24	1	3	15	10	24	95	105
2000	12	8	38	31	16	2	1	9	6	19	66	52
2001	22	8	71	36	29	2	2	5	8	15	122	54
2002	20	4	68	42	22	1	4	10	9	15	110	64
2003	20	4	46	24	28	0	0	2	17	6	94	43
2004	20	7	41	39	14	5	0	2	14	14	75	56
2005	16	5	65	24	25	1	1	6	12	12	106	43
2006	24	6	46	28	19	1	0	1	6	8	89	39
2007	27	6	68	43	30	0	0	4	16	10	125	64
2008	27	4	47	25	32	1	0	3	11	8	106	38
2009	35	5	60	48	33	1	0	10	18	16	128	73
2010	26	5	65	37	36	2	1	6	14	13	127	59
2011	34	10	70	55	36	1	0	1	24	12	140	83

OPCW

Again, in the first step I create a corpus from the annual codings and pre-process the texts to remove stopwords, punctuation and upper case letters.

```r
corpus <- Corpus(DirSource("../data/corpora/opcw-part-events/",
                  encoding="UTF-8"), readerControl=list(language="en"))
corpusVars <- data.frame(var1=factor(rep("", length(corpus))),
                  row.names=names(corpus))
dtmCorpus <- corpus
dtmCorpus <- tm_map(dtmCorpus, content_transformer(tolower))
dtmCorpus <- tm_map(dtmCorpus,
    content_transformer(function(x)
    gsub("(["”\n]|[[:punct:]]|[[:space:]]|[[:cntrl:]])+", " ", x)))
dtmCorpus <- tm_map(dtmCorpus, removeNumbers)
dtm <- DocumentTermMatrix(dtmCorpus,
                  control=list(tolower=FALSE, wordLengths=c(2, Inf)))
rm(dtmCorpus)
dictionary <- data.frame(row.names=colnames(dtm),
                  "Occurrences"=col_sums(dtm),
                  "Stopword"=ifelse(colnames(dtm) %in% stopwords("en"),
                  "Stopword", ""),   stringsAsFactors=FALSE)
dtm <- dtm[, !colnames(dtm) %in% stopwords("en")]
attr(dtm, "dictionary") <- dictionary
rm(dictionary)
meta(corpus, type="corpus", tag="language") <-
    attr(dtm, "language") <- "en"
meta(corpus, type="corpus", tag="processing") <-
    attr(dtm, "processing") <- c(lowercase=TRUE, punctuation=TRUE,
                  digits=TRUE, stopwords=TRUE, stemming=FALSE,
                  customStemming=FALSE, twitter=FALSE,
                  removeHashtags=NA, removeNames=NA)
corpus


## «VCorpus (documents: 15, metadata (corpus/indexed): 2/0)»


dtm


## «DocumentTermMatrix (documents: 15, terms: 2238)»
## Non-/sparse entries: 7251/26319
## Sparsity           : 78%
## Maximal term length: 24
## Weighting          : term frequency (tf)
```

In the second step, I first collect all search terms that still have different orthography. Second, I group them together according to the overarching topics of Science, Training, and Advice.

```r
terms <- as.data.frame(as.matrix(dtm))
terms$Year <- 1997:2011

## combine relevant terms
terms$WORKSHOP <- terms$workshop + terms$workshops + terms$workshopin
terms$SEMINAR <- terms$seminar + terms$seminars +terms$seminarfrom
terms$TRAINING <- terms$training
terms$MEETING <- terms$meeting + terms$meetings
terms$COURSE <- terms$course + terms$courseswere +
    terms$coursebefore + terms$coursefor + terms$courses +
    terms$courseswere
terms$PANEL <- terms$panelists
terms$SYMPOSIA <- terms$symposium
terms$NETWORK <- terms$network
terms$ADVISOR <- terms$advisory + terms$adviser

## create term categories
terms$GROUP_SCIENCE <- terms$SEMINAR + terms$PANEL + terms$SYMPOSIA
terms$GROUP_TRAINING <- terms$TRAINING + terms$COURSE + terms$WORKSHOP
terms$GROUP_ADVICE <- terms$MEETING + terms$NETWORK + terms$ADVISOR


write.csv(terms, file = "coding_terms_opcw.csv")


terms2 <- terms %>% select(Year, WORKSHOP, SEMINAR, TRAINING,
                   MEETING, COURSE, PANEL, SYMPOSIA, NETWORK,
                   GROUP_SCIENCE, GROUP_TRAINING, GROUP_ADVICE)
write.csv(terms2, file = "coding_terms3.csv")
```

Year	WORKSHOP	SEMINAR	TRAINING	MEETING	COURSE	PANEL	SYMPOSIA	NETWORK	GROUP_SCIENCE	GROUP_TRAINING	GROUP_ADVICE
1997	1	4	6	1	10	0	0	0	4	17	2
1998	3	9	4	4	9	0	5	2	14	16	11
1999	7	8	22	8	25	0	3	3	11	54	15
2000	18	3	22	12	21	0	0	5	3	61	19
2001	13	2	10	12	8	1	1	2	4	31	17
2002	6	3	12	9	17	0	0	1	3	35	12
2003	9	3	6	8	6	0	0	6	3	21	16
2004	12	1	9	7	9	0	0	4	1	30	14
2005	13	1	11	5	10	0	0	0	1	34	8
2006	12	3	7	7	14	0	0	0	3	33	9
2007	11	0	9	4	9	0	0	0	0	29	6
2008	13	2	12	9	11	0	0	0	2	36	11
2009	16	3	15	17	19	0	0	1	3	50	20
2010	12	4	20	12	27	0	0	1	4	59	15
2011	11	9	14	8	14	0	0	1	9	39	11

C QCA Analysis details

In the following appendix, I present the R Code to reproduce the truth tables and analyses in Chapter 5. I do not print the truth tables, here, as they are already included in the chapter. In addition, I add some illustrations and graphs for the QCA analyses. Also, I show the results of some individual analyses that I do not present in chapter 5. They are for illustration purposes.

First, I load the required R packages[32]:

```
library(QCA)
library(QCA3)
library(wordcloud)
library(SetMethods)
library(car)
```

Next, I import the raw data and create an empty data-set for the QCA data:

```
data <- read.csv("../data/raw-data.csv")
data$X <- NULL # clean up import artifact
data$cases <- paste(data$IO, data$Year, sep = "") # name cases
data_qca <- as.data.frame(matrix(0, ncol = 0, nrow = 70))
data_qca$cases <- data$cases
# add case names as row names
row.names(data_qca) <- data_qca$cases
```

C.1 CALIBRATION

The following code-blocks show the steps I took to calibrate the data-set. Again, the detailed description is included in Chapter 5.

---

[32]Dusa, Adrian and Alrik Thiem (2014). QCA: A Package for Qualitative Comparative Analysis. R package version 1.1-3. URL: http://cran.r-project.org/package=QCA. Fellows, Ian (2014). wordcloud: Word Clouds. R package version 2.5. URL: http://CRAN.R-project.org/package=wordcloud. Fox, John and Sanford Weisberg (2011). An {R} Companion to Applied Regression, Second Edition. Thousand Oaks CA: Sage. URL: http://socserv.socsci.mcmaster.ca/jfox/Books/Companion. Huang, Ronggui. (2014). QCA3: Yet another package for Qualitative Comparative Analysis. R package version 0.0-7. URL: http://asrr.r-forge.r-project.org/. Quaranta, Mario (2013). SetMethods: A Package Companion to "Set-Theoretic Methods for the Social Sciences". R package version 1.0. URL: http://CRAN.R-project.org/package=SetMethods.

259

C.1.1   TALK

```
thr1 <- 1
data_qca$TALK.Part <- c(thr1, 1, 1, thr1, thr1, rep(0, 31), rep(thr1, 5),
            1,thr1, rep(1, 3), rep(thr1, 3), 1, rep(thr1, 4), 1, 0, 1, 1,
            rep(thr1, 10), 1, 1)
data_qca$TALK.Trans <- c(rep(0, 36), rep(thr1, 9), 1, rep(thr1, 8), 1, 0,
            rep(thr1, 2), 1, thr1, thr1, 1, rep(thr1, 7), 1)
```

C.1.2   DECISION

```
thr1 <- 0
thr2 <- 1
data_qca$DEC.Part <- c(rep(0, 15), rep(1, 4), rep(0, 36), rep(1, 7),
            rep(0,8))

data_qca$DEC.Trans <- c(rep(0, 29), rep(thr1, 7), rep(thr2, 7),
            rep(1, 12), 0, thr1, rep(thr2, 11), rep(1, 2))
```

C.1.3   ACTION

```
data_qca$ACT.Part.1 <-  c(0, rep(1, 7), rep(0, 26), rep(1, 21), rep(1, 4),
            rep(0, 8), rep(1, 3))
data_qca$ACT.Part.2 <-  c(rep(0, 51), rep(1, 4), rep(0, 12), rep(1, 3))
data_qca$ACT.Part.4 <-  c(rep(0, 25), rep(1, 13), rep(0, 3), rep(1, 5),
            rep(0, 2), rep(1, 7), rep(0, 7), rep(1, 3),0, 0, 1, 1, 1)
data_qca$ACT.Trans <- c(rep(0, 4), rep(1, 3), rep(0, 38), rep(1, 10),
            rep(0, 7), rep(1, 4), rep(0, 4))
```

C.1.4   RESOURCE-BASED CONDITIONS

```
thr1 <- 1
data_qca$RB.Budget <-  c(rep(0, 26), rep(thr1, 4), rep(0, 6), rep(thr1, 9),
            rep(0, 10), rep(0, 2), rep(1, 4), rep(0, 6), rep(thr1, 3))
data_qca$RB.Inequality <-  recode(data$RB.Inequality,
            recodes = "0:0.8126000=0; 0.8126313:0.9=1")
data_qca$RB.Complexity <- c(rep(1, 55), rep(0, 15))
```

C.1.5   NORM-BASED CONDITIONS

```
thr1 <- 1
data_qca$NB.visibility.all <-  c(rep(0, 29), rep(thr1, 5), rep(1, 4),
          rep(thr1, 7), rep(1, 6), rep(thr1, 3), 1, rep(0, 15))
data_qca$NB.visibility.hl <-  c(rep(0, 29), rep(1, 3), rep(0, 10),
          rep(1, 5), rep(0, 5), rep(1, 3), rep(0, 15))
data_qca$NB.gov.depth <- c(rep(0, 13), rep(0, 21), rep(1, 21), rep(0, 15))
data_qca$NB.dem.mem <-  c(rep(0, 36), rep(1, 19), rep(0, 7), rep(1, 8))
data_qca$NB.og.norm <-  c(rep(0, 33), rep(thr1, 6), rep(1, 16), rep(1, 15))
```

C.2 QCA ANALYSES

Next, I present the analysis of the individual outcome variables and of some
combined outcomes. In the analysis for sufficiency, I limit the presentation
to the intermediate solution for those analyses I do not present in more
detail in Chapter 5.

C.2.1 PARTICIPATION TALK

```
#truth table w/o IAEA1957:1961, OPCW 1997
data_qca$TALKPART <- data_qca$TALK.Part # for QCA package conventions
tt <- truthTable(data_qca[c(6:55, 57:70), c(18, 10:17)], outcome =
          c("TALKPART"), incl.cut1=1, sort.by="incl",
          show.cases = TRUE)


# necessary conditions for participation talk
superSubset(data_qca[c(6:55, 57:70), c(18, 10:17)], outcome =
          "TALKPART", relation="necessity", incl.cut=1, cov.cut=0.8)


##
##                                   incl   cov.r
## ————————————————————
## 1   NB.OG.NORM                    1.000  0.917
## 2   rb.complexity+NB.DEM.MEM      1.000  1.000
## 3   rb.complexity+NB.GOV.DEPTH    1.000  0.943
## 4   rb.complexity+NB.VISIBILITY.ALL 1.000  0.825
## 5   RB.INEQUALITY+NB.DEM.MEM      1.000  1.000
## 6   RB.INEQUALITY+NB.GOV.DEPTH    1.000  0.943
## 7   RB.INEQUALITY+NB.VISIBILITY.ALL 1.000  0.825
## ————————————————————


# neg. outcome, to check for contradictions
superSubset(data_qca[c(6:55, 57:70), c(18, 10:17)], outcome =
          "TALKPART", relation="necessity", incl.cut=1, cov.cut=1,
          neg.out = T)
```

```
##
##                                                 incl   cov.r
## ─────────────────────────
## 1   RB.COMPLEXITY*nb.dem.mem                     1.000  1.000
## 2   rb.inequality*nb.dem.mem                     1.000  1.000
## 3   rb.inequality*RB.COMPLEXITY*nb.dem.mem       1.000  1.000
## ─────────────────────────


## sufficient conditions without nc og.norm
tt <- truthTable(data_qca[c(6:55, 57:70), c(18, 10:16)],
          outcome = c("TALKPART"), incl.cut1=1, sort.by="incl",
          show.cases = TRUE)
eqmcc(tt, include="?", show.cases = TRUE, details = TRUE,
          dir.exp = c(rep(1, 7)))


##
## n OUT = 1/0/C: 33/31/0
##   Total     : 64
##
## p.sol: NB.DEM.MEM + rb.complexity
##
## Number of multiple-covered cases: 0
##
## M1:     RB.INEQUALITY*rb.complexity +
##         RB.COMPLEXITY*NB.VISIBILITY.ALL*NB.GOV.DEPTH*NB.DEM.MEM
##         <=> TALKPART
##
##                                                      incl   cov.r  cov.u
## ─────────────────────────────
## 1   RB.INEQUALITY*rb.complexity                       1.000  0.424  0.424
## 2   RB.COMPLEXITY*NB.VISIBILITY.ALL*NB.GOV.DEPTH*NB.DEM.MEM  1.000  0.576  0.576
## ─────────────────────────────
##     M1                                                1.000  1.000
##
##                                                      cases
## ─────────────────────────────
## 1   RB.INEQUALITY*rb.complexity        OPCW1998,OPCW2003;
##                                        OPCW2004,OPCW2005,OPCW2006,OPCW2007,
##                                        OPCW2008;OPCW1999,OPCW2000,OPCW2001,
##                                        OPCW2002;OPCW2009,OPCW2010,OPCW2011
## 2   RB.COMPLEXITY*NB.VISIBILITY.ALL*
##         NB.GOV.DEPTH*NB.DEM.MEM        IAEA2004,IAEA2005,IAEA2006,IAEA2007,
##                                        IAEA2008;IAEA2002,IAEA2003;
##                                        IAEA2009,IAEA2010,IAEA2011;
##                                        IAEA1993,IAEA1994,IAEA1995,IAEA1996,
##                                        IAEA1997,IAEA1998;IAEA1999,IAEA2000,
##                                        IAEA2001
## ─────────────────────────────
##
##
## p.sol: NB.DEM.MEM + RB.INEQUALITY
##
```

```
## Number of multiple-covered cases: 3
##
## M1:      RB.INEQUALITY +
##          RB.COMPLEXITY*NB.VISIBILITY.ALL*NB.GOV.DEPTH*NB.DEM.MEM
##          <=> TALKPART
##
##
##                                                                    incl   cov.r  cov.u
## ---------------------------------------------
## 1   RB.INEQUALITY                                                  1.000  0.515  0.424
## 2   RB.COMPLEXITY*NB.VISIBILITY.ALL*NB.GOV.DEPTH*NB.DEM.MEM        1.000  0.576  0.485
## ---------------------------------------------
##      M1                                                            1.000  1.000
##
##                                                                    cases
## ----------------------------------------
## 1   RB.INEQUALITY                        OPCW1998,OPCW2003;
##                                          OPCW2004,OPCW2005,OPCW2006,OPCW2007,
##                                          OPCW2008;IAEA2009,IAEA2010,IAEA2011;
##                                          OPCW1999,OPCW2000,OPCW2001,OPCW2002;
##                                          OPCW2009,OPCW2010,OPCW2011
## 2   RB.COMPLEXITY*NB.VISIBILITY.ALL*
##          NB.GOV.DEPTH*NB.DEM.MEM         IAEA2004,IAEA2005,IAEA2006,IAEA2007,
##                                          IAEA2008;IAEA2002,IAEA2003;
##                                          IAEA2009,IAEA2010,IAEA2011;
##                                          IAEA1993,IAEA1994,IAEA1995,IAEA1996,
##                                          IAEA1997,IAEA1998;IAEA1999,IAEA2000,
##                                          IAEA2001
## ----------------------------------------


# neg. outcome, to check for contradictions
tt <- truthTable(data_qca[c(6:55, 57:70), c(18, 10:16)],
          outcome = c("TALKPART"), incl.cut1=1, sort.by="incl",
          show.cases = TRUE, neg.out = T)
eqmcc(tt, include="?", show.cases = TRUE, details = TRUE)



##
## n OUT = 1/0/C: 31/33/0
##    Total      : 64
##
## Number of multiple-covered cases: 0
##
## M1: RB.COMPLEXITY*nb.dem.mem <=> talkpart
## M2: rb.inequality*nb.dem.mem <=> talkpart
##
##                                     ---------
##                            incl   cov.r  cov.u  (M1)   (M2)
## ----------------------------
## 1   RB.COMPLEXITY*nb.dem.mem   1.000  1.000  0.000    -
## 2   rb.inequality*nb.dem.mem   1.000  1.000  0.000           -
## ----------------------------
##      M1                        1.000  1.000
##      M2                        1.000  1.000
```

```
##
##                                     cases
## ──────────-
## 1   RB.COMPLEXITY*nb.dem.mem   IAEA1962,IAEA1963,IAEA1964,IAEA1965,IAEA1966,IAEA1967,
##                                IAEA1968,IAEA1969,IAEA1970,IAEA1971,IAEA1972,IAEA1973,
##                                IAEA1974,IAEA1975,IAEA1976,IAEA1977,IAEA1978,IAEA1979,
##                                IAEA1980,IAEA1981,IAEA1982;IAEA1989,IAEA1990; IAEA1991,
##                                IAEA1992; IAEA1987,IAEA1988;IAEA1983,IAEA1984,IAEA1985;
##      IAEA1986
## 2   rb.inequality*nb.dem.mem   IAEA1962,IAEA1963,IAEA1964,IAEA1965,IAEA1966,IAEA1967,
##                                IAEA1968,IAEA1969,IAEA1970,IAEA1971,IAEA1972,IAEA1973,
##                                IAEA1974,IAEA1975,IAEA1976,IAEA1977,IAEA1978,IAEA1979,
##                                IAEA1980,IAEA1981,IAEA1982;IAEA1989,IAEA1990; IAEA1991,
##                                IAEA1992; IAEA1987,IAEA1988;IAEA1983,IAEA1984,IAEA1985;
##                                IAEA1986
## ──────────-
```

C.2.2 Transparency Talk

```
data_qca$TALKTRANS <- data_qca$TALK.Trans # for QCA package conventions
tt <- truthTable(data_qca[c(1:55, 57:70), c(19, 10:17)],
          outcome = c("TALKTRANS"), incl.cut1=1, sort.by="incl",
          show.cases = TRUE)
# necessary conditions
superSubset(data_qca[c(1:55, 57:60), c(19, 10:17)], outcome = "TALKTRANS",
          relation="nec", incl.cut=0.9, cov.cut=0.76)
```

```
##
##                                   incl   cov.r
## ─────────────────
## 1   NB.OG.NORM                    1.000  0.885
## 2   rb.complexity+NB.DEM.MEM      1.000  1.000
## 3   rb.complexity+NB.GOV.DEPTH    1.000  0.920
## 4   rb.complexity+NB.VISIBILITY.ALL  1.000  0.767
## 5   RB.INEQUALITY+NB.DEM.MEM      1.000  1.000
## 6   RB.INEQUALITY+NB.GOV.DEPTH    1.000  0.920
## 7   RB.INEQUALITY+NB.VISIBILITY.ALL  1.000  0.767
## 8   RB.BUDGET+NB.DEM.MEM          0.957  0.846
## 9   RB.BUDGET+NB.GOV.DEPTH        0.957  0.786
## ─────────────────
```

```
# neg. outcome, to check for contradictions
superSubset(data_qca[c(1:55, 57:60), c(19, 10:17)], outcome = "TALKTRANS",
          relation="nec", incl.cut=0.9, cov.cut=0.76, neg.out = T)
```

```
##
##                                              incl   cov.r
## ─────────────────────────────
## 1   nb.og.norm                               0.917  1.000
## 2   nb.dem.mem                               1.000  0.900
```

```
##  3   nb.gov.depth                                          0.944  0.895
##  4   nb.dem.mem*nb.og.norm                                 0.917  1.000
##  5   nb.gov.depth*nb.og.norm                               0.917  1.000
##  6   nb.gov.depth*nb.dem.mem                               0.944  0.895
##  7   nb.visibility.hl*nb.dem.mem                           0.917  0.892
##  8   RB.COMPLEXITY*nb.og.norm                              0.917  1.000
##  9   RB.COMPLEXITY*nb.dem.mem                              1.000  1.000
## 10   RB.COMPLEXITY*nb.gov.depth                            0.944  1.000
## 11   rb.inequality*nb.og.norm                              0.917  1.000
## 12   rb.inequality*nb.dem.mem                              1.000  1.000
## 13   rb.inequality*nb.gov.depth                            0.944  1.000
## 14   nb.gov.depth*nb.dem.mem*nb.og.norm                    0.917  1.000
## ...
## ---------------------------
```

```r
# sufficient conditions, w/o og. norm
tt <- truthTable(data_qca[c(1:55, 57:70), c(19, 10:16)],
          outcome = c("TALKTRANS"), incl.cut1=1, sort.by="incl",
          show.cases = TRUE)
eqmcc(tt, include="?", show.cases = TRUE, details = TRUE,
          dir.exp = c(rep(1, 7)))
```

```
##
## n OUT = 1/0/C: 33/36/0
##   Total      : 69
##
## p.sol: NB.DEM.MEM + rb.complexity
##
## Number of multiple-covered cases: 0
##
## M1:    RB.INEQUALITY*rb.complexity +
##        RB.COMPLEXITY*NB.VISIBILITY.ALL*NB.GOV.DEPTH*NB.DEM.MEM
##        <=> TALKTRANS
##
##                                                       incl   cov.r  cov.u
## ---------------------------
## 1   RB.INEQUALITY*rb.complexity                       1.000  0.424  0.424
## 2   RB.COMPLEXITY*NB.VISIBILITY.ALL*NB.GOV.DEPTH*NB.DEM.MEM  1.000  0.576  0.576
## ---------------------------
##     M1                                                1.000  1.000
##
##                                                       cases
## ---------------------------
## 1   RB.INEQUALITY*rb.complexity       OPCW1998,OPCW2003;
##                                       OPCW2004,OPCW2005,OPCW2006,OPCW2007,
##                                       OPCW2008;OPCW1999,OPCW2000,OPCW2001,
##                                       OPCW2002;OPCW2009,OPCW2010,OPCW2011
## 2   RB.COMPLEXITY*NB.VISIBILITY.ALL*
##              NB.GOV.DEPTH*NB.DEM.MEM  IAEA2004,IAEA2005,IAEA2006,IAEA2007,
##                                       IAEA2008;IAEA2002,IAEA2003;
##                                       IAEA2009,IAEA2010,IAEA2011;
##                                       IAEA1993,IAEA1994,IAEA1995,IAEA1996,
```

```
##                                              IAEA1997,IAEA1998;IAEA1999,IAEA2000,
##                                              IAEA2001
## ------------------------------
##
##
## p.sol: NB.DEM.MEM + RB.INEQUALITY
##
## Number of multiple-covered cases: 3
##
## M1:    RB.INEQUALITY +
##        RB.COMPLEXITY*NB.VISIBILITY.ALL*NB.GOV.DEPTH*NB.DEM.MEM
##        <=> TALKTRANS
##
##
##                                                    incl   cov.r  cov.u
## ----------------------------
## 1   RB.INEQUALITY                                  1.000  0.515  0.424
## 2   RB.COMPLEXITY*NB.VISIBILITY.ALL*NB.GOV.DEPTH*NB.DEM.MEM  1.000  0.576  0.485
## ----------------------------
##    M1                                              1.000  1.000
##
##                                                    cases
## ----------------------------
## 1   RB.INEQUALITY                 OPCW1998,OPCW2003;
##                                   OPCW2004,OPCW2005,OPCW2006,OPCW2007,
##                                   OPCW2008;IAEA2009,IAEA2010,IAEA2011;
##                                   OPCW1999,OPCW2000,OPCW2001,OPCW2002;
##                                   OPCW2009,OPCW2010,OPCW2011
## 2   RB.COMPLEXITY*NB.VISIBILITY.ALL*
##         NB.GOV.DEPTH*NB.DEM.MEM   IAEA2004,IAEA2005,IAEA2006,IAEA2007,
##                                   IAEA2008;IAEA2002,IAEA2003;
##                                   IAEA2009,IAEA2010,IAEA2011;
##                                   IAEA1993,IAEA1994,IAEA1995,IAEA1996,
##                                   IAEA1997,IAEA1998;IAEA1999,IAEA2000,
##                                   IAEA2001
## ----------------------------


# neg. outcome, to check for contradictions
tt <- truthTable(data_qca[c(1:55, 57:70), c(19, 10:16)],
          outcome = c("TALKTRANS"), incl.cut1=0.8, sort.by="incl",
          show.cases = TRUE, neg.out = T)
eqmcc(tt, include="?", show.cases = TRUE, details = TRUE)


##
## n OUT = 1/0/C: 36/33/0
##   Total      : 69
##
## Number of multiple-covered cases: 0
##
## M1: RB.COMPLEXITY*nb.dem.mem <=> talktrans
## M2: rb.inequality*nb.dem.mem <=> talktrans
##
##                                         ------
```

```
##                               incl  cov.r  cov.u  (M1)    (M2)
## -----------------------------
## 1  RB.COMPLEXITY*nb.dem.mem   1.000  1.000  0.000   -
## 2  rb.inequality*nb.dem.mem   1.000  1.000  0.000           -
## -----------------------------
##     M1                        1.000  1.000
##     M2                        1.000  1.000
##
##                               cases
## -----------------------------
## 1  RB.COMPLEXITY*nb.dem.mem   IAEA1957,IAEA1958,IAEA1959,IAEA1960,IAEA1961,IAEA1962,
##                               IAEA1963,IAEA1964,IAEA1965,IAEA1966,IAEA1967,IAEA1968,
##                               IAEA1969,IAEA1970,IAEA1971,IAEA1972,IAEA1973,IAEA1974,
##                               IAEA1975,IAEA1976,IAEA1977,IAEA1978,IAEA1979,IAEA1980,
##                               IAEA1981,IAEA1982;IAEA1989,IAEA1990; IAEA1991,IAEA1992;
##                               IAEA1987,IAEA1988;IAEA1983,IAEA1984,IAEA1985; IAEA1986
## 2  rb.inequality*nb.dem.mem   IAEA1957,IAEA1958,IAEA1959,IAEA1960,IAEA1961,IAEA1962,
##                               IAEA1963,IAEA1964,IAEA1965,IAEA1966,IAEA1967,IAEA1968,
##                               IAEA1969,IAEA1970,IAEA1971,IAEA1972,IAEA1973,IAEA1974,
##                               IAEA1975,IAEA1976,IAEA1977,IAEA1978,IAEA1979,IAEA1980,
##                               IAEA1981,IAEA1982;IAEA1989,IAEA1990; IAEA1991,IAEA1992;
##                               IAEA1987,IAEA1988;IAEA1983,IAEA1984,IAEA1985; IAEA1986
## -----------------------------
```

C.2.3   COMBINED TALK

```r
#truth table
data_qca$TALK <- fsor(data_qca$TALK.Part,
          data_qca$TALK.Trans) # for QCA package conventions


tt <- truthTable(data_qca[c(20, 10:11, 13:17)], outcome =
          c("TALK"), incl.cut1=1, sort.by="incl",
          show.cases = TRUE)


# necessary conditions for participation talk
superSubset(data_qca[c(20, 10:17)], outcome =
          "TALK", relation="necessity", incl.cut=0.8, cov.cut=0.8)
```

```
##
##                                    incl   cov.r
## -----------------------------
## 1  NB.OG.NORM                      0.868  0.892
## 2  rb.complexity+NB.DEM.MEM        0.868  0.971
## 3  rb.complexity+NB.GOV.DEPTH      0.868  0.917
## 4  rb.complexity+NB.VISIBILITY.ALL 0.868  0.805
## 5  RB.INEQUALITY+NB.DEM.MEM        0.868  0.971
## 6  RB.INEQUALITY+NB.GOV.DEPTH      0.868  0.917
## 7  RB.INEQUALITY+NB.VISIBILITY.ALL 0.868  0.805
## 8  RB.BUDGET+NB.DEM.MEM            0.816  0.886
## -----------------------------
```

```
# neg. outcome, to check for contradictions
superSubset(data_qca[c(20, 10:17)], outcome =
            "TALK", relation="necessity", incl.cut=0.8, cov.cut=0.8,
            neg.out = T)
```

```
##
##                                                     incl   cov.r
## ----------------------------------------------
## 1   nb.og.norm                                      0.875  0.848
## 2   nb.dem.mem*nb.og.norm                           0.875  0.848
## 3   nb.gov.depth*nb.og.norm                         0.875  0.848
## 4   RB.COMPLEXITY*nb.og.norm                        0.875  0.848
## 5   RB.COMPLEXITY*nb.dem.mem                        0.969  0.861
## 6   RB.COMPLEXITY*nb.gov.depth                      0.906  0.853
## 7   rb.inequality*nb.og.norm                        0.875  0.848
## 8   rb.inequality*nb.dem.mem                        0.969  0.861
## 9   rb.inequality*nb.gov.depth                      0.906  0.853
## 10  rb.budget*nb.dem.mem                            0.875  0.800
## ...
## ----------------------------------------------
```

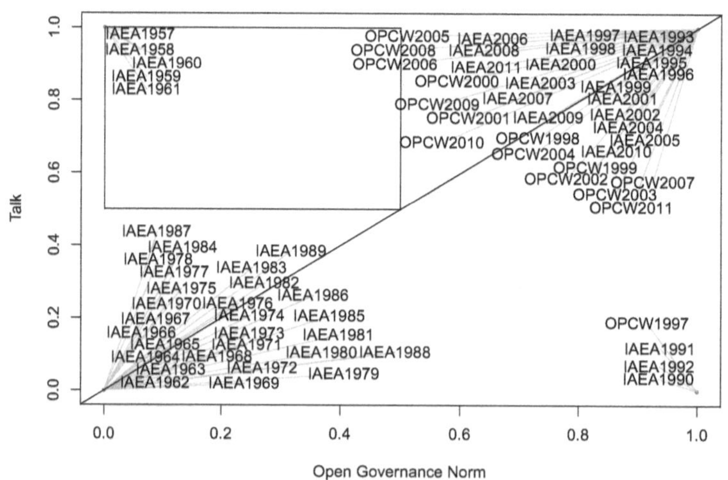

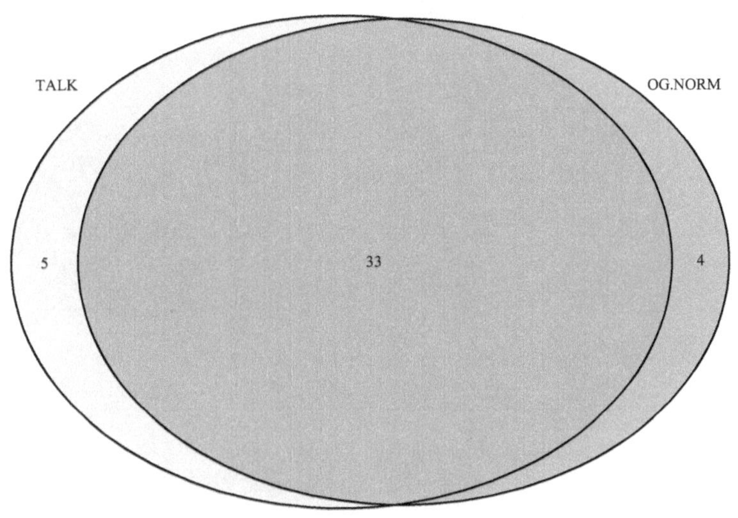


```
## sufficient conditions without nc og.norm
tt <- truthTable(data_qca[c(20, 10:11, 13:16)],
          outcome = c("TALK"), incl.cut1=1, sort.by="incl",
          show.cases = TRUE)
# conservative solution
eqmcc(tt, show.cases = TRUE, details = TRUE)


##
## n OUT = 1/0/C: 31/39/0
##   Total     : 70
##
## Number of multiple-covered cases: 5
##
## M1: rb.inequality*NB.VISIBILITY.ALL*NB.GOV.DEPTH*NB.DEM.MEM +
##     rb.budget*NB.VISIBILITY.ALL*NB.VISIBILITY.HL*NB.GOV.DEPTH*NB.DEM.MEM +
##     RB.BUDGET*RB.INEQUALITY*nb.visibility.all*nb.visibility.hl*nb.gov.depth +
##     RB.INEQUALITY*nb.visibility.all*nb.visibility.hl*nb.gov.depth*NB.DEM.MEM
##     => TALK
##
##                                                               incl  cov.r  cov.u
## ───────────────────────────────────────────────
## 1   rb.inequality*NB.VISIBILITY.ALL*NB.GOV.DEPTH*NB.DEM.MEM    1.000  0.421  0.368
## 2   rb.budget*NB.VISIBILITY.ALL*NB.VISIBILITY.HL*NB.GOV.DEPTH*
##                                            NB.DEM.MEM          1.000  0.132  0.079
## 3   RB.BUDGET*RB.INEQUALITY*nb.visibility.all*nb.visibility.hl*
##                                            nb.gov.depth        1.000  0.184  0.105
## 4   RB.INEQUALITY*nb.visibility.all*nb.visibility.hl*
##                        nb.gov.depth*NB.DEM.MEM                 1.000  0.211  0.132
```

```
## ----------------------------------------
##    M1                                                               1.000  0.816
##
##                                                                              cases
## -----------------------------------------
## 1  rb.inequality*NB.VISIBILITY.ALL*NB.GOV.DEPTH*NB.DEM.MEM          IAEA2004,IAEA2005,
##                                                                     IAEA2006,IAEA2007,
##                                                                     IAEA2008;
##                                                                     IAEA2002,IAEA2003;
##                                                                     IAEA1993,IAEA1994,
##                                                                     IAEA1995,IAEA1996,
##                                                                     IAEA1997,IAEA1998;
##                                                                     IAEA1999,IAEA2000,
##                                                                     IAEA2001
## 2  rb.budget*NB.VISIBILITY.ALL*NB.VISIBILITY.HL*NB.GOV.DEPTH*
##                                                 NB.DEM.MEM          IAEA2002,IAEA2003;
##                                                                     IAEA2009,IAEA2010,
##                                                                     IAEA2011
## 3  RB.BUDGET*RB.INEQUALITY*nb.visibility.all*nb.visibility.hl*
##                                                 nb.gov.depth        OPCW1999,OPCW2000,
##                                                                     OPCW2001,OPCW2002;
##                                                                     OPCW2009,OPCW2010,
##                                                                     OPCW2011
## 4  RB.INEQUALITY*nb.visibility.all*nb.visibility.hl*
##                               nb.gov.depth*NB.DEM.MEM               OPCW2004,OPCW2005,
##                                                                     OPCW2006,OPCW2007,
##                                                                     OPCW2008;OPCW2009,
##                                                                     OPCW2010,OPCW2011
## -----------------------------------------


# intermediary solution
eqmcc(tt, include="?", show.cases = TRUE, details = TRUE,
          dir.exp = c(rep(1, 6)))


##
## n OUT = 1/0/C: 31/39/0
##    Total      : 70
##
## p.sol: NB.DEM.MEM + RB.BUDGET*RB.INEQUALITY
##
## Number of multiple-covered cases: 6
##
## M1:    RB.BUDGET*RB.INEQUALITY + RB.INEQUALITY*NB.DEM.MEM +
##        NB.VISIBILITY.ALL*NB.GOV.DEPTH*NB.DEM.MEM => TALK
##
##                                                 incl   cov.r  cov.u
## -----------------------------------
## 1  RB.BUDGET*RB.INEQUALITY                      1.000  0.184  0.105
## 2  RB.INEQUALITY*NB.DEM.MEM                     1.000  0.289  0.132
## 3  NB.VISIBILITY.ALL*NB.GOV.DEPTH*NB.DEM.MEM    1.000  0.500  0.421
## -----------------------------
##    M1                                           1.000  0.816
```

```
##
##                                               cases
## ─────────────────────
## 1   RB.BUDGET*RB.INEQUALITY            OPCW1999,OPCW2000,OPCW2001,OPCW2002;
##                                        OPCW2009,OPCW2010,OPCW2011
## 2   RB.INEQUALITY*NB.DEM.MEM           OPCW2004,OPCW2005,OPCW2006,OPCW2007,OPCW2008;
##                                        IAEA2009,IAEA2010,IAEA2011; OPCW2009,OPCW2010,
##                                        OPCW2011
## 3   NB.VISIBILITY.ALL*NB.GOV.DEPTH*
##                        NB.DEM.MEM      IAEA2004,IAEA2005,IAEA2006,IAEA2007,IAEA2008;
##                                        IAEA2002,IAEA2003; IAEA2009,IAEA2010,IAEA2011;
##                                        IAEA1993,IAEA1994,IAEA1995,IAEA1996,IAEA1997,
##                                        IAEA1998;IAEA1999,IAEA2000,IAEA2001
## ─────────────────────


# parsimonious solution
eqmcc(tt, include="?", show.cases = TRUE, details = TRUE)


##
## n OUT = 1/0/C: 31/39/0
##    Total      : 70
##
## Number of multiple-covered cases: 3
##
## M1: NB.DEM.MEM + RB.BUDGET*RB.INEQUALITY => TALK
##
##                             incl   cov.r  cov.u
## ───────────────────
## 1   NB.DEM.MEM              1.000  0.711  0.632
## 2   RB.BUDGET*RB.INEQUALITY 1.000  0.184  0.105
## ───────────────────
##    M1                       1.000  0.816
##
##                             cases
## ─────────────
## 1   NB.DEM.MEM              IAEA2004,IAEA2005,IAEA2006,IAEA2007,IAEA2008; IAEA2002,
##                            IAEA2003;OPCW2004,OPCW2005,OPCW2006,OPCW2007,OPCW2008;
##                            IAEA2009,IAEA2010,IAEA2011;IAEA1993,IAEA1994,IAEA1995,
##                            IAEA1996,IAEA1997,IAEA1998;IAEA1999,IAEA2000,IAEA2001;
##                            OPCW2009,OPCW2010,OPCW2011
## 2   RB.BUDGET*RB.INEQUALITY OPCW1999,OPCW2000,OPCW2001,OPCW2002; OPCW2009,OPCW2010,
##                            OPCW2011
## ─────────────


# neg. outcome, to check for contradictions
tt <- truthTable(data_qca[c(20, 10:11, 13:16)],
          outcome = c("TALK"), incl.cut1=1, sort.by="incl",
          show.cases = TRUE, neg.out = T)
sc <- eqmcc(tt, include="?", show.cases = TRUE, details = TRUE,
          dir.exp = c(rep(1, 6)))
```

```
sc$i.sol$C1P1$IC
```

```
##
##
##
##                                           incl   cov.r  cov.u
## ————————————————-
## 1   NB.VISIBILITY.ALL*nb.dem.mem          1.000  0.219  0.188
## 2   RB.BUDGET*rb.inequality*nb.dem.mem    1.000  0.125  0.094
## ————————————————-
##      M1                                   1.000  0.312
##
##                                           cases
## ————————————————-
## 1   NB.VISIBILITY.ALL*nb.dem.mem          IAEA1989,IAEA1990; IAEA1991,IAEA1992;
##                                           IAEA1987,IAEA1988; IAEA1986
## 2   RB.BUDGET*rb.inequality*nb.dem.mem    IAEA1983,IAEA1984,IAEA1985; IAEA1986
## ————————————————-
```

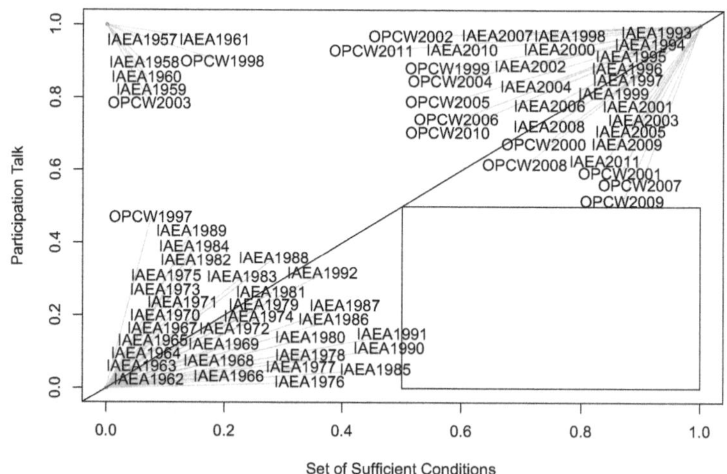

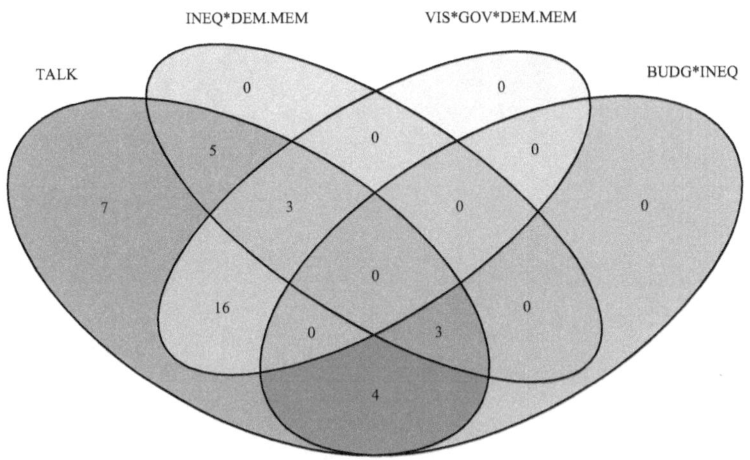

C.2.4 Participation Decision

```
data_qca$DECPART <- data_qca$DEC.Part # for QCA package conventions


tt <- truthTable(data_qca[c(21, 10:17)],
          outcome = c("DECPART"), incl.cut1=1, sort.by="incl",
          show.cases = TRUE)
superSubset(data_qca[c(21, 10:17)], outcome = "DECPART",
          relation="nec", incl.cut=0.6, cov.cut=0.7)



##
##                                      incl   cov.r
## ---------------------------------------------
## 1   nb.dem.mem*NB.OG.NORM            0.636  0.700
## 2   rb.complexity*nb.dem.mem         0.636  1.000
## 3   RB.INEQUALITY*nb.dem.mem         0.636  1.000
## ...
## ---------------------------------------------


# neg. outcome, to check for contradictions
superSubset(data_qca[c(21, 10:17)], outcome = "DECPART",
          relation="nec", incl.cut=0.8, cov.cut=0.9, neg.out = T)



##
##                               incl   cov.r
```

```
## ————————————
## 1  RB.COMPLEXITY                 0.864  0.927
## 2  rb.inequality                 0.814  0.923
## 3  rb.inequality*RB.COMPLEXITY   0.814  0.923
## 4  NB.DEM.MEM+nb.og.norm         0.949  0.933
## 5  NB.GOV.DEPTH+nb.og.norm       0.847  0.926
## 6  NB.VISIBILITY.ALL+nb.og.norm  0.864  0.927
## ————————————
```

```r
# sufficient conditions
eqmcc(tt, include="?", show.cases = TRUE, details = TRUE,
          dir.exp = c(rep(1, 8)))
```

```
##
## n OUT = 1/0/C: 7/63/0
##    Total      : 70
##
## p.sol: rb.complexity*nb.dem.mem
##
## Number of multiple-covered cases: 0
##
## M1:    RB.INEQUALITY*rb.complexity*nb.visibility.all*nb.visibility.hl*
##        nb.gov.depth*nb.dem.mem*NB.OG.NORM => DECPART
##
##
##                                                       incl  cov.r  cov.u
## ——————————————————————————————————————————-
## 1  RB.INEQUALITY*rb.complexity*nb.visibility.all*
##    nb.visibility.hl*b.gov.depth*nb.dem.mem*NB.OG.NORM  1.000  0.636   -
## ——————————————————————————————————————————-
##    M1                                                  1.000  0.636
##
##                                                       cases
## ——————————————————————————————————————————-
## 1  RB.INEQUALITY*rb.complexity*nb.visibility.all*
##    nb.visibility.hl*nb.gov.depth*nb.dem.mem*NB.OG.NORM  OPCW1997,OPCW1998,OPCW2003;
##                                                         OPCW1999,OPCW2000,OPCW2001,
##                                                         OPCW2002
## ——————————————————————————————————————————-
##
##
## p.sol: RB.INEQUALITY*nb.dem.mem
##
## Number of multiple-covered cases: 0
##
## M1:    RB.INEQUALITY*rb.complexity*nb.visibility.all*nb.visibility.hl*
##        nb.gov.depth*nb.dem.mem*NB.OG.NORM => DECPART
##
##
##                                                       incl  cov.r  cov.u
## ——————————————————————————————————————————-
## 1  RB.INEQUALITY*rb.complexity*nb.visibility.all*
##    nb.visibility.hl*nb.gov.depth*nb.dem.mem*NB.OG.NORM  1.000  0.636   -
## ——————————————————————————————————————————-
```

```
##     M1                                                      1.000   0.636
##
##                                                            cases
## ---------------------------------------------
## 1  RB.INEQUALITY*rb.complexity*nb.visibility.all*
##     nb.visibility.hl*nb.gov.depth*nb.dem.mem*NB.OG.NORM    OPCW1997,OPCW1998,OPCW2003;
##                                                            OPCW1999,OPCW2000,OPCW2001,
##                                                            OPCW2002
## ---------------------------------------------
##
##
## p.sol: nb.visibility.all*nb.dem.mem*NB.OG.NORM
##
## Number of multiple-covered cases: 0
##
## M1:    RB.INEQUALITY*rb.complexity*nb.visibility.all*nb.visibility.hl*
##        nb.gov.depth*nb.dem.mem*NB.OG.NORM => DECPART
##
##                                                       incl   cov.r  cov.u
## -----------------------------------------------
## 1  RB.INEQUALITY*rb.complexity*nb.visibility.all*
##     nb.visibility.hl*nb.gov.depth*nb.dem.mem*NB.OG.NORM   1.000   0.636    -
## -----------------------------------------------
##     M1                                                    1.000   0.636
##
##                                                          cases
## ---------------------------------------------
## 1  RB.INEQUALITY*rb.complexity*nb.visibility.all*
##     nb.visibility.hl*nb.gov.depth*nb.dem.mem*NB.OG.NORM   OPCW1997,OPCW1998,OPCW2003;
##                                                           OPCW1999,OPCW2000,OPCW2001,
##                                                           OPCW2002
## ---------------------------------------------
```

```r
# neg. outcome, to check for contradictions
tt <- truthTable(data_qca[c(1:15, 20:70), c(21, 10:17)],
          outcome = c("DECPART"), incl.cut1=1, sort.by="incl",
          show.cases = TRUE, neg.out = T)
eqmcc(tt, include="?", show.cases = TRUE, details = TRUE,
          dir.exp = c(rep(1, 8)))
```

```
##
## n OUT = 1/0/C: 59/7/0
##   Total      : 66
##
## p.sol: NB.DEM.MEM + RB.COMPLEXITY
##
## Number of multiple-covered cases: 3
##
## M1:    RB.COMPLEXITY + RB.INEQUALITY*NB.DEM.MEM*NB.OG.NORM <=> decpart
##
##                                      incl    cov.r  cov.u
## ---------------------------
```

```
## 1   RB.COMPLEXITY                                1.000   0.864   0.814
## 2   RB.INEQUALITY*NB.DEM.MEM*NB.OG.NORM  1.000   0.186   0.136
## ---------------------------
## 
##    M1                                          1.000   1.000
## 
## 
##                                              cases
## -------------------
## 1   RB.COMPLEXITY          IAEA1957,IAEA1958,IAEA1959,IAEA1960,IAEA1961,IAEA1962,
##                            IAEA1963,IAEA1964,IAEA1965,IAEA1966,IAEA1967,IAEA1968,
##                            IAEA1969,IAEA1970,IAEA1971,IAEA1976,IAEA1977,IAEA1978,
##                            IAEA1979,IAEA1980,IAEA1981,IAEA1982;
##                            IAEA1989; IAEA1990; IAEA1991,IAEA1992;
##                            IAEA2004,IAEA2005,IAEA2006,IAEA2007,IAEA2008;
##                            IAEA1987,IAEA1988; IAEA2002,IAEA2003;
##                            IAEA2009,IAEA2010,IAEA2011; IAEA1983,IAEA1984,IAEA1985;
##                            IAEA1993,IAEA1994,IAEA1995,IAEA1996,IAEA1997,IAEA1998;
##                            IAEA1986; IAEA1999,IAEA2000,IAEA2001
## 2   RB.INEQUALITY*NB.DEM.MEM*
##                 NB.OG.NORM  OPCW2004,OPCW2005,OPCW2006,OPCW2007,OPCW2008;
##                            IAEA2009,IAEA2010,IAEA2011; OPCW2009,OPCW2010,OPCW2011
## ---------------------
## 
## 
## p.sol: NB.DEM.MEM + rb.inequality
## 
## Number of multiple-covered cases: 0
## 
## M1:    rb.inequality*RB.COMPLEXITY + RB.INEQUALITY*NB.DEM.MEM*NB.OG.NORM
##        <=> decpart
## 
##                                            incl  cov.r  cov.u
## ----------------------------
## 1   rb.inequality*RB.COMPLEXITY            1.000   0.814   0.814
## 2   RB.INEQUALITY*NB.DEM.MEM*NB.OG.NORM    1.000   0.186   0.186
## ----------------------------
##    M1                                      1.000   1.000
## 
##                                            cases
## -------------------
## 1   rb.inequality*RB.COMPLEXITY  IAEA1957,IAEA1958,IAEA1959,IAEA1960,IAEA1961,
##                                  IAEA1962,IAEA1963,IAEA1964,IAEA1965,IAEA1966,
##                                  IAEA1967,IAEA1968,IAEA1969,IAEA1970,IAEA1971,
##                                  IAEA1976,IAEA1977,IAEA1978,IAEA1979,IAEA1980,
##                                  IAEA1981,IAEA1982;IAEA1989; IAEA1990; IAEA1991,
##                                  IAEA1992;IAEA2004,IAEA2005,IAEA2006,IAEA2007,
##                                  IAEA2008;IAEA1987,IAEA1988; IAEA2002,IAEA2003;
##                                  IAEA1983,IAEA1984,IAEA1985; IAEA1993,IAEA1994,
##                                  IAEA1995,IAEA1996,IAEA1997,IAEA1998;
##                                  IAEA1986; IAEA1999,IAEA2000,IAEA2001
## 2   RB.INEQUALITY*NB.DEM.MEM*
##                 NB.OG.NORM       OPCW2004,OPCW2005,OPCW2006,OPCW2007,OPCW2008;
##                                  IAEA2009,IAEA2010,IAEA2011; OPCW2009,OPCW2010,
##                                  OPCW2011
## ---------------
```

```
##
##
## p.sol: NB.DEM.MEM + RB.COMPLEXITY
##
## Number of multiple-covered cases: 3
##
## M1:    RB.COMPLEXITY + RB.INEQUALITY*NB.DEM.MEM*NB.OG.NORM <=> decpart
##
##                                      incl   cov.r  cov.u
## ---------------------------------
## 1  RB.COMPLEXITY                     1.000  0.864  0.814
## 2  RB.INEQUALITY*NB.DEM.MEM*NB.OG.NORM 1.000  0.186  0.136
## ---------------------------------
##    M1                                1.000  1.000
##
##                                      cases
## -------------------
## 1  RB.COMPLEXITY              IAEA1957,IAEA1958,IAEA1959,IAEA1960,IAEA1961,IAEA1962,
##                               IAEA1963,IAEA1964,IAEA1965,IAEA1966,IAEA1967,IAEA1968,
##                               IAEA1969,IAEA1970,IAEA1971,IAEA1976,IAEA1977,IAEA1978,
##                               IAEA1979,IAEA1980,IAEA1981,IAEA1982;
##                               IAEA1989; IAEA1990; IAEA1991,IAEA1992;
##                               IAEA2004,IAEA2005,IAEA2006,IAEA2007,IAEA2008;
##                               IAEA1987,IAEA1988; IAEA2002,IAEA2003;
##                               IAEA2009,IAEA2010,IAEA2011; IAEA1983,IAEA1984,IAEA1985;
##                               IAEA1993,IAEA1994,IAEA1995,IAEA1996,IAEA1997,IAEA1998;
##                               IAEA1986; IAEA1999,IAEA2000,IAEA2001
## 2  RB.INEQUALITY*NB.DEM.MEM*
##               NB.OG.NORM     OPCW2004,OPCW2005,OPCW2006,OPCW2007,OPCW2008;
##                               IAEA2009,IAEA2010,IAEA2011; OPCW2009,OPCW2010,OPCW2011
## -------------------
##
##
## p.sol: NB.DEM.MEM + rb.inequality
##
## Number of multiple-covered cases: 0
##
## M1:    rb.inequality*RB.COMPLEXITY + RB.INEQUALITY*NB.DEM.MEM*NB.OG.NORM
##        <=> decpart
##
##                                      incl   cov.r  cov.u
## ---------------------------------
## 1  rb.inequality*RB.COMPLEXITY       1.000  0.814  0.814
## 2  RB.INEQUALITY*NB.DEM.MEM*NB.OG.NORM 1.000  0.186  0.186
## ---------------------------------
##    M1                                1.000  1.000
##
##                                      cases
## -------------------
## 1  rb.inequality*RB.COMPLEXITY  IAEA1957,IAEA1958,IAEA1959,IAEA1960,IAEA1961,
##                                 IAEA1962,IAEA1963,IAEA1964,IAEA1965,IAEA1966,
##                                 IAEA1967,IAEA1968,IAEA1969,IAEA1970,IAEA1971,
##                                 IAEA1976,IAEA1977,IAEA1978,IAEA1979,IAEA1980,
##                                 IAEA1981,IAEA1982;IAEA1989; IAEA1990; IAEA1991,
```

```
##                                      IAEA1992;IAEA2004,IAEA2005,IAEA2006,IAEA2007,
##                                      IAEA2008;IAEA1987,IAEA1988; IAEA2002,IAEA2003;
##                                      IAEA1983,IAEA1984,IAEA1985; IAEA1993,IAEA1994,
##                                      IAEA1995,IAEA1996,IAEA1997,IAEA1998;
##                                      IAEA1986; IAEA1999,IAEA2000,IAEA2001
## 2  RB.INEQUALITY*NB.DEM.MEM*
##               NB.OG.NORM     OPCW2004,OPCW2005,OPCW2006,OPCW2007,OPCW2008;
##                                      IAEA2009,IAEA2010,IAEA2011; OPCW2009,OPCW2010,
##                                      OPCW2011
## ------------------
##
##
## p.sol: NB.DEM.MEM + RB.COMPLEXITY
##
## Number of multiple-covered cases: 3
##
## M1:    RB.COMPLEXITY + RB.INEQUALITY*NB.DEM.MEM*NB.OG.NORM <=> decpart
##
##                                           incl   cov.r  cov.u
## ----------------------
## 1  RB.COMPLEXITY                          1.000  0.864  0.814
## 2  RB.INEQUALITY*NB.DEM.MEM*NB.OG.NORM    1.000  0.186  0.136
## ----------------------
##    M1                                     1.000  1.000
##
##                                           cases
## ----------------
## 1  RB.COMPLEXITY              IAEA1957,IAEA1958,IAEA1959,IAEA1960,IAEA1961,IAEA1962,
##                               IAEA1963,IAEA1964,IAEA1965,IAEA1966,IAEA1967,IAEA1968,
##                               IAEA1969,IAEA1970,IAEA1971,IAEA1976,IAEA1977,IAEA1978,
##                               IAEA1979,IAEA1980,IAEA1981,IAEA1982;
##                               IAEA1989; IAEA1990; IAEA1991,IAEA1992;
##                               IAEA2004,IAEA2005,IAEA2006,IAEA2007,IAEA2008;
##                               IAEA1987,IAEA1988; IAEA2002,IAEA2003;
##                               IAEA2009,IAEA2010,IAEA2011; IAEA1983,IAEA1984,IAEA1985;
##                               IAEA1993,IAEA1994,IAEA1995,IAEA1996,IAEA1997,IAEA1998;
##                               IAEA1986; IAEA1999,IAEA2000,IAEA2001
## 2  RB.INEQUALITY*NB.DEM.MEM*
##               NB.OG.NORM      OPCW2004,OPCW2005,OPCW2006,OPCW2007,OPCW2008;
##                               IAEA2009,IAEA2010,IAEA2011; OPCW2009,OPCW2010,OPCW2011
## ----------------
##
##
## p.sol: NB.DEM.MEM + rb.inequality
##
## Number of multiple-covered cases: 0
##
## M1:    rb.inequality*RB.COMPLEXITY + RB.INEQUALITY*NB.DEM.MEM*NB.OG.NORM
##        <=> decpart
##
##                                           incl   cov.r  cov.u
## -----------------------
## 1  rb.inequality*RB.COMPLEXITY            1.000  0.814  0.814
## 2  RB.INEQUALITY*NB.DEM.MEM*NB.OG.NORM    1.000  0.186  0.186
```

```
## --------------------
## 
   M1                                     1.000  1.000
## 
## 
                                          cases
## ------------------
## 1  rb.inequality*RB.COMPLEXITY  IAEA1957,IAEA1958,IAEA1959,IAEA1960,IAEA1961,
## 
                                   IAEA1962,IAEA1963,IAEA1964,IAEA1965,IAEA1966,
## 
                                   IAEA1967,IAEA1968,IAEA1969,IAEA1970,IAEA1971,
## 
                                   IAEA1976,IAEA1977,IAEA1978,IAEA1979,IAEA1980,
## 
                                   IAEA1981,IAEA1982;IAEA1989; IAEA1990; IAEA1991,
## 
                                   IAEA1992;IAEA2004,IAEA2005,IAEA2006,IAEA2007,
## 
                                   IAEA2008;IAEA1987,IAEA1988; IAEA2002,IAEA2003;
## 
                                   IAEA1983,IAEA1984,IAEA1985; IAEA1993,IAEA1994,
## 
                                   IAEA1995,IAEA1996,IAEA1997,IAEA1998;
## 
                                   IAEA1986; IAEA1999,IAEA2000,IAEA2001
## 2  RB.INEQUALITY*NB.DEM.MEM*
## 
              NB.OG.NORM   OPCW2004,OPCW2005,OPCW2006,OPCW2007,OPCW2008;
## 
                           IAEA2009,IAEA2010,IAEA2011; OPCW2009,OPCW2010,
## 
                           OPCW2011
## ------------------
## 
## 
## p.sol: NB.DEM.MEM + RB.COMPLEXITY
## 
## Number of multiple-covered cases: 3
## 
## M1:    RB.COMPLEXITY + RB.INEQUALITY*NB.DEM.MEM*NB.OG.NORM <=> decpart
## 
## 
                                     incl  cov.r  cov.u
## --------------------------
## 1  RB.COMPLEXITY                   1.000  0.864  0.814
## 2  RB.INEQUALITY*NB.DEM.MEM*NB.OG.NORM  1.000  0.186  0.136
## --------------------------
## 
   M1                                1.000  1.000
## 
## 
                                     cases
## ------------------
## 1  RB.COMPLEXITY            IAEA1957,IAEA1958,IAEA1959,IAEA1960,IAEA1961,IAEA1962,
## 
                              IAEA1963,IAEA1964,IAEA1965,IAEA1966,IAEA1967,IAEA1968,
## 
                              IAEA1969,IAEA1970,IAEA1971,IAEA1976,IAEA1977,IAEA1978,
## 
                              IAEA1979,IAEA1980,IAEA1981,IAEA1982;
## 
                              IAEA1989; IAEA1990; IAEA1991,IAEA1992;
## 
                              IAEA2004,IAEA2005,IAEA2006,IAEA2007,IAEA2008;
## 
                              IAEA1987,IAEA1988; IAEA2002,IAEA2003;
## 
                              IAEA2009,IAEA2010,IAEA2011; IAEA1983,IAEA1984,IAEA1985;
## 
                              IAEA1993,IAEA1994,IAEA1995,IAEA1996,IAEA1997,IAEA1998;
## 
                              IAEA1986; IAEA1999,IAEA2000,IAEA2001
## 2  RB.INEQUALITY*NB.DEM.MEM*
## 
              NB.OG.NORM   OPCW2004,OPCW2005,OPCW2006,OPCW2007,OPCW2008;
## 
                           IAEA2009,IAEA2010,IAEA2011; OPCW2009,OPCW2010,OPCW2011
## ------------------
## 
## 
## p.sol: NB.DEM.MEM + rb.inequality
```

```
##
## Number of multiple-covered cases: 0
##
## M1:     rb.inequality*RB.COMPLEXITY + RB.INEQUALITY*NB.DEM.MEM*NB.OG.NORM
##         <=> decpart
##
##                                           incl   cov.r  cov.u
## ------------------------------
## 1   rb.inequality*RB.COMPLEXITY           1.000  0.814  0.814
## 2   RB.INEQUALITY*NB.DEM.MEM*NB.OG.NORM   1.000  0.186  0.186
## ------------------------------
##     M1                                    1.000  1.000
##
##                                           cases
## ----------------
## 1   rb.inequality*RB.COMPLEXITY  IAEA1957,IAEA1958,IAEA1959,IAEA1960,IAEA1961,IAEA1962,
##                                  IAEA1963,IAEA1964,IAEA1965,IAEA1966,IAEA1967,IAEA1968,
##                                  IAEA1969,IAEA1970,IAEA1971,IAEA1976,IAEA1977,IAEA1978,
##                                  IAEA1979,IAEA1980,IAEA1981,IAEA1982;
##                                  IAEA1989; IAEA1990; IAEA1991,IAEA1992;
##                                  IAEA2004,IAEA2005,IAEA2006,IAEA2007,IAEA2008;
##                                  IAEA1987,IAEA1988; IAEA2002,IAEA2003;
##                                  IAEA1983,IAEA1984,IAEA1985; IAEA1993,IAEA1994,
##                                  IAEA1995,IAEA1996,IAEA1997,IAEA1998;
##                                  IAEA1986; IAEA1999,IAEA2000,IAEA2001
## 2   RB.INEQUALITY*NB.DEM.MEM*
##                     NB.OG.NORM   OPCW2004,OPCW2005,OPCW2006,OPCW2007,OPCW2008;
##                                  IAEA2009,IAEA2010,IAEA2011; OPCW2009,OPCW2010,OPCW2011
## ----------------
```

C.2.5 Transparency Decision

```r
data_qca$DECTRANS <- data_qca$DEC.Trans # for QCA package conventions
tt <- truthTable(data_qca[c(1:55, 57:70), c(22, 10:17)],
          outcome = c("DECTRANS"), incl.cut1=1, sort.by="incl",
          show.cases = TRUE)
# necessary conditions
superSubset(data_qca[c(1:55, 57:70), c(22, 10:17)], outcome = "DECTRANS",
          relation="nec", incl.cut=0.9, cov.cut=0.8)
```

```
##
##                                  incl   cov.r
## ----------------
## 1   NB.OG.NORM                   1.000  0.889
## 2   rb.complexity+NB.DEM.MEM     1.000  0.970
## 3   rb.complexity+NB.GOV.DEPTH   1.000  0.914
## 4   rb.complexity+NB.VISIBILITY.ALL  1.000  0.800
## 5   RB.INEQUALITY+NB.DEM.MEM     1.000  0.970
## 6   RB.INEQUALITY+NB.GOV.DEPTH   1.000  0.914
## 7   RB.INEQUALITY+NB.VISIBILITY.ALL  1.000  0.800
## 8   RB.BUDGET+NB.DEM.MEM         0.969  0.886
## ----------------
```

```
# neg. outcome, to check for contradictions
superSubset(data_qca[c(1:55, 57:70), c(22, 10:17)], outcome = "DECTRANS",
            relation="nec", incl.cut=0.9, cov.cut=0.8, neg.out = T)
```

```
##
##                                                          incl   cov.r
## ------------------------------
## 1   nb.dem.mem                                           1.000  0.881
## 2   nb.gov.depth*nb.dem.mem                              0.946  0.875
## 3   nb.visibility.hl*nb.dem.mem                          0.919  0.872
## 4   RB.COMPLEXITY*nb.dem.mem                             0.973  1.000
## 5   RB.COMPLEXITY*nb.gov.depth                           0.919  1.000
## 6   rb.inequality*nb.dem.mem                             0.973  1.000
## 7   rb.inequality*nb.gov.depth                           0.919  1.000
## 8   RB.COMPLEXITY*nb.gov.depth*nb.dem.mem                0.919  1.000
## 9   rb.inequality*nb.gov.depth*nb.dem.mem                0.919  1.000
## 10  rb.inequality*RB.COMPLEXITY*nb.dem.mem               0.973  1.000
## 11  rb.inequality*RB.COMPLEXITY*nb.gov.depth             0.919  1.000
## 12  rb.inequality*RB.COMPLEXITY*nb.gov.depth*nb.dem.mem  0.919  1.000
## ------------------------------
```

```
# sufficient conditions w/o og.norm
tt <- truthTable(data_qca[c(1:55, 57:70), c(22, 10:16)],
            outcome = c("DECTRANS"), incl.cut1=1, sort.by="incl",
            show.cases = TRUE)
eqmcc(tt, include="?", show.cases = TRUE, details = TRUE,
            dir.exp = c(rep(1, 7)))
```

```
##
## n OUT = 1/0/C: 31/38/0
##    Total      : 69
##
## p.sol: NB.DEM.MEM + RB.BUDGET*rb.complexity
##
## Number of multiple-covered cases: 6
##
## M1:    RB.INEQUALITY*NB.DEM.MEM + RB.BUDGET*RB.INEQUALITY*rb.complexity +
##        RB.COMPLEXITY*NB.VISIBILITY.ALL*NB.GOV.DEPTH*NB.DEM.MEM => DECTRANS
##
##                                                          incl   cov.r  cov.u
## ---------------------------------
## 1   RB.INEQUALITY*NB.DEM.MEM                             1.000  0.344  0.156
## 2   RB.BUDGET*RB.INEQUALITY*rb.complexity                1.000  0.219  0.125
## 3   RB.COMPLEXITY*NB.VISIBILITY.ALL*NB.GOV.DEPTH*NB.DEM.MEM 1.000 0.594 0.500
## ---------------------------------
##     M1                                                   1.000  0.969
##
##                                                          cases
## ---------------------------------
## 1   RB.INEQUALITY*NB.DEM.MEM              OPCW2004,OPCW2005,OPCW2006,OPCW2007,
##                                          OPCW2008;IAEA2009,IAEA2010,IAEA2011;
```

```
##                                          OPCW2009,OPCW2010,OPCW2011
## 2  RB.BUDGET*RB.INEQUALITY*rb.complexity   OPCW1999,OPCW2000,OPCW2001,OPCW2002;
##                                          OPCW2009,OPCW2010,OPCW2011
## 3  RB.COMPLEXITY*NB.VISIBILITY.ALL*
##          NB.GOV.DEPTH*NB.DEM.MEM          IAEA2004,IAEA2005,IAEA2006,IAEA2007,
##                                          IAEA2008;IAEA2002,IAEA2003;
##                                          IAEA2009,IAEA2010,IAEA2011;
##                                          IAEA1993,IAEA1994,IAEA1995,IAEA1996,
##                                          IAEA1997,IAEA1998;
##                                          IAEA1999,IAEA2000,IAEA2001
## ----------------------------
##
##
## p.sol: NB.DEM.MEM + RB.BUDGET*RB.INEQUALITY
##
## Number of multiple-covered cases: 6
##
## M1:    RB.BUDGET*RB.INEQUALITY + RB.INEQUALITY*NB.DEM.MEM +
##        RB.COMPLEXITY*NB.VISIBILITY.ALL*NB.GOV.DEPTH*NB.DEM.MEM => DECTRANS
##
##
##                                             incl   cov.r  cov.u
## --------------------------------
## 1  RB.BUDGET*RB.INEQUALITY                  1.000  0.219  0.125
## 2  RB.INEQUALITY*NB.DEM.MEM                 1.000  0.344  0.156
## 3  RB.COMPLEXITY*NB.VISIBILITY.ALL*
##          NB.GOV.DEPTH*NB.DEM.MEM            1.000  0.594  0.500
## --------------------------------
##    M1                                       1.000  0.969
##
##                              cases
## --------------------------------
## 1  RB.BUDGET*RB.INEQUALITY       OPCW1999,OPCW2000,OPCW2001,OPCW2002;
##                                  OPCW2009,OPCW2010,OPCW2011
## 2  RB.INEQUALITY*NB.DEM.MEM      OPCW2004,OPCW2005,OPCW2006,OPCW2007,
##                                  OPCW2008;IAEA2009,IAEA2010,IAEA2011;
##                                  OPCW2009,OPCW2010,OPCW2011
## 3  RB.COMPLEXITY*NB.VISIBILITY.ALL*  IAEA2004,IAEA2005,IAEA2006,IAEA2007,
##    NB.GOV.DEPTH*NB.DEM.MEM        IAEA2008;IAEA2002,IAEA2003;
##                                  IAEA2009,IAEA2010,IAEA2011;
##                                  IAEA1993,IAEA1994,IAEA1995,IAEA1996,
##                                  IAEA1997,IAEA1998;IAEA1999,IAEA2000,
##                                  IAEA2001
## --------------------------------


# neg. outcome, to check for contradictions
tt <- truthTable(data_qca[c(1:55, 57:70), c(22, 10:16)],
          outcome = c("DECTRANS"), incl.cut1=0.8, sort.by="incl",
          show.cases = TRUE, neg.out = T)
eqmcc(tt, include="?", show.cases = TRUE, details = TRUE,
          dir.exp = c(rep(1, 7)))


##
```

```
## n OUT = 1/0/C: 36/33/0
##   Total      : 69
##
## p.sol: RB.COMPLEXITY*nb.dem.mem
##
## Number of multiple-covered cases: 0
##
## M1:     rb.budget*rb.inequality*RB.COMPLEXITY*NB.VISIBILITY.ALL*nb.visibility.hl*
##         nb.dem.mem + rb.inequality*RB.COMPLEXITY*nb.visibility.all*nb.visibility.hl*
##         nb.gov.depth*nb.dem.mem + rb.inequality*RB.COMPLEXITY*NB.VISIBILITY.ALL*
##         NB.VISIBILITY.HL*nb.gov.depth*nb.dem.mem <=> dectrans
##
##                                                          incl   cov.r  cov.u
## ------------------------------------------------
## 1  rb.budget*rb.inequality*RB.COMPLEXITY*NB.VISIBILITY.ALL*
##    nb.visibility.hl*nb.dem.mem                           1.000  0.108  0.108
## 2  rb.inequality*RB.COMPLEXITY*nb.visibility.all*
##    nb.visibility.hl*nb.gov.depth*nb.dem.mem              1.000  0.784  0.784
## 3  rb.inequality*RB.COMPLEXITY*NB.VISIBILITY.ALL*
##    NB.VISIBILITY.HL*nb.gov.depth*nb.dem.mem              1.000  0.081  0.081
## ------------------------------------------------
##   M1                                                     1.000  0.973
##
##                                                          cases
## ------------------------------------------------
## 1  rb.budget*rb.inequality*RB.COMPLEXITY*
##    NB.VISIBILITY.ALL*nb.visibility.hl*nb.dem.mem         IAEA1989,IAEA1990;
##                                                          IAEA1991,IAEA1992
## 2  rb.inequality*RB.COMPLEXITY*nb.visibility.all*
##    nb.visibility.hl*nb.gov.depth*nb.dem.mem              IAEA1957,IAEA1958,IAEA1959,
##                                                          IAEA1960,IAEA1961,IAEA1962,
##                                                          IAEA1963,IAEA1964,IAEA1965,
##                                                          IAEA1966,IAEA1967,IAEA1968,
##                                                          IAEA1969,IAEA1970,IAEA1971,
##                                                          IAEA1972,IAEA1973,IAEA1974,
##                                                          IAEA1975,IAEA1976,IAEA1977,
##                                                          IAEA1978,IAEA1979,IAEA1980,
##                                                          IAEA1981,IAEA1982;
##                                                          IAEA1983,IAEA1984,IAEA1985
## 3  rb.inequality*RB.COMPLEXITY*NB.VISIBILITY.ALL*
##    NB.VISIBILITY.HL*nb.gov.depth*nb.dem.mem              IAEA1987,IAEA1988;IAEA1986
##
## ------------------------------------------------
##
##
## p.sol: rb.inequality*nb.dem.mem
##
## Number of multiple-covered cases: 0
##
## M1:     rb.budget*rb.inequality*RB.COMPLEXITY*NB.VISIBILITY.ALL*nb.visibility.hl*
##         nb.dem.mem + rb.inequality*RB.COMPLEXITY*nb.visibility.all*nb.visibility.hl*
##         nb.gov.depth*nb.dem.mem +rb.inequality*RB.COMPLEXITY*NB.VISIBILITY.ALL*
##         NB.VISIBILITY.HL*nb.gov.depth*nb.dem.mem <=> dectrans
##
```

```
##                                                      incl   cov.r  cov.u
## ----------------------------------------------------
## 1   rb.budget*rb.inequality*RB.COMPLEXITY*NB.VISIBILITY.ALL*
##     nb.visibility.hl*nb.dem.mem                      1.000  0.108  0.108
## 2   rb.inequality*RB.COMPLEXITY*nb.visibility.all*
##     nb.visibility.hl*nb.gov.depth*nb.dem.mem         1.000  0.784  0.784
## 3   rb.inequality*RB.COMPLEXITY*NB.VISIBILITY.ALL*
##     NB.VISIBILITY.HL*nb.gov.depth*nb.dem.mem         1.000  0.081  0.081
## ----------------------------------------------------
##     M1                                               1.000  0.973
##
##                                                      cases
## ------------------------------------------------
## 1   rb.budget*rb.inequality*RB.COMPLEXITY*
##     NB.VISIBILITY.ALL*nb.visibility.hl*nb.dem.mem    IAEA1989,IAEA1990;IAEA1991,
##                                                      IAEA1992
## 2   rb.inequality*RB.COMPLEXITY*nb.visibility.all*
##     nb.visibility.hl*nb.gov.depth*nb.dem.mem         IAEA1957,IAEA1958,IAEA1959,
##                                                      IAEA1960,IAEA1961,IAEA1962,
##                                                      IAEA1963,IAEA1964,IAEA1965,
##                                                      IAEA1966,IAEA1967,IAEA1968,
##                                                      IAEA1969,IAEA1970,IAEA1971,
##                                                      IAEA1972,IAEA1973,IAEA1974,
##                                                      IAEA1975,IAEA1976,IAEA1977,
##                                                      IAEA1978,IAEA1979,IAEA1980,
##                                                      IAEA1981,IAEA1982;
##                                                      IAEA1983,IAEA1984,IAEA1985
## 3   rb.inequality*RB.COMPLEXITY*NB.VISIBILITY.ALL*
##     NB.VISIBILITY.HL*nb.gov.depth*nb.dem.mem         IAEA1987,IAEA1988;IAEA1986
## ------------------------------------------------
```

C.2.6 COMBINED DECISION

```
data_qca$DECISION <- fsor(data_qca$DEC.Part, data_qca$DEC.Trans)


tt <- truthTable(data_qca[c(23, 10:11, 13:17)], outcome = c("DECISION"),
          incl.cut1=1, sort.by="incl", show.cases = TRUE)
# necessary conditions
superSubset(data_qca[c(23, 10:11, 13:17)], outcome = "DECISION",
          relation="nec", incl.cut=0.8, cov.cut=0.5)


##
##                                          incl   cov.r
## ------------------------------------
## 1   NB.OG.NORM                           0.895  0.919
## 2   NB.DEM.MEM+nb.og.norm                0.816  0.517
## 3   nb.gov.depth+NB.DEM.MEM              1.000  0.559
## 4   nb.visibility.hl+NB.DEM.MEM          1.000  0.567
## 5   nb.visibility.hl+NB.GOV.DEPTH        1.000  0.567
## 6   nb.visibility.all+NB.DEM.MEM         1.000  0.603
## 7   nb.visibility.all+NB.GOV.DEPTH       1.000  0.585
```

```
##  8  NB.VISIBILITY.ALL+nb.gov.depth                      1.000  0.543
##  9  NB.VISIBILITY.ALL+nb.visibility.hl                  1.000  0.543
## ...
## ─────────────────────────
```

```r
# neg. outcome, to check for contradictions
superSubset(data_qca[c(23, 10:11, 13:17)], outcome = "DECISION",
            relation="nec", incl.cut=0.8, cov.cut=0.878,
            neg.out = T)
```

```
##
##                                                       incl   cov.r
## ─────────────────────────
##  1  nb.og.norm                                        0.906  0.879
##  2  nb.dem.mem*nb.og.norm                              0.906  0.879
##  3  nb.gov.depth*nb.og.norm                            0.906  0.879
##  4  rb.inequality*nb.og.norm                           0.906  0.879
##  5  rb.inequality*nb.dem.mem                           1.000  0.889
##  6  rb.inequality*nb.gov.depth                         0.938  0.882
##  7  nb.gov.depth*nb.dem.mem*nb.og.norm                 0.906  0.879
##  8  rb.inequality*nb.dem.mem*nb.og.norm                0.906  0.879
##  9  rb.inequality*nb.gov.depth*nb.og.norm              0.906  0.879
## 10  rb.inequality*nb.gov.depth*nb.dem.mem              0.938  0.882
## 11  rb.inequality*nb.visibility.hl*nb.dem.mem          0.906  0.879
## 12  rb.inequality*nb.gov.depth*nb.dem.mem*nb.og.norm   0.906  0.879
## ─────────────────────────
```

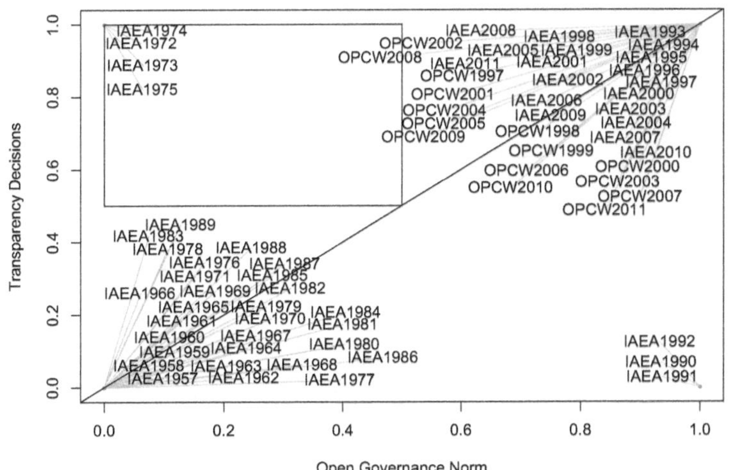

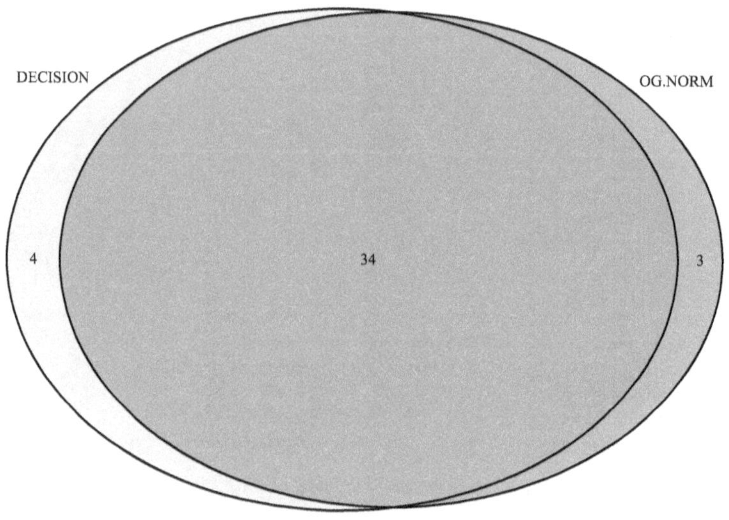


```
# sufficient conditions, w/o OG.Norm
tt <- truthTable(data_qca[c(23, 10:11, 13:16)], outcome = c("DECISION"),
          incl.cut1=1, sort.by="incl", show.cases = TRUE)


# conservative
eqmcc(tt, show.cases = TRUE, details = TRUE)


##
## n OUT = 1/0/C: 34/36/0
##   Total      : 70
##
## Number of multiple-covered cases: 2
##
## M1: rb.inequality*NB.VISIBILITY.ALL*NB.GOV.DEPTH*NB.DEM.MEM +
##     RB.INEQUALITY*nb.visibility.all*nb.visibility.hl*nb.gov.depth +
##     rb.budget*NB.VISIBILITY.ALL*NB.VISIBILITY.HL*NB.GOV.DEPTH*NB.DEM.MEM
##     => DECISION
##
##
##                                                         incl  cov.r  cov.u
## ---------------------------------------------
## 1  rb.inequality*NB.VISIBILITY.ALL*NB.GOV.DEPTH*NB.DEM.MEM 1.000  0.421  0.368
## 2  RB.INEQUALITY*nb.visibility.all*nb.visibility.hl*
##                                         nb.gov.depth       1.000  0.395  0.395
## 3  rb.budget*NB.VISIBILITY.ALL*NB.VISIBILITY.HL*
##                     NB.GOV.DEPTH*NB.DEM.MEM                1.000  0.132  0.079
## ---------------------------------------------
##    M1                                                      1.000  0.895
##
```

```
##                                                                  cases
## ─────────────────────────────
## 1   rb.inequality*NB.VISIBILITY.ALL*NB.GOV.DEPTH*
##                                  NB.DEM.MEM        IAEA2004,IAEA2005,IAEA2006,
##                                                    IAEA2007,IAEA2008;
##                                                    IAEA2002,IAEA2003;
##                                                    IAEA1993,IAEA1994,IAEA1995,
##                                                    IAEA1996,IAEA1997,IAEA1998;
##                                                    IAEA1999,IAEA2000,IAEA2001
## 2   RB.INEQUALITY*nb.visibility.all*nb.visibility.hl*
##                                  nb.gov.depth      OPCW1997,OPCW1998,OPCW2003;
##                                                    OPCW2004,OPCW2005,OPCW2006,
##                                                    OPCW2007,OPCW2008;
##                                                    OPCW1999,OPCW2000,OPCW2001,
##                                                    OPCW2002;
##                                                    OPCW2009,OPCW2010,OPCW2011
## 3   rb.budget*NB.VISIBILITY.ALL*NB.VISIBILITY.HL*
##                        NB.GOV.DEPTH*NB.DEM.MEM     IAEA2002,IAEA2003;
##                                                    IAEA2009,IAEA2010,IAEA2011
## ─────────────────────────────


# intermediate
eqmcc(tt, include="?", show.cases = TRUE, details = TRUE,
        dir.exp = c(rep(1, 6)))


##
## n OUT = 1/0/C: 34/36/0
##   Total      : 70
##
## p.sol: NB.DEM.MEM + RB.INEQUALITY
##
## Number of multiple-covered cases: 3
##
## M1:    RB.INEQUALITY + NB.VISIBILITY.ALL*NB.GOV.DEPTH*NB.DEM.MEM
##        => DECISION
##
##                                              incl   cov.r  cov.u
## ─────────────────────────────
## 1   RB.INEQUALITY                            1.000  0.474  0.395
## 2   NB.VISIBILITY.ALL*NB.GOV.DEPTH*NB.DEM.MEM 1.000  0.500  0.421
## ─────────────────────────────
##    M1                                         1.000  0.895
##
##                                              cases
## ─────────────────────────────
## 1   RB.INEQUALITY                            OPCW1997,OPCW1998,OPCW2003; OPCW2004,
##                                              OPCW2005,OPCW2006,OPCW2007,OPCW2008;
##                                              IAEA2009,IAEA2010,IAEA2011; OPCW1999,
##                                              OPCW2000,OPCW2001,OPCW2002;OPCW2009,
##                                              OPCW2010,OPCW2011
## 2   NB.VISIBILITY.ALL*NB.GOV.DEPTH*NB.DEM.MEM IAEA2004,IAEA2005,IAEA2006,IAEA2007,
##                                              IAEA2008;IAEA2002,IAEA2003; IAEA2009,
```

```
##                                         IAEA2010,IAEA2011;IAEA1993,IAEA1994,
##                                         IAEA1995,IAEA1996,IAEA1997,IAEA1998;
##                                         IAEA1999,IAEA2000,IAEA2001
## ------------------


# parsimonious
eqmcc(tt, include="?", show.cases = TRUE, details = TRUE)


##
## n OUT = 1/0/C: 34/36/0
##   Total      : 70
##
## Number of multiple-covered cases: 11
##
## M1: NB.DEM.MEM + RB.INEQUALITY => DECISION
##
##                   incl   cov.r  cov.u
## ----------------
## 1  NB.DEM.MEM      1.000  0.711  0.421
## 2  RB.INEQUALITY   1.000  0.474  0.184
## ----------------
##    M1              1.000  0.895
##
##                   cases
## ----------
## 1  NB.DEM.MEM      IAEA2004,IAEA2005,IAEA2006,IAEA2007,IAEA2008; IAEA2002,IAEA2003;
##                    OPCW2004,OPCW2005,OPCW2006,OPCW2007,OPCW2008; IAEA2009,IAEA2010,
##                    IAEA2011;IAEA1993,IAEA1994,IAEA1995,IAEA1996,IAEA1997,IAEA1998;
##                    IAEA1999,IAEA2000,IAEA2001;OPCW2009,OPCW2010,OPCW2011
## 2  RB.INEQUALITY  OPCW1997,OPCW1998,OPCW2003; OPCW2004,OPCW2005,OPCW2006,OPCW2007,
##                    OPCW2008;IAEA2009,IAEA2010,IAEA2011; OPCW1999,OPCW2000,OPCW2001,
##                    OPCW2002;OPCW2009,OPCW2010,OPCW2011
## ----------


#factorize(sc)
# neg. outcome, to check for contradictions
tt <- truthTable(data_qca[c(23, 10:11, 13:17)], outcome = c("DECISION"),
          incl.cut1=1, sort.by="incl", show.cases = TRUE,
          neg.out = T)
eqmcc(tt, include="?", show.cases = TRUE, details = TRUE)


##
## n OUT = 1/0/C: 10/60/0
##   Total      : 70
##
## Number of multiple-covered cases: 1
##
## M1: NB.VISIBILITY.ALL*nb.dem.mem + (RB.BUDGET*nb.og.norm) => decision
## M2: NB.VISIBILITY.ALL*nb.dem.mem + (RB.BUDGET*rb.inequality*nb.dem.mem)
##     => decision
```

```
## M3: NB.VISIBILITY.ALL*nb.dem.mem + (RB.BUDGET*rb.inequality*nb.gov.depth)
##      => decision
## M4: NB.VISIBILITY.ALL*nb.dem.mem +
##      (RB.BUDGET*rb.inequality*nb.visibility.all) => decision
##
##
##                                                          ‾‾‾‾
##                                                  incl  cov.r  cov.u  (M1)
## ─────────────────────────────────────
## 1  NB.VISIBILITY.ALL*nb.dem.mem                  1.000  0.219  0.188  0.188
## ─────────────────────────────────────
## 2  RB.BUDGET*nb.og.norm                          1.000  0.125  0.000  0.094
## 3  RB.BUDGET*rb.inequality*nb.dem.mem            1.000  0.125  0.000
## 4  RB.BUDGET*rb.inequality*nb.gov.depth          1.000  0.125  0.000
## 5  RB.BUDGET*rb.inequality*nb.visibility.all     1.000  0.094  0.000
## ─────────────────────────────────────
##    M1                                            1.000  0.312
##    M2                                            1.000  0.312
##    M3                                            1.000  0.312
##    M4                                            1.000  0.312
##
## ───────────────────────────────────────
##                                                  (M2)   (M3)   (M4)
## ───────────────────────────────────────
## 1  NB.VISIBILITY.ALL*nb.dem.mem                  0.188  0.188  0.219
## ───────────────────────────────────────
## 2  RB.BUDGET*nb.og.norm
## 3  RB.BUDGET*rb.inequality*nb.dem.mem            0.094
## 4  RB.BUDGET*rb.inequality*nb.gov.depth                 0.094
## 5  RB.BUDGET*rb.inequality*nb.visibility.all                   0.094
## ───────────────────────────────────────
##
##                                                  cases
## ─────────────────────────
## 2  NB.VISIBILITY.ALL*nb.dem.mem             IAEA1989; IAEA1990; IAEA1991,IAEA1992;
##                                        IAEA1987,IAEA1988; IAEA1986
## ─────────────────────────
## 2  RB.BUDGET*nb.og.norm                     IAEA1983,IAEA1984,IAEA1985; IAEA1986
## 3  RB.BUDGET*rb.inequality*nb.dem.mem       IAEA1983,IAEA1984,IAEA1985; IAEA1986
## 4  RB.BUDGET*rb.inequality*nb.gov.depth     IAEA1983,IAEA1984,IAEA1985; IAEA1986
## 5  RB.BUDGET*rb.inequality*nb.visibility.all  IAEA1983,IAEA1984,IAEA1985
## ─────────────────────────
```

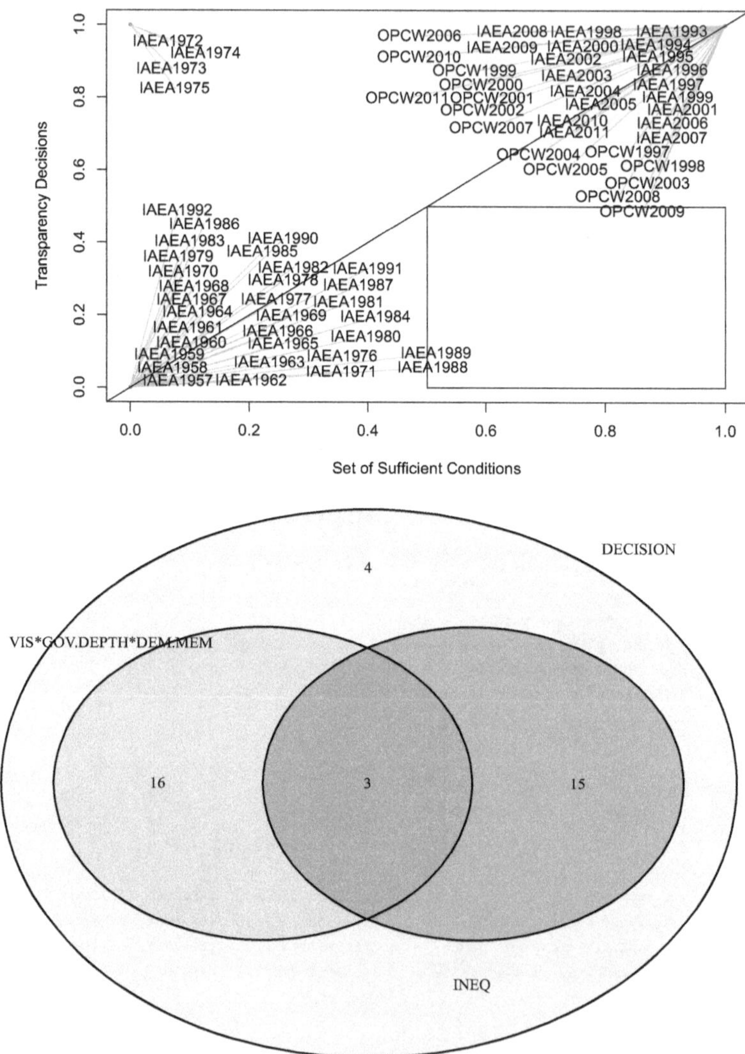

C.2.7   PARTICIPATION ACTION: NO. OF NGOS

```
data_qca$ACTPART1 <- data_qca$ACT.Part.1 # for QCA package conventions
tt <- truthTable(data_qca[c(24, 10:17)], outcome = c("ACTPART1"),
          incl.cut1=1, sort.by="incl", show.cases = TRUE)
```

```
# necessary conditions
superSubset(data_qca[c(24, 10:17)], outcome = "ACTPART1",
            relation="nec", incl.cut=0.8, cov.cut=0.6)



##
##                                  incl  cov.r
## ───────────────────
## 1   NB.OG.NORM                    0.800  0.757
## 2   rb.complexity+NB.GOV.DEPTH    0.800  0.778
## 3   rb.complexity+NB.VISIBILITY.ALL  0.800  0.683
## 4   RB.INEQUALITY+NB.GOV.DEPTH    0.800  0.778
## 5   RB.INEQUALITY+NB.VISIBILITY.ALL  0.800  0.683
## ───────────────────


# neg. outcome, to check for contradictions
superSubset(data_qca[c(24, 10:17)], outcome = "ACTPART1",
            relation="nec", incl.cut=0.9, cov.cut=0.6, neg.out = T)



##
##                                  incl  cov.r
## ─────────────────────-
## 1   nb.gov.depth                  1.000  0.714
## 2   nb.visibility.hl*nb.gov.depth 0.914  0.696
## 3   nb.visibility.all+nb.og.norm  0.971  0.708
## 4   nb.visibility.all+nb.dem.mem  1.000  0.686
## 5   nb.visibility.all+NB.VISIBILITY.HL  0.943  0.600
## 6   rb.complexity+nb.og.norm      0.971  0.708
## 7   rb.complexity+nb.dem.mem      1.000  0.686
## 8   RB.INEQUALITY+nb.og.norm      0.971  0.667
## 9   RB.INEQUALITY+nb.dem.mem      1.000  0.648
## 10  rb.budget+nb.og.norm          0.943  0.611
## 11  rb.budget+nb.dem.mem          1.000  0.603
## ─────────────────────-


# sufficient conditions
eqmcc(tt, include="?", show.cases = TRUE, details = TRUE,
      dir.exp = c(rep(1, 8)))



##
## n OUT = 1/0/C: 24/46/0
##    Total      : 70
##
## p.sol: NB.GOV.DEPTH + RB.BUDGET*NB.DEM.MEM
##
## Number of multiple-covered cases: 0
##
## M1:    RB.BUDGET*RB.INEQUALITY*NB.DEM.MEM*NB.OG.NORM +
##        RB.COMPLEXITY*NB.VISIBILITY.ALL*NB.GOV.DEPTH*NB.OG.NORM => ACTPART1
##
```

```
##                                                             incl   cov.r  cov.u
## -----------------------------------
## 1   RB.BUDGET*RB.INEQUALITY*NB.DEM.MEM*NB.OG.NORM            1.000  0.086  0.086
## 2   RB.COMPLEXITY*NB.VISIBILITY.ALL*NB.GOV.DEPTH*NB.OG.NORM  1.000  0.600  0.600
## -----------------------------------
##      M1                                                      1.000  0.686
##
##                                                             cases
## -----------------------------------
## 1   RB.BUDGET*RB.INEQUALITY*NB.DEM.MEM*NB.OG.NORM            OPCW2009,OPCW2010,OPCW2011
## 2   RB.COMPLEXITY*NB.VISIBILITY.ALL*NB.GOV.DEPTH*            IAEA1991,IAEA1992;
##      NB.OG.NORM                                             IAEA2004,IAEA2005,IAEA2006,
##                                                             IAEA2007,IAEA2008;IAEA2002,
##                                                             IAEA2003;IAEA2009,IAEA2010,
##                                                             IAEA2011;IAEA1993,IAEA1994,
##                                                             IAEA1995,IAEA1996,IAEA1997,
##                                                             IAEA1998;IAEA1999,IAEA2000,
##                                                             IAEA2001
## -----------------------------------
```

```r
# neg. outcome, to check for contradictions
tt <- truthTable(data_qca[c(24, 10:17)], outcome = c("ACTPART1"),
          incl.cut1=1, sort.by="incl", show.cases = TRUE,
          neg.out = T)
sc <- eqmcc(tt, include="?", show.cases = TRUE, details = TRUE)
sc$essential
```

```
## [1] "NB.VISIBILITY.ALL*nb.gov.depth"
```

C.2.8   Participation Action: No. of NGO representatives

```r
data_qca$ACTPART2 <- data_qca$ACT.Part.2 # for QCA package conventions
tt <- truthTable(data_qca[c(25, 10:17)], outcome = c("ACTPART2"),
          incl.cut1=1, sort.by="incl", show.cases = TRUE)
# necessary conditions
superSubset(data_qca[c(25, 10:17)], outcome = "ACTPART2",
          relation="nec", incl.cut=0.8, cov.cut=0.5)
```

```
##
##                                    incl   cov.r
## -----------------------
## 1   RB.INEQUALITY*NB.DEM.MEM             0.857  0.545
## 2   RB.INEQUALITY*NB.DEM.MEM*NB.OG.NORM  0.857  0.545
## -----------------------
```

```r
# neg. outcome, to check for contradictions
superSubset(data_qca[c(25, 10:17)], outcome = "ACTPART2",
          relation="nec", incl.cut=0.8, cov.cut=0.92,
          neg.out = T)
```

```
##
##                                              incl   cov.r
## ----------------------
## 1   nb.visibility.hl                         0.873  0.932
## 2   RB.COMPLEXITY                            0.810  0.927
## 3   rb.inequality                            0.810  0.981
## 4   rb.inequality*RB.COMPLEXITY              0.810  0.981
## 5   NB.GOV.DEPTH+nb.dem.mem                  0.921  0.935
## 6   NB.VISIBILITY.ALL+nb.og.norm             0.810  0.927
## 7   NB.VISIBILITY.ALL+nb.dem.mem             0.921  0.935
## 8   rb.budget+nb.dem.mem                     0.857  0.931
## 9   rb.budget+NB.GOV.DEPTH                   0.873  0.932
## 10  rb.budget+NB.VISIBILITY.ALL              0.889  0.933
## 11  RB.BUDGET+nb.dem.mem                     0.825  0.945
## 12  RB.BUDGET+nb.gov.depth                   0.873  0.948
## 13  RB.BUDGET+nb.visibility.all              0.810  0.944
## 14  rb.budget+NB.VISIBILITY.HL+nb.og.norm    0.841  0.930
## 15  RB.BUDGET+rb.complexity+nb.og.norm       0.857  0.947
## ----------------------


# sufficient conditions
eqmcc(tt, include="?", show.cases = TRUE, details = TRUE,
         dir.exp = c(rep(1, 8)))



##
## n OUT = 1/0/C: 6/64/0
##   Total     : 70
##
## p.sol: RB.INEQUALITY*NB.GOV.DEPTH + RB.BUDGET*nb.gov.depth*NB.DEM.MEM
##
## Number of multiple-covered cases: 0
##
## M1:   RB.BUDGET*RB.INEQUALITY*nb.gov.depth*NB.DEM.MEM*NB.OG.NORM +
##       RB.INEQUALITY*RB.COMPLEXITY*NB.VISIBILITY.ALL*NB.VISIBILITY.HL*
##       NB.GOV.DEPTH*NB.DEM.MEM*NB.OG.NORM
##       => ACTPART2
##
##                                                       incl   cov.r  cov.u
## ------------------------------------------
## 1   RB.BUDGET*RB.INEQUALITY*nb.gov.depth*NB.DEM.MEM*
##                              NB.OG.NORM               1.000  0.429  0.429
## 2   RB.INEQUALITY*RB.COMPLEXITY*NB.VISIBILITY.ALL*
##     NB.VISIBILITY.HL*NB.GOV.DEPTH*NB.DEM.MEM*NB.OG.NORM  1.000  0.429  0.429
## ------------------------------------------
##   M1                                                  1.000  0.857
##
##                                                       cases
## ------------------------------------------
## 1   RB.BUDGET*RB.INEQUALITY*nb.gov.depth*NB.DEM.MEM*
##                              NB.OG.NORM               OPCW2009,OPCW2010,OPCW2011
## 2   RB.INEQUALITY*RB.COMPLEXITY*NB.VISIBILITY.ALL*
##     NB.VISIBILITY.HL*NB.GOV.DEPTH*NB.DEM.MEM*NB.OG.NORM  IAEA2009,IAEA2010,IAEA2011
```

```
## ----------------------------------------
## 
## 
## p.sol: RB.INEQUALITY*NB.GOV.DEPTH + RB.BUDGET*nb.visibility.all*NB.DEM.MEM
## 
## Number of multiple-covered cases: 0
## 
## M1:    RB.BUDGET*RB.INEQUALITY*nb.visibility.all*NB.DEM.MEM*NB.OG.NORM +
##        RB.INEQUALITY*RB.COMPLEXITY*NB.VISIBILITY.ALL*NB.VISIBILITY.HL*
##        NB.GOV.DEPTH*NB.DEM.MEM*NB.OG.NORM
##        => ACTPART2
## 
## 
##                                                    incl   cov.r  cov.u
## ------------------------------------------------- 
## 1  RB.BUDGET*RB.INEQUALITY*nb.visibility.all*NB.DEM.MEM*
##                                         NB.OG.NORM   1.000  0.429  0.429
## 2  RB.INEQUALITY*RB.COMPLEXITY*NB.VISIBILITY.ALL*
##    NB.VISIBILITY.HL*NB.GOV.DEPTH*NB.DEM.MEM*NB.OG.NORM  1.000  0.429  0.429
## ------------------------------------------------- 
##    M1                                               1.000  0.857
## 
##                                                    cases
## ------------------------------------------------- 
## 1  RB.BUDGET*RB.INEQUALITY*nb.visibility.all*NB.DEM.MEM*
##                                         NB.OG.NORM   OPCW2009,OPCW2010,OPCW2011
## 2  RB.INEQUALITY*RB.COMPLEXITY*NB.VISIBILITY.ALL*
##    NB.VISIBILITY.HL*NB.GOV.DEPTH*NB.DEM.MEM*NB.OG.NORM  IAEA2009,IAEA2010,IAEA2011
## ------------------------------------------------- 
## 
## 
## p.sol: RB.INEQUALITY*NB.GOV.DEPTH + RB.BUDGET*rb.complexity*NB.DEM.MEM
## 
## Number of multiple-covered cases: 0
## 
## M1:    RB.BUDGET*RB.INEQUALITY*rb.complexity*NB.DEM.MEM*NB.OG.NORM +
##        RB.INEQUALITY*RB.COMPLEXITY*NB.VISIBILITY.ALL*NB.VISIBILITY.HL*
##        NB.GOV.DEPTH*NB.DEM.MEM*NB.OG.NORM
##        => ACTPART2
## 
## 
##                                                    incl   cov.r  cov.u
## ------------------------------------------------- 
## 1  RB.BUDGET*RB.INEQUALITY*rb.complexity*NB.DEM.MEM*
##                                         NB.OG.NORM   1.000  0.429  0.429
## 2  RB.INEQUALITY*RB.COMPLEXITY*NB.VISIBILITY.ALL*
##    NB.GOV.DEPTH*NB.DEM.MEM*NB.OG.NORM                 1.000  0.429  0.429
## ------------------------------------------------- 
##    M1                                               1.000  0.857
## 
##                                                    cases
## ------------------------------------------------- 
## 1  RB.BUDGET*RB.INEQUALITY*rb.complexity*NB.DEM.MEM*
##                                         NB.OG.NORM   OPCW2009,OPCW2010,OPCW2011
## 2  RB.INEQUALITY*RB.COMPLEXITY*NB.VISIBILITY.ALL*
##    NB.VISIBILITY.HL*NB.GOV.DEPTH*NB.DEM.MEM*NB.OG.NORM  IAEA2009,IAEA2010,IAEA2011
```

```
## ------------------------------------------
##
##
## p.sol: RB.INEQUALITY*NB.GOV.DEPTH + RB.BUDGET*RB.INEQUALITY*NB.DEM.MEM
##
## Number of multiple-covered cases: 0
##
## M1:    RB.BUDGET*RB.INEQUALITY*NB.DEM.MEM*NB.OG.NORM +
##        RB.INEQUALITY*RB.COMPLEXITY*NB.VISIBILITY.ALL*NB.VISIBILITY.HL*
#         NB.GOV.DEPTH*NB.DEM.MEM*NB.OG.NORM
##        => ACTPART2
##
##
##                                                        incl   cov.r  cov.u
## -------------------------------------------
## 1  RB.BUDGET*RB.INEQUALITY*NB.DEM.MEM*NB.OG.NORM        1.000  0.429  0.429
## 2  RB.INEQUALITY*RB.COMPLEXITY*NB.VISIBILITY.ALL*
##     NB.VISIBILITY.HL*NB.GOV.DEPTH*NB.DEM.MEM*NB.OG.NORM  1.000  0.429  0.429
## -------------------------------------------
##    M1                                                   1.000  0.857
##
##                                                          cases
## -------------------------------------------
## 1  RB.BUDGET*RB.INEQUALITY*NB.DEM.MEM*NB.OG.NORM        OPCW2009,OPCW2010,OPCW2011
## 2  RB.INEQUALITY*RB.COMPLEXITY*NB.VISIBILITY.ALL*
##     NB.VISIBILITY.HL*NB.GOV.DEPTH*NB.DEM.MEM*NB.OG.NORM  IAEA2009,IAEA2010,IAEA2011
## -------------------------------------------
##
##
## p.sol: RB.INEQUALITY*NB.VISIBILITY.ALL + RB.BUDGET*nb.gov.depth*NB.DEM.MEM
##
## Number of multiple-covered cases: 0
##
## M1:    RB.BUDGET*RB.INEQUALITY*nb.gov.depth*NB.DEM.MEM*NB.OG.NORM +
##        RB.INEQUALITY*RB.COMPLEXITY*NB.VISIBILITY.ALL*NB.VISIBILITY.HL*
##        NB.GOV.DEPTH*NB.DEM.MEM*NB.OG.NORM
##        => ACTPART2
##
##                                                        incl   cov.r  cov.u
## -------------------------------------------
## 1  RB.BUDGET*RB.INEQUALITY*nb.gov.depth*NB.DEM.MEM*
##                                  NB.OG.NORM            1.000  0.429  0.429
## 2  RB.INEQUALITY*RB.COMPLEXITY*NB.VISIBILITY.ALL*
##     NB.VISIBILITY.HL*NB.GOV.DEPTH*NB.DEM.MEM*NB.OG.NORM  1.000  0.429  0.429
## -------------------------------------------
##    M1                                                   1.000  0.857
##
##                                                          cases
## -------------------------------------------
## 1  RB.BUDGET*RB.INEQUALITY*nb.gov.depth*NB.DEM.MEM*
##                                  NB.OG.NORM            OPCW2009,OPCW2010,OPCW2011
## 2  RB.INEQUALITY*RB.COMPLEXITY*NB.VISIBILITY.ALL*
##     NB.VISIBILITY.HL*NB.GOV.DEPTH*NB.DEM.MEM*NB.OG.NORM  IAEA2009,IAEA2010,IAEA2011
## -------------------------------------------
##
```

```
##
## p.sol: RB.INEQUALITY*NB.VISIBILITY.ALL +
##        RB.BUDGET*nb.visibility.all*NB.DEM.MEM
##
## Number of multiple-covered cases: 0
##
## M1:    RB.BUDGET*RB.INEQUALITY*nb.visibility.all*NB.DEM.MEM*NB.OG.NORM +
##        RB.INEQUALITY*RB.COMPLEXITY*NB.VISIBILITY.ALL*NB.VISIBILITY.HL*
#         NB.GOV.DEPTH*NB.DEM.MEM*NB.OG.NORM
##        => ACTPART2
##
##                                                             incl   cov.r  cov.u
## ----------------------------------------------------
## 1  RB.BUDGET*RB.INEQUALITY*nb.visibility.all*NB.DEM.MEM*
#                                                 NB.OG.NORM  1.000  0.429  0.429
## 2  RB.INEQUALITY*RB.COMPLEXITY*NB.VISIBILITY.ALL*
##     NB.VISIBILITY.HL*NB.GOV.DEPTH*NB.DEM.MEM*NB.OG.NORM     1.000  0.429  0.429
## ----------------------------------------------------
##    M1                                                       1.000  0.857
##
##                                                             cases
## ----------------------------------------------------
## 1  RB.BUDGET*RB.INEQUALITY*nb.visibility.all*NB.DEM.MEM*
##                                                 NB.OG.NORM  OPCW2009,OPCW2010,OPCW2011
## 2  RB.INEQUALITY*RB.COMPLEXITY*NB.VISIBILITY.ALL*
##     NB.VISIBILITY.HL*NB.GOV.DEPTH*NB.DEM.MEM*NB.OG.NORM     IAEA2009,IAEA2010,IAEA2011
## ----------------------------------------------------
##
##
## p.sol: RB.INEQUALITY*NB.VISIBILITY.ALL +
##        RB.BUDGET*rb.complexity*NB.DEM.MEM
##
## Number of multiple-covered cases: 0
##
## M1:    RB.BUDGET*RB.INEQUALITY*rb.complexity*NB.DEM.MEM*NB.OG.NORM +
##        RB.INEQUALITY*RB.COMPLEXITY*NB.VISIBILITY.ALL*NB.VISIBILITY.HL*
##        NB.GOV.DEPTH*NB.DEM.MEM*NB.OG.NORM
##        => ACTPART2
##
##                                                             incl   cov.r  cov.u
## ----------------------------------------------------
## 1  RB.BUDGET*RB.INEQUALITY*rb.complexity*NB.DEM.MEM*
##                                                 NB.OG.NORM  1.000  0.429  0.429
## 2  RB.INEQUALITY*RB.COMPLEXITY*NB.VISIBILITY.ALL*
##     NB.GOV.DEPTH*NB.DEM.MEM*NB.OG.NORM                      1.000  0.429  0.429
## ----------------------------------------------------
##    M1                                                       1.000  0.857
##
##                                                             cases
## ----------------------------------------------------
## 1  RB.BUDGET*RB.INEQUALITY*rb.complexity*NB.DEM.MEM*
##                                                 NB.OG.NORM  OPCW2009,OPCW2010,OPCW2011
## 2  RB.INEQUALITY*RB.COMPLEXITY*NB.VISIBILITY.ALL*
##     NB.VISIBILITY.HL*NB.GOV.DEPTH*NB.DEM.MEM*NB.OG.NORM     IAEA2009,IAEA2010,IAEA2011
```

```
## ----------------------------------------------
##
##
## p.sol: RB.INEQUALITY*NB.VISIBILITY.ALL +
##        RB.BUDGET*RB.INEQUALITY*NB.DEM.MEM
##
## Number of multiple-covered cases: 0
##
## M1:    RB.BUDGET*RB.INEQUALITY*NB.DEM.MEM*NB.OG.NORM +
##        RB.INEQUALITY*RB.COMPLEXITY*NB.VISIBILITY.ALL*NB.VISIBILITY.HL*
##        NB.GOV.DEPTH*NB.DEM.MEM*NB.OG.NORM
##        => ACTPART2
##
##
##                                                       incl   cov.r  cov.u
## -----------------------------------------------
## 1  RB.BUDGET*RB.INEQUALITY*NB.DEM.MEM*NB.OG.NORM       1.000  0.429  0.429
## 2  RB.INEQUALITY*RB.COMPLEXITY*NB.VISIBILITY.ALL*
##    NB.VISIBILITY.HL*NB.GOV.DEPTH*NB.DEM.MEM*NB.OG.NORM 1.000  0.429  0.429
## -----------------------------------------------
##    M1                                                  1.000  0.857
##
##                                                       cases
## -----------------------------------------------
## 1  RB.BUDGET*RB.INEQUALITY*NB.DEM.MEM*NB.OG.NORM       OPCW2009,OPCW2010,OPCW2011
## 2  RB.INEQUALITY*RB.COMPLEXITY*NB.VISIBILITY.ALL*
##    NB.VISIBILITY.HL*NB.GOV.DEPTH*NB.DEM.MEM*NB.OG.NORM IAEA2009,IAEA2010,IAEA2011
## -----------------------------------------------
##
##
## p.sol: RB.INEQUALITY*NB.VISIBILITY.HL + RB.BUDGET*nb.gov.depth*NB.DEM.MEM
##
## Number of multiple-covered cases: 0
##
## M1:    RB.BUDGET*RB.INEQUALITY*nb.gov.depth*NB.DEM.MEM*NB.OG.NORM +
##        RB.INEQUALITY*RB.COMPLEXITY*NB.VISIBILITY.ALL*NB.VISIBILITY.HL*
##        NB.GOV.DEPTH*NB.DEM.MEM*NB.OG.NORM
##        => ACTPART2
##
##
##                                                       incl   cov.r  cov.u
## -----------------------------------------------
## 1  RB.BUDGET*RB.INEQUALITY*nb.gov.depth*NB.DEM.MEM*
##                                      NB.OG.NORM        1.000  0.429  0.429
## 2  RB.INEQUALITY*RB.COMPLEXITY*NB.VISIBILITY.ALL*
##    NB.VISIBILITY.HL*NB.GOV.DEPTH*NB.DEM.MEM*NB.OG.NORM 1.000  0.429  0.429
## -----------------------------------------------
##    M1                                                  1.000  0.857
##
##                                                       cases
## -----------------------------------------------
## 1  RB.BUDGET*RB.INEQUALITY*nb.gov.depth*NB.DEM.MEM*
##                                      NB.OG.NORM        OPCW2009,OPCW2010,OPCW2011
## 2  RB.INEQUALITY*RB.COMPLEXITY*NB.VISIBILITY.ALL*
##    NB.VISIBILITY.HL*NB.GOV.DEPTH*NB.DEM.MEM*NB.OG.NORM IAEA2009,IAEA2010,IAEA2011
## -----------------------------------------------
```

```
## 
## 
## p.sol: RB.INEQUALITY*NB.VISIBILITY.HL +
##        RB.BUDGET*nb.visibility.all*NB.DEM.MEM
## 
## Number of multiple-covered cases: 0
## 
## M1:    RB.BUDGET*RB.INEQUALITY*nb.visibility.all*NB.DEM.MEM*NB.OG.NORM +
##        RB.INEQUALITY*RB.COMPLEXITY*NB.VISIBILITY.ALL*NB.VISIBILITY.HL*
##        NB.GOV.DEPTH*NB.DEM.MEM*NB.OG.NORM
##        => ACTPART2
## 
## 
##                                                           incl   cov.r  cov.u
## ----------------------------------------------------------
## 1  RB.BUDGET*RB.INEQUALITY*nb.visibility.all*NB.DEM.MEM*
##                                              NB.OG.NORM    1.000  0.429  0.429
## 2  RB.INEQUALITY*RB.COMPLEXITY*NB.VISIBILITY.ALL*
##    NB.VISIBILITY.HL*NB.GOV.DEPTH*NB.DEM.MEM*NB.OG.NORM     1.000  0.429  0.429
## ----------------------------------------------------------
##    M1                                                      1.000  0.857
## 
##                                                           cases
## ----------------------------------------------------------
## 1  RB.BUDGET*RB.INEQUALITY*nb.visibility.all*NB.DEM.MEM*
##                                              NB.OG.NORM    OPCW2009,OPCW2010,OPCW2011
## 2  RB.INEQUALITY*RB.COMPLEXITY*NB.VISIBILITY.ALL*
##    NB.VISIBILITY.HL*NB.GOV.DEPTH*NB.DEM.MEM*NB.OG.NORM     IAEA2009,IAEA2010,IAEA2011
## ----------------------------------------------------------
## 
## 
## p.sol: RB.INEQUALITY*NB.VISIBILITY.HL + RB.BUDGET*rb.complexity*NB.DEM.MEM
## 
## Number of multiple-covered cases: 0
## 
## M1:    RB.BUDGET*RB.INEQUALITY*rb.complexity*NB.DEM.MEM*NB.OG.NORM +
##        RB.INEQUALITY*RB.COMPLEXITY*NB.VISIBILITY.ALL*NB.VISIBILITY.HL*
##        NB.GOV.DEPTH*NB.DEM.MEM*NB.OG.NORM
##        => ACTPART2
## 
## 
##                                                           incl   cov.r  cov.u
## ----------------------------------------------------------
## 1  RB.BUDGET*RB.INEQUALITY*rb.complexity*NB.DEM.MEM*
##                                              NB.OG.NORM    1.000  0.429  0.429
## 2  RB.INEQUALITY*RB.COMPLEXITY*NB.VISIBILITY.ALL*
##    NB.VISIBILITY.HL*NB.GOV.DEPTH*NB.DEM.MEM*NB.OG.NORM     1.000  0.429  0.429
## ----------------------------------------------------------
##    M1                                                      1.000  0.857
## 
##                                                           cases
## ----------------------------------------------------------
## 1  RB.BUDGET*RB.INEQUALITY*rb.complexity*NB.DEM.MEM*
##                                              NB.OG.NORM    OPCW2009,OPCW2010,OPCW2011
## 2  RB.INEQUALITY*RB.COMPLEXITY*NB.VISIBILITY.ALL*
##    NB.VISIBILITY.HL*NB.GOV.DEPTH*NB.DEM.MEM*NB.OG.NORM     IAEA2009,IAEA2010,IAEA2011
```

```
## ------------------------------------------
##
##
## p.sol: RB.INEQUALITY*NB.VISIBILITY.HL + RB.BUDGET*RB.INEQUALITY*NB.DEM.MEM
##
## Number of multiple-covered cases: 0
##
## M1:     RB.BUDGET*RB.INEQUALITY*NB.DEM.MEM*NB.OG.NORM +
##         RB.INEQUALITY*RB.COMPLEXITY*NB.VISIBILITY.ALL*NB.VISIBILITY.HL*
##         NB.GOV.DEPTH*NB.DEM.MEM*NB.OG.NORM
##         => ACTPART2
##
##                                                         incl   cov.r  cov.u
## ------------------------------------------------
## 1  RB.BUDGET*RB.INEQUALITY*NB.DEM.MEM*NB.OG.NORM        1.000  0.429  0.429
## 2  RB.INEQUALITY*RB.COMPLEXITY*NB.VISIBILITY.ALL*
##    NB.VISIBILITY.HL*NB.GOV.DEPTH*NB.DEM.MEM*NB.OG.NORM  1.000  0.429  0.429
## ------------------------------------------------
##    M1                                                   1.000  0.857
##
##                                                         cases
## ------------------------------------------------
## 1  RB.BUDGET*RB.INEQUALITY*NB.DEM.MEM*NB.OG.NORM        OPCW2009,OPCW2010,OPCW2011
## 2  RB.INEQUALITY*RB.COMPLEXITY*NB.VISIBILITY.ALL*
##    NB.VISIBILITY.HL*NB.GOV.DEPTH*NB.DEM.MEM*NB.OG.NORM  IAEA2009,IAEA2010,IAEA2011
## ------------------------------------------------
##
##
## p.sol: RB.INEQUALITY*RB.COMPLEXITY + RB.BUDGET*nb.gov.depth*NB.DEM.MEM
##
## Number of multiple-covered cases: 0
##
## M1:     RB.BUDGET*RB.INEQUALITY*nb.gov.depth*NB.DEM.MEM*NB.OG.NORM +
##         RB.INEQUALITY*RB.COMPLEXITY*NB.VISIBILITY.ALL*NB.VISIBILITY.HL*
##         NB.GOV.DEPTH*NB.DEM.MEM*NB.OG.NORM
##         => ACTPART2
##
##                                                         incl   cov.r  cov.u
## ------------------------------------------------
## 1  RB.BUDGET*RB.INEQUALITY*nb.gov.depth*NB.DEM.MEM*
##                                        NB.OG.NORM       1.000  0.429  0.429
## 2  RB.INEQUALITY*RB.COMPLEXITY*NB.VISIBILITY.ALL*
##    NB.VISIBILITY.HL*NB.GOV.DEPTH*NB.DEM.MEM*NB.OG.NORM  1.000  0.429  0.429
## ------------------------------------------------
##    M1                                                   1.000  0.857
##
##                                                         cases
## ------------------------------------------------
## 1  RB.BUDGET*RB.INEQUALITY*nb.gov.depth*NB.DEM.MEM*
##                                        NB.OG.NORM       OPCW2009,OPCW2010,OPCW2011
## 2  RB.INEQUALITY*RB.COMPLEXITY*NB.VISIBILITY.ALL*
##    NB.VISIBILITY.HL*NB.GOV.DEPTH*NB.DEM.MEM*NB.OG.NORM  IAEA2009,IAEA2010,IAEA2011
## ------------------------------------------------
##
```

```
##
## p.sol: RB.INEQUALITY*RB.COMPLEXITY +
##        RB.BUDGET*nb.visibility.all*NB.DEM.MEM
##
## Number of multiple-covered cases: 0
##
## M1:    RB.BUDGET*RB.INEQUALITY*nb.visibility.all*NB.DEM.MEM*NB.OG.NORM +
##        RB.INEQUALITY*RB.COMPLEXITY*NB.VISIBILITY.ALL*NB.VISIBILITY.HL*
##        NB.GOV.DEPTH*NB.DEM.MEM*NB.OG.NORM
##        => ACTPART2
##
##                                                       incl  cov.r  cov.u
## -----------------------------------------------------
## 1  RB.BUDGET*RB.INEQUALITY*nb.visibility.all*NB.DEM.MEM*
##                                          NB.OG.NORM    1.000  0.429  0.429
## 2  RB.INEQUALITY*RB.COMPLEXITY*NB.VISIBILITY.ALL*
##    NB.VISIBILITY.HL*NB.GOV.DEPTH*NB.DEM.MEM*NB.OG.NORM  1.000  0.429  0.429
## -----------------------------------------------------
##    M1                                                  1.000  0.857
##
##                                                       cases
## -----------------------------------------------------
## 1  RB.BUDGET*RB.INEQUALITY*nb.visibility.all*NB.DEM.MEM*
##                                          NB.OG.NORM    OPCW2009,OPCW2010,OPCW2011
## 2  RB.INEQUALITY*RB.COMPLEXITY*NB.VISIBILITY.ALL*
##    NB.VISIBILITY.HL*NB.GOV.DEPTH*NB.DEM.MEM*NB.OG.NORM  IAEA2009,IAEA2010,IAEA2011
## -----------------------------------------------------
##
##
## p.sol: RB.INEQUALITY*RB.COMPLEXITY + RB.BUDGET*rb.complexity*NB.DEM.MEM
##
## Number of multiple-covered cases: 0
##
## M1:    RB.BUDGET*RB.INEQUALITY*rb.complexity*NB.DEM.MEM*NB.OG.NORM +
##        RB.INEQUALITY*RB.COMPLEXITY*NB.VISIBILITY.ALL*NB.VISIBILITY.HL*
##        NB.GOV.DEPTH*NB.DEM.MEM*NB.OG.NORM
##        => ACTPART2
##
##                                                       incl  cov.r  cov.u
## -----------------------------------------------------
## 1  RB.BUDGET*RB.INEQUALITY*rb.complexity*NB.DEM.MEM*NB.OG.NORM  1.000  0.429  0.429
## 2  RB.INEQUALITY*RB.COMPLEXITY*NB.VISIBILITY.ALL*
##    NB.VISIBILITY.HL*NB.GOV.DEPTH*NB.DEM.MEM*NB.OG.NORM  1.000  0.429  0.429
## -----------------------------------------------------
##    M1                                                  1.000  0.857
##
##                                                       cases
## -----------------------------------------------------
## 1  RB.BUDGET*RB.INEQUALITY*rb.complexity*NB.DEM.MEM*
##                                          NB.OG.NORM    OPCW2009,OPCW2010,OPCW2011
## 2  RB.INEQUALITY*RB.COMPLEXITY*NB.VISIBILITY.ALL*
##    NB.VISIBILITY.HL*NB.GOV.DEPTH*NB.DEM.MEM*NB.OG.NORM  IAEA2009,IAEA2010,IAEA2011
## -----------------------------------------------------
##
```

```
##
## p.sol: RB.INEQUALITY*RB.COMPLEXITY + RB.BUDGET*RB.INEQUALITY*NB.DEM.MEM
##
## Number of multiple-covered cases: 0
##
## M1:    RB.BUDGET*RB.INEQUALITY*NB.DEM.MEM*NB.OG.NORM +
##        RB.INEQUALITY*RB.COMPLEXITY*NB.VISIBILITY.ALL*NB.VISIBILITY.HL*
##        NB.GOV.DEPTH*NB.DEM.MEM*NB.OG.NORM
##        => ACTPART2
##
##                                                           incl  cov.r  cov.u
## ————————————————————————————————————————————-
## 1   RB.BUDGET*RB.INEQUALITY*NB.DEM.MEM*NB.OG.NORM          1.000  0.429  0.429
## 2   RB.INEQUALITY*RB.COMPLEXITY*NB.VISIBILITY.ALL*
##     NB.VISIBILITY.HL*NB.GOV.DEPTH*NB.DEM.MEM*NB.OG.NORM    1.000  0.429  0.429
## ————————————————————————————————————————————-
##     M1                                                     1.000  0.857
##
##                                                           cases
## ————————————————————————————————————————————-
## 1   RB.BUDGET*RB.INEQUALITY*NB.DEM.MEM*NB.OG.NORM          OPCW2009,OPCW2010,OPCW2011
## 2   RB.INEQUALITY*RB.COMPLEXITY*NB.VISIBILITY.ALL*
##     NB.VISIBILITY.HL*NB.GOV.DEPTH*NB.DEM.MEM*NB.OG.NORM    IAEA2009,IAEA2010,IAEA2011
## ————————————————————————————————————————————-
```

```r
# neg. outcome, to check for contradictions
tt <- truthTable(data_qca[c(25, 10:17)], outcome = c("ACTPART2"),
          incl.cut1=1, sort.by="incl", show.cases = TRUE,
          neg.out = T)
sc <- eqmcc(tt, include="?", show.cases = TRUE, details = TRUE)
sc$essential
```

```
## [1] "nb.dem.mem"                "rb.inequality*NB.VISIBILITY.HL"
```

C.2.9 PARTICIPATION ACTION: PARTICIPATION EVENTS

```r
data_qca$ACTPART4 <- data_qca$ACT.Part.4 # for QCA package conventions
tt <- truthTable(data_qca[c(26, 10:17)], outcome = c("ACTPART4"),
          incl.cut1=1, sort.by="incl", show.cases = TRUE)
# necessary conditions
superSubset(data_qca[c(26, 10:17)], outcome = "ACTPART4",
          relation="nec", incl.cut=0.9, cov.cut=0.7)
```

```
##
##                                                      incl  cov.r
## ———————————————————————————-
## 1   RB.BUDGET+NB.VISIBILITY.ALL+NB.DEM.MEM           0.968  0.732
## 2   RB.BUDGET+NB.VISIBILITY.HL+NB.GOV.DEPTH+NB.DEM.MEM  0.903  0.718
## ———————————————————————————-
```

```r
# neg. outcome, to check for contradictions
superSubset(data_qca[c(26, 10:17)], outcome = "ACTPART4",
            relation="nec", incl.cut=0.9, cov.cut=0.63,
            neg.out = T)
```

```
##
##                                            incl   cov.r
## ————————————————————
## 1  nb.visibility.hl                        0.974  0.644
## 2  rb.budget+rb.complexity                 0.923  0.632
## 3  rb.budget+RB.INEQUALITY                 0.923  0.632
## 4  RB.BUDGET+nb.gov.depth                  0.949  0.638
## 5  RB.BUDGET+nb.visibility.all             0.949  0.685
## 6  RB.BUDGET+rb.complexity+nb.og.norm      0.949  0.649
## ————————————————————
```

```r
# sufficient conditions
tt <- truthTable(data_qca[c(26, 10:17)], outcome = c("ACTPART4"),
            incl.cut1=0.8, sort.by="incl", show.cases = TRUE)
# use parsimonious solution here.
sc <- eqmcc(tt, include="?", show.cases = TRUE, details = TRUE)
sc$essential
```

```
## [1] "RB.BUDGET*NB.VISIBILITY.HL"
```

```r
# neg. outcome, to check for contradictions
tt <- truthTable(data_qca[c(26, 10:17)], outcome = c("ACTPART4"),
            incl.cut1=1, sort.by="incl", show.cases = TRUE,
            neg.out = T)
eqmcc(tt, include="?", show.cases = TRUE, details = TRUE,
            dir.exp = c(rep(1, 8)))
```

```
##
## n OUT = 1/0/C: 7/63/0
##    Total      : 70
##
## p.sol: rb.complexity*nb.dem.mem
##
## Number of multiple-covered cases: 0
##
## M1:    RB.INEQUALITY*rb.complexity*nb.visibility.all*nb.visibility.hl*
##        nb.gov.depth*nb.dem.mem*NB.OG.NORM => actpart4
##
##                                                            incl   cov.r  cov.u
## ————————————————————————————————————————-
## 1  RB.INEQUALITY*rb.complexity*nb.visibility.all*
##    nb.visibility.hl*nb.gov.depth*nb.dem.mem*NB.OG.NORM      1.000  0.179   -
## ————————————————————————————————————————-
```

```
##    M1                                                       1.000  0.179
##
##
##                                                             cases
## ---------------------------------------------------------
## 1  RB.INEQUALITY*rb.complexity*nb.visibility.all*
##    nb.visibility.hl*nb.gov.depth*nb.dem.mem*NB.OG.NORM      OPCW1997,OPCW1998,OPCW2003;
##                                                             OPCW1999,OPCW2000,OPCW2001,
##                                                             OPCW2002
## ---------------------------------------------------------
##
##
## p.sol: RB.INEQUALITY*nb.dem.mem
##
## Number of multiple-covered cases: 0
##
## M1:    RB.INEQUALITY*rb.complexity*nb.visibility.all*nb.visibility.hl*
##        nb.gov.depth*nb.dem.mem*NB.OG.NORM => actpart4
##
##
##                                                             incl   cov.r  cov.u
## ----------------------------------------------------------
## 1  RB.INEQUALITY*rb.complexity*nb.visibility.all*
##    nb.visibility.hl*nb.gov.depth*nb.dem.mem*NB.OG.NORM      1.000  0.179    -
## ----------------------------------------------------------
##    M1                                                       1.000  0.179
##
##                                                             cases
## ---------------------------------------------------------
## 1  RB.INEQUALITY*rb.complexity*nb.visibility.all*
##    nb.visibility.hl*nb.gov.depth*nb.dem.mem*NB.OG.NORM      OPCW1997,OPCW1998,OPCW2003;
##                                                             OPCW1999,OPCW2000,OPCW2001,
##                                                             OPCW2002
## ---------------------------------------------------------
##
##
## p.sol: nb.visibility.all*nb.dem.mem*NB.OG.NORM
##
## Number of multiple-covered cases: 0
##
## M1:    RB.INEQUALITY*rb.complexity*nb.visibility.all*nb.visibility.hl*
##        nb.gov.depth*nb.dem.mem*NB.OG.NORM => actpart4
##
##
##                                                             incl   cov.r  cov.u
## ----------------------------------------------------------
## 1  RB.INEQUALITY*rb.complexity*nb.visibility.all*
##    nb.visibility.hl*nb.gov.depth*nb.dem.mem*NB.OG.NORM      1.000  0.179    -
## ----------------------------------------------------------
##    M1                                                       1.000  0.179
##
##                                                             cases
## ---------------------------------------------------------
## 1  RB.INEQUALITY*rb.complexity*nb.visibility.all*
##    nb.visibility.hl*nb.gov.depth*nb.dem.mem*NB.OG.NORM      OPCW1997,OPCW1998,OPCW2003;
##                                                             OPCW1999,OPCW2000,OPCW2001,
##                                                             OPCW2002
## ---------------------------------------------------------
```

C.2.10 PARTICIPATION ACTION

```
data_qca$ACTPART <- fsor(data_qca$ACTPART1,
          data_qca$ACTPART2, data_qca$ACTPART4)
tt <- truthTable(data_qca[c(27, 10:11, 13:17)],
          outcome = c("ACTPART"), incl.cut1=1, sort.by="incl",
          show.cases = TRUE)
# necessary conditions
superSubset(data_qca[c(27, 10:11, 13:17)], outcome = "ACTPART",
          relation="nec", incl.cut=1, cov.cut=0.6)
```

```
##
##                                              incl   cov.r
## ------------------------------
##  1   nb.dem.mem+NB.OG.NORM                   1.000  0.671
##  2   nb.gov.depth+NB.OG.NORM                 1.000  0.671
##  3   NB.VISIBILITY.ALL+nb.gov.depth          1.000  0.671
##  4   NB.VISIBILITY.ALL+nb.visibility.hl      1.000  0.671
##  5   rb.inequality+NB.OG.NORM                1.000  0.671
##  ...
## ------------------------------
```

```
# neg. outcome, to check for contradictions
superSubset(data_qca[c(27, 10:11, 13:17)], outcome = "ACTPART",
          relation="nec", incl.cut=0.9, cov.cut=0.4, neg.out = T)
```

```
##
##                                              incl   cov.r
## ------------------------------
##  1   nb.dem.mem                              0.913  0.488
##  2   nb.gov.depth                            1.000  0.469
##  3   nb.visibility.all                       1.000  0.523
##  4   rb.budget                               0.913  0.420
##  5   nb.gov.depth*nb.dem.mem                 0.913  0.512
##  6   nb.visibility.hl*nb.dem.mem             0.913  0.525
##  7   nb.visibility.hl*nb.gov.depth           1.000  0.500
##  8   nb.visibility.all*nb.dem.mem            0.913  0.583
##  9   nb.visibility.all*nb.gov.depth          1.000  0.523
## 10   nb.visibility.all*nb.visibility.hl      1.000  0.523
## 11   rb.budget*nb.gov.depth                  0.913  0.553
## 12   rb.budget*nb.visibility.hl              0.913  0.488
## 13   rb.budget*nb.visibility.all             0.913  0.618
##  ...
## ------------------------------
```

```
# conservative solution
sc <- eqmcc(tt, show.cases = T, details = T)
sc$essential
```

```
## [1] "rb.inequality*NB.VISIBILITY.ALL*NB.GOV.DEPTH*NB.DEM.MEM*NB.OG.NORM"
## [2] "rb.budget*NB.VISIBILITY.ALL*NB.VISIBILITY.HL*NB.GOV.DEPTH*NB.DEM.MEM*NB.OG.NORM"
## [3] "rb.inequality*NB.VISIBILITY.ALL*NB.VISIBILITY.HL*nb.gov.depth*nb.dem.mem*
##      nb.og.norm"
## [4] "RB.BUDGET*rb.inequality*nb.visibility.all*nb.visibility.hl*nb.gov.depth*
##      nb.dem.mem*nb.og.norm"
## [5] "RB.BUDGET*RB.INEQUALITY*nb.visibility.all*nb.visibility.hl*nb.gov.depth*
##      NB.DEM.MEM*NB.OG.NORM"
```

```r
  # intermediate solution
  intermed.sol <- eqmcc(tt, include="?", show.cases = TRUE, details = TRUE,
          dir.exp = c(rep(1, 7)))
intermed.sol
```

```
##
## n OUT = 1/0/C: 32/38/0
##   Total      : 70
##
## p.sol: NB.VISIBILITY.ALL + RB.BUDGET*NB.DEM.MEM + RB.BUDGET*nb.og.norm
##
## Number of multiple-covered cases: 1
##
## M1:    NB.VISIBILITY.ALL + RB.BUDGET*nb.og.norm +
##        RB.BUDGET*RB.INEQUALITY*NB.DEM.MEM => ACTPART
##
##
##                                    incl   cov.r  cov.u
## -------------------------------------
## 1   NB.VISIBILITY.ALL              1.000  0.553  0.532
## 2   RB.BUDGET*nb.og.norm           1.000  0.085  0.064
## 3   RB.BUDGET*RB.INEQUALITY*NB.DEM.MEM  1.000  0.064  0.064
## -------------------------------------
##    M1                              1.000  0.681
##
##                                    cases
## -------------------------------------
## 1   NB.VISIBILITY.ALL              IAEA1989; IAEA1990; IAEA1991,IAEA1992;
##                                    IAEA2004,IAEA2005,IAEA2006,IAEA2007,IAEA2008;
##                                    IAEA1987,IAEA1988; IAEA2002,IAEA2003;
##                                    IAEA2009,IAEA2010,IAEA2011; IAEA1993,IAEA1994,
##                                    IAEA1995,IAEA1996,IAEA1997,IAEA1998;
##                                    IAEA1986; IAEA1999,IAEA2000,IAEA2001
## 2   RB.BUDGET*nb.og.norm           IAEA1983,IAEA1984,IAEA1985; IAEA1986
## 3   RB.BUDGET*RB.INEQUALITY*NB.DEM.MEM  OPCW2009,OPCW2010,OPCW2011
## -------------------------------------
##
##
## p.sol: NB.VISIBILITY.ALL + RB.BUDGET*NB.DEM.MEM + RB.BUDGET*rb.inequality
##
## Number of multiple-covered cases: 10
##
## M1:    NB.VISIBILITY.ALL + RB.BUDGET*rb.inequality +
##        RB.BUDGET*NB.DEM.MEM*NB.OG.NORM => ACTPART
```

```
##
##                                        incl  cov.r  cov.u
## ----------------------------
## 1   NB.VISIBILITY.ALL             1.000  0.553  0.340
## 2   RB.BUDGET*rb.inequality       1.000  0.277  0.064
## 3   RB.BUDGET*NB.DEM.MEM*NB.OG.NORM 1.000  0.255  0.064
## ----------------------------
##     M1                            1.000  0.681
##
##                                        cases
## ------------------
## 1   NB.VISIBILITY.ALL             IAEA1989; IAEA1990; IAEA1991,IAEA1992; IAEA2004,
##                                   IAEA2005,IAEA2006,IAEA2007,IAEA2008;IAEA1987,
##                                   IAEA1988; IAEA2002,IAEA2003; IAEA2009,IAEA2010,
##                                   IAEA2011;IAEA1993,IAEA1994,IAEA1995,IAEA1996,
##                                   IAEA1997,IAEA1998;IAEA1986; IAEA1999,IAEA2000,
##                                   IAEA2001
## 2   RB.BUDGET*rb.inequality       IAEA1983,IAEA1984,IAEA1985; IAEA1993,IAEA1994,
##                                   IAEA1995,IAEA1996,IAEA1997,IAEA1998;
##                                   IAEA1986; IAEA1999,IAEA2000,IAEA2001
## 3   RB.BUDGET*NB.DEM.MEM*NB.OG.NORM IAEA1993,IAEA1994,IAEA1995,IAEA1996,IAEA1997,
##                                   IAEA1998;IAEA1999,IAEA2000,IAEA2001; OPCW2009,
##                                   OPCW2010,OPCW2011
## ------------------
##
##
## p.sol: NB.VISIBILITY.ALL + RB.BUDGET*NB.DEM.MEM + RB.BUDGET*nb.og.norm
##
## Number of multiple-covered cases: 1
##
## M1:    NB.VISIBILITY.ALL + RB.BUDGET*nb.og.norm +
##        RB.BUDGET*RB.INEQUALITY*NB.DEM.MEM => ACTPART
##
##                                        incl  cov.r  cov.u
## -----------------------------
## 1   NB.VISIBILITY.ALL             1.000  0.553  0.532
## 2   RB.BUDGET*nb.og.norm          1.000  0.085  0.064
## 3   RB.BUDGET*RB.INEQUALITY*NB.DEM.MEM 1.000  0.064  0.064
## -----------------------------
##     M1                            1.000  0.681
##
##                                        cases
## ------------------
## 1   NB.VISIBILITY.ALL             IAEA1989; IAEA1990; IAEA1991,IAEA1992;
##                                   IAEA2004,IAEA2005,IAEA2006,IAEA2007,IAEA2008;
##                                   IAEA1987,IAEA1988; IAEA2002,IAEA2003;
##                                   IAEA2009,IAEA2010,IAEA2011; IAEA1993,IAEA1994,
##                                   IAEA1995,IAEA1996,IAEA1997,IAEA1998;
##                                   IAEA1986; IAEA1999,IAEA2000,IAEA2001
## 2   RB.BUDGET*nb.og.norm          IAEA1983,IAEA1984,IAEA1985; IAEA1986
## 3   RB.BUDGET*RB.INEQUALITY*NB.DEM.MEM OPCW2009,OPCW2010,OPCW2011
## ------------------
##
##
```

```
## p.sol: NB.VISIBILITY.ALL + RB.BUDGET*NB.DEM.MEM + RB.BUDGET*rb.inequality
##
## Number of multiple-covered cases: 10
##
## M1:     NB.VISIBILITY.ALL + RB.BUDGET*rb.inequality +
##         RB.BUDGET*NB.DEM.MEM*NB.OG.NORM => ACTPART
##
##                                       incl   cov.r  cov.u
## ------------------------------
## 1  NB.VISIBILITY.ALL                  1.000  0.553  0.340
## 2  RB.BUDGET*rb.inequality            1.000  0.277  0.064
## 3  RB.BUDGET*NB.DEM.MEM*NB.OG.NORM    1.000  0.255  0.064
## ------------------------------
##     M1                                1.000  0.681
##
##                                       cases
## ------------------------------
## 1  NB.VISIBILITY.ALL                  IAEA1989; IAEA1990; IAEA1991,IAEA1992; IAEA2004,
##                                       IAEA2005,IAEA2006,IAEA2007,IAEA2008;IAEA1987,
##                                       IAEA1988; IAEA2002,IAEA2003; IAEA2009,IAEA2010,
##                                       IAEA2011;IAEA1993,IAEA1994,IAEA1995,IAEA1996,
##                                       IAEA1997,IAEA1998;IAEA1986; IAEA1999,IAEA2000,
##                                       IAEA2001
## 2  RB.BUDGET*rb.inequality            IAEA1983,IAEA1984,IAEA1985; IAEA1993,IAEA1994,
##                                       IAEA1995,IAEA1996,IAEA1997,IAEA1998;
##                                       IAEA1986; IAEA1999,IAEA2000,IAEA2001
## 3  RB.BUDGET*NB.DEM.MEM*NB.OG.NORM    IAEA1993,IAEA1994,IAEA1995,IAEA1996,IAEA1997,
##                                       IAEA1998;IAEA1999,IAEA2000,IAEA2001; OPCW2009,
##                                       OPCW2010,OPCW2011
## ------------------------------
##
##
## p.sol: NB.VISIBILITY.ALL + RB.BUDGET*NB.DEM.MEM + RB.BUDGET*nb.og.norm
##
## Number of multiple-covered cases: 1
##
## M1:     NB.VISIBILITY.ALL + RB.BUDGET*nb.og.norm +
##         RB.BUDGET*RB.INEQUALITY*NB.DEM.MEM => ACTPART
##
##                                       incl   cov.r  cov.u
## ------------------------------
## 1  NB.VISIBILITY.ALL                  1.000  0.553  0.532
## 2  RB.BUDGET*nb.og.norm               1.000  0.085  0.064
## 3  RB.BUDGET*RB.INEQUALITY*NB.DEM.MEM 1.000  0.064  0.064
## ------------------------------
##     M1                                1.000  0.681
##
##                                       cases
## ------------------------------
## 1  NB.VISIBILITY.ALL                  IAEA1989; IAEA1990; IAEA1991,IAEA1992;
##                                       IAEA2004,IAEA2005,IAEA2006,IAEA2007,IAEA2008;
##                                       IAEA1987,IAEA1988; IAEA2002,IAEA2003;
##                                       IAEA2009,IAEA2010,IAEA2011; IAEA1993,IAEA1994,
##                                       IAEA1995,IAEA1996,IAEA1997,IAEA1998;
```

```
##                                   IAEA1986; IAEA1999,IAEA2000,IAEA2001
## 2   RB.BUDGET*nb.og.norm          IAEA1983,IAEA1984,IAEA1985; IAEA1986
## 3   RB.BUDGET*RB.INEQUALITY*NB.DEM.MEM  OPCW2009,OPCW2010,OPCW2011
## -----------------
##
##
## p.sol: NB.VISIBILITY.ALL + RB.BUDGET*NB.DEM.MEM + RB.BUDGET*rb.inequality
##
## Number of multiple-covered cases: 10
##
## M1:    NB.VISIBILITY.ALL + RB.BUDGET*rb.inequality +
##        RB.BUDGET*NB.DEM.MEM*NB.OG.NORM => ACTPART
##
##
##                                   incl   cov.r  cov.u
## ---------------------
## 1   NB.VISIBILITY.ALL             1.000  0.553  0.340
## 2   RB.BUDGET*rb.inequality       1.000  0.277  0.064
## 3   RB.BUDGET*NB.DEM.MEM*NB.OG.NORM  1.000  0.255  0.064
## ---------------------
##     M1                            1.000  0.681
##
##                                   cases
## ---------------------
## 1   NB.VISIBILITY.ALL             IAEA1989; IAEA1990; IAEA1991,IAEA1992; IAEA2004,
##                                   IAEA2005,IAEA2006,IAEA2007,IAEA2008;IAEA1987,
##                                   IAEA1988; IAEA2002,IAEA2003; IAEA2009,IAEA2010,
##                                   IAEA2011;IAEA1993,IAEA1994,IAEA1995,IAEA1996,
##                                   IAEA1997,IAEA1998;IAEA1986; IAEA1999,IAEA2000,
##                                   IAEA2001
## 2   RB.BUDGET*rb.inequality       IAEA1983,IAEA1984,IAEA1985; IAEA1993,IAEA1994,
##                                   IAEA1995,IAEA1996,IAEA1997,IAEA1998;IAEA1986;
##                                   IAEA1999,IAEA2000,IAEA2001
## 3   RB.BUDGET*NB.DEM.MEM*NB.OG.NORM  IAEA1993,IAEA1994,IAEA1995,IAEA1996,IAEA1997,
##                                   IAEA1998;IAEA1999,IAEA2000,IAEA2001; OPCW2009,
##                                   OPCW2010,OPCW2011
## -----------------

# parsimonious solution
eqmcc(tt, include="?", show.cases = TRUE, details = TRUE)


##
## n OUT = 1/0/C: 32/38/0
##   Total      : 70
##
## Number of multiple-covered cases: 10
##
## M1: NB.VISIBILITY.ALL + RB.BUDGET*NB.DEM.MEM + (RB.BUDGET*nb.og.norm)
##     => ACTPART
## M2: NB.VISIBILITY.ALL + RB.BUDGET*NB.DEM.MEM + (RB.BUDGET*rb.inequality)
##     => ACTPART
##
##                                   ------
##                          incl   cov.r  cov.u  (M1)   (M2)
```

```
## ---------------------------

## 1 NB.VISIBILITY.ALL        1.000   0.553   0.340   0.340   0.340
## 2 RB.BUDGET*NB.DEM.MEM      1.000   0.255   0.064   0.064   0.064
## ---------------------------

## 3  RB.BUDGET*nb.og.norm     1.000   0.085   0.000   0.064
## 4  RB.BUDGET*rb.inequality  1.000   0.277   0.000           0.064
## ---------------------------

##    M1                       1.000   0.681
##    M2                       1.000   0.681
##

##                            cases
## ---------------

## 1   NB.VISIBILITY.ALL       IAEA1989; IAEA1990; IAEA1991,IAEA1992; IAEA2004,
##                             IAEA2005,IAEA2006,IAEA2007,IAEA2008;IAEA1987,
##                             IAEA1988; IAEA2002,IAEA2003; IAEA2009,IAEA2010,
##                             IAEA2011;IAEA1993,IAEA1994,IAEA1995,IAEA1996,
##                             IAEA1997,IAEA1998;IAEA1986; IAEA1999,IAEA2000,IAEA2001
## 2   RB.BUDGET*NB.DEM.MEM    IAEA1993,IAEA1994,IAEA1995,IAEA1996,IAEA1997,IAEA1998;
##                             IAEA1999,IAEA2000,IAEA2001; OPCW2009,OPCW2010,OPCW2011
## ---------------

## 3  RB.BUDGET*nb.og.norm     IAEA1983,IAEA1984,IAEA1985; IAEA1986
## 4  RB.BUDGET*rb.inequality  IAEA1983,IAEA1984,IAEA1985; IAEA1993,IAEA1994,IAEA1995,
##                             IAEA1996,IAEA1997,IAEA1998;IAEA1986; IAEA1999,IAEA2000,
##                             IAEA2001
## ---------------
```

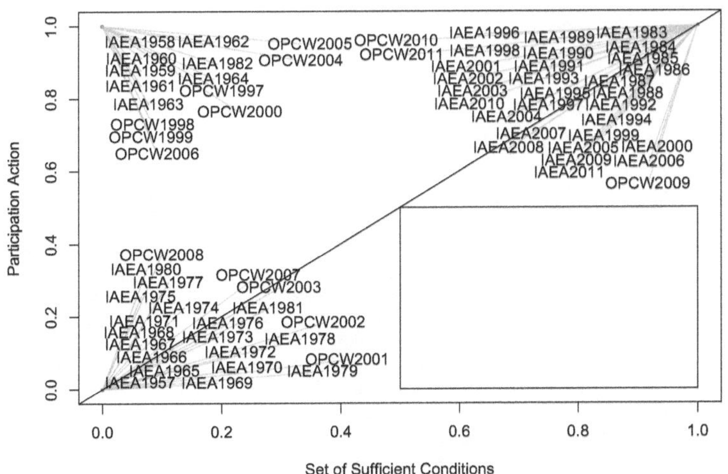

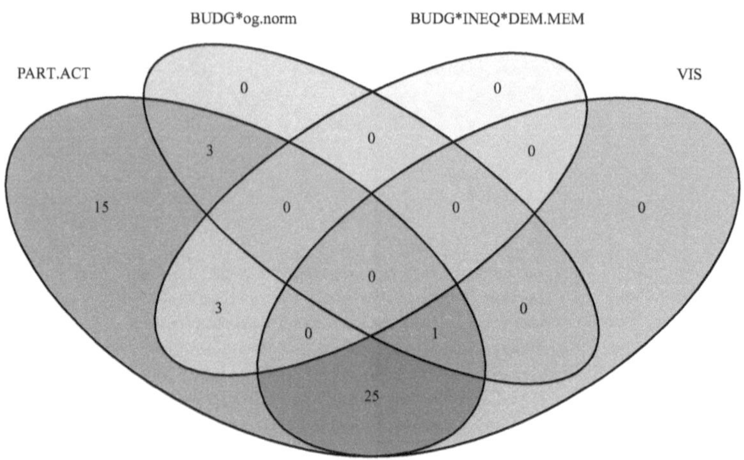

C.2.11   TRANSPARENCY ACTION

```
data_qca$ACTTRANS <- data_qca$ACT.Trans # for QCA package conventions
tt <- truthTable(data_qca[c(28, 10:11, 13:17)],
          outcome = c("ACTTRANS"), incl.cut1=0.8, sort.by="incl",
          show.cases = TRUE)
# necessary conditions
superSubset(data_qca[c(28, 10:11, 13:17)], outcome = "ACTTRANS",
          relation="nec", incl.cut=0.8, cov.cut=0.37)


##
##                                     incl   cov.r
## ————————————
## 1  NB.OG.NORM                       0.824  0.378
## 2  NB.DEM.MEM                       0.824  0.519
## 3  NB.DEM.MEM*NB.OG.NORM            0.824  0.519
## 4  rb.budget*NB.OG.NORM             0.824  0.667
## 5  rb.budget*NB.DEM.MEM             0.824  0.933
## 6  rb.budget*NB.DEM.MEM*NB.OG.NORM  0.824  0.933
## 7  RB.INEQUALITY+NB.GOV.DEPTH       0.824  0.389
## ————————————


# neg. outcome, to check for contradictions
superSubset(data_qca[c(28, 10:11, 13:17)], outcome = "ACTTRANS",
          relation="nec", incl.cut=1, cov.cut=0.4, neg.out = T)
```

```
## 
##                                                             incl   cov.r
## ─────────────────────────────────
## 1   nb.dem.mem+NB.OG.NORM                                    1.000  0.757
## 2   nb.gov.depth+NB.OG.NORM                                  1.000  0.757
## 3   NB.VISIBILITY.ALL+nb.gov.depth                           1.000  0.757
## 4   NB.VISIBILITY.ALL+nb.visibility.hl                       1.000  0.757
## 5   rb.inequality+NB.OG.NORM                                 1.000  0.757
## 6   rb.inequality+nb.gov.depth                               1.000  0.791
## 7   rb.inequality+nb.visibility.hl                           1.000  0.791
## 8   rb.inequality+nb.visibility.all                          1.000  0.791
## ...
## ─────────────────────────────────
```

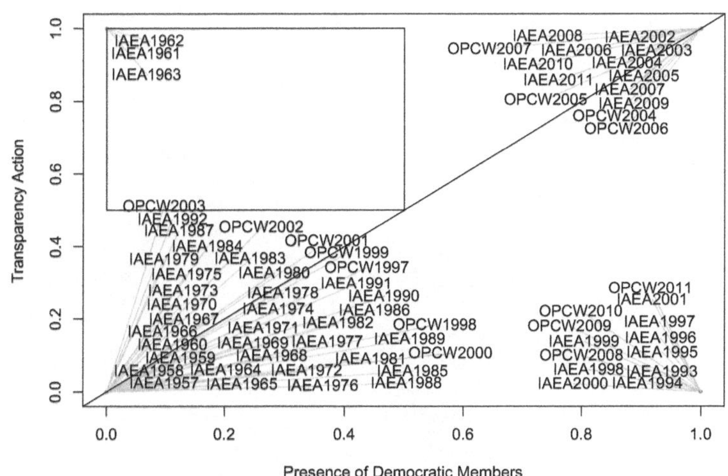

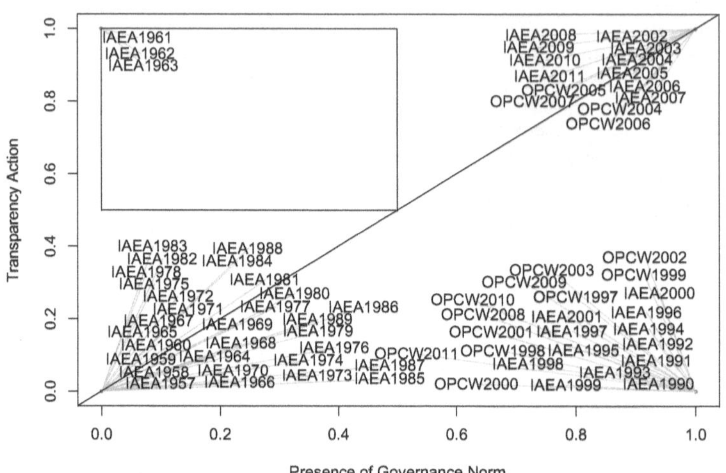

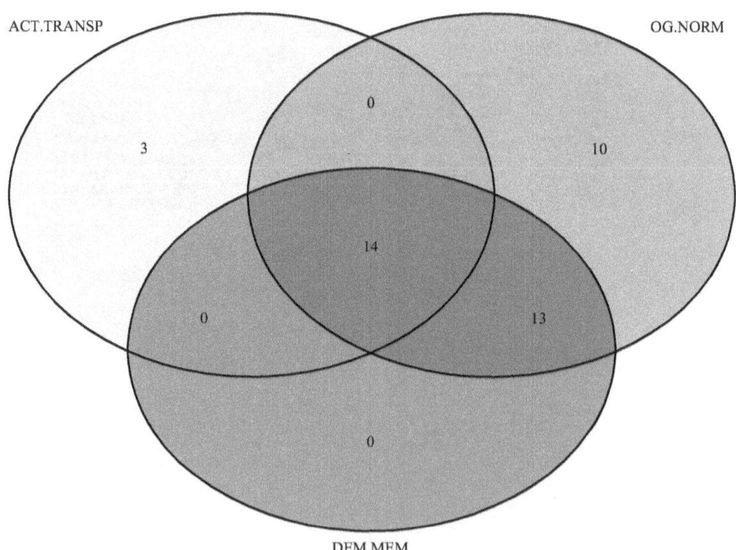


```
#sufficient condition, without democratic members
tt <- truthTable(data_qca[c(28, 10:11, 13:15, 17)],
        outcome = c("ACTTRANS"), incl.cut1=1, sort.by="incl",
        show.cases = TRUE)
```

```
# complex solution
eqmcc(tt, show.cases = TRUE, details = TRUE)


##
## n OUT = 1/0/C: 5/65/0
##   Total      : 70
##
## Number of multiple-covered cases: 0
##
## M1: rb.budget*NB.VISIBILITY.ALL*NB.VISIBILITY.HL*NB.GOV.DEPTH*
##                                   NB.OG.NORM => ACTTRANS
##
##                                                       incl  cov.r cov.u
## ----------------------------------
## 1  rb.budget*NB.VISIBILITY.ALL*NB.VISIBILITY.HL*NB.GOV.DEPTH
##                                   *NB.OG.NORM  1.000  0.294    -
## ----------------------------------
##    M1                                          1.000  0.294
##
##                                                       cases
## ----------------------------
## 1  rb.budget*NB.VISIBILITY.ALL*NB.VISIBILITY.HL*NB.GOV.DEPTH
##                                   *NB.OG.NORM  IAEA2002,IAEA2003;
##                                                IAEA2009,IAEA2010,
##                                                IAEA2011
## ----------------------------


# intermediate solution
eqmcc(tt, include="?", show.cases = TRUE, details = TRUE,
         dir.exp = c(rep(1, 6)))


##
## n OUT = 1/0/C: 5/65/0
##   Total      : 70
##
## p.sol: rb.budget*NB.VISIBILITY.HL*NB.GOV.DEPTH
##
## Number of multiple-covered cases: 0
##
## M1:    rb.budget*NB.VISIBILITY.ALL*NB.VISIBILITY.HL*NB.GOV.DEPTH
##                                   *NB.OG.NORM => ACTTRANS
##
##                                                       incl  cov.r cov.u
## ----------------------------------
## 1  rb.budget*NB.VISIBILITY.ALL*NB.VISIBILITY.HL*NB.GOV.DEPTH
##                                   *NB.OG.NORM  1.000  0.294    -
## ----------------------------------
##    M1                                          1.000  0.294
##
##                                                       cases
## ----------------------------
```

```
## 1   rb.budget*NB.VISIBILITY.ALL*NB.VISIBILITY.HL*NB.GOV.DEPTH*    IAEA2002,IAEA2003;
##                                                    NB.OG.NORM     IAEA2009,IAEA2010,
##                                                                   IAEA2011
## ───────────────────────────────
##
##
## p.sol: rb.budget*NB.VISIBILITY.HL*NB.OG.NORM
##
## Number of multiple-covered cases: 0
##
## M1:     rb.budget*NB.VISIBILITY.ALL*NB.VISIBILITY.HL*NB.GOV.DEPTH*
##         NB.OG.NORM => ACTTRANS
##
##                                                            incl   cov.r  cov.u
## ────────────────────────────────
## 1   rb.budget*NB.VISIBILITY.ALL*NB.VISIBILITY.HL*NB.GOV.DEPTH*
##                                         NB.OG.NORM  1.000  0.294     -
## ────────────────────────────────
##     M1                                              1.000  0.294
##
##                                                                   cases
## ───────────────────────────────
## 1   rb.budget*NB.VISIBILITY.ALL*NB.VISIBILITY.HL*NB.GOV.DEPTH*NB.OG.NORM  IAEA2002,
##                                                                   IAEA2003;
##                                                                   IAEA2009,
##                                                                   IAEA2010,
##                                                                   IAEA2011
## ───────────────────────────────


# parsimonious solution
sc <- eqmcc(tt, include="?", show.cases = TRUE, details = TRUE)
sc$solution


## [[1]]
## [1] "rb.budget*NB.VISIBILITY.HL*NB.GOV.DEPTH"
##
## [[2]]
## [1] "rb.budget*NB.VISIBILITY.HL*NB.OG.NORM"


# neg. outcome, to check for contradictions
tt <- truthTable(data_qca[c(28, 10:11, 13:15, 17)],
          outcome = c("ACTTRANS"), incl.cut1=1, sort.by="incl",
          show.cases = TRUE, neg.out = T)
eqmcc(tt, include="?", show.cases = TRUE, details = TRUE,
          dir.exp = c(rep(1, 6)))


##
## n OUT = 1/0/C: 24/46/0
##    Total      : 70
##
```

```
## p.sol: RB.BUDGET + NB.VISIBILITY.ALL*nb.gov.depth
##
## Number of multiple-covered cases: 1
##
## M1:    RB.BUDGET + NB.VISIBILITY.ALL*nb.gov.depth => acttrans
##
##                                  incl   cov.r  cov.u
## ---------------------
## 1  RB.BUDGET                      1.000  0.377  0.358
## 2  NB.VISIBILITY.ALL*nb.gov.depth 1.000  0.094  0.075
## ---------------------
##    M1                             1.000  0.453
##
##                                  cases
## ---------------------
## 1  RB.BUDGET                      IAEA1983,IAEA1984,IAEA1985; IAEA1993,IAEA1994,
##                                   IAEA1995,IAEA1996,IAEA1997,IAEA1998;IAEA1986;
##                                   IAEA1999,IAEA2000,IAEA2001; OPCW1999,OPCW2000,
##                                   OPCW2001,OPCW2002,OPCW2009,OPCW2010,OPCW2011
## 2  NB.VISIBILITY.ALL*nb.gov.depth IAEA1989; IAEA1990; IAEA1987,IAEA1988; IAEA1986
## ---------------------
```

Bibliography

Abbott, Kenneth W and Duncan Snidal. 1998. "Why states act through formal international organizations." *Journal of Conflict Resolution* 42(1):3–32.

Abbott, Kenneth W. and Duncan Snidal. 2000. "Hard and Soft Law in International Governance." *International Organization* 54(3):421–456.

Akbarzadeh, Shahram. 2006. "Iran punches hole in world treaty system." *Australian Financial Review* 24 Jan:47.

Allison, Graham and Phillip Zelikow. 1999. *Essence of Decison: Explainig the Cuban Missile Crisis*. New York: Longman.

Atkins, Gavin. 2011. "Fukushima facts obscured in fog of misinformation." *The Australian* 16 Mar:12.

Australia. 2006. "Statement to the Eleventh Session of the Conference of the States Parties to the Chemical Weapons Convention.".
URL: *https://www.opcw.org/index.php?eID=dam_frontend_push&docID=1207*

Balali-Mood, Mahdi, Pieter S. Steyn, Leiv K. Sydnes and Ralf Trapp. 2008. "Impact of scientific developments on the Chemical Weapons Convention (IUPAC Technical Report)." *Pure and Applied Chemistry* 80(1).

Balogh, Stefanie. 2007. "We won't budge: Iran." *The Advertiser* 27 Sep:35.

Baradei, M.E. and International Atomic Energy Agency. 2007. *Atoms for peace: a pictorial history of the International Atomic Energy Agency, 1957-2007*. International Atomic Energy Agency.
URL: *http://www-pub.iaea.org/books/IAEABooks/7773/Atoms-for-Peace-A-Pictorial-History-of-the-International-Atomic-Energy-Agency*

Barbeschi, Maurizio. 2002. "Organizational Culture of the OPCW Secretariat." *Disarmament Forum* 2002(4):45–53.

Barnett, Michael N and Martha Finnemore. 1999. "The Politics, Power, and Pathologies of International Organizations." *International Organization* 53(4):699–732.

Barnett, Michael N and Martha Finnemore. 2004. *Rules for the world: International organizations in global politics*. Ithaca, NY: Cornell University Press.

Bauer, Steffen, Frank Biermann, Klaus Dingwerth and Bernd Siebenhüner. 2009. Understanding International Bureaucracies: Taking Stock. In *Managers of Global Governance. The Influence of International Environmental Bureaucracies*, ed. Frank Biermann and Bernd Siebenhüner. Cambridge, MA: MIT Press pp. 15 – 36.

Bäckstrand, Karin. 2003. "Civic Science for Sustainability: Reframing the Role of Experts, Policy-Makers and Citizens in Environmental Governance." *Global Environmental Politics* 3(4):24–41.
URL: *http://dx.doi.org/10.1162/152638003322757916*

Bechhoefer, B. G. 1959. "Negotiating the Statute of the International Atomic Energy Agency." *International Organization* 13(1).

Bennett, Andrew. 2004. Case Study Methods: Design, Use, and Comparative Advantage. In *Models, Numbers & Cases. Methods for Studying International Relations*, ed. Detlef F Sprinz and Yael Wolinsky-Nahmias. Ann Arbor, MI: University of Michigan Press chapter 2, pp. 19–55.

Berg-Schlosser, Dirk, Gisèle De Meur, Benoît Rihoux and Charles C. Ragin. 2008. Qualitative Comparative Analysis (QCA) as an Approach. In *Qualitative Comparative Analysis (QCA) as an Approach*, ed. Benoît Rihoux and Charles C. Ragin. Los Angeles: Sage pp. 1–18.

Betsill, Michele and Elisabeth Corell. 2001. "NGO Influence in International Environmental Negotiations: A Framework for Analysis." *Global Environmental Politics* 1(4):65–85.

Bexell, Magdalena, Jonas Tallberg and Anders Uhlin. 2010. "Democracy in Global Governance: The Promises and Pitfalls of Transnational Actors." *Global Governance* 16(1):81–101.

Böhmelt, Tobias. 2013. "A closer look at the information provision rationale: Civil society participation in states delegations at the UNFCCC." *The Review of International Organizations* 8(1):55–80.

Bluemel, Erik B. 2005. "Overcoming NGO Accountability Concerns in International Governance." *Brooklin Journal of International Law* 31:139.

Bradley, Curtis A. and Judith G. Kelley. 2008. "The Concept of International Delegation." *Law and Contemporary Problems* 71(1):1–36.

Brunsson, Nils. 2002. *The organization of hypocrisy. Talk, decisions, and action in organizations*. Malmö: Liber.

Caren, Neil and Aaron Panofsky. 2005. "TQCA." *Sociological Methods & Research* 34(2):147.

Charnovitz, Steve. 1997. "Two centuries of participation: NGOs and international governance." *Michigan Journal of International Law* 18:183–286.

Charnovitz, Steve. 2000. "Economic and Social Actors in the World Trade Organization." *ILSA Journal of International & Comparative Law* 7:259.

Charnovitz, Steve. 2003. "The Emergence of Democratic Participation in Global Governance (Paris, 1919)." *Indiana Journal of Global Legal Studies* 10(1):45–77.

Clark, Ann Marie, Elisabeth J Friedman and Kathryn Hochstetler. 1998. "The Sovereign Limits of Global Civil Society. A Comparison of NGO Participation in UN World Conferences on the Environment, Human Rights and Women." *World Politics* 51(1):1–35.

Clark, Ian. 2005. *Legitimacy in International Society*. Oxford: Oxford University Press.

Coll, Steve. 1994. "Nuclear Debate Shaped by Post-Cold War Flux; North Korean Crisis Proving to Be Test Case for New Global Security Regime." *The Washington Post* 25 Jun:A1.

Collingwood, Vivien and Louis Logister. 2005. "State of the art: Addressing the INGO 'legitimacy deficit'." *Political Studies Review* 3(2):175–192.

Cooke, Bill and Uma Kothari, eds. 2001. *Participation: The new tyranny?* London: Zed Books.

Cowell, F. A. 2000. Measurement of inequality. In *Handbook of Income Distribution*, ed. Anthony B. Atkinson and François Bourguignon. Vol. 1 Elsevier pp. 87–166.

Cox, Richard W and Harold K Jacobson. 1973. *The anatomy of influence. Decision making in International Organization*. Yale University Press.

CWC. 1994. "Convention on the Prohibition of the Development, Production, Stockpiling and Use of Chemical Weapons and on their Destruction.".
URL: *http://www.opcw.org/index.php?eID=dam_frontend_push&docID=6357*

Dahl, Robert A. 1994. "A Democratic Dilemma: System Effectiveness versus Citizen Participation." *Political Science Quarterly* 109(1):23–24.

Daily News. 2009. "So long, Sucker." *Daily News* 1 Dec:20.

Dingwerth, Klaus, Ina Lehmann, Ellen Reichel and Tobias Weise. 2015. "Democracy Is Democracy Is Democracy? Changes in Evaluations of International Institutions in Academic Textbooks, 1970–2010." *International Studies Perspectives* 16(2):173–189.

Dingwerth, Klaus and Tobias Weise. 2012. Legitimitätspolitik jenseits des Staats: Der Beitrag nichtstaatlicher Akteure zum Wandel grenzüberschreitender Governance-Normen. In *Der Aufstieg der Legitimitätspolitik. Rechtfertigung und Kritik politisch-ökonomischer Ordnungen*, ed. Anna Geis, Frank Nullmeier and Christopher Daase. Number 27 *in* "Leviathan Sonderband" Baden-Baden: Nomos pp. 100–117.

Dobbs, Michael. 1986. "Soviet Troubleshooter Finds Work at IAEA Session." *The Washington Post* 23 May.

Dorn, Walter. 1993. "The Organization for the Prohibition of Chemical Weapons and the IAEA. A comparative Overview." *IAEA Bulletin* 3:44–47.

Doub, W. O. and J.M. Dukert. 1975. "Making nuclear energy safe and secure." *Foreign Affairs* 53(4):756–772.

Dunworth, Treasa. 2008. "Towards a Culture of Legality in International Organizations: The Case of the OPCW." *International Organizations Law Review* 5(1):119–139.

Elman, Colin and Diana Kapiszewski. 2014. "Data Access and Research Transparency in the Qualitative Tradition." *PS: Political Science & Politics* 47(01):43–47.

Enia, Jason and Jeffrey Fields. 2014. "The Relative Efficacy of the Biological and Chemical Weapon Regimes." *The Nonproliferation Review* 21(1):43–64.

Feakes, Daniel. 2007. Keeping Peaceful Uses Peaceful: Article VI. In *The Creation of the Organisation for the Prohibition of Chemical Weapons. A Case Study in the Birth of an Intergovernmental Organisation*, ed. Ian R. Kenyon and Daniel Feakes. Cambridge University Press pp. 179–204.

Findlay, Trevor. 2012. *Unleashing The Nuclear Watchdog. Strengthening and reform of the IAEA*. Waterloo, Ontario: The Cenre for International Governance Innovation.

Finnemore, Martha. 1996. "Norms, Culture, and world politics: insights from sociology's institutionalism." *International Organization* 50(2):325–347.

Finnemore, Martha and Kathryn Sikkink. 1998. "International Norm Dynamics and Political Change." *International Organization* 52(4):887–917.

Fioretos, Orfeo. 2011. "Historical Institutionalism in International Relations." *International Organization* 65(02):367–399.

Fischer, David. 2000. Nuclear Safeguards: Evolution and Future. In *Verification Yearbok 2000*. London: VERTIC pp. 43–56.

Fischer, David and IAEA. 1997. *History of the International Atomic Energy Agency: the first forty years*. A 40th anniversary publication International Atomic Energy Agency.

Fitzpatrick, Stephen. 2006. "SBY takes a grip on Iran crisis." *The Australian* 11 May:1.

Flick, Uwe. 2007. *Triangulation: Eine Einführung*. Wiesbaden: VS Verlag.

Florini, Ann M. 2002. "Increasing Transparency in Government." *International Journal on World Peace* 19(3):3–37.

Gerring, John. 2007. *Case Study Research. Principles and Practices*. New York, NY: Cambridge University Press.

Glick, Caroline B. 2007. "ElBaradei's nuclear policy." *The Jerusalem Post* 28 Aug:15.

Grigorescu, Alexandru. 2003. "International Organizations and Government Transparency: Linking the International and Domestic Realms." *International Studies Quarterly* 47(4):643–667.

Grigorescu, Alexandru. 2007. "Transparency of Intergovernmental Organizations: The Roles of Member States, International Bureaucracies and Non-governmental Organizations." *International Studies Quarterly* 51(3):625–648.

Grigorescu, Alexandru. 2015. *Democratic intergovernmental organizations?: normative pressures and decision-making rules*. New York, NY: Cambridge University Press.

Göthel, V, G Voigt and W Burkart. 2007. Atomenergie zum Nutzen von Umwelt und Gesundheit. In *50 Jahre Internationale Atomenergie-Organisation IAEO. Ein Wirken für Frieden und Sicherheit im nuklearen Zeitalter*. Baden-Baden: Nomos.

Hale, Thomas N. 2008. "Transparency, Accountability, and Global Governance." *Global Governance* 14(1):73–94.

Hall, Rodney B and Thomas J Biersteker. 2002. The emergence of private authority in the international system. In *The Emergence of Private Authority in Global Governance*, ed. Rodney B Hall and Thomas J Biersteker. Cambridge: Cambridge University Press chapter 1, pp. 3–22.

Harrer, Gudrun. 2014. *Dismantling the Iraqi nuclear programme : the inspections of the International Atomic Energy Agency, 1991-1998*. 1. publ. ed. London: Routledge.

Hawkins, Darren G, David A Lake, Daniel L Nielson and Michael J Tierney. 2006. Delegation under anarchy: states, international organizations, and principal-agent theory. In *Delegation and Agency in International Organizations*, ed. Darren G Hawkins, David A Lake, Daniel L Nielson and Michael J Tierney. New York: Oxford University Press pp. 3–38.

Held, David. 1995. Democracy and the New International Order. In *Cosmopolitan Democracy: An Agenda for a New World Order*, ed. Danielle Archibugi and David Held. Oxford: Polity Press chapter 4, pp. 96–120.

Hirsch, Theodore. 2004. "The IAEA additional protocol: What it is and why it matters." *The Nonproliferation Review* 11(3):140–166.

Hurd, Ian. 1999. "Legitimacy and Authority in International Politics." *International Organization* 53(2):379 – 408.

Hurd, Ian. 2011. *International Organizations: Politics, Law, Practice*. Cambridge: Cambridge University Press.

IAEA. 1956. *The Statute of the IAEA*.
  URL: *http://www.iaea.org/About/statute.html*

IAEA. 1977. *Twenty years International Atomic Energy Agency (1957-1977)*. Vienna: IAEA.

IAEA. 1995. *Annual Report 1994*. Wien: International Atomic Energy Agency.
  URL: *http://iaea.org/Publications/Reports/Anrep94/index.html*

IAEA. 1997. *International Atomic Energy Agency: personal reflections*. A 40th anniversary publication Vienna: IAEA.

IAEA. 2000. "Medium Term Strategy 2001-2005.".
  URL: *https://www.iaea.org/sites/default/files/mts2001_2005.pdf*

IAEA. 2005. "Medium Term Strategy 2006-2011.".
  URL: *https://www.iaea.org/sites/default/files/mts2006_2011.pdf*

IAEA. 2013. *INPRO – In Brief. International Project on Innovative Nuclear Reactors and Fuel Cycles*. Vienna: International Atomic Energy Agency.

IAEA Archives. 1970. "Data Processing, General Scientific Information, International Nuclear Information System, Cooperation with NGOs." *DAT / 233-8, Box 09741* .

IAEA Archives. 1975*a*. "Scientific and Technical Cooperation, Participation and Cooperation, IGOs." *STI / 222, Box 09025* .

IAEA Archives. 1975*b*. "Scientific and Technical Cooperation, Participation and Cooperation, Non-Governmental Organizations." *STI / 223, Box 09025* .

IAEA Archives. 1975*c*. "Scientific and Technical Cooperation, Participation and Cooperation, UN and specialized Agencies." *STI / 221, Box 09025* .

IAEA Archives. 1977. "Scientific and Technical Cooperation, Participation and Cooperation, Member States - general." *STI / 224, Box 09025* .

Jönsson, Christer and Jonas Tallberg, eds. 2010. *Transnational Actors in Global Governance. Patterns, Explanations and Implications*. Basingstoke: Palgrave Macmillan.

Kelle, Alexander. 2003. "The CWC after its first Review Conference: is the glass half full or half empty?" *Disarmament Diplomacy* 71:31–40.

Kelle, Alexander. 2004. "Assessing the Effectiveness of Security Regimes — The Chemical Weapons Control Regime's First Six Years of Operation." *International Politics* 41(2):221–242.

Kelle, Alexander. 2013. "The Third Review Conference of the Chemical Weapons Convention and beyond: key themes and the prospects of incremental change." *International Affairs* 89(1):143–158.

Kenyon, Ian R. 2007*a*. Establishing the Preparatory Commission and Creating the OPCW Technical Scretariat. In *The Creation of the Organisation for the Prohibition of Chemical Weapons. A Case Study in the Birth of an Intergovernmental Organisation*, ed. Ian R. Kenyon and Daniel Feakes. Cambridge University Press pp. 31–67.

Kenyon, Ian R. 2007*b*. Why We Need a Chemical Weapons Convention and an OPCW? In *The Creation of the Organisation for the Prohibition of Chemical Weapons. A Case Study in the Birth of an Intergovernmental Organisation*, ed. Ian R. Kenyon and Daniel Feakes. Cambridge University Press pp. 1–19.

Kenyon, Ian R. and Sergei Kisselev. 2007. Cooperation in Peaceful Uses: Article XI. In *The Creation of the Organisation for the Prohibition of Chemical Weapons. A Case Study in the Birth of an Intergovernmental Organisation*, ed. Ian R. Kenyon and Daniel Feakes. Cambridge University Press pp. 249–260.

Keohane, Robert O. and Joseph S. Nye. 1977. *Power and Interdependence. World Politics in Transition.* Boston: Little & Brown.

King, Gary, Robert O Keohane and Sidney Verba. 1994. *Designing social inquiry : scientific inference in qualitative research.* Princeton, NJ: Princeton Univ. Press.

Kissling, Claudia. 2008. The Evolution of CSO's Legal Status in International Governance and Its Relevance for the Legitimacy of International Organizations. *in* Steffek, Kissling and Nanz (2008) chapter 2, pp. 30–52.

Krippendorf, Klaus. 1980. *Content Analysis. An Introduction to Its Methodology.* Newsbury Park, CA: Sage.

Krogslund, Chris, Donghyun Danny Choi and Mathias Poertner. 2015. "Fuzzy Sets on Shaky Ground: Parameter Sensitivity and Confirmation Bias in fsQCA." *Political Analysis* 23(1):21–41.

Kubig, Bernd W., Matthias Dembinski and Alexander Kelle. 2000. "Unilateralism as Sole Foreign-Policy Strategy? American Policy toward the UN, and the OPCW in the Clinton Era." *Peace Research Institute Frankfurt Reports* 57.

Lak, Maarten W. J. 2009. "Note on the Chemical Weapons Convention's Second Review Conference, Held at The Hague on 7–18 April 2008." *Journal of Conflict and Security Law* 14(2):353–381.

Liese, Andrea. 2010. Explaining Varying Degrees of Openness in the Food and Agriculture Organization of the United Nations (FAO). *in* Jönsson and Tallberg (2010) pp. 88–109.

Lipson, Michael. 2007. "Peacekeeping: organized hypocrisy?" *European Journal of International Relations* 13(1):5.

Lucas, Samuel R. and Alisa Szatrowski. 2014. "Qualitative Comparative Analysis in Critical Perspective." *Sociological Methodology* 44(1):1–79.

Lupia, Arthur and Colin Elman. 2014. "Openness in Political Science: Data Access and Research Transparency." *PS: Political Science & Politics* 47(01):19–42.

Manley, Ron G. 2007a. Preparing for Disarmament: Articles III, IV and V. In *The Creation of the Organisation for the Prohibition of Chemical Weapons. A Case Study in the Birth of an Intergovernmental Organisation,* ed. Ian R. Kenyon and Daniel Feakes. Cambridge University Press pp. 139–178.

Manley, Ron G. 2007*b*. Recruiting and Training of Inspectors. In *The Creation of the Organisation for the Prohibition of Chemical Weapons. A Case Study in the Birth of an Intergovernmental Organisation*, ed. Ian R. Kenyon and Daniel Feakes. Cambridge University Press pp. 105–112.

March, James G and Johan P Olsen. 2004. "The logic of appropriateness." Arena Working Paper No. 9.
URL: *http://www.sv.uio.no/arena/english/research/publications/ arena-publications/workingpapers/working-papers2004/wp04_9.pdf*

Marshall, Monty G., Keith Jaggers and Ted R. Gurr. 2014. *Polity IV Project. Political Regime Characteristics and Transitions, 1800-2013*.
URL: *http://www.systemicpeace.org/inscr/p4manualv2013.pdf*

Martin, Lisa L and Beth A Simmons. 1998. "Theories and Empirical Studies of International Institutions." *International Organization* 52(4):729–757.

Mathews, RJ. 2002. The OPCW at five: balancing verification in evolving circumstances. In *Verification Yearbook 2002*. Verification Research, Training and Information Centre pp. 53–73.

Mayer, Peter. 2008. Civil Society Participation in International Security Organizations: The Cases of NATO and the OSCE. In *Civil Society Participation in European and Global Governance. A Cure for the Democratic Deficit?*, ed. Jens Steffek, Claudia Kissling and Patrizia Nanz. New York: Palgrave Macmillan pp. 116–139.

Mayring, Philipp. 2010. *Qualitative Inhaltsanalyse. Grundlagen und Techniken*. Weinheim: Beltz.

Meyer, John W and Brian Rowan. 1977. "Institutionalized organizations: Formal structure as myth and ceremony." *American journal of sociology* 83(2):340–363.

Meyer, John W, Gili S Drori and Hokyu Hwang. 2006. World society and the proliferation of formal organization. In *Globalization and organization: World society and organizational change*, ed. Gili S Drori, John W Meyer and Hokyu Hwang. Oxford: Oxford University Press pp. 25–49.

Michel, Jean-Baptiste, Yuan Kui Shen, Aviva Presser Aiden, Adrian Veres, Matthew K. Gray, Joseph P. Pickett, Dale Hoiberg, Dan Clancy, Peter Norvig, Jon Orwant, Steven Pinker, Martin A. Nowak and Erez Lieberman Aiden. 2011. "Quantitative Analysis of Culture Using Millions of Digitized Books." *Science* 331(6014):176–182.

Moravcsik, Andrew. 2014. "Transparency: The Revolution in Qualitative Research." *PS: Political Science & Politics* 47(01):48–53.

Nasiritousi, Naghmeh and Björn-Ola Linnér. 2014. "Open or closed meetings? Explaining nonstate actor involvement in the international climate change negotiations." *International Environmental Agreements: Politics, Law and Economics* pp. 1–18.

Niehaus, F. 2007. Internationale Zusammenarbeit bei der Nuklearen Sicherheit. In *50 Jahre Internationale Atomenergie-Organisation IAEO. Ein Wirken für Frieden und Sicherheit im nuklearen Zeitalter*, ed. Dirk Schriefer, Walter Sandtner and Wolfgang Rudischhauser. Baden-Baden: Nomos.

Olwell, Russell B. 2008. *The International Atomic Energy Agency*. Global Organizations 1st ed. Chelsea House Publications.

OPCW. 1997. *OPCW Media and Public Affairs Policy*. The Hague: Organization for the Prohibition of Chemical Weapons (C-I/DEC.55).

OPCW. 2011*a*. *Components of an Agreed Framework for the Full Implementation of Article XI*. The Hague: Organization for the Prohibition of Chemical Weapons (C-16/DEC.10).

OPCW. 2011*b*. *Report of the Advisory Panel on Future Priorities of the Organization for the Prohibition of Chemical Weapons*. The Hague: Organization for the Prohibition of Chemical Weapons (S/951/2011).

OPCW. 2013. *Report of the OPCW on the Implementation of the Convention on the Prohibition of the Development, Production, Stockpiling and Use of Chemical Weapons and on their Destruction in 2012*. The Hague: The Organization for the Prohibition of Chemical Weapons (C-18/4).

Pakistan. 2006. "Eleventh Session of the Conference of States Parties to the Chemical Weapons Convention Statement in the General Debate.".
URL: *https://www.opcw.org/index.php?eID=dam_frontend_push&docID=1237*

Parshall, G. W., G. S. Pearson, T. D. Inch and Edwin D. Becker. 2002. "Impact of scientific developments on the Chemical Weapons Convention (IUPAC Technical Report)." *Pure and Applied Chemistry* 74(12).

Ragin, Charles C. 1987. *The comparative method: Moving beyond qualitative and quantitative strategies*. Berkeley: University of California Press.

Ragin, Charles C. 2000. *Fuzzy-set social science*. Chicago: University of Chicago Press.

Raustiala, Kal. 1997. "States, NGOs, and International Environmental Institutions." *International Studies Quarterly* 41(4):719–740.

Reimann, Kim D. 2006. "A View from the Top: International Politics, Norms and the Worldwide Growth of NGOs." *International Studies Quarterly* 50(1):45–68.

Reus-Smit, Christian. 2007. "International crises of legitimacy." *International Politics* 44(2):157–174.

Risse-Kappen, Thomas. 1995. "Reden ist nicht billig." *Zeitschrift für Internationale Beziehungen* 2(1):171–184.

Risse, Thomas. 2000. ""Let's Argue!": Communicative Action in World Politics." *International Organization* 54(01):1–39.

Rixen, Thomas and Lora A Viola. 2009. "Uses and Abuses of the Concept of Path Dependence: Notes towards a Clearer Theory of Institutional Change.".
URL: *http://www.wiwiss.fu-berlin.de/forschung/pfadkolleg/downloads/ summer_school_2009/Paper_Rixen_Viola.pdf*

Robinson, J. P. Perry. 1996. "Implementing the Chemical Weapons Convention." *International Affairs* 72(1):73–89.

Robinson, J. P. Perry. 2008. "Difficulties Facing the Chemical Weapons Convention." *International Affairs* 84(2):223–239.

Rosenau, James N and Ernst O Czempiel. 1992. *Governance without Government: Order and Change in World Politics.* Cambridge: Cambridge University Press.

Ryan, Maria. 2014. "Wilful Blindness or Blissful Ignorance? The United States and the Successful Denuclearization of Iraq." *Intelligence & National Security* 29(3):458–486.

Saxby, John. 2003. "Local ownership and development co-operation – the role of Northern civil society." *Canadian Council for International Co-operation Resource Document, Ontario* .

Schein, Edgar H. 1996. "Culture: The missing concept in organization studies." *Administrative Science Quarterly* pp. 229–240.

Scheinman, Lawrence. 1987. *The International Atomic Energy Agency and world nuclear order.* Washington D.C.: Resources for the Future.

Schneider, Carsten Q and Claudius Wagemann. 2012. *Set-theoretic methods for the social sciences. A guide to qualitative comparative analysis.* Cambridge: Cambridge University Press.

Scholte, Jan A. 2002. "Civil society and democracy in global governance." *Global Governance* 8(3):281–304.

Schriefer, Dirk, Walter Sandtner and Wolfgang Rudischhauser, eds. 2007. *50 Jahre Internationale Atomenergie-Organisation IAEO. Ein Wirken für Frieden und Sicherheit im nuklearen Zeitalter*. Baden-Baden: Nomos.

Scott, Richard W. 2003. *Organizations: Rational, Natural, and Open Systems*. 5 ed. Upper Saddle River, NJ: Prentice Hall.

Sebenius, James K. 1983. "Negotiation Arithmetic; Adding and Subtracting Issues and Parties." *International Organization* 37(2):281–316.

Seevaratnam, James I. 2006. "The Australia Group." *The Nonproliferation Review* 13(2):401–415.

Smallwood, Katie, Ralf Trapp, Robert Mathews, Beat Schmidt and Leiv K. Sydnes. 2013. "Impact of scientific developments on the Chemical Weapons Convention (IUPAC Technical Report)." *Pure and Applied Chemistry* 85(4).

South China Morning Post. 2011. "Atomic report puts Iran on the spot." *South China Morning Post* 11 Nov:16.

Steffek, Jens. 2013. "Explaining cooperation between IGOs and NGOs – push factors, pull factors, and the policy cycle." *Review of International Studies* 39:993–1013.

Steffek, Jens, Claudia Kissling and Patrizia Nanz, eds. 2008. *Civil Society Participation in European and Global Governance. A Cure for the Democratic Deficit?* New York: Palgrave Macmillan.

Steffek, Jens and Patrizia Nanz. 2008. Emergent Patterns of Civil Society Participation in Global and European Governance. In *Civil Society Participation in European and Global Governance. A Cure for the Democratic Deficit?*, ed. Jens Steffek, Claudia Kissling and Patrizia Nanz. New York: Palgrave Macmillan pp. 1–29.

Steffek, Jens and Ulrike Ehling. 2008. Civil Society Participation at the Margins: The Case of the WTO. In *Civil Society Participation in European and Global Governance. A Cure for the Democratic Deficit?*, ed. Jens Steffek, Claudia Kissling and Patrizia Nanz. New York: Palgrave Macmillan pp. 95–115.

Stiles, Kendall W. 1998. "Civil Society Empowerment and Multilateral Donors: International Institutions on New International Norms." *Global Governance* 4(2):199–216.

Suchman, Mark C. 1995. "Managing legitimacy: Strategic and institutional approaches." *The Academy of Management Review* 20(3):571–610.

Szasz, Paul. 1970. *The Law and Practices of the International Atomic Energy Agency*. Legal Series No. 7 Vienna: IAEA.

Tallberg, Jonas. 2002. "Delegation to supranational institutions: why, how, and with what consequences?" *West European Politics* 25(1):23–46.

Tallberg, Jonas. 2010. Transnational Access to International Institutions: Three Approaches. *in* Jönsson and Tallberg (2010) pp. 45–66.

Tallberg, Jonas and Christer Jönsson. 2010. Transnational Actor Participation in International Institutions: Where, Why, and What Consequences? *in* Jönsson and Tallberg (2010) chapter 1, pp. 1–21.

Tallberg, Jonas, Thomas Sommerer, Theresa Squatrito and Christer Jönsson. 2013. *The opening up of international organizations. Transnational access in global governance*. Cambridge: Cambridge University Press.

Taylor, Paul. 1991. "The United Nations System under Stress: Financial Pressures and Their Consequences." *Review of International Studies* 17(4):365–382.

The Globe and Mail. 2004. "Uranium enrichment will resume, Iran says." *The Globa and Mail* 11 May:A16.

The Washington Times. 2003. "The IAEA and Iraqi nukes." *The Washington Times* 29 Jan:A20.

Thiem, Alrik. 2011. "Conditions of intergovernmental armaments cooperation in Western Europe, 1996–2006." *European Political Science Review* 3(01):1–33.

Trapp, Ralf. 2007. The First Ten Years. In *The Creation of the Organisation for the Prohibition of Chemical Weapons. A Case Study in the Birth of an Intergovernmental Organisation*, ed. Ian R. Kenyon and Daniel Feakes. Cambridge University Press pp. 261–289.

Trapp, Ralf. 2012. The OPCW in Transition. From Stockpile Elimination to Maintaining a World Free of Chemical Weapons. In *Agent of Change? The CW Regime*. United Nations Institute for Disarmament Research (UNIDIR), Geneva, Switzerland pp. 41–54.

Trapp, Ralf. 2014. "Elimination of the Chemical Weapons Stockpile of Syria." *Journal of Conflict and Security Law* 19(1):7–23.

Traub, James. 2004. "The Netherworld of Nonproliferation." *The New York Times* 13 Jun:49.

Tucker, Jonathan B. 2012. "The Role of the Chemical Weapons Convention in Countering Chemical Terrorism." *Terrorism and Political Violence* 24(1):105–119.

Ukraine. 2006. "Statement to the Eleventh Session of the Conference of States Parties to the Convention on the Prohibition of Chemical Weapons.".
URL: *https://www.opcw.org/index.php?eID=dam_frontend_push&docID=1242*

UNHCR. 2011. "Report on the Annual Consultations with NGOs.".
URL: *http://www.unhcr.org/ngo-consultations/ngo-consultations-2011/Final-Full-Report-on-UNHCR-Annual-Consultations-with-NGOs-28-30June2011.pdf*

Vabulas, Felicity. 2011. What is a Seat on the ECOSOC NGO Committee Worth? Exploring the State Motivations and Benefits of Granting UN Access to NGOs. In *Paper prepared for the American Political Science Association Annual Conference.*
URL: *http://ssrn.com/abstract=1900279*

Washington, Monica J. 1997. "The Practice of Peer Review in the International Nuclear Safety Regime." *NYU Law Review* 72(2):430 – 469.

Watt, Nicholas, Ewen MacAskill and Matthew Engel. 2002. "Bush: Saddam's trying to fool us: Weapons offer scorned despite signs of split in coalition." *The Guardian* 18 Sep:1.

Weise, Tobias. 2015. "Between Functionality and Legitimacy: German Diplomatic Talk About the Opening of Intergovernmental Organizations." *Global Governance: A Review of Multilateralism and International Organizations* 21(1):99–117.

Weiss, Thomas George and Leon Gordenker, eds. 1996. *NGOs, the UN, and global governance.* Emerging global issues Boulder: Rienner. Literaturverz. S. 227 - 240.

Wiener, Antje. 2007. "The dual quality of norms and governance beyond the state: Sociological and normative approaches to 'Interaction'." *Critical Review of International Social and Political Philosophy* 10(1):47–69.

Willetts, Peter. 2000. "From "Consultative Arrangements" to "Partnership": The Changing Status of NGOs in Diplomacy at the UN." *Global Governance* 6(2):191–212.

Willetts, Peter. 2011. *Non-Governmental Organizations in World Politics*. New York: Routledge.

Wing, Christine and Fiona Simpson. 2013. *Detect, Dismantle, and Disarm. IAEA Verification, 1992-2005*. Washington, DC: United States Institute of Peace Press.

Zürn, Michael. 2000. "Democratic Governance Beyond the Nation State: The EU and Other International Institutions." *European Journal of International Relations* 6(2):183–221.

Zürn, Michael, Martin Binder and Matthias Ecker-Ehrhardt. 2012. "International authority and its politicization." *International Theory* 4(01):69–106.